Circuits and Systems: Design and Applications

Volume IV

Circuits and Systems: Design and Applications
Volume IV

Edited by **Helena Walker**

CLANRYE INTERNATIONAL

New Jersey

Published by Clanrye International,
55 Van Reypen Street,
Jersey City, NJ 07306, USA
www.clanryeinternational.com

Circuits and Systems: Design and Applications
Volume IV
Edited by Helena Walker

International Standard Book Number: 978-1-63240-100-7 (Hardback)

Printed in the United States of America.

Contents

Preface

At a very fundamental level, a circuit refers to an overall, complex arrangement of components such as resistors, conductors etc. which are connected in order to ensure a steady flow of current. It is only through circuits that signals or information is conveyed to the destination. Without a proper circuit system, the functional ability of any device becomes more or less redundant. The complexity and design of electronic circuits is ever increasing. Circuits are classified into analog circuits, digital circuits and mixed-signal circuits.

Circuits and systems in this book explain the handling of theory and applications of circuits and systems, signal processing, and system design methodology. The practical implementation of circuits, and application of circuit theoretic techniques to systems and to signal processing are the topics covered under this discipline. From radio astronomy to wireless communications and biomedical applications, the application of circuits and systems can be found across a varying range of subjects.

Circuits and Systems is an interesting discipline and is emerging as a coveted career option for many students. A lot of research, to develop more efficient systems is also being conducted.

I'd like to thank all the contributors for sharing their studies with us and make this book an enlightening read. I would also like to thank them for submitting their work within the set time parameters. Lastly, I wish to thank my family, whose support has been crucial for the completion of this book.

Editor

Transient and Permanent Fault Injection in VHDL Description of Digital Circuits

Parag K. Lala

Department of Electrical Engineering, Texas A&M University, Texarkana, USA

ABSTRACT

The ability to evaluate the testability of digital circuits before they are actually implemented is critical for designing highly reliable systems. This feature enables designers to verify the fault detection capability of online as well as offline testable digital circuits for both permanent and transient faults, during the design stage of the circuits. This paper presents a technique for transient and permanent fault injection at the VHDL level description of both combinational and sequential digital circuits. Access to all VHDL blocks a system is straight forward using a specially designed single fault injection block. This capability of inserting transient and permanent faults should help in evaluating the testability of a digital system before it is actually implemented.

Keywords: On-Line Fault Detection; VHDL; Transient Faults; Fault Injection; LFSR

1. Introduction

Modern digital systems are typically specified in a high level language such as VHDL. The actual implementation of the system is then performed using this specification. Several important criteria of a system to be designed e.g. testability, power consumption, need to be evaluated. The capability to ascertain the testability of a system at the VHDL level before it is implemented, allows design modifications to achieve the desired goal. A fault injection system provides the capability of introducing a fault at any desired location into the VHDL model of a circuit [1]. The injection technique allows faults to be injected at varying levels of VHDL hierarchy and hence help in evaluating the performance of a testable system.

In general, faults are grouped into two categories: *permanent* and *temporary*. Permanent faults that exist in logic circuits are normally identified during offline testing by the manufacturer of ICs, temporary faults on the other hand are of major concern after an IC chip is used in a particular application. Temporary faults can be one of two types: intermittent and transient [2]. Some work has been reported on the development of VHDL model for intermittent faults [3,4], however not much has been reported on transient (soft) fault injection in VHDL-based circuit descriptions [5,6]. The ability to simulate the occurrence of a transient fault in the VHDL description of a circuit is extremely important if the circuit has built-in on-line fault detection capability. In addition the

ability to insert permanent faults on single bits or a data word must also be taken into consideration. These features enable the performance of a circuit or a system under faulty conditions to be effectively evaluated before it is implemented.

Fault injection is crucial in an online testable system. It enables a designer to test whether the functional circuit and the checker within the system are operating as specified. Faults in an online testable system are assumed to be mainly single bit faults where a single bit is flipped from a logic 1 to a 0 or vice-versa. They can be both transient and permanent in nature. For (offline) testable systems fault injection helps in evaluating the testability of the entire system before the system is actually implemented. Any internal signal can be accessed at the VHDL level for the purposes of injecting faults, thus ensuring greater controllability and observability of the system.

The fault injection system proposed in this paper will be contained within the instruction VHDL of a system. This maintains the system as platform independent, able to simulate on any VHDL simulation software without extensive knowledge of simulation VHDL, which is a very tedious approach. Delong *et al.* [7] proposed a technique to accomplish the same goal, offering a different approach to fault injection. Other approaches such as the one offered by Parrotta *et al.* [8] or the one offered by Vargas *et al.* [9] involve injection techniques that must be used within simulation VHDL. Other papers approached fault injection differently by using methodologies based on scan paths [10], using outside logic sources to inject faults into VHDL descriptions [11], or by modifying existing circuit architecture [12-14]. Incorporating an injection technique in a VHDL description instead of the simulation code is more easily handled and is portable between design packages. A realistic fault injection system must have the capability to access most signals within a VHDL description including the inputs and outputs of the description; this is crucial for both on- and off-line testing.

The organization of the paper is follows. Section 2 discusses the general concept of the proposed fault injection system, and how each of the constituent blocks of the system is implemented in VHDL code. Section 3 illustrates the application of the fault injection system using several examples. Section 4 shows how permanent and transient faults are injected into a system specified in VHDL language. Section 5 is the conclusion.

2. Fault Injection in VHDL Description

A user-friendly fault injection system must evolve from a basic set of specifications. It must allow designers the ability to verify an online testable system, and therefore support injection of transient faults. Furthermore, it needs to have the capability to observe how a circuit behaves in the presence of a fault in an offline testing environment.

The transient fault injection feature proposed in this paper does not just randomly insert faults on its own into the system. It allows predetermination of a rate at which faults are inserted into a data word or data bit; as far as the authors are aware of this feature is not available in any system studied to date. During transient fault injection, random bits in a data word are selected by the system fault insertion. This is a key component of the proposed injection system that enables the designer to simulate faults at more realistic intervals on varying bits in a data word without having to modify the VHDL description every time a fault is inserted in the system. If there is a single input bit or a signal that is directed to the system, a transient fault will always occur on that bit at the interval chosen by the user. This allows the user to focus solely on a single bit when transient fault insertion is desired. If a larger data word is sent to the injection system, it will choose on which bit the fault be injected. This is especially useful in on and offline testing by focusing in on a specific bit or inserting faults randomly across a data word.

The proposed fault injection system is comprised of five blocks with three levels of hierarchy as shown in **Figure 1**. To invoke the system one component instantiation block is necessary for each data word where faults are to be inserted.

2.1. LFSR Blocks

A major feature of the fault injection system is the ability to insert faults at desired intervals. To accomplish this task the injection system uses pseudo-random sequences. Pseudo-random sequences of maximal length are generated using LFSR's. The two 16-bit LFSR's run in parallel constantly generating pseudo-random sequences. Based on the percentage of time that is chosen to insert a fault, a certain number of bits in the two LFSR's are compared by the fault injection logic block. If that number of bits matches, then a fault is inserted into the system. The data flow through the system that accomplishes this is shown in **Figure 2**.

Figure 3 presents resulted from a program that was written to simulate two 16-bit LFSR's running in parallel and certain numbers of bits being matched. A 4-bit control code (Ctrl) which is processed by the Control Logic block determines how many bits need to be matched in the two LFSR's to control the percentage at which faults are injected. The initial seed to each of the LFSR's must

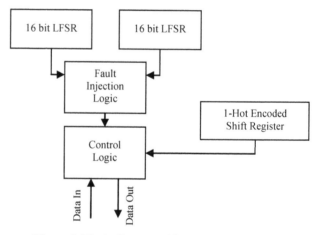

Figure 1. Block diagram of fault injection system.

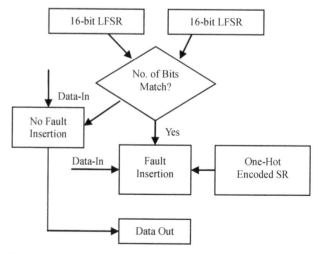

Figure 2. Basic flow chart of data through system during transient fault injection.

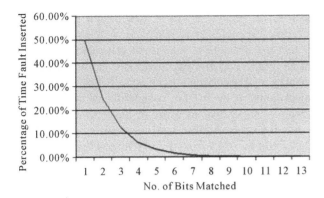

Figure 3. Percentage on the left is the percent of time a fault is inserted in the system.

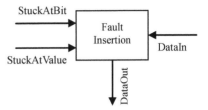

Figure 4. Data flow for permanent fault injection.

be different in order to produce two different pseudo-random binary sequences.

Certain easy to use control settings are employed in order to insert a stuck-at-0 or stuck-at-1 fault at a location selected by the user. Bits can be targeted easily with permanent injection by means of the StuckAtBit and StuckAtValue in the injection block. StuckatBit is the location of the permanent fault and StuckAtValue is the logic value of the stuck-at fault. The flow for data that will have permanent injection of a fault is shown in **Figure 4**.

The easiest way to accomplish control of the system is with a simple generic port map in VHDL that is used for the fault injection logic block in the system. A control code that is 4 bits wide is used in the highest level block, the control logic module, in order to let the user to change the rates of fault injection.

2.2. Fault Injection Logic Block and One-Hot Encoded Shift Register

The Fault Injection Logic block is the heart of the injection system that bears the work of incorporating data from the two LFSR's and also the One-Hot Encoded shift register. The block monitors the control inputs to the circuit to evaluate whether it needs to perform transient or permanent fault injection in the data that is sent to it. The control code which initializes permanent fault injection is "1111". If "1111" is sent to the injection system, the fault injection logic inserts a stuck-at fault at the location that is specified by the user (StuckAtBit) to the value (StuckAtValue) that is specified by the user. Otherwise, injection is determined to be of the transient nature. It must be made clear that the system operates differently when this "1111" is passed to it in the form of a control code. That code is the only one that uses StuckAtBit and StuckAtValue.

Other control codes are for transient injection and range from "0001" → 50% injection to "1110" → < 0.01% injection. A control code of "0000" is 0% fault

injection while a control code of "1111" is 100% fault injection. The control code is used to control the point in time at which the fault is injected. By incrementing this control code by "1" for each code, fault injection is dropped by 1/2 from the previous rate.

In order to determine the bit on which a fault will be inserted during transient fault injection, a one-hot encoded shift register is used. Every clock cycle, a logic "1" is shifted through a data word that is the length of the data word sent to the injection system. The purpose of the "1" is to determine on which bit the fault will be injected. When the control logic has seen that a fault is to be injected, it views the data output word of the one-hot encoded shift register. On the bit which is a "1" the control logic flips the bit in the data word.

The Fault Injection Logic block constantly monitors the output of both of the LFSR's, determining whether a fault is to be injected or not. It also determines on which bit a fault will occur if more than one bit is sent to the injection system. The Fault Injection Logic block sends to the Control block the same data word that was passed into the system or a faulty data word based on whether a fault has been calculated to occur.

2.3. Control Logic for Fault Insertion

The Control logic allows the user to change rates of fault insertion during operation. It does this by operating in parallel 15 different Fault Injection Logic blocks. The output of a certain Fault Injection Logic block is directed to the output of the injection system by multiplexing the 16 total different signals to the output of the injection block based on the 4-bit wide control code, as discussed in the previous section. If the fault injection system is not activated, the data that is sent into the system is directed out. But if the system is active, then a fault is inserted on the data word coming into the system and directed to the data out word.

2.4. Component Instantiation

In behavioral or structural design approach within VHDL, the component instantiation is the same. With predominately behavioral design approaches being used in system design especially in describing complex state machines, it is not possible to predict the structure of the circuit generated by the synthesis tool. Therefore, a generic instantiation block as shown in **Figure 5** is employed in the proposed fault injection technique.

In **Figure 5** DataLength is the length of the primary input or internal signal on which a fault will be injected. It is just a positive integer that is needed in order for the fault injection system to operate, and should be the same as the number of bits that are contained in a signal or primary input that is being fed to the system for fault injection. For example, for a single bit that is sent to the system for injection, DataLength is 1. For a 4-bit wide word whereby faults will be inserted, DataLength is 4. DataIn is the signal or primary input from the VHDL block that is calling this instantiation for which a fault will be inserted. DataOut corresponds to the output of the block that may contain a fault. Faults injected by the system are placed on the data coming from DataIn and seen on DataOut. DataIn and DataOut must be of the same width and must be DataLength bits long. Ctrl codes are 4 bits wide and range from "0000" to "1111". "0000" corresponds to no fault injection and "1111" corresponds to permanent fault injection. Clk is a system clock that is needed to be turned on for both transient and permanent fault injection. The Reset signal resets all flip flops in the system and must be enabled for at least one clock cycle at the beginning of a simulation followed by the load signal one to two clock cycles later. Match is simply an output signal denoting a fault has occurred and enable allows the system to inject faults onto incoming data. StuckAtBit and StuckAtValue are only useful when permanent fault injection in the system with a control code of "1111". StuckAtBit is the bit on which a permanent fault is injected, and StuckAtValue is the logic value (0 or 1) that the bit selected by StuckAtBit is set to.

2.5. Injection Block Placement

The proposed fault injection system is able to inject faults into both combinational and sequential parts of VHDL descriptions and into behavioral or structural VHDL coding. With predominately behavioral design

```
inserter: faultblock
     generic map( DataLength => 4,
                  StuckAtBit => 1)
     port map ( DataIn => DataIn,
                DataOut => DataOut,
                ctrl => ctrl,
                clk => clk,
                reset => reset,
                StuckAtValue => '0',
                load => load,
                match => match,
                enable => faultenable);
```

Figure 5. Generic fault injection system instantiation in VHDL.

approaches being used in system design especially in describing complex state machines, it is not possible to predict the structure of the circuit generated by the synthesis tool. Since in most cases only the behavioral description of a sequential circuit is available, the ability to inject faults in the VHDL description of the sequential circuit is imperative in order to have the capability to assess the controllability and observability of the eventual circuit resulting from the VHDL description.

The fault injection block is *not* meant to be able to inject faults on every signal within a VHDL description, but to reach as many low-level VHDL blocks containing primary inputs and outputs, internal signals therein as possible.

3. Fault Injection System in Practice

The application of the proposed fault injection system is illustrated through several examples. The VHDL coding and compilation in the following examples utilized the Xilinx Foundation 5.1.03i, and the simulation was performed in ModelSim XE II 5.6a. In order to write VHDL in the in the Xilinx Foundation, a specific FPGA had to be chosen; the FPGA XC2V500-4FG456C was selected for this purpose.

3.1. Transient Fault Injection in Online Testable Systems

To illustrate the use of fault injection in an on-line testable circuit, the fault injection block must be inserted into a VHDL block that is meant to be self-checking. A self-checking circuit can determine whether a fault has propagated to an output data word or not. Thus, a coding system must be employed to accomplish the self-checking aspect of the circuit and a checker that accepts coded data. For this example, a 2-out-of-4 code is used for the method of data encoding. In other words, for every 4-bit word of data that is going through the system, 2 bits in each word are 1s and the other two are 0s. The fault injection block is placed as shown in **Figure 6**. Subsequently, data is fed from the fault injection block to the 2-out-of-4 code checker which is shown in **Figure 7**. When $Z1\ Z2 = 01$ or 10, the circuit under test is fault-free, where as $Z1\ Z2 = 00$ or 11 indicates the presence of a fault.

The 2-out-of-4 Code Generator circuit is assumed to have 3 inputs (I1, I2, I3) and a 2-out-of-4 code as the output (O1, O2, O3, O4). The sum of products notation for the example circuit is:

$O1 = \sum (0, 3, 5, 6)$
$O2 = \sum (1, 3, 4, 6)$
$O3 = \sum (2, 4, 5, 7)$
$O4 = \sum (0, 1, 2, 7)$

The VHDL code for the circuit is shown below:

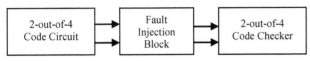

Figure 6. Placement of fault injection block in VHDL code.

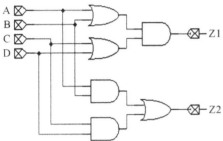

Figure 7. 2-out-of-4 checker [9].

```
library IEEE;
use IEEE.STD_LOGIC_1164.ALL;
use IEEE.STD_LOGIC_ARITH.ALL;
use IEEE.STD_LOGIC_UNSIGNED.ALL;

library work;
use work.lfsr_pkg.all;

entity test1 is
    Port (DataOut: out std_logic_vector(3 downto 0);
    clk,reset,load,faultenable : in std_logic;
    ctrl : in std_logic_vector(3 downto 0);
    CircuitIn : out std_logic_vector(2 downto 0);
    match : out std_logic;
    fault : out std_logic;
    Z1,Z2 : out std_logic);
end test1;

architecture Behavioral of test1 is
    signal i : std_logic_vector(2 downto 0);
    signal DataIn : std_logic_vector(3 downto 0);
    signal subdata : std_logic_vector(3 downto 0);
begin

-- The LFSR serves the function of feeding inputs to the
-- circuit so it will not have to be done manually in the
-- simulator

LFSR1: LFSR_GENERIC
        generic map (Width => 3)
        port map  (clock => clk,
                    reset => reset,
                    load => load,
                    seed => "101",
                    parallel out => i);
    CircuitIn <= i;

-- DataIn(3) = O1, DataIn(2) = O2, DataIn(1) = O3,
```

DataIn(0) = O4
```
    DataIn(3) <= (NOT i(0) AND (i(1) XNOR i(2))) OR
(i(0) AND (i(1) XOR i(2)));
    DataIn(2) <= i(0) XOR i(2);
    DataIn(1) <= (NOT i(2) AND (i(0) XOR i(1))) OR
(i(0) AND i(2));
    DataIn(0) <= (NOT i(0) AND NOT i(1)) OR (i(1)
AND (i(0) XNOR i(2)));

-- Fault insertion block instantiation
inserter: faultblock
generic map(DataLength => 4,
            StuckAtBit => 0)
-- The value for StuckAtBit does not matter in this case
-- because a transient fault is going to be injected, thus
-- letting the injection system handle when and where the
-- fault occurs
-- The 4 indicates the length of the data word for which a
-- fault shall be injected
port map (DataIn => DataIn,
            DataOut => subdata,
            StuckAtValue => '0',
-- StuckAtValue does not matter in this case because
-- once again, the system in transient injection is han-
dling
-- the location and what the fault will be
            ctrl => ctrl,
-- Set ctrl anywhere between "0001" and "1110" for
-- transient fault injection
-- If ctrl is used as an input to the circuit, it can be
changed
-- during operation or it can be set manually within the
-- injection block (ctrl => "0001")
            clk => clk,
            reset => reset,
            load => load,
            enable => faultenable);

    DataOut <= subdata;

-- 2 out of 4 checker
Z1 <= (subdata(0) OR subdata(1)) AND (subdata(2) OR
subdata(3));
Z2 <= (subdata(0) AND subdata(1)) OR (subdata(2)
AND subdata(3));
end Behavioral;
```

Figure 8 shows the simulation results of the 2-out-of-4 encoder operating at 100 MHz without fault injection occurring. The circuit inputs are generated by a 3-bit linear feedback shift register (LFSR) and are fed directly to the circuitry described above in O1, O2, O3, & O4. The resulting 2-out-of-4 code words are verified by the code checker as shown in Z1 and Z2.

Figure 9 shows simulation results with the fault inject-

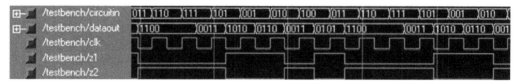

Figure 8. Example circuit for online testing without fault injection.

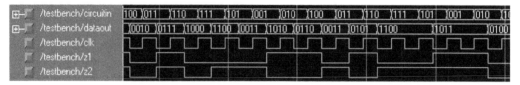

Figure 9. Example circuit for online testing with transient fault injection.

tion block turned on; the control code is set at 0001 *i.e.* the rate of fault appearance is 50%. As can be seen in the diagram for certain input combinations Z1 and Z2 are either 00 or 11. After a few clock cycles, fault insertion stops briefly to allow normal operation. This makes Z1 and Z2 to become 01 or 10. Towards the end of the diagram Z1 and Z2 become 11 and then 00 indicating the presence of a fault in the data word. This can be verified by observing the "dataout" word which is producing a non-code word.

3.2. Permanent Fault Injection in an Off-Line Testing Environment

To further illustrate the functionality of the system, an example showing permanent injection of a single stuck-at fault is provided. The test pattern generator in this case is a 3-bit LFSR. The control code is set at 1111.

There is no on-line checker in this case, the outputs need to be observed to ascertain the effect of the stuck-at-1 fault being introduced on the 0-bit in the data word. The fault injection block is shown in **Figure 10**.

Figure 11 shows the simulation results in the absence of a fault. The expected outputs can be observed on the Datout line. From the simulation results in **Figure 12**, it can be concluded that the circuit is operating with a stuck-at-1 fault on bit 0 in the data word, as indicated in the specifications of the injection block in **Figure 10**. It should be noted that that the fault injection block of **Figure 10** can insert either a transient or a permanent fault simply by changing the control code even during normal operation. However, the location of the permanent cannot be changed during operation.

4. Transient and Permanent Fault Injection in a Sequential Circuit

The fault insertion technique proposed in [5] considered combinational logic circuits only With predominately behavioral design approaches currently being used in system design especially in describing complex state

```
inserter: faultblock
generic map(DataLength => 4,
            StuckAtBit => 0)
-- StuckAtBit being set to 0 makes the system
-- insert a stuck-at fault on bit 0 in the data word
port map (DataIn => DataIn,
          DataOut => subdata,
          ctrl => ctrl,
-- For permanent fault injection in simulation set
-- ctrl to "1111"
          clk => clk,
          reset => reset,
          load => load,
          match => match,
          StuckAtValue => '1',
-- The stuck-at fault that will occur will be a
-- stuck-at-1
          enable => faultenable);
```

Figure 10. Fault injection block for offline testing example.

machines, it is not possible to predict the structure of the circuit generated by the synthesis tool. Since in most cases only the behavioral description of a sequential circuit is available, the ability to inject faults in the VHDL description of the sequential circuit is imperative in order to have the capability to assess the controllability and observability of the eventual circuit resulting from the VHDL description. The fault injection block is *not* meant to be able to inject faults on every signal within a VHDL description, but to reach as many low-level VHDL blocks containing primary inputs and outputs, internal signals therein as possible

If Z1, Z2 = "01" or "10"
→ Circuit is behaving normally

If Z1, Z2 = "00" or "11"
→ Circuit is operating with a fault

For sequential circuits, the states must be set outside a process statement in order for the injection system to

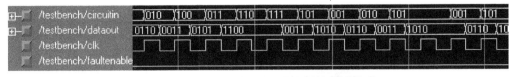

Figure 11. Example circuit for offline testing without fault injection.

Figure 12. Example circuit for offline testing with permanent fault injection.

```
ARCHITECTURE Behavior OF upcount IS
SIGNAL Count:
        STD_LOGIC_VECTOR(3 DOWNTO 0);
BEGIN
-- Q is the state of the machine and is a BUFFER
    PROCESS(Clock,Resetn)
      BEGIN
      IF Resetn = '0' THEN
Count <= "0000";
        ELSIF (Clock' EVENT AND Clock = '1') THEN
            IF E = '1' THEN
                Count <= subdata + 1;
            ELSE Count <= subdata;
            END IF;
        END IF;
    END PROCESS;
-- Fault insertion block instantiation
-- The set of registers, Q or subdata, is set after the process
-- block even in normal operation for this circuit.
inserter: faultblock
generic map(DataLength => 4,
            StuckAtBit => 1)
-- When permanent injection is chosen by means of
-- ctrl = "1111", bit 1 will have a permanent stuck-at
-- fault that is StuckAtValue, in this case '0'
port map (DataIn => Count,
            DataOut => subdata,
            ctrl => "1111",
            clk => clk,
                reset => reset,
            StuckAtValue => '1',
            load => load,
            match => match,
enable => faultenable);
  Q <= subdata;
END Behavior;
            enable => faultenable);
  Q <= subdata;
END Behavior;
```

Figure 13. Up-counter with injection system in place.

operate. The process statement may however contain a signal representing the state of the machine. The signal that identifies the new state of the machine is used in the DataIn assignment in the injection block. The new state of the machine is on DataOut. The new state may or may not contain an injected fault. The component instantiation for the system cannot be implemented within a process statement. An example sequential circuit that includes a fault injection block is shown in **Figure 13**. **Figure 14** shows the simulation results of the sequential circuit described in **Figure 13** operating under normal conditions. **Figure 15** shows the circuit operation with a 50% fault injection rate. As can be seen in the diagram the counter is going through erroneous state transitions. **Figure 16** shows the circuit operation with permanent fault injection for a stuck-at-1 on bit 0 of the counter registers. It should be clear from the diagram that the circuit states are erroneous.

5. Conclusion

A fault injection technique that enables designers the access to a VHDL package to insert a fault on any signal within the block of a VHDL code, has been presented. It allows the injection of transient faults randomly across a data word, and allows the insertion of a permanent fault at any chosen point in a data word. A number of examples are provided to illustrate the use of the proposed fault injection system in on- and off-line testing environments for both combinational and sequential circuits. A major advantage of the proposed approach is that the fault insertion process is significantly simpler than other currently available approaches. Since the fault insertion block is included in a package, much like a library in other forms of programming, only a simple call at the beginning of the VHDL description and a component instantiation is needed to activate the insertion mechanism.

6. Acknowledgements

This work was supported in part by the National Science

Figure 14. Sequential Circuit (Counter) operating normally.

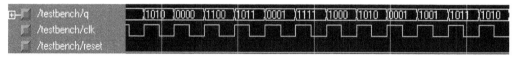

Figure 15. Sequential Circuit (Counter) operating with 50% fault injection.

Figure 16. Sequential Circuit (Counter) operating with stuck-at-1 on bit 0.

Foundation, USA under Grant 0925080.

REFERENCES

[1] A. Benso and P. Prinetto, "Fault Injection Techniques and Tools for Embedded Systems Reliability Evaluation," Kluwer Academic Publishers, Holland, 2003.

[2] P. K. Lala, "Self-Checking and Fault Tolerant Digital Design," Morgan Kaufmann Publishers, Waltham, 2001.

[3] J. Gracia, L. Saiz, J. C. Baraza, D. Gil and P. Gil, "Analysis of the Influence of Intermittent Faults in a Microcontroller," 11th IEEE International Workshop on Design and Diagnostics of Electronic Circuits and Systems, Bratislava, 16-18 April 2008, pp. 80-85.

[4] L. J. Saiz, J. Gracia, J. C. Baraza, D. Gil and P. J. Gil, "Applying Fault Injection to Study the Effects of Intermittent Faults," 7th European Dependable Computing Conference, Kaunas, 7-9 May 2008, pp. 67-69.

[5] S. R. Seward and P. K. Lala, "Fault Injection for Verifying Testability at the VHDL Level," Proceedings of International Test Conference, Baltimore, 30 September-2 October, 2003, pp. 131-137.

[6] W. Sheng, L. Xiao and Z. Mao, "An Automated Fault Injection Technique Based on VHDL Syntax Analysis and Stratified Sampling," 4th IEEE International Symposium on Electronic Design, Test and Applications (Delta), Hong Kong, 23-25 January 2008, pp. 587-591.

[7] T. A. Delong, B. W. Johnson and J. A. Profeta III, "A Fault Injection Technique for VHDL Behavioral-Level Models," IEEE Design & Test of Computers, Vol. 13, No. 4, 1996, pp. 24-33.

[8] B. Parrotta, M. Rebaudengo, M. S. Reorda and M. Vi-
olante, "New Techniques for Accelerating Fault Injection in VHDL Descriptions," Proceedings of 6th IEEE Online Testing Workshop, Palma de Mallorca, 3-5 July 2000, pp. 61-66.

[9] F. Vargas, A, Amory and R. Velazco, "Estimating Circuit Fault-Tolerance by Means of Transient-Fault Injection in VHDL," Proceedings of 6th IEEE Online Testing Workshop, Palma de Mallorca, 3-5 July 2000, pp. 67-72.

[10] N. Z. Basturkmen, S. M. Reddy and I. Pomeranz, "A Low Power Pseudo-Random BIST Technique," Proceedings of IEEE International Conference on Computer Design: VLSI in Computers and Processors, Freiberg, 16-18 September 2002, pp. 468-473.

[11] A. Manzone and D. De Costantini, "Fault Tolerant Insertion and Verification: A Case Study," Proceedings of IEEE Memory Technology Design and Testing Workshop, Isle of Bendor, 10-12 July 2002, pp. 44-48.

[12] R. J. Hayne and B. W. Johnson, "Behavioral Fault Modeling in a VHDL Synthesis Environment," Proceed- ings of VLSI Test Symposium, Dana Point, 25-29 April 1999, pp. 333-340.

[13] D. G. Mavis and P. H. Eaton, "SEU and SET Mitigation Techniques for FPGA Circuit and Configuration Bit Storage Design," Proceedings of Military and Aerospace Applications of Programmable Devices and Technologies Confenerce, Laurel, 10-12 September 2000, pp. 1-15.

[14] P. Civera, L. Macchiarulo, M. Rebaudengo, M. S. Reorda and A. Violante, "Exploiting FPGA for Accelerating Fault Injection Experiments," Proceedings of IEEE Online Testing Workshop, Taormina, 9-11 July 2001, pp. 9-13.

2

Dynamic and Leakage Power Estimation in Register Files Using Neural Networks

Assim A. Sagahyroon, Jamal A. Abdalla
American University of Sharjah, Sharjah, UAE

ABSTRACT

Efficient power consumption and energy dissipation in embedded devices and modern processors is becoming increasingly critical due to the limited energy supply available from the current battery technologies. It is vital for chip architects, circuit, and processor designers to evaluate the energy per access, the power consumption and power leakage in register files at an early stage of the design process in order to explore power/performance tradeoffs, and be able to adopt power efficient architectures and layouts. Power models and tools that would allow architects and designers the early prediction of power consumption in register files are vital to the design of energy-efficient systems. This paper presents a Radial Base Function (RBF) Artificial Neural Network (ANN) model for the prediction of energy/access and leakage power in standard cell register files designed using optimized Synopsys Design Ware components and an UMC 130 nm library. The ANN model predictions were compared against experimental results (obtained using detailed simulation) and a nonlinear regression-based model, and it is observed that the ANN model is very accurate and outperformed the nonlinear model in several statistical parameters. Using the trained ANN model, a parametric study was carried out to study the effect of the number of words in the file (D), the number of bit in one word (W) and the total number of Read and Write Ports (P) on the values of energy/access and the leakage power in standard cell register files.

Keywords: Component; Formatting; Style; Styling; Insert

1. Introduction

Reducing the energy consumption of modern processors is critical to the extension of battery life time in portable devices. Various studies have shown that register files are major consumers of energy in modern processors [1-3]. Different architectures and techniques have been proposed in the literature [4-9] where the primary objective was to optimize the energy consumption of register files. Hence, there exists a justifiable need for the accurate power modeling of these components taking into consideration the current nanometer processing technologies. Different modeling techniques have been discussed in the literature but mostly assuming micrometer technologies; a discussion of the various modeling approaches and their advantages and shortcomings can be found in [10,11].

In recent years, there has been a great advancement in the field of ANN, both from theoretical and applications points of view. ANN has been used in classification, pattern matching, pattern recognition, optimization and control-related problems. In electrical engineering, neural networks have been used to solve a wide variety of VLSI-

related problems [12-16]. A neural network (NN) approach for modeling the time characteristics of fundamental gates of digital integrated circuits that include Iinverters, NAND, NOR, and XOR gates is discussed in [2]. The modeling approach presented in the article is technology independent, fast, and accurate, which makes it suitable for circuit simulators. The application of an artificial neural network (ANN) to the study of the nanoscale CMOS circuits is presented in [13]. A novel method of testing analog VLSI circuits, using wavelet transform for analog circuit response analysis and artificial neural networks (ANN) for fault detection is proposed in [14]. Power consumption using neural network of analog components at the system level is discussed in [15]. The method provides estimation of the instantaneous power consumption of analog blocks. In [16], the authors proposed an ANN-based approach for modeling performance of nano-scale CMOS Inverters. The inputs to the network are the channel width of the PMOS and NMOS transistors and the load capacitor. The outputs are rise time and fall times of the output, inverter switching point, and average power consumption.

In this work, we propose the use of neural networks in

modeling energy/access and leakage power of standard cell based register files designed using 130 nm technologies. Three parameters that influence the power consumed by a register file, namely, the number of words in the register file (Depth), the number of bits in one word (Width), and the total number of Read and Write Ports (Port) are used as inputs to the ANN. The output parameters of the ANN are the energy/access and the leakage power. To the best of the authors' knowledge this is the first work that attempts to create power models for register files using ANN.

2. Background

In their work, Praveen and others [10], used low level simulation that takes into account the layout details as well as detailed transistor characterization provided by a standard cell library to collect data on the power consumption of various structures of register files. They used optimized Synopsys Design Ware components from the UMC 130 nm library to design various register files structures. Layouts were generated for register files with a varying number of ports ranging from 3 to 12, a depth that varies from 4 to 64 words, and a width that varies from 8 to 128 bits. All these combinations of register files were designed; patristic capacitances in the routing wires and gate capacitances of each transistor were extracted from the layouts. The extracted netlist was then simulated using ModelSim with different switching activity factors to obtain power estimates. After completing over 100 register file design for the 130 nm technology node, the dynamic and leakage energy of each design was tabulated. Curve fitting was performed on each variable using register file depth, width, number of ports as well as the activity factor as independent input variables. For the designs it is assumed that each of the ports of the register file is driving a load of F04. To a first degree of approximation and to keep the problem tractable, the authors assumed that the energy/access scales linearly with the Hamming Distance between consecutive read/written words. The assumption is validated using different Hamming Distances. Equations (1) and (2) below are the derived model equations, where Energy/Access and Leakage power are the subjects of the two equations respectively; the authors in [10] referred to it as the Empire Model. For a complete description of the steps taken to arrive to this model, readers are referred to [10].

$$
\begin{aligned}
E/\text{Access}\left(\text{in}:J\right) = &\Big[2.23\times10^{-11} - 8.06\times10^{-13}\times D \\
&- 5.89\times10^{-13}\times W - 3.35\times10^{-12}\times P \\
&+ 2.06\times10^{-14}\times D\times W + 7.57\times10^{-14}\times D\times P \\
&+ 6.34\times10^{-14}\times W\times P + 2.48\times10^{-15}\times D^2 \\
&+ 9.93\times10^{-16}\times W^2 + 8.72\times10^{-14}\times P^2\Big]\times\left(HD/P\right)
\end{aligned}
\tag{1}
$$

$$
\begin{aligned}
\text{Leakage Power}&\left(\text{in}:\mu W\right) \\
= &\,5.43\times10^{1} - 1.76\times D - 1.62\times W \\
&- 8.42\times P + 8.55\times10^{-2}\times D\times W \\
&+ 2.15\times10^{-1}\times D\times P + 1.61\times10^{-1}\times W\times P \\
&+ 1.73\times10^{-3}\times D^2 + 4.23\times10^{-3}\times W^2 \\
&+ 2.10\times10^{-1}\times P^2
\end{aligned}
\tag{2}
$$

In the equations above: D represents the number of words in the file, W represents the number of bit in one word, P represents the total number of ports (read and write), HD is the total number of bits that switch (either from 1 to 0 or from 0 to 1) on the data and address lines from one read/write cycle to another.

To validate the curve-fitted formulae described by Equations (1) and (2), they were compared against results obtained using low level detailed implementations. It is reported that the Empire models exhibit on average about 10% error when compared to the values obtained using detailed simulation.

In this work, data sets obtained from detailed simulation using the power estimation framework proposed in [10] were used to train and test the proposed ANN model. The performance of the ANN model is compared with results obtained using Empire model, as well as power measurements obtained using detailed low-level design simulations of the register files.

3. Neural Network Model and Architecture

The field of Artificial Neural Networks is one of the main branches of artificial intelligence that found many applications in several engineering disciplines. ANNs are processing elements that are capable of learning relationships between input and output and they can be used for classification, prediction, clustering and function approximation, among others. Several neural network architectures with different learning algorithms such as backpropagation were used over the years. In general, an ANN consists of massive parallel computational processing elements (neurons) that are connected with weighted connections and have learning capability that simulates the behavior of a brain [17]. The network weights and the network threshold values are initially set to random values and new values of the network weights and bias values are computed during the network training phase. The neurons output are calculated using Equation (3) below:

$$
y_i = F\left(\sum\left(x_j\times w_{ij}\right)+b_j\right)
\tag{3}
$$

where y_i is the output of the neuron i, x_j are the input of j neurons of the previous layer; value, w_{ij} is the neuron weights, b_j is the bias for modeling the threshold; and F is the transfer or activation function [17,18]. The transfer function also known as the *processing element* is the portion of the neural network where all the computing is performed. The activation function maps the input domain (infinite) to an output domain (finite). The ANN Error (E) for a given training pattern i is given by Equation (4):

$$E = \frac{1}{2}\sum_{i=1}^{n}\sum_{j=1}^{m}\left(O_j^i - T_j^i\right)^2 \qquad (4)$$

where O_j^i is the output and T_j^i is the target. For a thorough discussion of neural network theory and applications readers are referred to [17].

The Radial Basis Function (RBF) ANN together with the Gaussian activation function, and the Multi-Layer Perceptron (MLP) together with the hyperbolic tangent (tanh) activation function are among the most widely used feed-forward universal approximators. In this study a hybrid of these two universal approximators is used. Specifically, a RBF ANN topology with one additional hidden layer and 15 neurons (processing elements) in first hidden layer, and four processing element in the second hidden layer are used. The RBF neural network has a Gaussian activation function in the first hidden layer while the additional hidden layer has a tangent hyperbolic (tanh) activation function and the output layer has a bias axon activation function as shown in **Figure 1**. The performance of this combination of activation functions for the data set used in this work proved to outperform the standard RBF or standard MLP, when used separately.

As depicted in **Figure 1**, the neural network architecture used in this study, has one input layer, two hidden layers and one output layer. The input layer consists of three nodes, mainly, the number of words in the register file Depth (D), the number of bits in one word Width (W), and the total number of Read and Write Ports (P). The output layer of the ANN consists of two nodes which are the energy/access, and the leakage power as shown.

The data collected from the detailed simulation runs is divided into two categories referred to as the training data, and the test data. The training of the network is conducted using the training data set. The test data is used to validate the performance of the network by comparing its outputs with the values reported from the detailed simulation of the register files design. **Table 1** shows the range of maximum and minimum values of the training and testing data sets that is used in this study. The ranges of Energy/Access and Leakage Power indicate the minimum and maximum values reported from detailed simulation results within each selected category. Initial random values are used for the weight of the neural network and different learning rates (step sizes) were used for the different layers of the RBF neural network. The learning rate used for the first and second hidden layers is 1.0 and for the output layer is 0.1. A momentum factor of 0.7 was used for the model all through. The total number of data items used for training the neural network is 60, and the number of data items used for testing the neural network is 20. The neural network was trained 20 times with 2000 epochs in each training cycle and the average performance was recorded. The average minimum normalized mean square error (NMSE) for the training data was 0.00045 with standard deviation of 0.00019.

4. Results and Discussions

In this section we discuss results of power estimates obtained using the following:

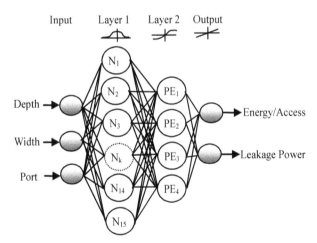

Figure 1. A multilayer RBF neural network topology.

Table 1. Range of training and testing parameters.

Parameter	Training Data		Testing Data	
	Maximum	Minimum	Maximum	Minimum
Depth	64	4	64	4
Width	64	8	64	8
Ports	12	3	12	3
Energy/Access (J)	1.38998E–10	3.14246E–13	1.70584E–11	6.77792E–13
Leakage Power (µW)	492.5446	1.2387	107.862	3.3823

1) Empire Model (Empire Prediction);

2) ANN Model (ANN Prediction);

3) Detailed simulation-based power measurements (Experimental Values).

The ANN model was trained using 60 data sets, and for verification the trained ANN model is tested on 20 randomly selected testing data sets. **Tables 2** and **3** show the performance indicators of the 20 testing samples for the two outputs (Energy/Access and Leakage Power) respectively. As shown in **Table 2**, for the Energy/Access, the normalized mean square error (NMSE) obtained is 0.05951 and the correlation co-efficient (r) is 0.97445, while from **Table 3** for Leakage Power, the normalized mean square error (NMSE) is 0.045778 and the correlation coefficient is 0.9823. This indicates that the measured and the ANN predicted values correlate very well for both parameters. It is clear from the tabulated results that the ANN model outperformed the Empire model in all performance criteria.

Figures 2 and **3** show the prediction and accuracy of the ANN model and the Empire model based on the test data set when compared to the detailed simulation values of energy/access and leakage power. The ANN prediction is clearly better than the prediction computed using the Empire model.

It is observed that 75% of ANN model predictions of the test data are within 10% of the measured values of energy/access compared to only 15% of Empire model predictions of the test data are within 10% of the measured values of energy/access. Also, 75% of the ANN predictions of the test data are within 20% of the measured values of the leakage power while only 30% of Empire model predictions of the test data are within 20% of

Table 2. Performance of the ANN prediction of energy/access on the test data.

Performance Criterion	ANN Model	Empire Model
Root Mean Square Error (RMSE) (J)	1.1968E–12	3.8685E–12
Mean Absolute Error (MAE) (J)	7.556E–13	2.9502E–12
Mean Absolute Percent Error (MAPE) (%)	10.94	90.10
Minimum Absolute Error (J)	8.123E–15	2.2498E–13
Maximum Absolute Error (J)	3.940E–12	9.714E–12
Normalized Mean Square Error (NMSE)	0.05951	0.62173
Correlation Coefficient (r)	0.97445	0.86255

Table 3. Performance of the ANN prediction of leakage power on the test data.

Performance Criterion	ANN Model	Empire Model
Root Mean Square Error (RMSE) (µW)	6.59782	9.77937
Mean Absolute Error (MAE) (µW)	4.579615	7.61819
Mean Absolute Percent Error (MAPE) (%)	17.29	50.09
Minimum Absolute Error (µW)	0.31224	0.41176
Maximum Absolute Error (µW)	17.294355	21.39266
Normalized Mean Square Error (NMSE)	0.045778	0.100572
Correlation Coefficient (r)	0.982399	0.952308

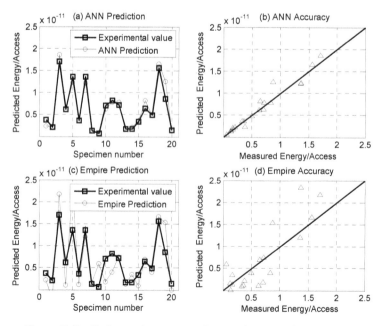

Figure 2. Prediction and accuracy of energy/access using test data.

the measured values of leakage power. Furthermore, some of Empire predictions have relative percent error well above 100%.

5. Parametric Study

To further compare the performance of the Empire model and the ANN model in predicting the Energy/Access and the Leakage Power, we varied the input parameters (width, ports, and depth) and computed the resulting outputs. **Figures 4** and **5** depict comparative plots showing the

predictions of energy and power respectively. From **Figure 4(a)**, Empire seems to overestimate the Energy/Access prediction for wider designs with relatively fewer ports since from **Figure 4(b)**, the estimates of both models for 32 ports is closer. Similar overestimates occurred when the number of ports and depth is varied (**Figures 4(d)** and **4(e)**). Interestingly from **Figure 4(f)**, the Empire model underestimated the energy per access in the case of wider and deeper designs.

From the plots of **Figure 5**, the performance of the two

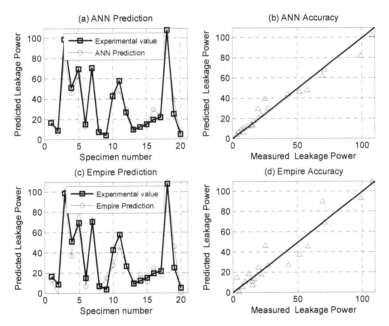

Figure 3. Prediction and accuracy of leakage power of test data.

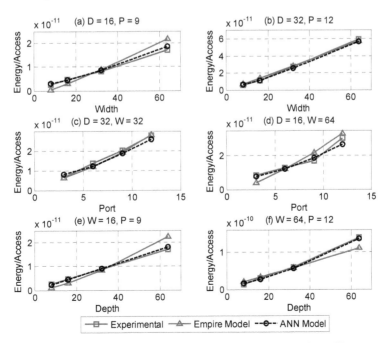

Figure 4. Comparison of energy/access for selected register files.

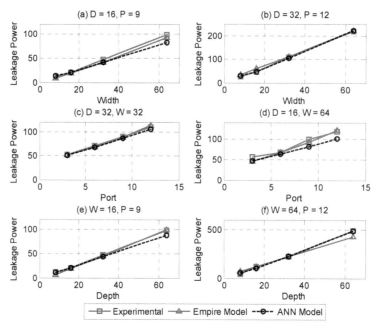

Figure 5. Comparison of leakage power for selected register files.

models for the tested instances was comparable with the ANN model underestimating in three instances (**Figures 5(a)**, **5(d)** and **5(e)**). Although Empire performance seem to be better in these instances, however, for 20 randomly selected test cases, the overall performance of ANN model was better in as demonstrated by the several performance criteria shown in **Table 3**.

From the aforementioned analysis of results and validation of the ANN model, it is evident that the proposed ANN model can be used to provide designers with representative estimates of the energy/access and the leakage power of a perceived register file design before committing to silicon. The energy/access and the leakage power are shown in **Figures 6** and **7** for all the register file designs used in this study assuming 130 nm technology and a supply voltage of 1.2 V.

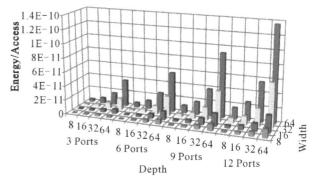

Figure 6. ANN model energy/access for all ports.

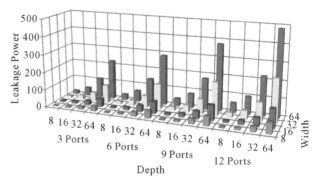

Figure 7. ANN model leakage power for all ports.

6. Conclusions

Register Files are becoming a major source of power dissipation in processor cores impacting the limited energy budget provided by batteries in portable devices. It is impractical to delay design decisions that impact the power consumption of a processor till the back-end design phase. It is becoming imperative that designers should be able to explore architectural tradeoffs at an early stage of the design cycle.

In this paper, we proposed a novel neural network model for estimating energy and leakage power in register files. The model is simple and efficient and can be used to provide estimates that are close to those expected when detailed and time consuming simulation is performed. The model is validated by comparing its results

to those produced by low level simulation, as well as by comparing it to the recently reported Empire model [10].

7. Acknowledgements

The authors would like to thank Dr. Praveen Raghavan of IMEC in Belgium for providing the register file designs data for the 130 nm technology node.

REFERENCES

[1] N. Sung and T. Mudge, "The Micorarchitecure of a Low Power Register File," *Proceedings of the International Symposium on Low Power Electronics and Design*, Seoul, 25-27 August 2003, pp. 384-389.

[2] X. Guan and Y. Fei, "Reducing Power Consumption of Embedded Processors through File Partitioning and Compiler Support," *Proceedings of the Conference on Application-Specific Systems, Architecture and Processors*, Leuven, 2-4 July 2008, pp. 269-274.

[3] Y. Zhou, H. Guo and J. Gu, "Register File Customization for Low Power Embedded Processors," *IEEE International Conference on Computer Science and Information Technology*, Beijing, 8-11 August 2009, pp. 92-96.

[4] M. Kondo and H. Nakamura, "A Small, Fast and Low-Power Register File by Bit-Partitioning," *11th International Symposium on High-Performance Computer Architecture*, San Francisco, 12-16 February 2005, pp. 40-49.

[5] M. Mueller *et al.*, "Low Power Register File Architecture for Application Specific DSPs," *IEEE International Symposium on Circuits and Systems*, 2002, Vol. 4, pp. 89-92.

[6] S. Wang, H. Yang, J. Hu and S. G. Ziavras, "Asymmetrically Banked Value-Aware Register Files for Low-Energy and High-Performance," *Microprocessors and Microsystems*, Vol. 32, No. 3, 2008, pp. 171-182.

[7] H. Takamura, K. Inoue and V. G. Moshnyaga, "Reducing Access Count to Register Files through Operand Reuse," *Advances in Computer Architecture, Lecture Notes in Computer Science*, Vol. 2823, 2003, pp. 112-121.

[8] W.-Y. Shieh and H.-D. Chen, "Saving Register-File Static Power by Monitoring Instruction Sequence in ROB," *Journal of Systems Architecture*, Vol. 57, No. 4, 2011, pp. 327-339.

[9] J. H. Tseng and K. Asanovic, "Energy-Efficient Register Access," *13th Symposium on Integrated Circuits and System Design*, Manaus, 18 September 2000, pp. 377-382.

[10] P. Raghavan, A. Lambrechts, M. Jayapala, F. Catthoor and D. Verkest, "EMPIRE: Empirical Power/Area/Timing Models for Register Files," *Microprocessors and Microsystems*, Vol. 33, No. 4, 2009, pp. 295-300.

[11] D. Brooks, V. Tiwari and M. Martonosi, "Wattch: A Framework for Architectural-Level Power Analysis and Optimizations," *Proceedings of the 27th International Symposium on Computer Architecture*, Vancouver, 14 June 2000, pp. 83-94.

[12] N. Kahraman and T. Yildirim, "Technology Independent Circuit Sizing for Standard Cell Based Design Using Neural Etworks," *Digital Signal Processing*, Vol. 19, No. 4, 2009, pp. 708-714.

[13] F. Djeffal, M. Chahdi, A. Benhaya and M. L. Hafiane, "An Approach Based on Neural Computation to Simulate the Nano-Scale CMOS Circuits: Application to the Simulation of CMOS Inverter," *Solid-State Electronics*, Vol. 51, No. 1, 2007, pp. 48-56.

[14] P. Kalpana and K. Gunavathi, "Wavelet Based Fault Detection in Analog VLSI Circuits Using Neural Networks," *Applied Soft Computing*, Vol. 8, No. 4, 2008, pp. 1592-1598.

[15] A. Suissa, O. Romain, J. Denoulet, K. Hachicha and P. Garda, "Empirical Method Based on Neural Networks for Analog Power Modeling," *IEEE Transactions on Computer-Aided Design of Integrated Circuits and Systems*, Vol. 29, No. 5, 2010, pp. 839-844.

[16] D. Dhabak and S. Pandit, "An Artificial Neural Network-Based Approach for Performance Modeling of Nano-Scale CMOS Inverter," *Institute of Engineering and Management Conference*, January 2011, pp. 165-170.

[17] S. Haykin, "Neural Networks: A Comprehensive Foundation," 2nd Edition, Prentice-Hall, Upper Saddle River, 1999.

[18] J. A. Abdalla and R. Hawileh, "Modeling and Simulation of Low-Cycle Fatigue Life of Steel Reinforcing Bars Using Artificial Neural Network," *Journal of the Franklin Institute*, Vol. 348, No. 7, 2011, pp. 1393-1403.

3

Area and Timing Estimation in Register Files Using Neural Networks

Assim Sagahyroon, Jamal Abdalla
American University of Sharjah, Sharjah, UAE

ABSTRACT

The increase in issue width and instructions window size in modern processors demand an increase in the size of the register files, as well as an increase in the number of ports. Bigger register files implies an increase in power consumed by these units as well as longer access delays. Models that assist in estimating the size of the register file, and its timing early in the design cycle are critical to the time-budget allocated to a processor design and to its performance. In this work, we discuss a Radial Base Function (RBF) Artificial Neural Network (ANN) model for the prediction of time and area for standard cell register files designed using optimized Synopsys Design Ware components and an UMC130 nm library. The ANN model predictions were compared against experimental results (obtained using detailed simulation) and a nonlinear regression-based model, and it is observed that the ANN model is very accurate and outperformed the non-linear model in several statistical parameters. Using the trained ANN model, a parametric study was carried out to study the effect of the number of words in the file (D), the number of bit in one word (W) and the total number of read and write ports (P) on the latency and area of standard cell register files.

Keywords: Register Files; Area Estimates; Timing Estimates; Neural Networks

1. Introduction

The access time, energy, and area of a register file are critical factors to the performance of modern processors. The access time and size of register files in wide-issue processors often play a critical role in determining cycle time. This is because such files need to be large to support multiple in-flight instructions, and multiported to avoid stalling the wide-issue. Large sized multiport architectures of register files often lead to significant increase in the processor's power consumption. For example, in the Alpha 21,464, the 512-entry 16-read and 8-write (16-r/8-w) ports register file consumed more power and was larger than the 64 KB primary caches. To reduce the cycle time impact, it was implemented as two 8-r/8-w split register files [1,2].

Register files are heavily-ported RAM structures. A processor capable of issuing eight integer instructions each cycle may need an integer register file with sixteen read ports (corresponding to two source operands per instruction), and eight write ports. It was reported in [3] that the access time for an 80-entry 24-ported register file can exceed 1.5 ns at 0.18 micron technology, potentially being on critical paths determining the cycle time.

Although, the adverse delays effects can be alleviated by pipelining, this complicates the bypass logic instead.

In addition, having a deep pipeline increases the branch misprediction penalty, lowering IPC or instructions completed per cycle. Therefore, it is difficult to remove the adverse effect of a large register file completely and it is important to optimize the register file size without performance degradation [4].

The access time of a register file consists of two distinct components: the wire propagation delay and the fan-in/fan-out delay. Register files typically contain long word-lines and bit-lines, which can take a long time to propagate a signal across their length. Bigger register file and an increased number of ports result in a taller register file layout, which translates to longer word-lines and bit-lines [5], thereby increasing wire propagation delay. Also, wire delays do not at all scale with the silicon technology improvements. Thus as register files grow in size, with faster transistors (smaller feature sizes), it only exacerbates their delay problem. A circuit diagram for a three ports register file is shown in **Figure 1**.

Additionally, the physical dimensions of a register file play a very important role in determining its power consumption. They influence the power consumption in more than one way: 1) they determine the length of the wires in the file, hence directly affects the power consumption by determining the capacitance of the nodes, and 2) they impose pipelining constraints, indirectly af-

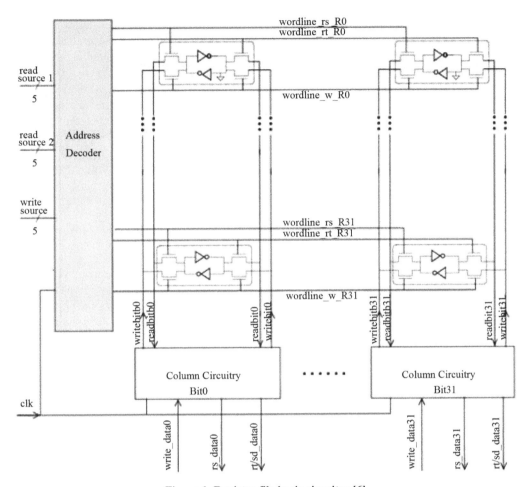

Figure 1. Register file basic circuitry [6].

fecting power by introducing additional power consuming nodes. Therefore, it is critical to have a good model that assists designers in estimating the physical dimensions of these files [7].

Models that can be used to evaluate architectural alternatives in register file design, and assist in making informed decisions prior to the back-end design phase are essential to realizing efficient designs in terms of area, delay, and power.

In recent years, there has been a great advancement in the field of ANN (Artificial Neural Networks), both from theoretical and applications points of view. ANNs have been used in classification, pattern matching, pattern recognition, optimization and control-related problems. In electrical engineering, neural networks have been used to solve a wide variety of VLSI related problems [8-11]. A neural network (NN) approach for modeling the time characteristics of fundamental gates of digital integrated circuits that include inverter, NAND, NOR, and XOR gates is discussed in [8]. The modeling approach presented is technology independent, fast, and accurate, which makes it suitable for circuit simulators. The application of an artificial neural network (ANN) to the study

of the nanoscale CMOS circuits is presented in [9]. A novel method of testing analog VLSI circuits, using wavelet transform for analog circuit response analysis and artificial neural networks (ANN) for fault detection is proposed in [10]. Power consumption using neural network of analog components at the system level is discussed in [11]. The proposed method provides estimation of the instantaneous power consumption of analog blocks.

In this work, we propose the use of neural networks to model timing and area for standard cell based register files designed using 130 nm technology. Three parameters that influence the power consumed by a register file, namely, the number of words in the register file (Depth), the number of bits in one word (Width), and the total number of read and write ports (Port) are used as input to the ANN. The output parameters of the ANN are delay and area estimates for the perceived design.

2. Background

Praveen *et al.* [12], used low level simulation that takes into account the layout details as well as detailed transistor characterization provided by a standard cell library to collect data on the size and delays exhibited by various structures of register files. They used optimized Synopsys Design Ware components from the UMC130 nm library to design various register files structures. Layouts were generated for register files with a varying number of ports ranging from 3 to 12, a depth that varies from 4 to 64 words, and a width that varies from 8 to 128 bits. All these combinations of register files were designed; patristic capacitances in the routing wires and gate capacitances of each transistor were extracted from the layouts. The extracted netlist was then simulated using ModelSim. After completing over 100 register file design for the 130 nm technology node, the timing and area of each design were tabulated. Curve fitting was performed on each variable using register file depth, width, number of ports, as well as the activity factor as independent input variables. For the designs it is assumed that each of the ports of the register file is driving a load of F04. Equations (1) and (2) below are the derived model equations, where Area and Timing are the subjects of the two equations respectively; the authors in [12] referred to it as the Empire Model. For a complete description of the steps taken to arrive to this model, readers are referred to [12].

$$\text{Area}\left(\text{in: } \mu m^2\right) = 7.36 \times 10^4 - 2.37 \times 10^3 \times D$$
$$- 2.12 \times 10^3 \times W - 1.21 \times 10^4 \times P + 1.24 \times 10^2 \times D \times W$$
$$+ 3.33 \times 10^2 \times D \times P + 2.58 \times 10^2 \times W \times P$$
$$- 4.98 \times 10^{-1} \times D^2 + 1.56 \times W^2 + 2.71 \times 10^2 \times P^2$$

$$\text{Timing}\left(\text{in: ns}\right) = 1.90 \times 10^{-1} + 1.57 \times 10^{-2} \times D + 1.72$$
$$\times 10^{-2} \times W + 4.08 \times 10^{-1} \times P + 5.91 \times 10^{-4} \times D \times W$$
$$+ 1.10 \times 10^{-3} \times D \times P + 1.62 \times 10^{-3} \times W \times P - 1.69 \tag{2}$$
$$\times 10^{-4} \times D^2 - 2.39 \times 10^{-4} \times W^2 - 1.74 \times 10^{-2} \times P^2$$

In the equations above: D represents the number of words in the file, W represents the number of bit in one word, P represents the total number of ports (read and write). To validate the curve-fitted formulae described by Equations (1) and (2), Praveen *et al.* in [12], compared them against results from the actual implementations. It is reported that the models exhibit on average about 10% error when compared to the values obtained using detailed simulation.

3. Neural Network Model and Architecture

The field of *Artificial Neural Networks* is one of the main branches of artificial intelligence that found many applications in several engineering disciplines. ANNs are processing elements that are capable of learning relationships between input and output and they can be used for

classification, prediction, clustering, and function approximation, among others. Several neural network architectures with different learning algorithms such as backpropagation were used over the years. In general, an ANN consists of massive parallel computational processing elements (neurons) that are connected with weighted connections and have learning capability that simulates the behavior of a brain [13,14]. The network weights and the network threshold values are initially set to random values and new values of the network weights and bias values are computed during the network training phase. The neurons output are calculated using Equation (3) below:

$$y_i = F\left(\sum \left(x_j \times w_{ij}\right) + b_j\right) \tag{3}$$

where y_i is the output of the neuron i, x_j are the input of j neurons of the previous layer; value, w_{ij} is the neuron weights, b_j is the bias for modeling the threshold; and F is the transfer or activation function [13,14]. The transfer function also known as the *processing element* is the portion of the neural network where all the computing is performed. The activation function maps the input domain (infinite) to an output domain (finite). The ANN error (E) for a given training pattern i is given by Equation (4):

$$E = \frac{1}{2} \sum_{i=1}^{n} \sum_{j=1}^{m} \left(O_j^i - T_j^i\right)^2 \tag{4}$$

where O_j^i is the output and T_j^i is the target. For a thorough discussion of neural network theory and applications readers are referred to [13].

The Radial Basis Function (RBF) ANN together with the Gaussian activation function, and the Multi-Layer Perceptron (MLP) together with the hyperbolic tangent (tanh) activation function are among the most widely used feed-forward universal approximators. In this study a hybrid of these two universal approximators is used. Specifically, a RBF ANN topology with one additional hidden layer and 15 neurons (processing elements) in first hidden layer, and four processing element in the second hidden layer are used. The RBF neural network has a Gaussian activation function in the first hidden layer while the additional hidden layer has a linear hyperbolic tangent (linear tanh) activation function and the output layer has a bias axon activation function as shown in **Figure 2**. The performance of this combination of activation functions for the data set used in this work proved to outperform the standard RBF or standard MLP, when used separately.

As depicted in **Figure 2**, the neural network architecture used in this study, has one input layer, two hidden layers and one output layer. The input layer consists of three nodes, mainly, the number of words in the register

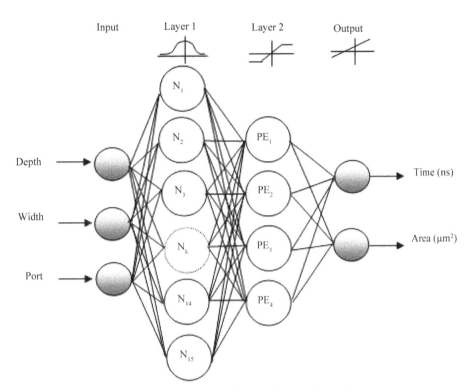

Figure 2. A multilayer RBF neural network topology.

file depth (D), the number of bits in one word width (W), and the total number of read and write ports (P). The output layer of the ANN consists of two nodes which are the *time* and the *area* estimates.

To train the NN, data collected from details simulation runs in [12] is divided into two categories, namely, the *training data set and, the testing data set.* For both sets the maximum Depth value used is 64 registers per file, the minimum is 4; the maximum width used is 64 bits and the minimum is 8, while for the ports parameter the maximum number of ports is 12 ports, and the minimum is 3 ports. For the training data set, the maximum timing computed is 7.55 nano-second (ns) and the minimum is 1.11 ns, while for the test data set, the maximum timing within the used set is 4.92 ns, and the minimum is 1.81 ns. The areas range is 721,383 μm^2 to 2512 μm^2 for the training set, and 164,590 μm^2 to 4902 μm^2 for the test set.

Initial random values are used for the weights of the neural network and different learning rates (step sizes) were used for the different layers of the RBF neural network. The learning rate used for the first and second hidden layers is 1.0 and for the output layer is 0.1. A momentum factor of 0.7 was used for the model all through with a back-propagation learning algorithm. The total number of data items used for training the neural network is 60 and the number of data items used for testing the neural network is 20. The neural network was trained four times with 2000 epochs in each training cycle and the average performance was taken. The computed aver-

age Normalized Mean Square Error (NMSE) for the training data was 0.00494 with a standard deviation of 0.000614. **Figure 3** shows the convergence rate of the four training runs. There is a sharp decrease in the NMSE during the first 15 epochs. As the number of epoch increases, the MSE remains almost constant.

4. Results and Discussions

The ANN model was trained using 60 data sets and for verification the trained ANN model is tested next using 20 randomly selected testing data sets. Parameters of the 20 test data sets were also used to predict the time and area using the Empire model. **Tables 1** and **2** show the performance indicators of the 20 testing samples. As shown

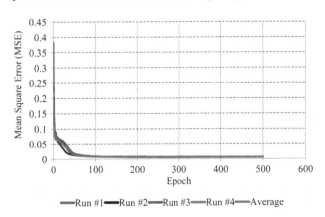

Figure 3. Training NMSE for the four runs of ANN models.

Table 1. Performance of the ANN on time prediction of the test data.

Performance Criterion	ANN Model	Empire Model
Mean Absolute Error (MAE) (ns)	0.37963	0.34450
Mean Absolute Percent Error (MAPE) (%)	11.208	10.649
Normalized Mean Square Error (NMSE)	0.39772	0.28300
Correlation Coefficient (r)	0.79835	0.86485

Table 2. Performance of the ANN on area prediction of the test data.

Performance Criterion	ANN Model	Empire Model
Mean Absolute Error (MAE) (μm^2)	5648.987	11153.388
Mean Absolute Percent Error (MAPE) (%)	16.130	47.413
Normalized Mean Square Error (NMSE)	0.02606	0.12030
Correlation Coefficient (r)	0.98722	0.94734

in **Tables 1** and **2**, the Normalized Mean Square Error (NMSE) is 0.3977 and 0.0261 and the correlation co-efficient (r) is 0.7983 and 0.9872 for time and area, respectively. This indicates that the measured and the ANN predicted values correlate very well for the area and to a lesser extent for the time. The performance of the

Empire model is slightly better than the performance of the ANN in all performance criteria in predicting time, however, the ANN model outperformed the Empire model by far in all performance criteria in predicting area estimates.

Table 3 shows the prediction and accuracy of the ANN model and the Empire model based on the test data set as compared to the measured values of *time*. In column 1, the case number specifies the depth (D), width (W), and number of ports (P) for each design tested. It is observed that 55% of the ANN model predictions of the test data are within 10% or less of the measured values of time compared to 50% of Empire model predictions of the test data are within 10% of the measured values of time. Furthermore, 80% of the ANN predictions of the test data are within 20% of the measured values of the time while 90% of Empire model predictions of the test data are within 20% of the measured values of time. It is clear that the Empire predictions of time are slightly better than the ANN model prediction which corroborate with the results from the performance criteria presented earlier.

Table 4 shows the prediction and accuracy of the ANN model and the Empire model based on the test data set as compared to the measured values of area. It is observed that 45% of ANN model predictions are within

Table 3. Prediction and accuracy of time of test data.

Case Number	Measured Value (ns)	ANN Prediction (ns)	Empire Prediction (ns)	ANN Error (%)	Empire Error (%)
DWP_8-32-6	2.41	2.84	2.94	17.93	22.16
DWP_8-8-12	3.03	3.29	3.12	8.67	2.83
DWP_16-64-9	3.9	4.20	4.47	7.75	14.68
DWP_64-16-3	2.51	2.79	2.68	11.12	6.63
DWP_64-8-12	3.71	4.29	4.32	15.54	16.37
DWP_8-16-12	2.91	3.60	3.40	23.60	16.83
DWP_32-32-6	3.65	3.91	3.77	7.12	3.31
DWP_4-32-3	1.86	1.89	1.86	1.73	0.23
DWP_4-16-3	1.81	1.83	1.66	1.38	−8.36
DWP_64-8-6	3.07	3.21	3.25	4.44	5.81
DWP_16-64-3	2.28	2.29	2.55	0.42	11.83
DWP_8-32-12	3.24	4.23	3.88	30.49	19.65
DWP_16-8-6	2.58	2.47	2.60	−4.17	0.78
DWP_16-16-3	2.08	2.03	1.96	−2.29	−5.79
DWP_16-8-12	3.39	3.49	3.35	2.87	−1.11
DWP_4-64-9	4.45	3.71	3.75	−16.63	−15.68
DWP_8-32-9	2.9	3.50	3.57	20.61	23.00
DWP_64-32-3	3.21	3.34	3.45	4.16	7.46
DWP_4-64-12	4.92	3.73	4.20	−24.27	−14.55
DWP_4-16-9	3.61	2.93	3.04	−18.95	−15.91

Table 4. Prediction and accuracy of area of test data.

Case Number	Measured Value (μm²)	ANN Prediction (μm²)	Empire Prediction (μm²)	ANN Error (%)	Empire Error (%)
DWP_8-32-6	25709.18	30363.05	22785.57	18.10	−11.37
DWP_8-8-12	12087.36	16958.01	−3756.03	40.30	−131.07
DWP_16-64-9	136007.4	125049	142849.3	−8.06	5.03
DWP_64-16-3	81561.6	87238.13	55794.55	6.96	−31.59
DWP_64-8-12	100,675	113386.6	140844	12.63	39.90
DWP_8-16-12	22,032	26109.32	12287.49	18.51	−44.23
DWP_32-32-6	108433.7	117453.4	108611.5	8.32	0.16
DWP_4-32-3	9671.616	14226.64	8644.472	47.10	−10.62
DWP_4-16-3	4902.336	6109.812	21046.39	24.63	329.31
DWP_64-8-6	60937.92	69793.9	43920.03	14.53	−27.93
DWP_16-64-3	78853.82	60670.06	64897.27	−23.06	−17.70
DWP_8-32-12	42265.15	44686.45	44973.57	5.73	6.41
DWP_16-8-6	13775.62	14572.04	16072.35	5.78	16.67
DWP_16-16-3	20043.07	20316.6	28282.87	1.36	41.11
DWP_16-8-12	23378.11	25364.64	17092.35	8.50	−26.89
DWP_4-64-9	32106.24	36923.01	40212.79	15.00	25.25
DWP_8-32-9	33170.69	22730.22	31440.57	−31.47	−5.22
DWP_64-32-3	164590.3	161332	162432.6	−1.98	−1.31
DWP_4-64-12	40272.77	42352.23	74517.79	5.16	85.03
DWP_4-16-9	8403.264	6266.601	718.392	−25.43	−91.45

10% or less of the measured values of area compared to 25% of Empire model predictions of the test data are within 10% of the measured values of area. Also, 70% of the ANN predictions of the test data are within 20% of the measured values of the area while only 45% of Empire model predictions of the test data are within 20% of the measured values of area. It is clear that the ANN predictions of area are better than the Empire model predictions. This corroborates the results of the performance criteria presented earlier in **Table 1**.

Parametric Study

To further compare the performance of the Empire model and the ANN model in predicting the time and the area, we varied the input parameters (width, ports, and depth) and computed the resulting outputs for 6 designs. **Figures 4** and **5** depict comparative plots showing the predictions of time and area respectively for varied combinations of parameters.

From **Figures 4(c)** and **(d)**, it is clear ANN model predictions are fairly accurate when the number of ports is varied with a fixed depth and width. **Figure 3(b)** shows that the ANN model when the width is increased with the depth and ports parameters fixed has underestimated the time specially with wider designs. Similarly, when the depth is varied while keeping the width and ports fixed

(**Figures 4(e)** and **(f)**), the ANN predications were relatively above and below the experimental values in few cases.

In the instances selected for area comparison (**Figure 6**), both models performed relatively well and the predicted areas were close to the experimental values obtained from detailed simulation. However, overall and as the statistical results of **Table 2** indicate, the ANN model has outperformed the Empire in area prediction.

From the aforementioned analysis of results and validation of the ANN model, it is evident that the proposed ANN model can be used to provide designers with representative estimates of the time and area of a perceived register file design before committing to silicon. The time and the area estimates for all the register file designs used in this study with 130 nm technology and a supply voltage of 1.2 V are shown in **Figures 6** and **7** respectively.

5. Conclusions

The continued trend in microprocessors design towards wider instruction issue and large instruction windows implies register files will have to be designed with large sizes and a large number of read/write ports. Consequently, this will lead to additional power consumption by these large-sized files and a noticeable impact on cy-

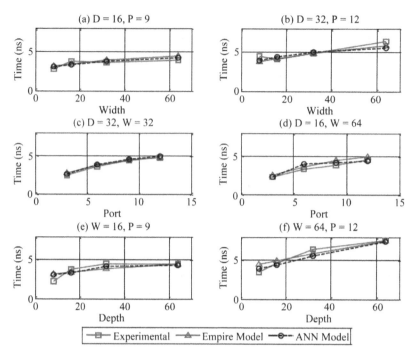

Figure 4. Comparison of time for selected register files.

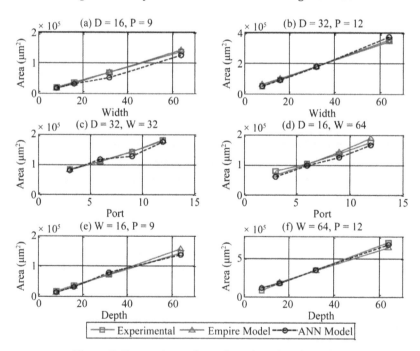

Figure 5. Comparison of area for selected register files.

cle time. Therefore, models and tools that allow designers to predict the area and the timing of a given design prior to committing to silicon are of great benefit to microprocessors designers. Evaluating architectural trade-offs early in the design cycle provides designers with insight into the performance of a design, and shortens the time-to-market window.

In this paper, we proposed a novel neural network model for estimating the timing and size or area for register file designs. The model is simple and efficient and can be used to provide estimates that are close to those expected when detailed and time consuming simulation is performed. The model is validated by comparing its results to those produced by low level simulation, as well as by comparing it to the recently reported Empire model [11].

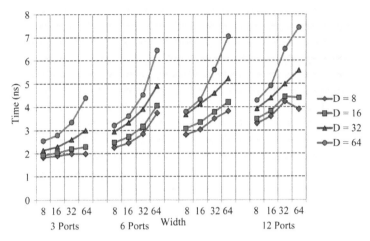

Figure 6. ANN model for time for all ports.

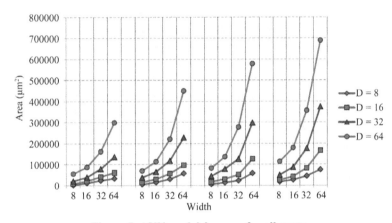

Figure 7. ANN model for area for all ports.

6. Acknowledgements

The authors would like to thank Dr. Praveen Raghavan of IMEC in Belgium for providing the register file designs data for the 130 nm technology node.

REFERENCES

[1] R. Preston, *et al.*, "Design of an 8-Wide Superscalar RISC Microprocessor with Simultaneous Multithreading," *Solid-State Circuits Conference*, Vol. 1, 7 February 2002, pp. 334-472.

[2] N. S. Kim and T. Mudge, "The Microarchitecture of a Low Power Register File," *Proceedings of the 2003 International Symposium on Low Power Electronics and Design*, Seoul, 25-27 August 2003, pp. 384-389.

[3] R. Balasubramonian, S. Dwarkadas and D. H. Albonesi, "Reducing the Complexity of the Register File in Dynamic Superscalar Processors," *Proceedings of the 34th annual ACM/IEEE International Symposium on Microarchitecture*, Austin, 1-5 December 2001, pp. 237-248.

[4] Y. Tanaka and H. Ando, "Reducing Register File Size through Instruction Pre-Execution Enhanced by Value Prediction," *Proceedings of the 2009 IEEE International Conference on Computer Design*, Nagoya, 4-7 October 2009, pp. 238-245.

[5] S. Rixner, W. J. Dally, B. Khailany, P. Mattson, U. J. Kapasi and J. D. Owens, "Register Organization for Media Processing," *Proceedings of the 6th International Symposium on High Performance Computer Architecture*, Stanford, January 2000, pp. 375-386.

[6] J. Tseng and K. Asanovic, "Energy Efficient Register Access," *Proceedings of the 13th Symposium on Integrated Circuits and Systems Design*, Cambridge, 2000, pp. 377-382.

[7] K. M. B Ahin, P. Patra and F. N. Najm, "ESTIMA: An Architectural-Level Power Estimator for Multi-Ported Pipelined Register Files," *Proceedings of 2003 International Symposium on Low Power Electronics and Design*, Hillsboro, 25-27 August 2003, pp. 294-297.

[8] N. Kahraman and T. Yildirim, "Technology Independent Circuit Sizing for Standard Cell Based Design Using Neural Networks," *Digital Signal Processing*, Vol. 19, No. 4, 2009, pp. 708-714.

[9] F. Djeffal, M. Chahdi, A. Benhaya and M. L. Hafiane, "An Approach Based on Neural Computation to Simulate the Nanoscale CMOS Circuits: Application to the Simulation of CMOS Inverter," *Solid-State Electronics*, Vol. 51, No. 1, 2007, pp. 48-56.

[10] P. Kalpana and K. Gunavathi, "Wavelet Based Fault De-

tection in Analog VLSI Circuits Using Neural Networks," *Applied Soft Computing*, Vol. 8, No. 4, 2008, pp. 1592-1598.

[11] A. Suissa, O. Romain, J. Denoulet, K. Hachicha and P. Garda, "Empirical Method Based on Neural Networks for Analog Power Modeling," *IEEE Transactions on Computer-Aided Design of Integrated Circuits and Systems*, Vol. 29, No. 5, 2010, pp. 839-844.

[12] P. Raghavan, A. Lambrechts and M. Jayapala, F. Catthoor and D. Verkest, "EMPIRE: Empirical Power/Area/

Timing Models for Register Files," *Microprocessors and Microsystems*, Vol. 33, 2009, pp. 295-300.

[13] S. Haykin, "Neural Networks: A Comprehensive Foundation," 2nd Edition, Prentice-Hall, Upper Saddle River, 1999.

[14] J. A. Abdalla and R. A. Hawileh, "Modeling and Simulation of Low-Cycle Fatigue Life of Steel Reinforcing Bars Using Artificial Neural Network," *Journal of the Franklin Institute*, Vol. 348, No. 7, 2011, pp. 1393-1403.

4

Voltage Mode Universal Filter Using Current Differencing Buffered Amplifier as an Active Device

Sheikh Ajaz Bashir*, **Nisar Ahmed Shah**

Department of Electronics & Instrumentation Technology, University of Kashmir, Srinagar, India

ABSTRACT

Integrated filter circuit design resulted in desire for replacement of Inductors by active elements like Operational Amplifiers which led to the introduction of active filters. Active filter design has evolved over a period of time. Starting with OP AMPs, we have witnessed phenomenal growth of active component usage in filter design and development catering to varying requirements. This has contributed greatly in emergence of circuits with minimal limitations and advantages in terms of wide Bandwidth and High slew rates. Current Differencing Buffered Amplifier (CDBA) based active filter design has resulted in introduction of many novel circuits. This paper proposes a new Voltage-mode three input and Single output (TISO) multifunction filter based on single CDBA, four resistors and two capacitors. This second order filter circuit is capable of realizing various filter functions by choosing values of the three inputs variably. The natural frequency (ω_0) can be tuned with passive components and the Q of the circuit is independent of (ω_0). The higher cascading capability of the circuit is ensured because of its low-output impedance. Further PSPICE-simulated results are in conformity with theoretical values.

Keywords: CDBA; Voltage Mode Circuits; Multifunction Filters; Slew Rate; Parasitic Capacitance

1. Introduction

CDBA, a current-mode component, has been introduced by C. Acar and S. Ozoguz in 1999 [1]. It offers advantageous features such as high slew rate, absence of parasitic capacitance, wide bandwidth, and simple implementation. Since the CDBA consists of a unity-gain current differential amplifier and a unity-gain voltage amplifier, this element would be suitable for the implementation of voltage and current-mode signal processing applications. As far as the applications of the CDBA are concerned, various voltage-mode and current-mode filters and oscillators have been reported in literature [2-10]. CDBA being a Current-mode universal active component, provides wide bandwidth and high slew-rate as distinct advantages.

In this paper we are implementing CDBA, a current mode active element, in voltage mode operation due to the fact that majority of analog signal processing applications require voltage-mode operation [2].

The circuit symbol of the CDBA is shown in **Figure 1(a)**, where p and n are the positive and negative current input terminals, respectively, z is the current output terminal, and w is the voltage output terminal. Its current and voltage characteristics can be described by the ma-

trix shown below.

$$\begin{bmatrix} I_z \\ V_w \\ V_p \\ V_n \end{bmatrix} = \begin{bmatrix} 0 & 0 & 1 & -1 \\ 1 & 0 & 0 & 0 \\ 0 & 0 & 0 & 0 \\ 0 & 0 & 0 & 0 \end{bmatrix} \begin{bmatrix} V_z \\ I_w \\ I_p \\ I_n \end{bmatrix}$$

Here we have

$$V_p = V_n, \; I_z = I_p - I_n \text{ and } V_w = V_z \qquad (1)$$

According to the above set of describing equations at (1) depicted by the Matrix, the terminal z behaves as a current source that takes the difference of currents at the inputs, and the terminal w behaves as a voltage source that copies the output voltage at the z terminal. Thus, the CDBA can be considered as a collection of a non inverting and an inverting current-mode, and non-inverting voltage-mode unity-gain cells, which can be realized by a cascade connection of a current subtractor and a voltage follower. Although the CDBA can be realized by using several well-known circuit techniques, one possible practical implementation is given in **Figure 1(b)** by use of two CFAs (AD844) [11]. Further a CMOS circuit realization of the CDBA is displayed in **Figure 2**.

The size of CDBA configuration shown in **Figure 2** is about the same as that of a CMOS II-generation Current

*Corresponding author.

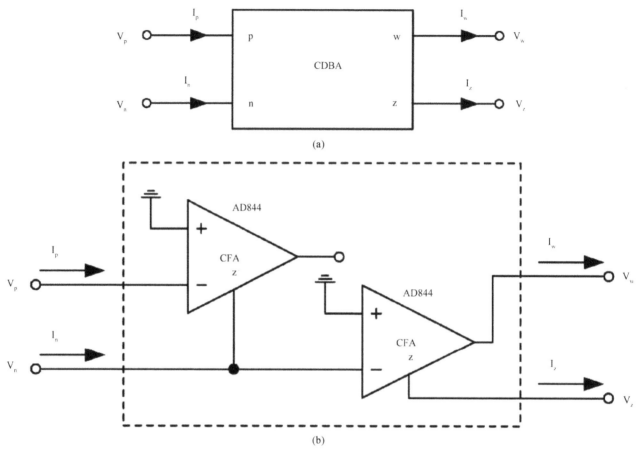

(a)

(b)

Figure 1. (a) CDBA symbol; (b) Implementation of CDBA using CFAs AD844.

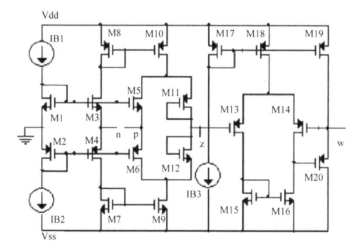

Figure 2. CMOS circuit realization of CDBA [11].

Conveyor (CC II) [12].

2. Purpose of Research

The aim of this research article is to present a Universal active second order filter with single active device and a few passive components and better cascadability. By suitable selection of inputs we should be able to realize all

filter functions. The natural frequency of Biquad has to be dependent on passive components only with Quality factor being independent of it.

3. Proposed Circuit

In this paper a Voltage Mode multifunction circuit based on single CDBA is proposed as shown in **Figure 3**. In the proposed circuit a single CDBA, four resistors and two capacitors are used and the circuit shapes as a three input and single Output unit (TISO).

From routine Circuit analysis, the characteristic equation of the proposed CDBA based VM TISO circuit can be written as at (2).

$$V_{out} = \frac{V_1 s^2 + V_2 s \dfrac{1}{R_4 C_1} + V_3 \dfrac{1}{R_3 R_5 C_1 C_6}}{s^2 + \dfrac{s}{C_1}\left(\dfrac{1}{R_3} + \dfrac{1}{R_4} + \dfrac{1}{R_5}\right) + \dfrac{1}{R_2 R_3 C_1 C_6}} \quad (2)$$

The natural frequency of the circuit (ω_0) will be as shown in Equation (3). Here the value of (ω_0) can be adjusted by changing the values of passive components R_2 and R_3.

$$\omega_o = \sqrt{\frac{1}{R_2 R_3 C_1 C_6}} \quad (3)$$

Further the Quality factor of the filter block will be derived from Equation (4) where its value will be independent of (ω_0) and can be adjusted with variation in R_4 only.

$$Q = \frac{R_4}{R_2 R_3 + R_4 R_3 + R_2 R_4} \sqrt{\frac{R_2 R_3 C_1}{C_6}} \quad (4)$$

Realization of various filter topologies is possible by varying the inputs as under

INPUT VALUES		FILTER REALIZATION
$V_2 = V_3 = 0$	$V_1 = V_{in}$	A Second Order High Pass Filter
$V_2 = V_3 = 0$	$V_2 = V_{in}$	A Second Order Band Pass Filter
$V_1 = V_2 = 0$	$V_3 = V_{in}$	A Second Order Low Pass Filter
$V_2 = 0$	$V_1 = V_3 = V_{in}$	A Second Order Notch Filter
$V_1 = -V_2 = V_3 = V_{in}$		A Second Order All Pass Filter

4. Circuit Simulation

The performances of the proposed circuit given in **Figure 3** has been simulated with PSPICE program. In the simulations, the CDBA was constructed employing commercially available current feedback amplifiers (CFAs), *i.e.*, AD844 of Analog Devices, as given in **Figure 1(b)**. The circuit was supplied with symmetrical voltages of ±12 V.

The simulated frequency characteristics of all the filter functions of the proposed CDBA-based VM multifunction TISO circuit in **Figure 3** are shown in **Figure 4** with the passive component values: $R_2 = R_3 = R_4 = R_5 = 1$ K Ohm, $C_1 = C_6 = 1$ nF leading to $f_0 = 159.15$ KHz and $Q = 1/3$ (Gain for BP response at $f_0 = 0.3$). The filter is de-

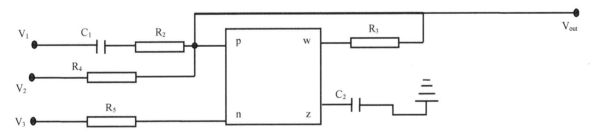

Figure 3. Proposed VM TISO multifunction filter.

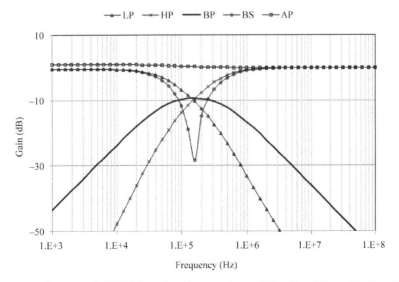

Figure 4. Magnitude response of proposed CDBA based voltage mode multifunction filter with $R_2 = R_3 = R_4 = R_5 = 1$ K ohm, $C_1 = C_6 = 1$ nF leading to $f_0 = 159.15$ KHz and $Q = 1/3$ (Gain for BP response at $f_0 = 0.3$).

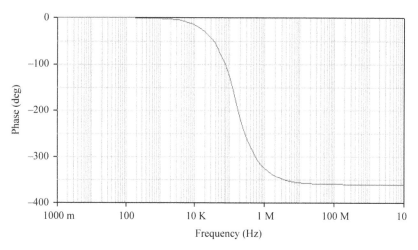

Figure 5. Phase response of all pass response.

signed for a natural angular frequency of $f_o = \omega_0/2\pi \cong$ 159.15 KHz and the quality factor of $Q = 1/3$. With the same setting, the simulated gain and phase responses of the AP filters verifying theory values are depicted in **Figure 5**. From the figures, it appears that the simulation results are in excellent agreement with theoretical values.

5. Conclusion

In this paper, VM TISO multifunction filter involving a single CDBA is introduced. The proposed circuit is able to realize Low Pass, High Pass, Band Pass, All Pass and Notch function as well. Besides employing a single CDBA, there are four resistive and two reactive components in the circuit block. Further incase of proposed circuit Q is independent of (ω_0) and can be varied by simply changing the value of R_4 only. The tuning of filter *i.e*; changing the value of (ω_0) is possible by changing the value of passive components R_2 and R_3 in the circuit.

REFERENCES

[1] C. Acar and S. O¨ Zog˘uz, "A New Versatile Building Block: Current Differencing Buffered Amplifier Suitable for Analog Signal Processing Filters," *Microelectronics Journal*, Vol. 30, No. 2, 1999, pp. 157-160.

[2] A. U. Keskin, "Voltage-Mode High-Q Band-Pass Filters and Oscillators Employing Single CDBA and Minimum Number of Components," *International Journal of Electronics*, Vol. 92, No. 8, 2005, pp. 479-487.

[3] S. O¨zog˘uz, A. Toker and C. Acar, "Current-Mode Continuous Time Fully-Integrated Universal Filter Using CDBAs," *Electronics Letters*, Vol. 35, No. 2, 1999, pp. 97-98.

[4] W. Tangsrirat and W. Surakampontorn, "Realization of Multiple-Output Biquadratic Filters Using Current Differencing Buffered Amplifiers," *International Journal of Electronics*, Vol. 92, No. 6, 2005, pp. 313-325.

[5] W. Tangsrirat, "Voltage-Mode Multifunction Biquadratic Filter and Sinusoidal Oscillator Using Only Two CDBAs," *Journal of Active and Passive Electronic Devices*, Vol. 4, No. 4, 2009, pp. 335-345.

[6] H. Sedef and C. Acar, "On the Realization of Voltage-Mode Filters Using CDBA," *Frequenz*, Vol. 54, No. 9-10, 2000, pp. 198-202.

[7] K. N. Salama and A. M. Soliman, "Voltage Mode Kerwin-Huelsman-Newcomb Circuit Using CDBAs," *Frequenz*, Vol. 54, No. 7-8, 2000, pp. 90-93.

[8] S. Maheshwari and I. A. Khan, "Novel Voltage-Mode Universal Filter Using Only Two CDBAs," *Journal of Circuits, Systems and Computers*, Vol. 14, No. 1, 2005, pp. 159-164.

[9] S. Ozoguz, A. Toker and C. Acar, "Current-Mode Continuous-Time Fully Integrated Universal Filter Using CDBAs," *Electronics Letters*, Vol. 35, No. 2, 1999, pp. 97-98.

[10] A. U. Keskin and E. Hancioglu, "Current Mode Multifunction Filter Using Two CDBAs," *International Journal of Electronics & Communications*, Vol. 59, No. 8, 2005, pp. 495-498.

[11] Anonymity, "Analog Devices Linear Products Data Book," Analog Devices, Norwood, 1990.

[12] W. S. Hassanein, I. A. Awad and A. M. Soliman, "New Wide Band Low Power CMOS Current Conveyors," *Analog Integrated Circuits Signal Process*, Vol. 40, No. 1, 2004, pp. 91-97.

5

Design and Implementation of an Analogue Tester Board*

Yousif Al Mashhadany, Semeh Jassam, Amead Sami, Hebaa Nassar

Electrical Engineering Department, Engineering College, University of Anbar, Al-Anbar, Iraq

ABSTRACT

The recent rapid development of electronics and continual increase of the complexity and variety of electronic circuits (chips, packets, micro- and embedded systems) creates a demand for viable test and diagnostic methods. These recent developments have led to a great deal of research interest in electronic diagnostic systems, especially of effective diagnosis methods of detection, localization and identification levels of hard (catastrophic) and soft (parametric) faults in analog circuits. At present, the majority of electronic devices (embedded systems) are designed based on digital circuits; however a lot of them also contain analog components that require more complicated testing techniques. This paper presents a novel, electronic components tester board with inside, outside of circuit under tested. The design is first simulated by using the electronic work-bench software Multisim 11 in order to obtain satisfactory theoretical results for each standalone element of the design. Thereafter, the design is practically implemented and experimentally verified to show agreement with the simulated results.

Keywords: Tester Board; Electronic Components; Electronic Diagnostic Systems

1. Introduction

The different type of electronic equipment that has invaded our offices and homes these days is mind boggling. Numerous appliances we use at home and office are remote-controlled, for example, television (TV), air-conditioners, audio equipment, telephone, etc. It almost seems like magic how even a child, can switch channels, or increase and decrease the volume on a TV set at home by just clicking on a few buttons sitting at the comfort of a sofa away from the television apparently without any physical wiring or connection [1]!

Again, it is astonishing how easy it is to communicate with people living several thousands of kilometers away, from any place at home, office, on the road in a car, or in a classroom by just clicking a few numbers on palm sized cellular phones. One of the most important concerns related with electrical and electronic gadgets and equipment is their power consumption. Nowadays, consumers would like to know the specifics of every electrical and electronic item before buying a product for residential or commercial purposes. So, commercial electrical and electronic devices must match international quality standards in terms of operation, efficiency and functionality to be able checking with standard [2,3].

For construction of the tester board discussed in this paper, it was a requirement that all the components should be able to be mounted on a small PC. There are a number of different suitable cases and even a small one will fit the board. Despite initial reluctance to use a soft casing for fears that it would not be suitable, subsequent testing proved that it was the best choice for the board the soft plastic is more durable and will not fracture if dropped or bumped. Rigid styrene cases tend to crack very easily and during development, one styrene case was crushed under foot when it fell on the floor [4].

The case is the first item to be purchased as it dictates the maximum height for the components. If some of the parts are too high, they can be bent over during assembly and it's important to know this before designing the remaining of the board. Next, the slide switch needs to be selected for the right size of the board. The switch supplied in the kit fits exactly into the holes and any mounting flanges must be cut off so that the board will slide neatly into the case. It should be noted during soldering of the switch that a long soldering job may cause flux leakage along the switch leads causing contact faults. Assembly should be started at one end of the board and each component fitted in sequence. The LED, transistors, diodes and electrolytic must be fitted around the correct way following the layout on the board. Finally, the probe tip is made from a small nail and soldered to the underside of the board. The two cells are soldered to the board with short lengths of tin [5,6].

The various types of electrical and electronic tester boards are classified according to the electronic components being tested. Any electronic component may be

---

*Design and Implement analogue electronic tester board.

classified as passive or active. The formal physics definition treats passive components as ones that cannot supply energy themselves; whereas a battery would be seen as an active component since it truly acts as a source of energy. However, electronic engineers performing circuit analysis use a more restrictive definition of component power consumption. When the concern is with the energy due to signals it is convenient to ignore the DC circuit and pretend that the power supplying components such as transistors or integrated circuits are absent (as if each such component had its own battery built in), although it may in reality be supplied by the DC circuit which is being ignored. Then, the analysis only concerns the so, called AC circuit; an abstraction which ignores the DC voltages and currents (and the power associated with them) present in the actual circuit. This technique, for instance, allows the modeling of an oscillator as "producing energy" even though in reality the oscillator consumes even more energy from a power supply, obtained through the DC circuit which has been ignored. Under such restrictions the following terms used in circuit analysis can be defined as follows [7-9]:

- **Passive components** are ones which cannot introduce net energy into the circuit they are connected to. They also cannot rely on a source of power except for what is available from the (AC) circuit they are connected to. Consequently, they are unable to amplify (increase the power of a signal), although they may well increase a voltage or current such as is done by a transformer or resonant circuit. Among passive components are familiar two-terminal components such as resistors, capacitors, inductors, and most sorts of diodes.
- **Active components** rely on a source of energy (usually from the ignored DC circuit) and are usually able to inject power into a circuit. This includes amplifying components such as transistors, triode vacuum tubes (valves), and tunnel diodes. Passive components can be further divided into lossless and lossy components [10-12].
- **Lossless** components do not have a net power flow into or out of the component. This would include ideal capacitors, inductors, transformers, and the (theoretical) gyrator.
- **Lossy** or **dissipative** components do not have that property and generally absorb power from the external circuit over time. The prototypical example is the resistor. In practice all non-ideal passive components are at least a little lossy, but these are typically modeled in circuit analysis as consisting of an ideal lossless component with an attached resistor to account for the loss.

Most passive components with more than two terminals can be described in terms of two-port parameters satisfying the principle of reciprocity. In contrast, active components generally lack the property of reciprocity. Such distinctions only apply to components modeled as elements within circuit analysis. Practical items, which act as transducers or have other connections to the outside world such as switches, cannot be subject to this form of classification since they defy the view of the electronic circuit as a closed system. This work consists of introduction, design of model of tester board, the hardware design of board, results and discussion of results and conclusions.

2. Design the Model of Tester Board

The design and implementation of the developed model has two phases. The first presents the theoretical design by software which consists of simulating the circuit to verify the correctness of the design and the second step presents the practical implementation and testing of the model with different components. Both these steps are explained in detail in the following sub-sections.

2.1. Simulation

The theoretical design of the electronic tester and its simulation is achieved by using the electronic workbench software MultiSim Ver. 11.0.1. Initially, the circuit was designed in order to test the operation of each component in a standalone fashion. Two types of checks are implemented for components: in context of the electric circuit and outside of the circuit (without any connection). Some of these circuits are shown in **Figures 1** and **2**. Thereafter, these circuits are reduced to a single circuit (as shown in **Figure 3**) that is used for the purpose of testing within the context of the circuit. The procedure of checking the electronic components can be carried out with this circuit by the following steps that are related to the type of component which is taken under test. An example that will be considered is that of a MOSFET. The operation of a MOSFET (N-channel and P-channel) when it is connected in the circuit or individually can be checked by the following procedure:

- Connect the transistor with the tester board with the source at position (a), gate at position (c) and drain at position (b).
- Connect plugs to J5 and J4 for N-channel MOSFET, or J2 for P-channel MOSFET.
- Press the push switch and check the two LED's. For an operative N-channel transistor, LED2 will flash repeatedly; and for an operative P-channel transistor, LED1 will flash repeatedly. If the opposite LED's flash, then the transistors are inoperative. If both LED's flash, then the transistor is in open circuit; and if both LED's are off, the transistor is in short-circuiting.

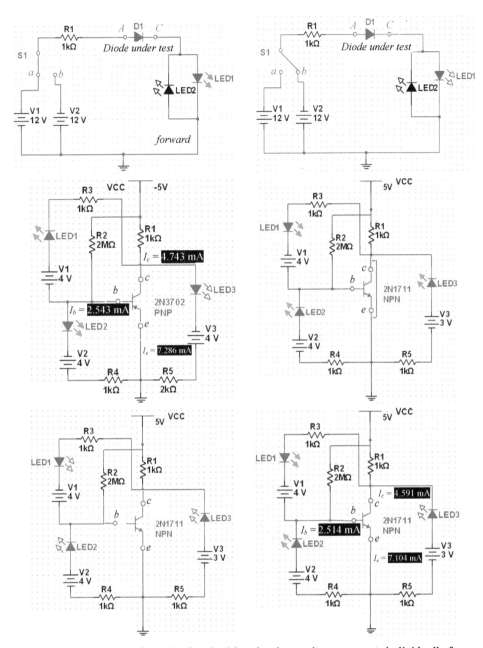

Figure 1. The first part of circuits for checking the electronic components individually form.

A summary of the procedure for checking all analogue electronic components in the circuit shown in **Figure 2** as well as the various expected outputs and their indication is given in **Table 1**.

2.2. The Hardware Design

After the simulation results proved the circuit in **Figure 3** could be used as a general design and the input-output configuration and connection procedure was derived for us in **Table 1**, it only remained to implement the circuit design in a practical way. The circuit was implemented with suitable biasing configuration and two options of

power supply (an internal 9 V battery or any external power supply). Images of the practical model are shown in **Figure 4**.

The procedure for connection and testing with the practical model are similar to the procedure as explained in the simulation setup. For example when we need check any component such as P-ch JFET (Junction field effect transistor) for operation can be done by the following procedure:

- Set the board that is shown in **Figure 4** for any select of power supply (external power supply or internal).
- Made the connection of JEFT piece according to connect table shown in **Table 1**. The point connection

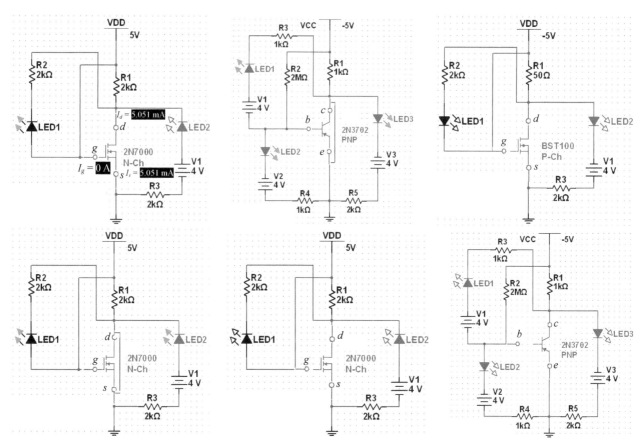

Figure 2. The second part of circuits for checking the electronic components individually form.

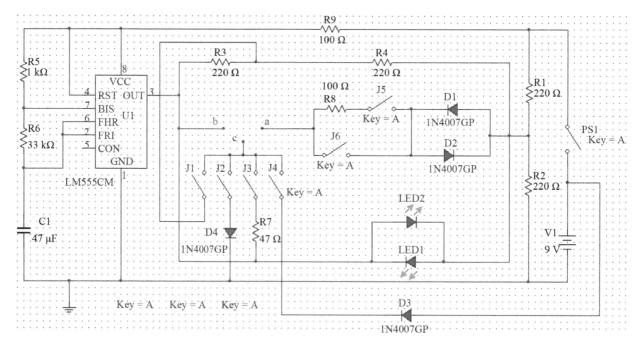

Figure 3. Simulation of model by software (Multisim 11.0).

is J3 and J6 to connect the terminals of JEFT at the points A, B and C according to **Table 1** and **Figure 4**.
• Check your connection then, press the push button S1

to get the results (see **Figure 4**). According to **Table 1**. When the JEFT is operating the LED1 is flash otherwise no response indicates to the JEFT is short cct

Table 1. The connection of components and testing decision (* ≡ Switch ON).

Element name	Symbol in cct	Switch connection						Operative	Short cct	Open cct
		J1	J2	J3	J4	J5	J6			
Diode		*	-	-	-	-	*	Led 2 flash	No response	Flash by two led's
Thyristor		*	-	-	-	-	*	Led 2 flash	No response	Flash by two led's
NPN-JBT		*	-	-	-	-	*	Led 2 flash	No response	Flash by two led's
PNP-JBT		*	-	-	-	-	*	Led 1 flash	No response	Flash by two led's
P-ch JFET		-	-	*	-	-	*	Led 1 flash	No response	Flash by two led's
N-ch JFET		-	-	*	-	-	*	Led 2 flash	No response	Flash by two led's
N-ch MOSFET		-	-	-	*	*	-	Led 2 flash	No response	Flash by two led's
P-ch MOSFET		-	*	-	-	-	*	Led 1 flash	No response	Flash by two led's

(damage) and flash by two LDE's is open cct.

The general procedure for using this trainer by checking the operation of any electronic piece by theoretical study after that made the procedure which shown above to take the suitable discussion about the piece under test.

3. Results and Discussion

Depending on the individual operation principles of the electronic components, the tester board was designed for checking the components outside of the circuit. However, as increased faults happen during the operation of the electronic components, this necessitated the requirement to design a tester to perform within a circuit that used the component under test. The first design that tested electronic components within a circuit was limited to diode and BJT. Since an electric circuit has many types of these components like ssSCR, MOSFET and JFET's, the general tester model was designed. After the initial design of **Figures 1** and **2**, was used in testing it became clear that it needed R9 (100 ohm) to limit the current which passes through the 555IC when the electronic device under test is shorted.

In addition, for MOSFET testing, it also became clear that if the MOSFET is shorted, the circuit would be shorted at the source. This prompted the use of a diode on the gate to prevent the source from being shorted. This design offers a very important facility for any designer in electronic circuits where by using the model for testing transistors it has ability to estimate the type of the transistor with the output configuration as follows:

- If only LED2 flashes, the type of the transistor is NPN for a BJT and P-channel for a JFET.
- If only LED1 flashes, the type of the transistor is PNP for a BJT and N-channel for a JFET.

To more explain the procedure of checking the types of transistor and its operation. The following example will discuss the Bipolar Junction Transistor (BJT) by the following steps:

- Connect the transistor in tester board where collector in position (a), base in position (c) and emitter in position (b), as shown in **Figure 4**.
- Connect the J1 and J6.
- Press bush switch, then check the two LED's. For NPN transistor if only LED2 will flash intermittently, this means that the transistor is operative, otherwise, it is in operative.
- If the transistor is PNP only LED1 will flash inter-

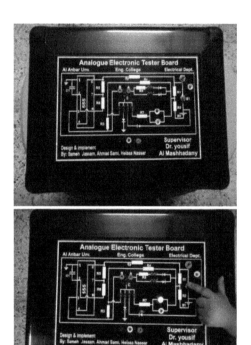

Figure 4. The practical model of electronic tester board.

mittently, this means that the transistor is operative.

- Otherwise, it is in operative. If the transistors are open-circuit the two LED's will flashes intermittently. If the transistors are short-circuiting the two LED's won't flash.

4. Conclusions

This paper presents a design for an electronic tester board and provides details of its development. From the simulation results and the practical implementation and experimentation of the board with many components it can be seen that the circuit implemented in the tester model offers several electronic component testing abilities as follows:

- It has the ability to check the electronic components as listed in **Table 1** independent of the external circuit.
- It has the ability to check the elements within the context of the electric circuit without removing the element from circuit. This option easily facilitates repairing of electrical boards by minimizing the cost and time for the designer.
- In transistor applications the board has the ability to determine the specific type of transistor being used

and classify it in the appropriate category of (ssSCR, MOSFET, JFET) transistor.

Finally, an additional advantage is that this design is small and light enough to be used in portable form, or also in the laboratory where it offers two power supply options.

REFERENCES

[1] Z. Czaja, "Testing of Analog Parts of Electronic Embedded Systems with Limited Access to Internal Nodes," 12*th IMEKO TC*1 *& TC*7 *Joint Symposium on Man Science & Measurement*, Annecy, 3-5 September 2008, pp. 305-312.

[2] I. Memis, "Testing to Eliminate Reliability Defects from Electronic Packages," 43*rd Annual Proceedings of Reliability Physics Symposium*, 17-21 April 2005, pp. 462-465.

[3] B. Betts, "Diagnosing and Fixing Motherboard Faults," 1997.
http://people.richland.edu/dkirby/mbdfaults.pdf

[4] Company Manual, "Front Panel I/O Connectivity Design Guide," Intel Corporation, Copyright 2000, Order Number A29286-001.

[5] L. Wang and M. S. Abadir, "On Efficiency Producing Quality Tests for Custom Circuits in Power PC^{TM} Microprocessors," *Journal of Electronic Testing*: *Theory and Applications*, Vol. 16, No. 1-2, 1999, pp. 121-130.

[6] Dell South, "Basic Electronics Testing Study Guide," *USA an Equal Opportunity Employer*, 2005.

[7] K. Warren, D. Roth, J. Kinnison and B. Carkuff, "Single Event Latchup and Total Dose Testing of Spacecfat Electronic Components," *Radiation Effects Data Workshop*, 2001, pp. 100-105.

[8] H. Livingston, "Avoiding Counterfeit Electronic Components—Part 2 Observations from Recent Counterfeit Detection Experiences," BAE Systems Information and Electronic Systems Integration Inc., 2007, pp. 1-4.

[9] J. Yong, "7 Ways on How to Save Your Time for Electronic Repairing Line," 2011.
http://www.Testingelectroniccomponents.com

[10] Altera DE2 Board, "Development and Education Board Getting Started Guide," Document Version 1.2, 2005.

[11] Instruction Sheet, "Thermo Scientific Orion Electronic Test Kit", 2011.
http://www.thermo.com/eThermo/CMA/PDFs/Various/File_9126.pdf

[12] J. Yong, "How to Solve No Power Problem in HP f1723 LCD Monitor," 2011.
http://ezinearticles.com/?HP-F1723-LCD-Monitor-Repair---No-Power&id=914512

6

Power Conversion Enhancement of CdS/CdTe Solar Cell Interconnected with Tunnel Diode

Wagah F. Mohammed, Omar Daoud, Munther Al-Tikriti
Communications and Electronics Department, Faculty of Engineering, Philadelphia University, Amman, Jordan

ABSTRACT

One of the most promising solar cell devices is cadmium telluride (CdTe) based. These cells however, have their own problems of stability and degradation in efficiency. Measurements show that CdS/CdTe solar cell has high series resistance which degrades the performance of solar cell energy conversion. Both active layers (CdS and CdTe) had been fabricated by thermal evaporation and tested individually. It was found that CdS window layer of 300 nm have the lowest series resistance with maximum light absorption. While 5 - 7 μm CdTe absorber layer absorbed more than 90% of the incident light with minimum series resistance. A complete CdS/CdTe solar cell was fabricated and tested. It was found that deposited cell without heat treatment shows that the short circuit current increment decreases as the light intensity increases. This type of deposited cell has low conversion efficiency. The energy conversion efficiency was improved by heat treatment, depositing heavily doped layer at the back of the cell and minimizing the contact resistivity by depositing material with resistivity less than 1 m$\Omega\cdot$cm^2. All these modifications were not enough because the back contact is non-ohmic. Tunnel diode of CdTe (p++)/CdS (n++) was deposited in the back of the cell. The energy conversion efficiency was improved by more than 7%.

Keywords: CdS/CdTe; Solar Cells; Energy Conversion; Efficiency

1. Introduction

Silicon-based solar cells are currently the most successful commercial photovoltaic product. The PV market, dominated by crystalline silicon, has grown on average more than twenty percent per year but faces the problem of profitability as it must compete with traditional sources and methods of energy conversion. To become competitive, PV materials are needed as they are much less expensive than single crystal silicon and are compatible with large scale manufacturing. Thin film materials and manufacturing processes are an obvious choice for lowering the cost. Thin film solar cells based on polycrystalline Cadmium Telluride (CdTe) reached record efficiencies of 16.5% [1] for laboratory scale device and of 10.9% for terrestrial module [2]. Since the record efficiency of such type solar cells is considerably lower than the theoretical limit of 28% - 30% [3], the performance of the modules can be improved, through new advances in fundamental material science and engineering, and device processing. CdTe is one of the most suitable materials for photovoltaic applications. CdTe has a direct band gap material (E$_g$ ≈ 1.5 eV at room temperature) with a high absorption coefficient (above 10^5 cm^{-1} at the wavelength of 700 nm). Few microns thick layer of CdTe absorbs more than 90% of the incident light with the photon energy higher than the band gap. The maximum theoretical efficiency corresponding to such band gap is about 27%. The small thickness required for an absorbing layer makes the cost of material for the solar cells relatively low. To date, CdTe has been deposited successfully by a variety of techniques [4].

CaCadmium sulfide (CdS) belonging to the II-VI group is one of the promising materials for optoelectronic devices. CdS has been the subject of intensive research because of its intermediate band gap (E$_g$ ≈ 2.42 eV) making the material suitable as window material for a heterojunction solar cell [5], high absorption coefficient, reasonable conversion efficiency, stability and low cost [6]. Knowledge of the optical properties of CdS films is very important in the field of optoelectronic devices like photo-detectors and solar cells. A broad variety of deposition techniques can be used to fabricate CdS films with desirable optical properties [7]. Although CdTe can be doped both p-type and n-type CdTe: homojunction cells have not shown very high efficiency. Due to high absorption coefficient and small diffusion length, the junction must be formed close to the surface, which reduces the carrier lifetime through surface recombination. The In-doped CdTe (p) thin film is of high bulk resistivity which largely affects its photovoltaic properties particularly the short circuit current [8]. It was noted that, the deteriorative effect of the high bulk resistivity increases by increasing the light intensity, which in turn limits the benefit of using light concentrators that improve the short circuit current.

Heterojunctions which consist of CdTe as one of the junction sides had been under investigation for many years [9]. The electrical properties of post-deposition annealed and as-deposited In-doped CdTe thin films were studied in details [10]. It was observed that the CdTe film was of modified Poole-Frenkel conduction mechanism and the resistivity of the film could be lowered by more than one order of magnitude due to indium doping. Also, considerable amount of work had been paid to develop the CdS/CdTe solar cells over the last twenty years [11]. Also the electrical, photoelectrical, and structural properties of CdS/CdTe heterostruture were studied [12]. Deposition of thin polycrystalline CdTe layers on the top of the CdS layer for solar cells has been successfully performed by using various methods. Considerably higher efficiencies were obtained by using n-CdS/p-CdTe heterojunctions. The CdS layer serves as a window layer and helps to reduce the interface recombination. Without special doping the CdS film has significantly higher carrier concentration ($\approx 10^{16}$ - 10^{17} cm^{-3}) than the CdTe adjacent to the interface ($\approx 10^{14}$ - 10^{15} cm^{-3}). As a result the built-in potential is applied mostly to the CdTe absorber layer, providing effective separation of the photo generated carriers. High efficiency solar cells of efficiencies up to 12.5% were developed with a CdTe low temperature (<450°C) process [13]. Efficient solar cell performance requires minimizing the forward recombination current and maximizing the light generated current. Collection losses can be minimized in thin film of high absorption and short diffusion length. Voltage dependent photocurrent collection losses in CdTe films were observed [14]. The voltage dependence of photocurrent of CdTe/CdS solar cells was characterized by separating the forward current from the photocurrent. Recently, preparation and performance of CdS/CdTe tandem solar cells is introduced [15,16]. Thinner layers at the top and thicker ones at the bottom managed to increase the open circuit voltage and improve the spectral response.

2. Laboratory Preparations and Solar Cell Structure

Cadmium Sulphide/Cadmium telluride (CdS/CdTe) solar cell is composed of four main layers deposited on a glass substrate. A transparent conducting oxide deposited directly on top of the glass to form the front contact. The second layer is the window layer, which is usually n-type semiconductor. CdS, with band gap of 2.4 eV at room temperature, is the most suitable material for CdTe-based solar cells. The work of [17-19] showed that without special doping, the CdS films have significantly higher carrier concentration than the CdTe. The third layer is the absorber layer of CdTe, which is usually from 5 - 10 μm thick film. The deposition parameters, optical and electrical properties of active layers will be discussed deeply later. Finally, the fourth step in the solar cell fabrication is the application of the back electrical contact to the CdTe layer. 2 μm Aluminum is used as metal back contact. It was recognized that this step is critical for CdS/CdTe solar cell performance due to low stability and resulted in a high contact resistance. In order to minimize this resistance (ρ_C < 1 mΩ·cm) tunnel diode is proposed to be connected in series with the solar cell [20]. These problems will be the main issues in this work and they will be addressed later.

Fabrication of CdS films of thickness up to 800 nm was carried out on a glass substrate using Balzer vacuum thermal evaporation system. The substrate temperature, vacuum pressure, deposition rate, film thickness and annealing temperature have been measured by the system. CdS film was evaporated at optimum evaporation parameters [18], under 10^{-6} mbar vacuum. The substrate temperature was 300°C and the deposition rate is 2° A/sec. Thickness of the layer and annealing temperature are varied to obtain maximum grain size at minimum thickness with very low resistivity. Few samples of CdTe thin film were prepared by thermal evaporation and deposited on glass substrate to be examined individually. A comprehensive study of CdTe layer in CdS/CdTe solar cell had been conducted [21], and the main parameters of CdTe material that affect the module efficiency had been discussed. Among these parameters are the lifetime, diffusion length, drift length of minority carriers and thickness of CdTe absorber layer. In this research; it is found that 7 μm of CdTe thickness deposited with 8° A/sec. rate of deposition on substrate with 100°C temperature is optimum for maximum absorption of radiation and produces large enough grain size [10]. The annealing temperature is varied for optimum optical and electrical properties of the film.

3. Optical and Electrical Properties of the Solar Cell Layers

Transmission and absorption coefficient spectrum have been carried out for each individual layer at different annealing temperature. **Figures 1** and **2** shows the transmission and absorption coefficients of CdS and CdTe layers respectively. CdS film exhibited high degree of transmittance in the infrared region and showed sharp falling of the absorption edge towards lower wavelength. The absorption edge is lowered as the annealing tem-

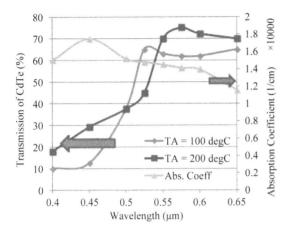

Figure 1. Transmittance and absorption coefficients of CdS layer at different annealing temperatures.

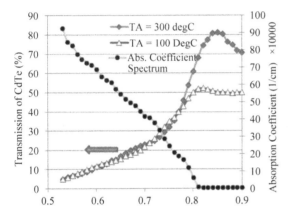

Figure 2. Transmittance and absorption coefficients of CdTe layer at different annealing temperatures.

perature of the film increased. It was found that small changes in the thickness of CdS had a greater influence on transmission. It must, however, be emphasized that more reduction of CdS will increase the resistivity of the layer which will deteriorate the electrical properties of the layer. Thicker CdTe layer is used in order that all light is absorbed in this layer. CdTe film exhibits transmittance at short wavelength ($\lambda \approx 500$ nm). The transmittance becomes more pronounced at wavelength higher than 800 nm. The absorption edge shifted toward lower wavelength at high annealing temperature (250°C).

Figures 3 and **4** show that the variation of resistivity and photo generated current of CdS and CdTe layers with wavelength at different annealing temperatures. It is clear that CdS sample annealed at 250°C gave minimum resistivity and of course maximum photo generated current. This is because that the absorption coefficient for this sample is very high which is inversely proportional to resistivity. The material becomes more n-type due to excessive Cadmium under layer and enhanced diffusion at grain boundaries or impurities incorporated in the deposit [7].

4. The Effect of Series Resistance

Figure 5(a) represents a schematic representation of the CdS/CdTe solar cell heterostructure. The layers succession and thicknesses are the one used in the present work. An electronic solar cell model can be considered, as shown in **Figure 5(b)**, taking into account the effect of the series resistance (R_s) and shunt resistance (R_{sh}). The solar cell current source generates a light current (I_{PH}) which is directly proportional to the solar illumination. The two resistors (R_{sh}) and (R_s) represent the losses incurred in the solar cell. The series resistor (R_s) caused by the ohmic losses in the surface of the solar cell. The par-

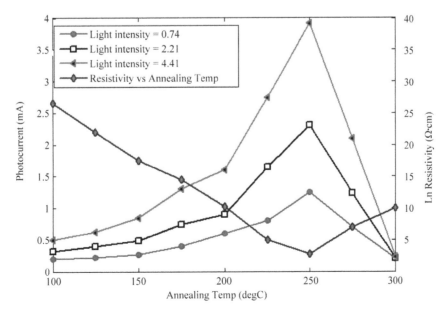

Figure 3. Variation of resistivity and photo generated current with annealing temperature for CdS layer.

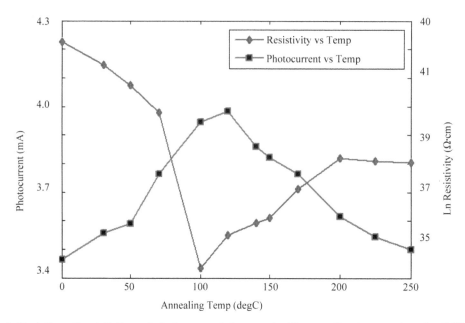

Figure 4. Variation of resistivity and photo generated current with annealing temperature for CdTe layer.

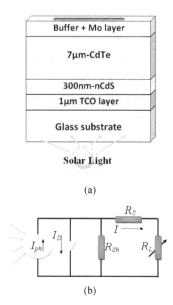

(a)

(b)

Figure 5. (a) Schematic representation of the CdS/CdTe solar cell heterostructure; (b) Electronic solar cell model.

allel shunt resistor (R_{sh}) denotes the losses due to leakage current in the solar cell.

Taking into account the effect of the series resistance (R_s) and shunt resistance (R_{sh}), the current supplied to the load (I) can be expressed as:

$$I = I_{ph} - I_o \left(e^{\left(\frac{V}{nV_T}\right)} - 1 \right) - \left(\frac{V + IR_s}{R_{sh}} \right) \qquad (1)$$

where I_{ph} is the photo generated current, I_o is the saturation current, V is the applied voltage, n is the identity factor and V_T is thermal voltage which is equal to 26 mV

at room temperature. The saturation current is measured to be equal to 2 µA. The series resistance is determined as [22].

$$R_{oc} = \frac{dV}{dj_{sc}}\bigg|_{V=V_{oc}} = R_s \left[1 + \frac{R_o}{R_s} + \frac{R_o}{R_{sh}} \right]\left[1 + \frac{R_o}{R_{sh}} \right]^{-1} \qquad (2)$$

where R_{oc} is the open circuit series resistance and R_o = [$nkT/q \cdot J_{sc}$]. Usually for CdTe based cells, $J_{sc} \approx 20$ mA/cm^2 and n = 2 [8], hence $R_o \approx 2.5$ Ω at room temperature. R_{sh} is usually of order of few several hundred Ohms which means $R_o/R_{sh} \ll 1$ leads to an approximate relation: $R_s \approx R_{oc} - R_o$. Hence the calculated range of series resistance is 5 - 10 Ω. I-V characteristics of CdS/CdTe show that the device has high series resistance [8]. The real value of measured series resistance is higher than the calculated one due to the parasitic resistance connected in series to the main cell. **Figure 6** shows the variation of the short circuit current with the light intensity measured practically. It can be seen that the short circuit current

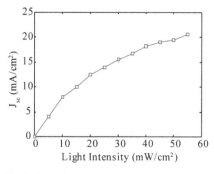

Figure 6. Variation of short circuit current density with light intensity.

varies rapidly at low intensity (<5 mW) while it saturates at high intensity. It can be suggested that this degradation in the cell performance at high light intensities is due to the high series resistance.

The solar cell model given by Equation (1) is simulated using MATLAB. The photo generated current density is measured using the following equation [8]:

$$J_{ph} = q \int F(\lambda)\left[1 - R(\lambda)\right]\left[1 - e^{-\alpha d}\right]\eta(\lambda) \cdot \partial\lambda \qquad (3)$$

q is the electron charge, F is the number of incident photons with energies greater than the band energy in $[cm^{-2} \cdot s^{-1}]$, R is the reflection coefficient, α is the absorption coefficient (cm^{-1}), d is the cell thickness which is nearly equal to CdTe, and η is the collection efficiency which varies from 0 - 1. The limits of integration are from 0.48 - 0.87 μm; out of this range the absorption process can be ignored. The reflection coefficient varies from 0.7 - 0.9 for the wavelength mentioned above. The absorption coefficient can be deduced from **Figure 2**, which is approximately equals to 1.3×10^{7} cm^{-1}. **Figure 7** shows that the simulation result and practical measurements of short circuit current versus photo generated current at different values of series resistance with shunt resistance is 10 KΩ. The results given in **Figure 8** were calculated at high light intensity (high photo generated currents) which in turn means high short circuit current.

Mathematical manipulation of Equation (1) at short circuit current condition when the voltage across the load resistance becomes zero yields:

$$\frac{dI_{sc}}{dI_{ph}} = \left[\left(\frac{I_{o}R_{s}}{nV_{T}}\right)e^{\left(\frac{I_{sc}R_{s}}{nV_{T}}\right)}\right]^{-1} \qquad (4)$$

It can be seen that the slope varies inversely with R_s that means the variation of I_{sc} will be less as the I_{ph} increases due to the high effect of R_s. That is evidently shown in **Figure 7**, when R_s becomes zero the slope $\left(dI_{sc}/dI_{ph}\right)$ will be equal to one; that means the change in the short circuit current equals to the change in photo generated current. The deterioration effect of the high series resistance increases by increasing the light intensity. This will limit the benefit of using light concentrators and improve the short circuit current. Many researches have been carried out to reduce the effect of series resistance. Post-deposition heat treatment with CdCl$_2$ to activate CdTe (p) would probably reduce the series resistance and possibly improve ohmic contact performance [23]. Another improvement of CdS/CdTe solar cell can be achieved in the fill-factor. The improvement is achieved by depositing a thin heavily doped p-type semiconductor with a high work function at the back of CdTe layer [24]. Small valence band (<0.2 eV) would be formed between CdTe layer and metal leads to a low or zero potential barrier at the interface and hence an easy hole transport between the two layers. **Figure 8** shows the improvement in quantum efficiency at different annealing temperatures (curves 1 & 2) and depositing thin layer of Te (curve 3) compared with theoretically calculated (curve 4).

More improvements have been made by varying the thickness of CdTe layer. Considering the information of the drift and diffusion components of the photocurrent will lead to the calculation of the short circuit current. Calculation of short circuit current gives an expression of quantum efficiency spectra [21]. In order to reach the total change collection at CdTe layer, the thickness should

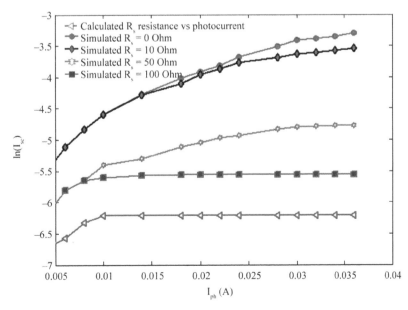

Figure 7. Simulated and calculated short circuit current versus photo current at different values of series resistance.

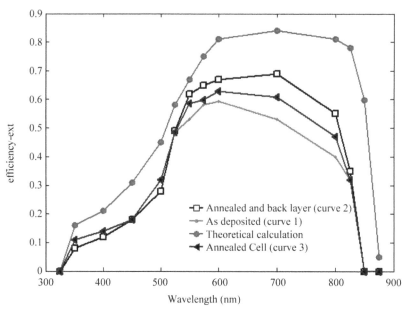

Figure 8. Improvement the quantum efficiency of the solar cell: (1) As deposited; (2) Annealed; (3) With deposited layer and (4) Theoretical calculated.

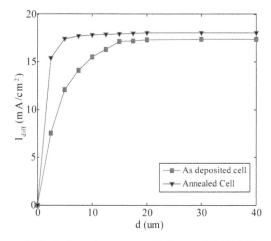

Figure 9. Variation of quantum efficiency of CdS/CdTe solar cell for different values of CdTe thickness: (1) As deposited cell; (2) Annealed cell.

be 50 μm or more [25]. Layer thickness can be reduced by shortening electron life time and hence electron diffusion length. **Figure 9** shows the variation of quantum efficiency of the annealed CdS/CdTe cell for different values of CdTe layer thickness. More than 83% efficiency has been detected at 10 μm thickness with the highest efficiency in the gradual transition between 500 nm and 800 nm (the characteristics of the intermixing between CdTe and CdS layer). High quantum efficiency at the thinner CdTe layer achieved due to the increasing of absorption coefficient. As soon as the photon energy exceeds the band gap of CdTe, the absorption coefficient becomes higher than 10^4 cm^{-1} *i.e.* the effective penetration depth becomes less than 10^{-4} cm (1 nm). This is the

reason behind the choice of a few microns (5 - 10 μm) thickness of the CdTe layers. It is evident that the resistance between the CdTe layer and metal back contact is non-ohmic [10]. Actually, there are two diode circuits; the first one is the CdS/CdTe junction (main diode) and the second one is the back contact Schottky diode, which they are connected opposite to each other. Thus, distribution of the applied voltage between the two diodes changes in favor of Schottky diode when applying forward bias voltage to the cell. There is a decrease in the resistance of the main diode and increase that of the Schottky diode.

The above discussions means that the value of the series resistance depends on the voltage applied and current flowing through the cell. According to Schottky theory, the formation of an ohmic contact between a p-type semiconductor and metal results in a high contact resistance due to high potential barrier. Creating a highly doped p++ layer at the surface of CdTe can reduce the effects of the back contact potential barrier. Thinner potential barrier (lower the depletion layer width) produces tunneling or thermally assisted tunneling carrier transport mechanism. The individual sub cell of multi-junction solar cell is interconnected via interband tunnel diode [20]. They feature both low electrical resistivity and high optical transmittance. Reliable simulations of the tunnel diode behavior are still a challenge for solar cell application. Theoretical and experimental measurements of current voltage (I-V) characteristics of tunnel diodes and solar cells had been studied [26]. It is concluded that as the short circuit current of the cell is lower than the maximum tunneling current, the tunnel diode is operated in the state with lower voltage drop. Hence, the tunnel diode acts like an almost ohmic resistor and will not reduce the maximum power output of the solar cell. If the short circuit current of the cell exceeds the maximum tunneling current, the tunnel diode works in the region where thermal current dominated and high voltage drop occurs over the tunnel diode. I-V curve of the solar cell will be sheared to lower voltages. The test structure consisting of CdS/CdTe solar cell with underlying tunnel diode can be regarded as a series of two diodes connected back-to-back as shown in the left side of **Figure 10**. The tunnel diode is formed by high doping thin layer of CdTe to produce p++ ($5 \times 10^{19}/cm^3$), then depositing another highly doped CdS to produce n++ ($3 \times 10^{19}/cm^3$). The tunnel diode is designed to be able to have a peak current may exceeds values of 50 mA/cm^2. Measured I-V characteristics of a CdS/CdTe solar cell with CdTe (p++) CdS (n++) tunnel diode is shown in the right side of **Figure 10**.

Circled line marks the measurement at low light concentration (<50 mW/cm^2), causing the short circuit current of the cell to be lower than the maximum tunneling current. The short circuit current is increased as long as the photo generated current is increased. Consequently the maximum power output with the solar cell is increased. Dashed line in **Figure 10** marks the measurements at higher light concentration (>50 mW/cm^2) causing the short circuit current to exceed the maximum tunneling current. When critical illumination is reached, the cell current exceeds the tunneling current of the tunnel diode and voltage dip appears in the I-V characteristics.

5. Conclusion

CdTe based solar cell is a leading technology in thin film energy conversion efficiency. Their energy conversion efficiency is degraded by the high series resistance of the cell. The resistance is a combination of contact resis-

tances, semiconductor resistance and non-ohmic ones of the back contact. The contact resistance and semiconductor resistances can be modified by annealing, fabrication parameter and using materials of low resistivity at the contacts. The non-ohmic contact can be modified by connecting tunnel diode at the back of the cell. The only limitation to this approach is that the short circuit current of the cell should not exceed the maximum tunneling current of the tunnel diode. More research and study about this point is needed. AC measurements in wide range of frequencies should be carried out to measure impedances of both diodes and then more adequate physical model can be suggested.

REFERENCES

[1] X. Wu, J. C. Keane, R. G. Dhere, C. DeHart, A. Duda, T. A. Gessert, S. Asher, D. H. Levi and Sheldon, "16.5% Efficient CdS/CdTe Polycrystalline Thin-Film Solar Cell," *Proceedings of the* 17th *E-PVSEC*, München, October 2001, pp. 995-1000.

[2] D. Cunningham, K. Davies, L. Grammond, E. Mopas, M. O'Connor, M. Rubcich, M. Sadeghi, D. Skinner and T. Trumbly, "Large Area Apollo Module Performance and Reliability," *Proceedings of the* 28th *IEEE Photovoltaic Specialists Conference*, Fairfield, 2000, pp. 13-18.

[3] S. Sze, "Physics of semiconductor Devices," 2nd Edition, Wiley, New York, 1981.

[4] R. Birkmire, "CdTe$_{1-x}$S$_x$ Absorber Layers for Thin-Film CdTe/CdS Solar Cells," 26th *IEEE Photovoltaic's Specialists Conference* (PVSC), Anaheim, Vol. 295, 1997, pp. 307- 312.

[5] M. V. Garcia-Cuenc, J. L. Morenza, E. Bertran and A. Lousa, "Electrical Conduction in Polycrystalline CdS Films: Comparison of Theory and Experiment," *Journal of Physics D: Applied Physics*, Vol. 20, No. 7, 1987, pp. 958-962.

[6] A. Sanchez, P. J. Sebastian and O. Gomez-Daza, "Low-Resistivity CdS Thin Films Formed by a New Chemical Vapor Transport Method," *Semiconductor Science and Technology*, Vol. 10, No. 1, 1995, pp. 87-90.

[7] W. F. Mohammed, "The Effect of Temperatures and Doped Level on CdS Thin Films," *Engineering & Technology Journal*, Vol. 14, No. 7, 1995, p. 34.

[8] W. F. Mohammed and M. A. Shehathah, "Effect of Series Resistance on Photovoltaic Properties of In-Doped CdTe (p) Thin Film Homojunction Structure," *Renewable Energy*, Vol. 21, No. 3, 2000, pp. 141-152.

[9] F. Zhou, X. C. Wang, H. C. Wu and C. Z. Zhao, "Achievements and Challenges of CdS/CdTe Solar Cells," *International Journal of Photo Energy*, Vol. 2011, 2011, pp. 1-8.

[10] W. F. Mohammed and M. A. Shehathah, "The Electrical Properties of Post-Deposition Annealed and As-Deposited In-Doped CdTe Thin Films," *Renewable Energy*, Vol.

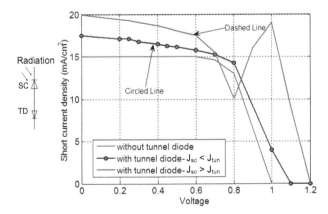

Figure 10. I-V characteristics of a CdS/CdTe solar cell. (a) Without tunnel diode; (b) With tunnel diode and $J_{sc} > J_{tun}$; (c) With tunnel diode and $J_{sc} < J_{tun}$.

26, 2002, pp. 285-249.

[11] M. M. Al-Jassim, R. G. Dhere, K. M. Jons, F. S. Hasoon and Sheldon, "The Morphology, Microstructure, and Luminescent Properties of CdS/CdTe Films," *2nd World Conference and Exhibition on Photovoltaic Solar Energy Conversion*, Vienna, 6-10 July 1998.

[12] D. H. Levi, L. M. Woods, D. S. Albin and T. A. Gessert, "The Influence of Grain Boundary Diffusion on the Electro-Optical Properties of CdTe/CdS Solar Cells," *2nd World Conference and Exhibition on Photovoltaic Solar Energy Conversion*, Vienna, 6-10 July 1998.

[13] G. Khrypunov, A. Romeo, F. Kurdesau, D. L. Batnzer, H. Zogg and D. L. Tiwari, "Recent Development in Evaporated CdTe Solar Cells," *Solar Energy Material and Solar Cells*, Vol. 90, No. 6, 2006, p. 664.

[14] S. Hegedus, D. Desai and C. Thompson, "Voltage Dependent Photocurrent Collection in CdTe/CdS Solar Cells," *Progress Photovoltaic: Research and Applications*, Vol. 15, No. 7, 2007, p. 587.

[15] Y. J. Li, *et al.*, "Preparation and Performance of CdS/CdTe Tandem Solar Cells," *Chinese Journal of Semiconductors*, Vol. 5, 2007, pp. 722-725.

[16] X. Mathew, J. Drayton, V. Parikh, N. R. Mathews, X. X. Liu and A. D. Compaan, "Development of a Semitransparent CdMgTe/CdS Top Cell for Applications in Tandem Solar Cells," *Semiconductor Science Technology*, Vol. 24, No. 1, 2009, Article ID: 015012.

[17] W. F. Mohammed and A. Nori, "The Photo-Electric and Thermal Properties of Vacuum Deposited CdS Thin Films," *Renewable Energy Journal*, Vol. 14, No. 1-4, 1998, pp. 129-134.

[18] W. F. Mohammed and A. Nori, "The Effect of Deposition Parameters on Hall Mobility and Carrier Concentration of CdS Thin Films," *Abhath Al-Yarmook Journal*, Vol. 11, No. 1B, 2002, pp. 402-412.

[19] H. A. Ahmed and L. S. Ali, "Characterization of In-Doped CdTe Thin Film," *Muutah Journal for Research and Studies*, Vol. 11, No. 5, 1996, pp. 207-218.

[20] W. Guter, F. Dimroth, M. Meusel and A. W. Bett, "Tunnel Diodes for III-V Multi-Junction Solar Cells," *20th European Photovoltaic Solar Energy Conference*, Barcelona, June 2005, pp. 515-518.

[21] L. Kosyachenko, "Efficiency of Thin-Film CdS/CdTe Solar Cells," In: R. D. Rugescu, Ed., *Solar Energy*, 2010, pp. 105-130.

[22] M. Wolf and H. Rauschenbusch, "Series Resistance Effects on Solar Cell Measurements," *Advanced Energy Conversion*, Vol. 3, 1963, pp. 455-479.

[23] A. W. Brinkman and S. M. Al-Amri, "Thin Film CdTe Based Solar Cell," *Proceedings of the 6th Arab International Solar Energy Conference*, Muscat, 1998.

[24] J. Sites and J. Pan, "Strategies to Increase CdTe Solar-Cell Voltage," *Thin Solid Films*, Vol. 515, No. 15, 2007, pp. 6099-6102.

[25] N. Amin, K. Sopian and M. Konagai, "Numerical Modeling of CdS/CdTe and CdS/CdTe/ZnTe Solar Cells as a Function of CdTe Thickness," *Solar Energy Materials and Solar Cells*, Vol. 91, No. 13, 2007, pp. 1202-1208.

[26] W. Guter and A. W. Bett, "I-V Characterization of Tunnel Diodes and Multijunction Solar Cells," *IEEE Transactions on Electron Devices*, Vol. 53, No. 9, 2006, pp. 2216-2222.

7

Estimation of Intermodulation Rejection Value as a Function of Frequency in Power Amplifier Using AM-AM and AM-PM Diagrams Based on Power Series Analysis

Aazar Saadaat Kashi[*], Mahmoud Kamarei, Mohsen Javadi
Department of Electrical and Computer Engineering, University of Tehran, Tehran, Iran

ABSTRACT

A method to predict intermodulation (IM) products of two tone test based on Amplitude to amplitude (AM-AM) and amplitude to phase (AM-PM) diagrams of power amplifier is proposed in this paper. An RF power amplifier is mathematically modeled by a power series in order of 13. Coefficients of the transfer function are obtained by odd-order polynomial fitting of the transfer function of the power amplifier that is modeled by power series, with AM-AM and AM-PM diagrams. Because of considering AM-PM distortion, coefficients have become complex. By using this transfer function, analytical expressions of IM products are derived. Frequency effect of IM products are modeled in suggested method to estimate the effects of changing in input frequency on output. With the mean of this factor the model is able to predict IM products of wideband frequency input. Simulated results agree well with the predicted method in comparisons.

Keywords: Intermodulation Product; Two Tone Test; RF Power Amplifier; Power Series; AM-AM and AM-PM Diagrams

1. Introduction

In modern communication systems, digital communication schemes, such as code division multiple access, where the information is carried are admitted by various systems. The purpose that makes CDMA spectrally efficient and popular in recent digital mobile communication systems lies in allocation a unique code for each user, so a certain number of users can communicate at the same time and frequency.

Although, the high spectral efficiency gained by using a CDMA scheme, it degrade at the cause of spectral regrowth that is inevitably generated when signal is passed through nonlinear devices of a RF transmitter.

As in other communication systems, one of the critical and costly components in digital cellular communication systems is RF power amplifier. The power amplifier is the major source of nonlinearity in a communication system. To increase their efficiency, power amplifiers are sometimes driven into their nonlinear region [1], thus causing spectral regrowth, increasing bit error rate, interference to adjacent channel, and intermodulation products to be generated. In extreme these IM products can interfere with signals that are being amplifies [2].

Since the spectral regrowth is stringently regulated and is mostly generated by a nonlinear RF power amplifier [3], it is very important for RF system designers to predict the distortion effects of power amplifiers and analyze its effect on the output.

Given certain power amplifier characteristics, it is desirable to be able to predict, without running time-domain simulations, whether the power amplifier can be used to amplify certain type of signals, *i.e.* the amount of spectral regrowth is within limits [4]. This is due to the fact that channel impairments like the intermodulation distortion can be readily estimated with the knowledge of the nonlinear characteristics of the power amplifier, and properly modeled it [5].

Since, third-order polynomials for modeling the nonlinearities are suitable for weakly nonlinear systems [6], this paper presents an analytical expression that predicts IM products of the output of power amplifier. With the mean of power series transfer function (in order of 13) and AM-AM and AM-PM distortions of power amplifier, it modeled and analyzed to predict first, third, and fifth order IM products of the output.

One of the advantages of the presented model is that it uses both AM-AM and AM-PM diagram to characterize power amplifier transfer function. The phase variations

[*]Corresponding author.

have an important effect on the spectral regrowth [7]. However, similar previous models only used AM-AM diagram to characterize power amplifier's transfer functions [3,8-11] while such an effect is considered in [7,12-15]. Although, in this case, transfer function's coefficients have become complex and this increases the difficulty of the calculations, but neglecting the AM-PM distortion causes many problems in predicting output spectrum [16-18]. Considering variation in output response of power amplifier with disparity on input frequency is the major factor that is deliberated in our model. It is found that adjacent channel power ratio performances is not only dependent on the input signal magnitude (or power) but also dependent on the bandwidth of the signal that is used [19]. Main advantage of this model is that we don't neglect the frequency dependence of power amplifier's transfer function coefficient that makes asymmetric spectrum in the upper and lower band which is not taking into consideration in [3,7,14,15]. The factor is added in our model with considering our transfer function's constants as a function of input frequency besides they are complex. With considering frequency effect, this model is able to be used for wide band frequency range inputs such as UWB systems, WCDMA input, and input signals with complexity in their phase or frequency. With the mean of this method we also can analyze power amplifier systems in the case that their circuit is not reachable.

2. Power Series Model of Power Amplifier

Estimating a perfect nonlinear model of power amplifier that can describe output characteristics is of the great importance. In this part power series model of power amplifier is described, and with using this model and AM-AM and AM-PM diagrams, output IM products will be predicted.

Generally speaking, a practical amplifier is only a linear device in its linear region, meaning that the amplifier output will not exactly a scaled copy of the input signal when the amplifier works beyond linear region [9].

Considering an amplifier as a function box it can be modeled by a power series [20,21]. The input signal is of the form:

$$x(t) = A(t) \cdot \cos(w_c t + \theta(t)) = \mathrm{Re}\left[\tilde{x}(t) \cdot e^{j\theta(t)} \cdot e^{j\omega_c t}\right] \quad (1)$$

where $A(t)$ is an amplitude and $\theta(t)$ is a phase of carrier, ω_c is the carrier angular frequency, and $\tilde{x}(t)$ denotes the base band equivalent input signal.

Because of nonlinearities of the power amplifier that can represent by AM-AM and AM-PM distortion the amplitude and phase of the output are affected, respectively.

The output can represent as follow [7]:

$$y(t) = \mathrm{Re}\left[\tilde{y}(t) \cdot e^{j\theta(t)} \cdot e^{j\omega_c t}\right]$$
$$= \mathrm{Re}\left[F(A(t)) \cdot e^{j\theta(t)} \cdot e^{j\omega_c t}\right] \quad (2)$$
$$= \left|F(A(t))\right| \cdot \cos\left(\omega_c t + \theta(t) + \angle F(A(t))\right)$$

where $y(t)$ represents the equivalent output signal and $F(A(t))$ denotes the complex envelope transfer function of the power amplifier. Function F can be represented by a power series or by an orthogonal function expansion or perhaps reasonably well approximated over the range of $x(t)$ by a polynomial in x [22]. With considering power series model and using baseband equivalent model for power amplifier, we can represent F as:

$$y(t) = F(x(t)) = \sum_{n}^{N} a_n x^n(t) \quad (3)$$

$$x(t) = \mathrm{Re}\left[\tilde{x}(t) \cdot e^{j\theta(t)} \cdot e^{j\omega_c t}\right]$$
$$= \frac{1}{2}\left[\tilde{x}(t) \cdot e^{j\theta(t)} \cdot e^{j\omega_c t} + \tilde{x}^*(t) \cdot e^{-j\theta(t)} \cdot e^{-j\omega_c t}\right] \quad (4)$$

By using the binomial expansion for $x^n(t)$ and considering only the first zone components we obtain [22]:

$$x^n(t) = \frac{1}{2^n}\sum_{k=0}^{n} C_n^k \left[\tilde{x}(t)\right]^k \left[\tilde{x}^*(t)\right]^{n-k} e^{(j\omega_c t + j\theta(t))(2k-n)}$$
$$= \frac{1}{2^{n-1}} C_n^{\frac{n+1}{2}} \left|\tilde{x}^*(t)\right|^{n-1} \tilde{x}(t) \quad \text{for } n \text{: odd} \quad (5)$$

The complex envelope of the first-zone component of $y(t)$ is:

$$\tilde{y}(t) = \tilde{x}(t) \sum_{m=0}^{\frac{N-1}{2}} \frac{a_{2m+1}}{2^{2m}} C_{2m+1}^{m+1} \left|\tilde{x}^*(t)\right|^{2m} \quad (6)$$

With simplify Equation (6), we can write the base band output signal as follow if we assume that the $\theta(t)$ (phase of carrier) is zero:

$$\tilde{y}(t) = \sum_{n=1}^{N} a_n \tilde{x}^n(t) \qquad n \text{: odd} \quad (7)$$

In power amplifier transfer function's coefficients characterization, if only AM-AM distortion is considered the coefficients that are obtained from the fitting of AM-AM diagram and proposed transfer function, have become real. Also neglecting the AM-PM distortion causes many problems in predicting IM products and then output spectrum.

In this model, the coefficients a_n would be obtained by fitting a polynomial of degree N to AM-AM and AM-PM diagrams of power amplifier that obtained by simulation of power amplifier in ADS. The coefficient a_n considered to be complex, because of using AM-PM distortion besides AM-AM. To obtain a good fit we would require a large value of N, which would reduce the efficiency of

Estimation of Intermodulation Rejection Value as a Function of Frequency in Power Amplifier Using AM-AM
and AM-PM Diagrams Based on Power Series Analysis

45

such model [22]. In this work we only consider first 13th terms of power series.

3. Predicting IM Products with the Mean of Power Amplifier Model

When multiple signals are passed through a common amplifier, the nonlinearity of amplifier cause intermodulation (IM) products to be generated [2]. One of the major areas in analyzing nonlinear effect of power amplifier is considering variation in output response of power amplifier with disparity on input frequency. Variation in IM product with frequency is deliberate in our model.

With considering frequency effect, the method is able to predict IM products of every type of input such as WCDMA or input signals with complexity in their phase or frequency. Also, it can use to analyze power amplifiers system when their circuit details are not reachable.

Generally, IM3 is used as a linearity parameter, but when an input signal becomes large, higher order IM products are also generated [3]. So, by using our model, an analytical expression that relates IM product in general order to the amplitude of the input of two tone test is derived.

Input signal of the two tone test can be considered as follow:

$$x(t) = \frac{s}{2}\cos\left[(\omega_c + \Delta\omega)t\right] + \frac{s}{2}\cos\left[(\omega_c - \Delta\omega)t\right]$$
$$= s\cos(\Delta\omega t)\cos(\omega_c t) = \text{Re}\left[s\cos(\Delta\omega t)\cdot e^{j\omega_c t}\right] \quad (8)$$

where $s/2$ is an amplitude of each tone. By comparing this equation with Equation (1), we can represent the baseband input signal as:

$$\tilde{x}(t) = s\cos(\Delta\omega t) \quad (9)$$

The baseband output signal with respect to Equation (8) can be represented as follow [7]:

$$\tilde{y}(t) = \sum_{n=1}^{N} a_{2n-1}\tilde{x}^{2n-1}(t) = \sum_{n=1}^{N} a_{2n-1}s^{2n-1}\cos^{2n-1}(\Delta\omega t)$$

$$= \left[a_1 s + \frac{3}{4}f_3 s^3 + \cdots + \frac{C_{N-1}^{2N-1}}{4^{N-1}}a_{2N-1}s^{2N-1}\right]\cos(\Delta\omega t)$$

$$+ \left[\frac{1}{4}f_3 s^3 + \cdots + \frac{C_{N-2}^{2N-1}}{4^{N-1}}a_{2N-1}s^{2N-1}\right]\cos(3\Delta\omega t) + \cdots$$

$$+ \left[\frac{1}{4^{N-1}}a_{2N-1}s^{2N-1}\right]\cos((2N-1)\Delta\omega t) \quad (10)$$

$$= \tilde{y}_1\cos(\Delta\omega t) + \tilde{y}_3\cos(3\Delta\omega t) + \tilde{y}_5\cos(5\Delta\omega t) + \cdots$$

$$+ \tilde{y}_{2N-1}\cos((2N-1)\Delta\omega t)$$

$$= \sum_{n=1}^{N} \tilde{y}_{2n-1}\cos((2n-1)\Delta\omega t)$$

where $\tilde{y}_{2n-1}$ is an output complex envelope of IM_{2n-1}.

So we can write an analytical expression for IM_{2n-1} as a function of amplifier characteristics and input amplitude "s", as follow:

$$\tilde{y}_{2n-1} = \sum_{j=n}^{N} \frac{C_{j-n}^{2j-1}}{4^{j-1}}a_{2j-1}s^{2j-1} \quad (11)$$

4. Simulation Results

Verify our derivation, a simulation of an RF power amplifier with ADS simulator is performed. The carrier frequency is 850 MHz. To predict the IM products, power amplifier's transfer function coefficients that are the function of input frequency must be obtained first. To evaluate these coefficients (a_{2n+1}) the amplifier is simulated with one-tone input in ADS and the input voltage is swept in its range to AM-AM and AM-PM diagrams are obtained.

Amplitude to amplitude and amplitude to phase distortions are two distortion effects in power amplifiers at high output power levels, causing out of band interference in the transmitted signal and a bit errors in the received signal [23]. Using diagrams and our analytical equation for the output, complex coefficients a_{2n+1} will be found by odd order polynomial fitting that perform in MATLAB. Power amplifier's coefficients must show its nonlinearity, so, we should simulate our circuit both in linear and nonlinear region. On the other hand, input voltage must sweep to voltages that make the circuit being in its nonlinear region.

Power amplifier's AM-AM and AM-PM diagrams that are simulated in wide range of V_{in} to shows nonlinear region are indicated in **Figure 1**. Also, the figure shows fitting diagram with different color that is used to calculate power amplifier's transfer function complex coefficients.

To obtain frequency function coefficients, 10 tests in ADS with previous condition are performed with different input frequency in each test and complex coefficients for each test are obtained with the method that is described. Input frequency varies between (850 + B) MHz and (850 – B) MHz to fill the range (B = 0.62 MHz). After these tests, 10 complex values for each coefficient are acquired. Hence, each coefficient with the mean of these 10 values has the equation which frequency is its-variable.

To validate our analysis, with the mean of our equations and coefficients we can draw $IM_{1,3,5}$ diagrams (amplitude and phase) as a function of input amplitude of two-tone test "s". We compare these diagrams with those we get from two-tone test of our power amplifier that simulated in ADS. For considering frequency effect in our analysis, we must posit our coefficients a_{2n+1} as a function of frequency.

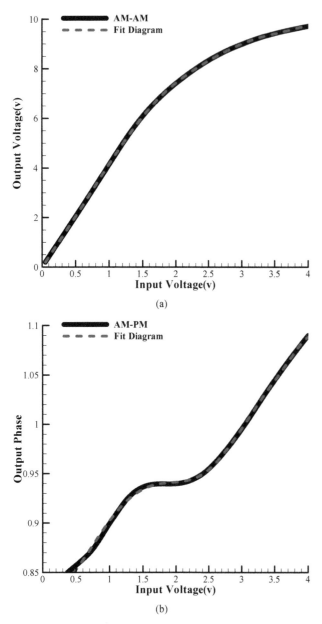

(a)

(b)

Figure 1. (a) Amplitude to amplitude (AM-AM) and (b) Magnitude to phase of output in compare with diagram that fitted in MATLAB.

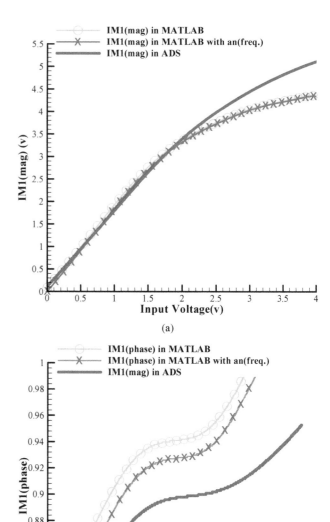

(a)

(b)

Figure 2. (a) Magnitude and (b) Phase of IM_1 in compare with analytical expression that plotted in MATLAB.

Result of our simulation in compare with analytical expression (with or without considering frequency effect) for $IM_{1,3,5}$ (phase and amplitude) are plotted in **Figures 2-4**. In all figures, diagrams that frequency effect isconsidered in their a_{2n+1} coefficients (blue), show better fit to simulated results (red) than the other one (green). In Equations (8) and (11), it is obvious that every coefficient related to one type of nonlinearity or are the dominate factor in them. For example a_1 is the dominate factor in IM_1. It shows that little variation in its value makes huge change in predicting IM_1. Without any doubt, errors that occurred in fitting make some errors in calculating

coefficients a_{2n+1}.

As we can see in **Figure 2**, the difference between predicted and simulated results is due to the a_{2n+1} but difference in IM_1 (magnitude or phase) is higher than IM_3 or IM_5. The cause of this error is due to the higher value of a_1, that is the dominate factor in calculating IM_1, than the other factors. The coefficient a_1 is related to the linear gain G of the amplifier, and the coefficients a_3 and a_5, that are the dominate factors in calculating IM_3 and IM_5, respectively, are directly related to IP_3 and IP_5. Because of distortion nature of a_3 and a_5 it is obvious that

Estimation of Intermodulation Rejection Value as a Function of Frequency in Power Amplifier Using AM-AM and AM-PM Diagrams Based on Power Series Analysis

47

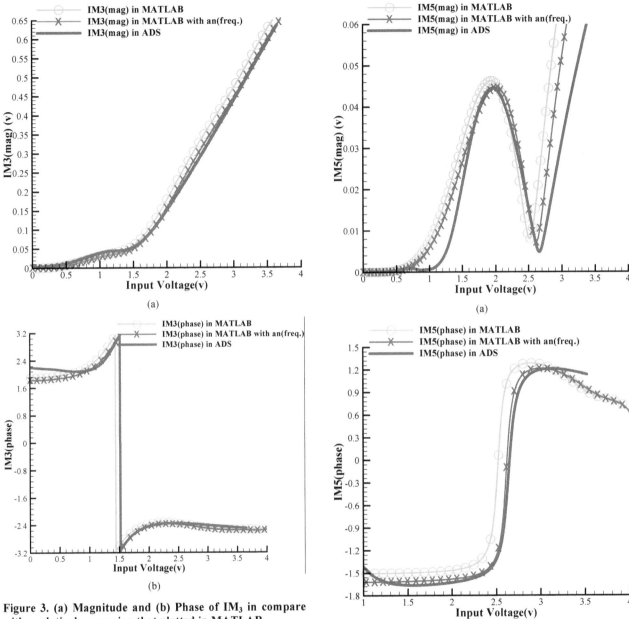

Figure 3. (a) Magnitude and (b) Phase of IM$_3$ in compare with analytical expression that plotted in MATLAB.

Figure 4. (a) Magnitude and (b) Phase of IM$_5$ in compare with analytical expression that plotted in MATLAB.

they have smaller values than a_1 and, so, error in a_1 shows higher difference than errors in a_3 and a_5, as we can see in **Figures 3** and **4**.

Totally, results show that both magnitude and phase of each frequency (each IM) are predicted well by Equation (11), and have better match if we consider frequency effect. Though we did not compare it with real measurement results, HB (Harmonic Balance) simulation in ADS is known as the most accurate simulation method for a real system.

5. Conclusion

In this paper, we proposed a method to predict inter mo-

dulation (IM) products based on AM-AM and AM-PM diagrams of the power amplifier. Our method shows not only input magnitude but also input frequency is affected output IM products. With the mean of this method and considering frequency effect in it, it is possible to predict IM products for wide band frequency range input, and input with complexity in their phase or frequency. In addition there is no need for circuit details of our power amplifier in our analyzing. Simulated results of power amplifier in compare with results that are gained from our method show good fitting with each other that shows our method is accurate.

REFERENCES

[1]   R. Raich, H. Qian and G. T. Zhou, "Orthogonal Polynomials for Power Amplifier Modeling and Predistorter Design," *IEEE Transactions on Vehicular Technology*, Vol. 53, No. 5, 2004, pp. 1468-1479.

[2]   B. Larkin, "Multiple-Signal Intermodulation and Stability Consideration in the Use of Linear Repeaters," *Proceeding of 41st IEEE Vehicular Technology*, St. Louis, 19-22 May 1991, pp. 747-752.

[3]   Q. Wu, M. Testa and R. Larkin, "Linear RF Power Amplifier Design for CDMA Signal," *IEEE MIT-S Digest*, Corvallis, June 1996, pp. 851-854.

[4]   G. T. Zhou and J. S. Kenney, "Predicting Spectral Regrowth of Nonlinear Power Amplifiers," *IEEE Transactions on Communications*, Vol. 50, No. 5, 2002, pp. 718-722.

[5]   C. H. Tseng, "Estimation of Cubic Nonlinear Bandpass Channels in Orthogonal Frequency-Division Multiplexing Systems," *IEEE Transaction on Communications*, Vol. 58, No. 5, 2010, pp. 1415-1425.

[6]   M. E. Gadringer, C. Schuberth and G. Magerl "Behavioral Modeling of the Frequency Translation Process in Direct Conversion Transmitters," *International Journal of RF and Microwave Computer-Aided Engineering*, Vol. 20, No. 3, 2010, pp. 347-359.

[7]   S. J. Yi, S. Nam, S. H. Oh and J. H. Han, "Prediction of a CDMA Output Spectrum Based on Intermodulation Products of Two-Tone Test," *IEEE Transaction on Microwave Theory and Techniques*, Vol. 49, No. 5, 2001, pp. 767-946.

[8]   A. H. Coskun and S. Demir, "A Mathematical Characterization and Analysis of a Feed forward Circuit for CDMA Applications," *IEEE Transaction on Microwave Theory and Techniques*, Vol. 51, No. 3, 2003, pp. 767-777.

[9]   C. Liu, H. Xiao, Q. Wu and F. Lit, "Linear RF Power Amplifier Design for Wireless Signals: A Spectrum Analysis Approach," *International Conference on Acoustics, Speech, and Signal Processing*, Vol. 4, 2003, pp. 568-571.

[10] A. M. A. Hemmatyar and F. Farzaneh, "Predicting of Inter-Modulation Rejection Values for the First and Second Adjacent Channels in Feed-Forward Linearised Microwave Amplifiers Using Closed-Form Expressions," *IET Microwaves Antennas & Propagation*, Vol. 1, No. 3, 2007, pp. 782-789.

[11] M. L. Ku, S. H. Lu, L. C. Wang and S. H. Yan, "Nonlinear Effect of Receiver Amplifier for 60 GHz Radio Communication," *IEEE International Conference on Vehicular Technology*, 5-8 September 2011, pp. 1-5.

[12] K. G. Gard, H. M. Gutierrez and M. B. Steer, "Characterization of Spectral Regrowth in Microwave Amplifiers Based on the Nonlinear Transformation of a Complex Gaussian Process," *IEEE Transaction on Microwave Theory and Techniques*, Vol. 47, No. 7, 1999, pp. 1059-1069.

[13] G. T. Zhou, "Analysis of Spectral Regrowth of Weakly Nonlinear Power Amplifiers," *IEEE Communication Letters*, Vol. 4, No. 11, 2000, pp. 357-359.

[14] C. Liu, H. Xiao, Q. Wu and F. Li, "Linear RF Power Amplifier Design for TDMA Signals: A Spectrum Analysis Approach," *Proceedings of International Conference on Acoustics, Speech, and Signal Processing*, Salt Lake City, Vol. 4, May 2001, pp. 2665-2668.

[15] M. M. Rahmati, A. Abdipour, A. Mohammadi and G. Moradi, "An Analytic Approach for CDMA Output of Feed forward Power Amplifier," *Analog Integrated Circuit and Signal Processing*, Vol. 66, No. 3, 2011, pp. 349-361.

[16] E. Cottais, Y. Wang and S. Toutain, "Spectral Regrowth at the Output of a Memoryless Power Amplifier with Multicarrier Signals," *IEEE Transactions on Communications*, Vol. 56, No. 7, 2008, pp. 1111-1118.

[17] J. P. Aikio and T. Rahkonen, "A Comprehensive Analysis of AM-AM and AM-PM Conversion in an LDMOS RF Power Amplifier," *IEEE Transactions on Microwave Theory and Techniques*, Vol. 57, No. 2, 2009, pp. 262-270.

[18] S. Meza, M. O'Droma, Y. Lei and A. Goacher, "Some New Memory Less Behavioral Models of Wireless Transmitter Solid State Power Amplifiers," *IEEE Automation, Quality and Testing, Robotics*, Vol. 1, 2008, pp. 96-98.

[19] M. Masood, J. Staudinger, J. Wood, M. Bokatius and J. S. Kenney, "Linearity Considerations for a High Power Doherty Amplifier," *IEEE International Conference on Power Amplifier for Wireless and Radio Applications*, Atlanta, 15-18 January 2012, pp. 77-80.

[20] L. W. Couch, "Digital and Analog Communication Systems," Prentice-Hall Inc., Upper Saddle River, 1996.

[21] T. S. Rappaport, "Wireless Communication Principle and Practice," Prentice-Hall Inc., Upper Saddle River, 1996.

[22] M. C. Jeruchim, P. Balabon and K. S. Shanmugan, "Simulation of Communication Systems," Kluwer Academic Publishers, Springer, New York, 2002.

[23] A. Chatterjee, S. Devarakond and S. Sen, "Phase Distortion to Amplitude Conversion-Based Low-Cost Measurement of AM-AM and AM-PM Effects in RF Power Amplifiers," *IEEE Transaction on Very Large Scale Integration (VLSI) Systems*, Vol. PP, No. 99, 2011, pp. 1-13.

8

Optimization of the Voltage Doubler Stages in an RF-DC Convertor Module for Energy Harvesting

Kavuri Kasi Annapurna Devi[1*], **Norashidah Md. Din**[2], **Chandan Kumar Chakrabarty**[2]

[1]Department of Electrical and Electronic Engineering, INTI International University, Nilai, Malaysia
[2]Department of Electronics and Communication Engineering, Universiti Tenega Nasional, Kajang, Malaysia

ABSTRACT

This paper presents an optimization of the voltage doubler stages in an energy conversion module for Radio Frequency (RF) energy harvesting system at 900 MHz band. The function of the energy conversion module is to convert the (RF) signals into direct-current (DC) voltage at the given frequency band to power the low power devices/circuits. The design is based on the Villard voltage doubler circuit. A 7 stage Schottky diode voltage doubler circuit is designed, modeled, simulated, fabricated and tested in this work. Multisim was used for the modeling and simulation work. Simulation and measurement were carried out for various input power levels at the specified frequency band. For an equivalent incident signal of –40 dBm, the circuit can produce 3 mV across a 100 kΩ load. The results also show that there is a multiplication factor of 22 at 0 dBm and produces DC output voltage of 5.0 V in measurement. This voltage can be used to power low power sensors in sensor networks ultimately in place of batteries.

Keywords: Energy Conversion; RF; Schottky Diode; Villard; Energy Harvesting

1. Introduction

RF energy harvesting is one type of energy harvesting that can be potentially harvested such as solar, vibration and wind. The RF energy harvesting uses the idea of capturing transmitted RF energy at ambient and either using it directly to power a low power circuit or storing it for later use. The concept needs an efficient antenna along with a circuit capable of converting RF signals to DC voltage. The efficiency of an antenna mainly depends on its impedance and the impedance of the energy converting circuit. If the two impedances aren't matched then it will be unable to receive all the available power from the free space at the desired frequency band. Matching of the impedances means that the impedance of the antenna is the complex conjugate of the impedance of the circuit (voltage doubler circuit).

The concept of energy harvesting system is shown in **Figure 1**, which consists of matching network, RF-DC conversion and load circuits. The authors in [1], used a 2.4 GHz operating frequency with an integrated zero bias detector circuit using BiCMOS technology which produced an output voltage of 1 V into a 1 MΩ load at an input power level of 0 dBm. H. Yan and co-authors revealed that a DC voltage of 0.8 volts can be achieved from a –20 dBm RF input signal at 868.3 MHz through

simulation results [2]. In [3], work was carried out on a firm frequency of 900 MHz by matching to a 50 Ω impedance and resonance circuit transformation in front of the Schottky diode which yields an output voltage of over 300 mV at an input power level of 2.5 μ. W. J. Wang, L. Dong and Y. Fu [4] used a Cockcroft-Walton multiplier circuit that produced a voltage level of 1.0 V into a 200 MΩ load for an input power level of less than –30 dBm at a fixed frequency of 2.4 GHz.

The energy conversion module designed in this paper is based on a voltage doubler circuit which can be able to output a DC voltage typically larger than a simple diode rectifier circuit as in [5], in which switched capacitor charge pump circuits are used to design two phase voltage doubler and a multiphase voltage doubler. The module presented in this can function as an AC to DC converter that not only rectifies the input AC signal but also elevates the DC voltage level. The output voltage of the

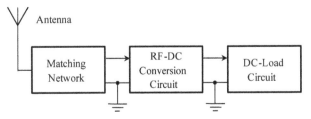

Figure 1. Schematic view of a RF energy harvesting system.

*Corresponding author.

energy conversion module can be used to energize the low power devices for example sensors for a sensor network in application to agriculture.

Section 2 of this paper discusses on the theoretical background of the voltage doubler circuit. Section 3 presents the simulation study and implementation of the circuit design. Section 4 provides the results and analysis. Section 5 concludes with a discussion on the findings from the simulated and measured results.

2. Voltage Multiplier

There are various voltage multiplier circuit topologies. The design used in this module is derived from the function of peak detector or a half wave peak rectifier. The Villard voltage multiplier circuit was chosen in the circuit design of this paper because it produces two times of the input signal voltage towards ground at a single output and can be cascaded to form a voltage multiplier with an arbitrary output voltage and its design simplicity.

2.1. Diode Modeling

The voltage multiplier circuit in this design uses zero bias Schottky diode HSMS-2850 from Agilent. The attractive feature of these Schottky diodes are low substrate losses and very fast switching but leads to a fabrication overhead. This diode has been modeled for the energy harvesting circuit which comes in a one-diode configuration. The modeling parameters for these diodes are given by Agilent in their data sheets. These parameters are used in Multisim for its own modeling purposes. The modeling is done by transforming the diode into an equivalent circuit using passive components which are described by the SPICE parameters in **Table 1** [6].

The diode used in this design is shown in **Figure 2** and its equivalent model is shown in **Figure 3**. The special features of HSMS-2850 diode is that it provides a low forward voltage, low substrate leakage and uses the non

Table 1. SPICE parameters.

Parameters	Units	HSMS 2850
B_V	V	3.8
C_{J0}	pF	0.18
E_G	Ev	0.69
I_{BV}	A	3E–4
I_S	A	3E–6
N	No unite	1.06
R_S	Ω	25
$P_B\ (V_J)$	V	0.35
$P_T\ (XTI)$	No units	2
M	No units	0.5

Figure 2. Schottky diode.

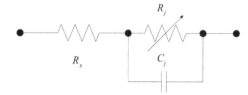

Figure 3. Linear circuit model of the Schottky diode [6].

symmetric properties of a diode that allows unidirectional flow of current under ideal condition.

The diodes are fixed and are not subject of optimization or tuning. This is described using the following derivations. By neglecting the effect of diode substrate, an equivalent linear model that can be used for the diode as shown in **Figure 3**. When C_j is the junction capacitance and R_j is the junction resistance, the admittance Y_z of the linear model is given by

$$Y_Z = Y_{C_j} + Y_{R_j} \tag{1}$$

Equation (1) related to the frequency of operation is given by

$$Y_Z = jwC_j + \frac{1}{R_j} \tag{2}$$

$$= \frac{jwC_jR_j + 1}{R_j} \tag{3}$$

The impedance Z of the linear model is given by

$$Z = \frac{R_j}{1 + jwR_jC_j} \tag{4}$$

The total impedance Z_T is given by

$$Z_T = R_S + \frac{R_j}{1 + jwR_jC_j} \tag{5}$$

where R_S is the series resistance of the circuit and R_j is given by

$$R_j = \frac{8.33 \times 10^{-5} \times N \times T}{I_b + I_S}$$

where:

I_b = bias current in μA;
I_s = saturation current in μA;
T = temperature (K);

N = ideality factor.

In Equation (5), R_j and C_j are constants and the frequency of operation (w) is the only variable parameter. As the frequency increases, the value of Z is almost negligible compared to the series resistance R_S of the diode. From this it is concluded that the function of the diode is independent of the frequency of operation.

2.2. Single Stage Voltage Multiplier

Figure 4 represents a single stage voltage multiplier circuit. The circuit is also called as a voltage doubler because in theory, the voltage that is arrived on the output is approximately twice that at the input. The circuit consists of two sections; each comprises a diode and a capacitor for rectification. The RF input signal is rectified in the positive half of the input cycle, followed by the negative half of the input cycle. But, the voltage stored on the input capacitor during one half cycle is transferred to the output capacitor during the next half cycle of the input signal. Thus, the voltage on output capacitor is roughly two times the peak voltage of the RF source minus the turn-on voltage of the diode.

The most interesting feature of this circuit is that when these stages are connected in series. This method behaves akin to the principle of stacking batteries in series to get more voltage at the output. The output of the first stage is not exactly pure DC voltage and it is basically an AC signal with a DC offset voltage. This is equivalent to a DC signal superimposed by ripple content. Due to this distinctive feature, succeeding stages in the circuit can get more voltage than the preceding stages. If a second stage is added on top of the first multiplier circuit, the only waveform that the second stage receives is the noise of the first stage. This noise is then doubled and added to the DC voltage of the first stage. Therefore, the more stages that are added, theoretically, more voltage will come from the system regardless of the input. Each independent stage with its dedicated voltage doubler circuit can be seen as a single battery with open circuit output voltage V_0, internal resistance R_0 with load resistance R_L, the output voltage, V_{out} is expressed as in Equation (7).

$$V_{out} = \frac{V_0}{R_0 + R_L} R_L \qquad (6)$$

When n number of these circuits are put in series and connected to a load of R_L in Equation (6) the output voltage V_{out} obtained is given by this change in RC value will make the time constant longer which in turn retains the multiplication effect of two in this design of seven stage voltage doubler.

$$V_{out} = \frac{nV_0}{nR_0 + R_L} = V_0 \frac{1}{\frac{R_0}{R_L} + \frac{1}{n}} \qquad (7)$$

The number of stages in the system has the greatest effect on the DC output voltage, as shown from Equations (6) and (7).

It is inferred that the output voltage V_{out} is determined by the addition of R_0/R_L and $1/n$, if V_0 is fixed. From this analysis it is observed that V_0, R_0 and R_L are all constants. Assume that $V_0 = 1$ V, $R_0/R_L = 0.25$, $n = 2, 3, 4, 5, 6$ and 7, the output voltage $V_{out} = 1.33$ V, 1.72 V, 2.0 V, 2.22 V, 2.43 V and 2.56 V respectively when substituted analytically in the Equation (7). This analysis can be compared with the results obtained in the circuit design of this module. In simulation at $n = 4$, $V_{out} = 1.42$ V, $n = 5$, $V_{out} = 1.67$ V; $n = 6$, $V_{out} = 1.92$; $n = 7$, $V_{out} = 2.15$ V; $n = 8$, $V_{out} = 1.92$ V; $n = 9$, $V_{out} = 1.81$ V. Also in measurement, for $n = 4$, $V_{out} = 2.1$ V; $n = 5$, $V_{out} = 2.9$ V; $n = 6$, $V_{out} = 3.72$ V; and $n = 7$, $V_{out} = 5$ V. As n increases, the increase in output voltage will be almost double the input voltage up to some number of stages. But at some point, *i.e.* beyond seven stages, in this circuit the output voltage gained (8 and 9 stages) will be negligible as shown in **Figure 5**.

The capacitors are charged to the peak value of the input RF signal and discharge to the series resistance (R_s) of the diode. Thus the output voltage across the capacitor of the first stage is approximately twice that of the input signal. As the signal swings from one stage to other, there is an additive resistance in the discharge path of the

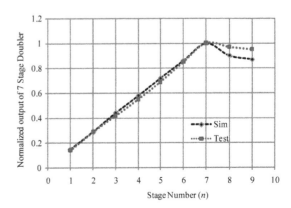

Figure 5. Normalized output voltage multiplier versus number of stages.

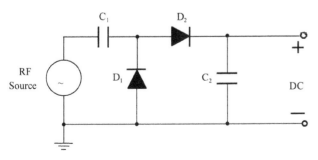

Figure 4. Single stage voltage multiplier circuit [7].

diode and increase of capacitance due to the stage capacitors.

2.3. Seven Stage Voltage Multiplier

The seven stage voltage multiplier circuit design implemented in this paper is shown in **Figure 6**. Starting on the left side, there is a RF signal source for the circuit followed by the first stage of the voltage multiplier circuit. Each stage is stacked onto the previous stage as shown in the **Figure 6**. Stacking was done from left to right for simplicity instead of conventional stacking from bottom to top.

The circuit uses eight zero bias Schottky surface-mount Agilent HSMS-285X series, HSMS-2850 diodes. The special features of these diode is that, it provides a low forward voltage, low substrate leakage and uses the non-symmetric properties of a diode that allows unidirectional flow of current under ideal conditions. The diodes are fixed and are not subject of optimization or tuning. This type of multiplier produces a DC voltage which depends on the incident RF voltage. Input to the circuit is a predefined RF source. The voltage conversion can be effective only if the input voltage is higher than the Schottky forward voltage.

The other components associated with the circuit are the stage capacitors. The chosen capacitors for this circuit are of through-hole type, which make it easier to modify for optimization, where in [8] the optimization was accomplished at the input impedance of the CMOS chip for a three stage voltage multiplier. The circuit design in this paper uses a capacitor across the load to store and provide DC leveling of the output voltage and its value only affects the speed of the transient response. Without a capacitor across the load, the output is not a good DC signal, but more of an offset AC signal.

In addition to the above, an equivalent load resistor is connected at the final node. The output voltage across the load decreases during the negative half cycle of the AC input signal. The voltage decreases is inversely proportional to the product of resistance and capacitance across the load. Without the load resistor on the circuit, the voltage would be hold indefinitely on the capacitor and look like a DC signal, assuming ideal components. In the design, the individual components of the stages need not to be rated to withstand the entire output voltage. Each component only needs to be concerned with the relative voltage differences directly across its own terminals and of the components immediately adjacent to it. In this type of circuitry, the circuit does not change the output voltage but increases the possible output current by a factor of two. The number of stages in the system is directly proportional to the amount of voltage obtained and has the greatest effect on the output voltage as explained in the Equation (7) and shown in **Figure 5**.

3. Simulation and Implementation

Multisim software was chosen for modeling and simulation which is a circuit simulation tool by Texas Instruments. The simulation and practical implementation were carried out with fixed RF at 945 MHz ± 100 MHz, which are close to the down link center radio frequency (947.5 MHz) of the GSM-900 transmitter. The voltages obtained at the final node V_{DC} of the multiplier circuit were recorded for various input power levels from –40 dBm - +5 dBm with power level interval (spacing) of 5 dBm.

The simulations were also carried out using same stage capacitance value (3.3 nF) and then with a varied capacitance value for all stages from 4 stages through 9 stages [9]. The capacitance value was varied in such a way that, from one stage to the next, it was halved. For example, if the first stage was 3.3 nF, the second stage was 1.65 nF, third stage was 825 pF, fourth stage was 415 pF and so on. But keeping in view of testing, the capacitance values were chosen to have a close match with the standard available values in the market.

Simulation was carried out through 4 to 9 voltage doubler stages. Based on results obtained a 7 stage doubler is best to implemented for this application.

The design of the printed circuit board (PCB) was carried out using DipTrace software. The material used to

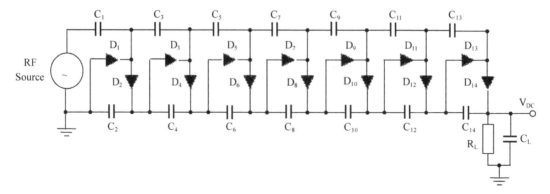

Figure 6. Schematic of 7 stage voltage multiplier.

manufacture the printed circuit board (PCB) is the standard Fiberglass Reinforced Epoxy (FR4), with the thickness of 1.6 mm and dielectric constant of 3.9. The topology is constructed on the PCB with the dimensions of 98 mm × 34 mm (W × H). The Sub Miniature version A (SMA) connectors are used at the input and output of PCB to carry out the measurements. The circuit components consist of active and passive components. The component used in circuit is shown in **Table 2**.

Special handling precautions have been taken to avoid Electro Static Discharge (ESD), while assembling of the surface-mount zero bias Schottky diodes. Also special attention has been given to mount other components and the SMA connectors on to the PCB. The Photograph of Assembled circuit board I shown in **Figure 7**.

4. Results and Analysis

The simulated and measured results at the output voltage of voltage multiplier circuit are shown graphically in **Figure 8**. From the graph analysis, the simulated and the measured results agree considerably with each other. The measured results are shown to be better than the simulation results. The reason behind this may be due to the uncertainty in series resistance value of the diode obtained from SPICE parameters in modeling as explained in Equation (5). This resistance vale of diodes in practical circuit may be lower than in the model, which provides fast discharge path, in turn rise in voltage as passes through the stages and reaches to final output. In this work, the DC output voltages obtained through simulation and measurement at 0 dBm re 2.12 V and 5.0 V respectively. These results are comparatively much better than in ref. [9], where in at 0 dBm, 900 MHz they achieved 0.5 V and 0.8 V through simulation and measurement

respectively.

Figures 9 and **10** show the result of a 4 stage voltage doubler circuit with equal and varied capacitance values between the stages as described in Section 3.

From the analysis of these two simulations, it can be observed that the resulting output voltages are equal. The only difference between these two graphs is the rise time of the circuit with varied capacitance value is a little bit slower. But, overall result on the performance of rise time is still under 20 μs to 24 μs and the difference is negligible. From these results, the use of equal stage capacitance of each being 3.3 nF was hence considered for the design of the multiplier.

The results from **Figure 11**, shows that the output voltage reaches to 1.0 V within 20 μS and then uniformly increasing to 1.4 V, 1.67 V, 1.87 V and 2.12 V for 4, 5, 6 and 7 stages respectively compared to 2 mS as shown in [10]. **Figure 12** shows that the conversion ratio of 22 is achieved at 0 dBm input power and drops to 2.5 at –40 dBm. The highest value at 0 dBm is due to the innate characteristics of the zero bias Schottky diodes which conduct fairly well at higher input voltages.

5. Conclusion

From the experimental results, it is found that the pro-

Table 2. Component used in 7 stage voltage multiplier.

Name of component	Label	Value
Stage capacitors	C_1 - C_{14}	3.3 nF
Stage diodes	D_1 - D_{14}	HSMS 2850
Filter capacitor	C_L	100 nF
Load resister	R_L	100 kΩ

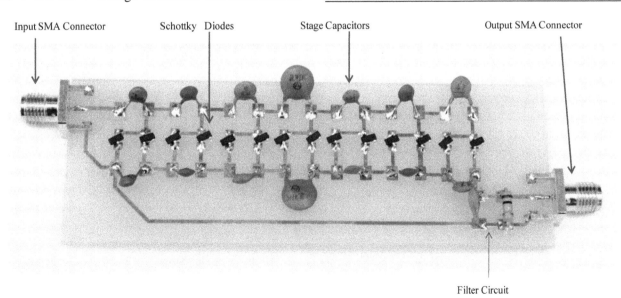

Input SMA Connector   Schottky Diodes   Stage Capacitors   Output SMA Connector

Filter Circuit

Figure 7. Photograph of assembled circuit board.

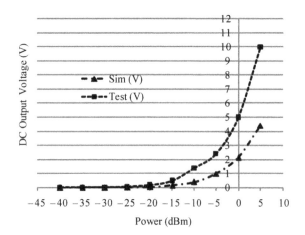

Figure 8. Simulated and test DC output voltage of multiplier as a function of input power.

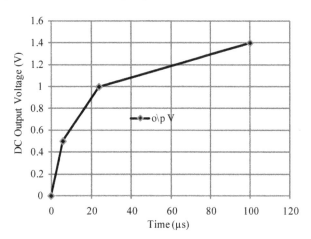

Figure 9. DC output voltage verses rise time of 4 stage voltage doubler circuit with equal stage capacitance [8].

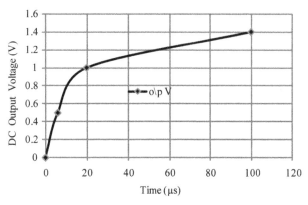

Figure 10. DC output voltage verses rise time of 4 stage voltage doubler with varied stage capacitance [8].

posed voltage multiplier circuit operates at the frequency of 945 MHz with the specified input power levels. The results have shown that there is multiplication of the input voltage. From **Figure 12**, it is shown that at 0 dBm input power, the multiplication factor is 22. This is sig-

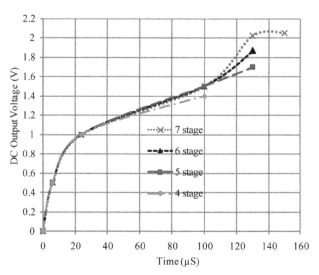

Figure 11. DC output voltage verses rise time of voltage doubler circuit through 4 - 7 stages with equal stage capacitance.

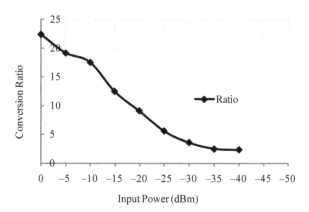

Figure 12. Conversion ratio as a function of input power.

nificant, as the work shows that RF energy in the GSM-900 band can be harvested from the ambient RF source using the Villard circuit topology. The power density levels from a GSM base station is expected from 0.1 mW/m^2 to 1 mW/m^2 for a distance ranging from 25 m - 100 m. These power levels may be elevated by a factor between one and three for the GSM-900 downlink frequency bands depending on the traffic density [10]. The next phase of the research work is to interface the voltage multiplier circuit through a matching network to the antenna at the input side and a low power device to power from the system at the output side to complete the RF energy harvesting system.

6. Acknowledgements

We would like to acknowledge and thank the Ministry of Higher Education Malaysia for funding this project under Fundamental Research Grant: FRGS/1/10/TK/UNITEN/ 02/13.

REFERENCES

[1] S. von der Mark and G. Boeck, "Ultra Low Power Wakeup Detector for Sensor Networks," *SBMO/IEEE MTT-S International Microwave & Optoelectronics Conference (IMOC* 2007), Berlin, 29 October-1 November 2007, pp. 865-868.

[2] H. Yan, J. G. M. Montero, A. Akhnoukh, L. C. N. de Vreede and J. N. Burghartz, "An Integration Scheme for RF Power Harvesting," *Proceedings of STW Annual Workshop on Semiconductor Advances for Future Electronics and Sensors*, Veldhoven, November 2005, pp. 64-66.

[3] T. Ungan and L. M. Reindl, "Concept for Harvesting Low Ambient RF-Sources for Microsystems," 2007. http://www.imtek.de/content/pdf/public/2007/powermems_2007_paper_ungan.pdf

[4] J. Wang, L. Dong and Y. Z. Fu, "Modeling of UHF Voltage Multiplier for Radio-Triggered Wake-Up Circuits," *International Journal of Circuit Theory and Application*, Vol. 39, No. 11, 2010, pp. 1189-1197.

[5] J. A. Starzyk, Y.-W. Jan and F. J. Qiu, "A DC-DC Charge Pump Design Based on Voltage Doublers," *IEEE Transactions on Circuits and Systems-I: Fundamental Theory and Applications*, Vol. 48, No. 3, 2001, pp. 350-359.

[6] HSMS-2850, "Surface Mount Zero Bias Schottky Detector Diodes." http://www.crystal-radio.eu/hsms285xdata.pdf

[7] D. W. Harrist, "Wireless Battery Charging System Using Radio Frequency Energy Harvesting," M.S. Thesis, University of Pittsburgh, Pittsburgh, 2004.

[8] E. Bergeret, J. Gaubert, P. Pannie and J. M. Gaultierr, "Modeling and Design of CMOS UHF Voltage Multiplier for RFID in an EEPROM Compatible Process," *IEEE Transactions on Circuits and Systems-I*, Vol. 54, No. 10, 2007, pp. 833-837.

[9] B. Emmanuel, J. Gaubert, P. Pannier and J. M. Gaultier, "Conception of UHF Voltage Multiplier for RFID Circui," *IEEE North-East Workshop on Circuits and Systems*, Gatineau, June 2006, pp. 217-220.

[10] H. J. Visser, A. C. F. Reniers and J. A. C. Theeuwes, "Ambient RF Energy Scavenging: GSM and WLAN Power Density Measurements," *Proceedings of the 38th European Microwave Conference*, Eindhoven, 27-31 October 2008, pp. 721-724.

9

Appropriate Placement of Fault Current Limiting Reactors in Different HV Substation Arrangements

Heresh Seyedi, Barzan Tabei
Faculty of Electrical and Computer Engineering, University of Tabriz, Tabriz, Iran

ABSTRACT

Short circuit currents of power systems are growing with an increasing rate, due to the fast development of generation and transmission systems. Current Limiting Reactor is one of the effective short circuit current limiting devices. This technique is known to be more practical than other available approaches. In this paper, proper application of CLR to HV substations is proposed, based on a comprehensive short circuit analysis of 4 well-known substation bus bar arrangements. Eventually, appropriate place and number of CLRs is recommended for each bus bar arrangement.

Keywords: Current Limiting Reactor; Fault Current Limiter; Bus Arrangement

1. Introduction

In modern power system, the increasing rate of energy demand imposes development of generation and transmission systems. As an unwelcome consequence of generation and transmission systems development, short circuit current are day-to-day increasing. Many utilities, all over the world, are experiencing the problem of astonishing short circuit levels. For instance, some utilities in Brazil, China, Iran and Kuwait may be mentioned [1-4]. Increasing rate of short circuit level causes undesired consequences which may be summarized as follows:

- Equipments are exposed to unacceptable thermal stresses;
- Equipments are exposed to unacceptable electro-dynamic forces;
- Short circuit breaking capability of high voltage circuit breakers is typically limited to 80 KA [5];
- In order to prevent equipment damage, faster circuit breakers are required. This requirement faces both technological and economical restrictions;
- Step and touch voltages are also increased as a result of increasing short circuit levels. This will cause safety problems to the personnel;
- Switching over voltage transients will become more severe, due to significant short circuit current.

Due to the above-mentioned problems, the subject of short circuit level reduction has gained a considerable attention in recent years among electric utilities. Numerous short circuit current limitation techniques have been introduced in the literature. One could mention the following important approaches:

- Current Limiting Reactor [1,2,6,7];
- Solid State Fault Current Limiters [8,9];
- Superconducting Fault Current Limiters [10-15];
- Fuse [16];
- Is limiter [17];
- Power system reconfiguration;
- Bus bar splitting techniques in the substations;
- Disconnection of some lines from the critical substations;
- Application of high impedance transformers;
- HVDC links [18];
- Design of higher voltage transmission networks [4];
- Application of neutral reactor.

The above mentioned approaches are briefly described in Section 2. Among these methods, Current Limiting Reactor may be the most practical approach. Methods such as SFCL are more or less passing their initial research stage. In addition they are still uneconomical. Other methods are either unacceptable due to their shortcomings or can not be economically justified.

In this paper, appropriate placement of CLR within the substation, considering four common busbar arrangements, is proposed. The main objective of this work is to find proper place for CLRs, which satisfy the following conditions:

- The short circuit level is reduced as much as possible;
- Minimum number of CLRs is applied.

The appropriate places are determined, based on comprehensive simulation studies followed by a complete analysis of the results. Using the results of this work, electric utilities could easily find the proper place of

CLRs whenever required.

In Section 2 of this paper, important short circuit limitation techniques are briefly described. In the third Section, characteristics of CLR are explained in detail. In Section 4, numerous possible places for the installation of CLRs are introduced. In Section 5, comprehensive simulation studies of this work are presented. Finally, in Section 6 results of simulations are discussed. Based on the discussion of Section 6, appropriate CLR places are recommended for each busbar arrangement.

2. Short Circuit Current Limitation Techniques

In this section, the previously-introduced short circuit reduction methods are briefly described.

2.1. Current Limiting Reactors

CLR is a will-known fault current limiting technique. Compared with many other methods, it is more economical. In addition its effect on the reliability of substation is negligible. However, it occupies a relatively large area in the substation, due to safety considerations. Moreover, it may degrade both voltage stability and transient stability of the system. More detail about CLR will be presented in Section 3 [1,2,6,7].

2.2. Solid State Fault Current Limiters

SSFCLs apply power electronic switches. These limiters are, practically, restricted to the distribution level. Moreover, they are complicated and expensive. Some types of SSFCLs apply series resonance or parallel resonance circuits [8,9].

2.3. Superconducting Fault Current Limiters

Superconducting material such as YBCO, NbTi and MgB_2 transit from superconducting state to the normal state, if exposed to high current levels. Due to this feature of superconductors, they can be applied as a fault current limiter. During normal operation of power system, SFCL resistance is negligible. However, as soon as the fault current shows up, SFCL quenches and consequently its resistance increases considerably. Resistive, inductive and transformer type SFCLs are important types of this device [10-15]. Although this limiter seems to be an ideal fault current limiter, it is still too expensive, especially due to the cost of its complicated cryogenic system.

2.4. Fuse

Fuse is a fast short circuit interrupting device. Therefore, it might be considered as a limiter. It is simple and cost-effective. However, it is technically restricted to below 40 kV nominal voltages and 200 A nominal currents. In addition to these restrictions, fuse must be replaced, following every interruption. Therefore, it may not be used when high speed auto-reclosing is required.

2.5. I_s Limiter

I_s Limiter is the improved version of fuse. In this device, during normal operation, major portion of current passes through a path parallel with the fuse. When the short circuit occurs, the parallel path is opened, using electrodynamic forces of fault current. Consequently, the fault current is commutated to the fuse. This way, the problem associated with the limited nominal current of fuse is resolved. I_s Limiter is claimed to be capable of interrupting fault currents up to 5 kA, within 1 ms after occurrence of the fault. However, it is still limited to 40 kV rated voltage [17].

2.6. Power System Reconfiguration

This approach is, to some extent, empirical. There is no definite rule for this method. In other words, it is case-dependent. It also depends on parameters such as creativity and familiarity of the engineer with the system under study. In many cases, it may result in considerable reduction of fault current level. Moreover, it may improve transient stability and voltage stability of the system.

2.7. Bus Bar Splitting Techniques in the Substations

In this approach, in order to reduce fault current level, bus section or/and bus coupler circuit breakers are opened. Power system operators are seriously opposed to this approach. Their disagreement is mainly due to the fact that bus bar splitting significantly decreases reliability of the substation. Moreover, it affects integrity of the system, which may result in lower transient stability and voltage stability margins. However, from the short circuit reduction point of view, this method is more effective than CLR. This is due the fact that bus bar splitting is equivalent to application of a CLR with infinite reactance. Meanwhile, this method may be considered as a temporary strategy which is acceptable only in emergency situations.

2.8. Disconnection of Some Lines from the Critical Substation

In this technique, in order to reduce bus bar short circuit level, 2 transmission lines are disconnected from the bus bar. Afterwards, these lines are reconnected together, outside the substation. Similar to the bus bar splitting method, this technique is not acceptable, from the power system operation point of view. Undesired effects on the reliability, transient stability and voltage stability of power system are known to be the main disadvantages of this approach.

2.9. Application of High Impedance Transformers

Using high impedance transformers may result in the considerable reduction of fault current level. However the undesired effects on transient stability and voltage stability might be significant.

2.10. HVDC

Replacement of tie lines with HVDC links will diminish inter-area short circuit currents. This will, obviously, restrict fault current levels. However, in most cases, this method is not economically justified.

2.11. Design of Higher Voltage Transmission Networks

In this method, the existing power system is split to several islands. Afterwards, a higher voltage system is designed and then the islands are reconnected through the higher voltage network [4]. This method seems not to be practical, as it is both complicated and costly.

2.12. Application of Neutral Reactor

Application of reactors in the neutral of transformers, will limit the earth fault current level. As the majority of faults include ground, this method may be considered as an effective approach [4].

Among the above mentioned approaches, CLR may be the most practical method. Since it does not affect reliability of the system, power system operators may accept it. However, as it might degrade voltage stability and transient stability margins of the system, its application requires careful attention.

3. Introduction to CLR

In this section important characteristics of CLR are introduced in detail.

3.1. Type of CLR

Dry type CLR and oil type CLR are the two well-known types of CLR. Dry type is an air-core reactor with copper or aluminum windings. Generally, iron cores are not used in CLRs, due to the possibility of saturation. Since this device is installed in series with the main circuit, possibility of iron core saturation, specially, during short circuit conditions, is high. Therefore, dry type air-core reactor is the common type of CLR, used in power systems. One of the main problems, associated with this device, is

the safety problem due to the magnetic flux distributed through the space around CLR. Therefore, air-core CLRs require proper fencing due to the personnel safety considerations.

Characteristics of oil type reactors are mainly similar to the dry type. However, the oil type is specifically designed for the heavily polluted environments. Moreover, oil type CLR has got the following advantages:
- Dielectric constant of oil is greater than air. This will result in the smaller size of oil type CLR, compared with the dry type.
- Heat transfer capability of oil is higher the air. This will result in some advantages and savings during the design stage.

3.2. Technical Specifications

Important technical parameters of CLRs may be listed as follows:
- Nominal voltage;
- Nominal frequency;
- Short circuit capacity of the system;
- Basic insulation level;
- Continuous operating current;
- Rated inductance;
- Type (dry or oil);
- Class (indoor or outdoor).

3.3. Practical Considerations

CLRs may significantly reduce short circuit level. However, some practical restrictions must be considered, before installing CLRs.
- **Voltage drop:** CLRs may affect voltage profile of the system. Hence, when CLR is recommended for a system, voltage stability studies of the system should be repeated.
- **Transient stability:** in addition to voltage stability, CLR may also degrade transient stability of the system.
- **Energy consumption:** since the main current of power system is continuously passing through the CLR, energy consumption of the device might be significant. This issue must be considered in the CLR design stage.
- **Distributed magnetic flux:** required safety clearances around the CLR should be double-checked, in order to consider the high magnetic flux, distributed through the space. This will necessitate careful fencing.
- **Transient recovery voltage:** when the circuit breakers interrupt short circuit or even normal load current, a transient voltage appears across the opened contacts. This voltage is known as Transient Recovery Voltage. TRV and its rate of rise, known as Rate of Rise of Recovery Voltage are considered as important pa-

rameters for the circuit breaker manufacturers. If either TRV or RRRV exceeds the circuit breaker capability, possibility of secondary arc will be increased. This will impose a significant stress on the circuit breaker and other equipments.

According to the analyses of [1] and [2], CLR affects both TRV and RRRV in the following manner:

- It reduces the peak of TRV. This is an advantage of CLR.
- It increases RRRV. This is a disadvantage of CLR. Unfortunately, RRRV is more critical than TRV. Therefore, prior to the installation of CLR, accurate transient studies are required.

3.4. Selection of CLR Inductance

Appropriate value of CLR inductance is dependent on the system, under study. In **Figure 1**, maximum short circuit current of a simulated system is depicted as a function of CLR reactance, ωL. The simulated system will be introduced in Section 5.

According to **Figure 1**, as L increases, slope of the I_{sc}-L curve decreases. Therefore, for the values of ωL greater than 50 Ω, variations of L will not significantly change I_{sc}. Therefore, in this simulation 50 Ω is a limit, which is called "efficiency limit" in [2]. From the short circuit reduction point of view, 50 Ω is an effective value for ωL. However, in practice since transient stability, voltage stability and also TRV restrictions should also be taken into consideration, ωL is not necessarily selected to be 50 Ω.

4. Candidate Places for CLR in the Substations

At least 4 locations in the substation may be the candidate places for installation of CLR. These candidates are introduced as follows.

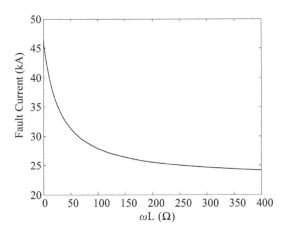

Figure 1. Effect of inductance on fault current level.

4.1. In Series with the Bus Section Breaker

In both single bus bar and double bus bar arrangements, the main bus is divided into 2 sections. These sections are connected by either circuit breaker or disconnecting switches. **Figure 2** depicts the double-bus bar arrangement. In this figure, breakers number 1 and number 2 are the bus section and bus coupler breakers, respectively.

Installation of CLR in series with the bus section breaker is a suitable option. This configuration is shown in **Figure 3**. Since in this configuration, CLR is not connected directly in series with any feeder, effects on the transient stability and voltage stability seem to be tolerable.

4.2. In Series with the Bus Coupler

This configuration is shown in **Figure 4**. In this case, CLR is installed in series with breaker number 2, the bus coupler breaker. Again, it is expected that degradation of voltage stability and transient stability margins will not be significant.

4.3. In Series with the Critical Feeders

Each feeder, connected to the bus bar, contributes to the

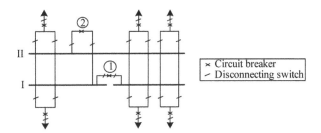

Figure 2. Double bus bar arrangement.

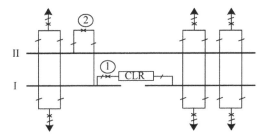

Figure 3. CLR in series with the bus section breaker.

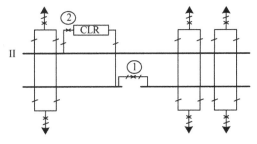

Figure 4. CLR in series with the bus coupler breaker.

short circuit level. However, contribution of some feeders is greater than others. Once the contribution of each feeder to the short circuit level has been evaluated, it is possible to recognize the critical feeders. Critical feeders are those which supply a great portion of short circuit current. Obviously, if CLRs are installed in series with the critical feeders, fault current level will significantly be decreased. This configuration is shown in **Figure 5**.

Since in this configuration, CLR is installed directly in series with feeder, significant decrease in transient stability and voltage stability margins is expected.

4.4. CLR, Connecting Adjacent Bus Bars or Substations

In some cases, there are adjacent bus bars or substations. In general, utilities tend to connect these adjacent sections to each other, due to its positive impact on the reliability, voltage stability and transient stability of the system. However, in many cases, high short circuit levels prevent this connection. In this situation, it is possible to connect the separated sections by CLRs. For instance, in Brazil, two 550 kV adjacent substations have been connected by a CLR [1]. In reference [4], connection of adjacent 1.5 breaker bus bars by CLRs, have been proposed. This configuration is depicted in **Figure 6**.

5. Appropriate CLR Placement in Different Arrangements

In this section a comprehensive short circuit study is

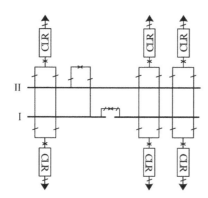

Figure 5. CLR in series with critical feeders.

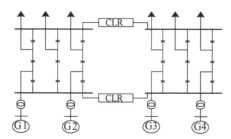

Figure 6. Connection of 1.5 breaker bus bars by CLRs.

performed. Four well-known bus bar arrangements are modeled in the Electro Magnetic Transients Program (EMTP). Six transmission lines with lengths of 60, 240, 170, 130, 250 and 75 km are connected to the simulated substation. For each bus bar arrangement, at the first stage, without any CLR, short circuit levels associated with different fault locations are obtained. Afterwards, CLRs are placed in different locations and the short circuit levels are again evaluated. Impedance of CLR is assumed to be 20 Ω in all simulation studies. Based on the simulation results followed by a complete discussion, the most appropriate locations of CLRs are introduced. The optimal placement is based on the impact of CLR on the short circuit level. However, the impacts on transient stability and voltage stability are also discussed. It is worth mentioning that, in order to save space, only a selected set of simulation results are presented in this section. However, all simulated cases have been considered in the discussion making conclusions.

5.1. Single Bus Bar with Bus Section Breaker

Configuration of this case study is shown in **Figure 7**.

In **Table 1**, results of the simulation study for fault occurring on Section A are listed. The results are related to different locations and different numbers of CLRs. In each case, both bus section current and total fault current are presented. At the next stage of simulation studies, assuming that fault occurs on Section B, case studies of **Table 1** are repeated. The results are presented in **Table 2**. The next stage, short circuit studies are performed for fault occurring at the beginning of line 6. The results are presented in **Table 3**.

According to the results of **Tables 1-3**, bus section is the most appropriate place for CLR installation. In some cases, impact of bus section CLR on fault current level is even greater than application of 6 CLRs, 1 in series with each line.

5.2. Double Bus Bar Arrangement

Configuration of the simulated substation for this section is depicted in **Figure 8**. In this configuration, lines number 1, 2 and 4 are connected to bus number 1, while lines number 3, 5 and 6 are connected to bus number 2. This is a typical operating condition. The results of short circuit studies for faults occurring on bus 1, bus 2, at the beginning of line 1 and at the beginning of line 3 are presented

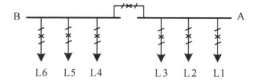

Figure 7. Single bus bar with bus section breaker.

Table 1. Bus bar arrangement, fault on Section A.

Case	Place of CLR	Bus section current (kA)	Fault current (kA)	Number of CLRs
1	Without CLR	23.9	46.25	0
2	Bus section	14.15	36.65	1
3	Series with Line 1	23.5	43.19	1
4	Series with Line 2	23.95	45.65	1
5	Series with Line 3	23.95	45.26	1
6	Series with Line 4	22.84	45.15	1
7	Series with Line 5	23.12	45.68	1
8	Series with Line 6	20.62	43.06	1
9	Series with (L1 + L6)	20.3	40	2
10	Series with (L1 + L6 + L4)	19.35	38.8	3
11	Series with (L1 + L6 + L4 + L3)	19.3	37.9	4
12	Series with (L1 + L6 + L4 + L3 + L2)	19.34	37.3	5
13	Series with all lines	18.8	36.82	6

Table 2. Single bus bar arrangement, fault on Section B.

Case	Place of CLR	Bus section current (KA)	Fault current (KA)	Number of CLRs
1	Without CLR	22.41	46.25	0
2	Bus section	13.70	37.35	1
3	Series with Line 1	19.65	43.18	1
4	Series with Line 2	21.73	45.65	1
5	Series with Line 3	21.3	45.25	1
6	Series with Line 4	22.33	45.15	1
7	Series with Line 5	22.57	45.67	1
8	Series with Line 6	22.41	43.03	1
9	Series with (L1 + L6)	19.67	40	2
10	Series with (L1 + L6 + L4)	19.46	38.8	3
11	Series with (L1 + L6 + L4 + L3)	18.55	37.85	4
12	Series with (L1 + L6 + L4 + L3 + L2)	18.03	37.33	5
13	Series with all lines	18	36.82	6

Table 3. Single bus bar arrangement, fault at the beginning of line 6.

Case	Place of CLR	Bus section current (KA)	Fault current (KA)	Number of CLRs
1	Without CLR	22.41	46.25	0
2	Bus section	13.69	37.33	1
3	Series with all lines	10	27.71	6

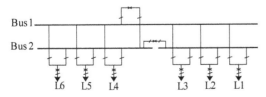

Figure 8. Double bus bar arrangement.

in **Tables 4-7**, respectively. Based on the results of **Tables 4-7**, installation of CLR in either bus coupler or bus section alone is not sufficient to limit fault current level

Table 4. Double bus bar arrangement, fault occurring at bus 1.

Case	Place of CLR	Peak current (kA)			Number of CLRs
		Bus section	Bus coupler	Fault	
1	Without CLR	6.4	23.7	46.31	0
2	Bus section	3.8	14	37	1
3	Bus coupler	5.5	22.6	45.3	1
4	Bus section + coupler	3.25	13.5	36.6	2
5	Series with all lines	5.25	18.4	36.85	6

Table 5. Double bus bar arrangement, fault occurring at bus 2.

| Case | Place of CLR | Peak current (kA) | | | Number of CLRs |
		Bus section	Bus coupler	Fault	
1	Without CLR	39.92	22.63	46.3	0
2	Bus section	30.72	13.9	37	1
3	Bus coupler	18.64	10.55	24.82	1
4	Bus section + coupler	16.33	7.5	22.5	2
5	Series with all lines	17	18.47	36.85	6

Table 6. Double busbar arrangement, fault occurring at the beginning of line 1.

| Case | Place of CLR | Peak current (kA) | | | Number of CLRs |
		Bus section	Bus coupler	Fault	
1	Without CLR	6.4	23.7	46.3	0
2	Bus section	3.8	13.9	36.96	1
3	Bus coupler	5.26	22.6	45.3	1
4	Bus section + coupler	3.25	13.55	36.6	2
5	Series with all lines	2.9	10	27	6

Table 7. Double bus bar arrangement, fault occurring at the beginning of line 3.

| Case | Place of CLR | Peak current (kA) | | | Number of CLRs |
		Bus section	Bus coupler	Fault	
1	Without CLR	40	23	46.3	0
2	Bus section	30.75	13.92	37	1
3	Bus coupler	18.64	10.57	24.82	1
4	Bus section + coupler	16.33	7.39	22.53	2
5	Series with all lines	16.7	9.72	22.8	6

for all fault locations. Therefore, in the double bus bar arrangement, it seems that simultaneous installation of CLR in series with both bus section and bus coupler breakers is necessary.

To illustrate the effect of CLR on the fault current level, waveforms of the fault current, with and without CLR, are depicted in **Figure 9**. The dotted curve is related to the case without CLR. While, in the normal curve, CLRs are placed in series with both bus section and bus coupler breakers.

5.3. Double Breaker Arrangement

The double breaker arrangement is shown in **Figure 10**. In this configuration, each feeder is connected to both bus bars, through 2 sets of circuit breakers. Hence, the results of faults on bus bars 1 and 2 are identical. The

results of fault analysis for faults on bus bar 1 and at the beginning of line 1 are presented in **Tables 8** and **9**, respectively.

In the double breaker arrangement, there is no bus coupler breaker. However, there might be a bus section breaker. Since all lines are connected to both bus bars at the same time, the bus section is always shorted through several parallel paths. Therefore, even if a bus section exists, it is not possible to apply CLR to this place. Hence, the bus section has not been considered in this

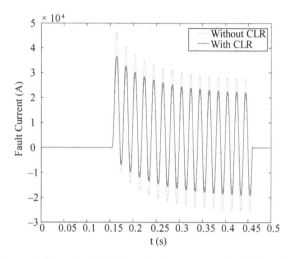

Figure 9. Impact of CLR on fault current, double bus bar arrangement.

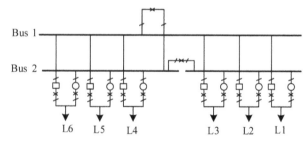

Figure 10. Double breaker arrangement.

Table 8. Double breaker arrangement, fault at bus 1.

Case	Place of CLR	Fault current (kA)	Number of CLRs
1	Without CLR	46.3	0
2	Series with L1	43.31	1
3	Series with (L1 + L6)	40.1	2
4	Series with (L1 + L6 + L4)	38.9	3
5	Series with (L1 + L6 + L4 + L3)	37.94	4
6	Series with all lines	36.85	6
7	Square locations	38	6
8	Circle locations	46.3	6
9	Circle + square locations	37.25	12

case. Instead, the circle and square positions are considered, as depicted in **Figure 10**. Based on the results of **Tables 8** and **9**, installation of CLR in either circle or square locations alone is not sufficient. On the other hand, installation of CLRs on both circle and square positions will require a large number of reactors, *i.e.* twice the number of lines. Therefore, these options are not acceptable. Instead, it recommended to install reactors in series with 1 or 2 critical lines, for example lines 1 and 6 in this study.

5.4. Breaker and a Half (1.5 Breaker) Arrangement

1.5-breaker arrangement is depicted in **Figure 11**. The results of simulation studies for faults at bus bar 1, the beginning of line 1 and bus bar 2 are listed in **Tables 10-12**, respectively.

In the 1.5 breaker arrangement, if CLRs are to be installed between 2 bus bars, there must be at least 1 CLR in each bay. Even if one bay is without CLR, it will bypass all CLRs of other bays. For example if CLRs are installed in series with just B1 and B4 breakers, both of these CLRs will be bypassed through the B7-B8-B9 path. Therefore, for the three-bay arrangement shown in **Figure 11**, at least 3 CLRs are required. Based on the results of **Tables 10-12**, if CLRs are installed adjacent to one of the bus bars, for some fault locations CLRs will have no impact on the fault current. On the other hand, installa-

Table 9. Double breaker arrangement, fault at the beginning of line 1.

Case	Place of CLR	Fault current (kA)	Number of CLRs
1	Without CLR	46.3	0
2	Series with L1	28.67	1
3	Series with L6	43.1	1
4	Series with (L6 + L4)	42	2
5	Series with (L6 + L4 + L3)	40.9	3
6	Series with (L6 + L4 + L3 + L1)	27.25	4
7	Series with (L6 + L4 + L1)	27.5	3

Table 10. 1.5 breaker arrangement, fault at bus 1.

Case	Place of CLR	Fault current (kA)	Number of CLRs
1	Without CLR	46.33	0
2	Series with B1, B4, B7	32	3
3	Series with B2, B5, B8	41.9	3
4	Series with B3, B6, B9	46.31	3
5	Series with B1, B3, B4, B6, B7, B9	31.62	6
6	Series with L1	43.3	1
7	Series with L2	45.66	1
8	Series with L3	45.3	1
9	Series with L4	45.2	1
10	Series with L5	45.73	1
11	Series with L6	43.05	1
12	Series with L1 + L6	40	2
13	Series with L1 + L6 + L4	38.9	3
14	Series with L1 + L6 + L4 + L3	37.92	4
15	Series with L1, 6, 4, 3, 2	37.38	5
16	Series with all lines	36.84	6

Table 11. 1.5 breaker arrangement, fault at the beginning of line 1.

Case	Place of CLR	Fault current kA	Number of CLRs
1	Without CLR	46.31	0
2	Series with B1, B4, B7	46.1	3
3	Series with B2, B5, B8	41.9	3
4	Series with B3, B6, B9	46.31	3
5	Series with B1, B3, B4, B6, B7, B9	35.5	6
6	Series with L1 + L6	27.85	2
7	Series with L1 + L6 + L4	27.52	3

tion of CLRs in series with the intermediate breakers, *i.e.* B2, B5 and B8, will reduce fault current for any fault location. However, the degree of reduction is not significant.

Figure 12 depicts the impact of CLR on the fault current level. Fault occurs on bus 1. In the dotted curve, no CLR is applied, while in the normal curve, three CLRs are connected in series with lines 1, 4 and 6.

6. Discussion

6.1. Single Bus Bar with Bus Section

According to the results of **Tables 1** to **3**, the following conclusions are made:
- Bus section is the most appropriate location for the installation of CLR. This is due to the fact that the bus section CLR restricts the current of 3 out of 6 feeders,

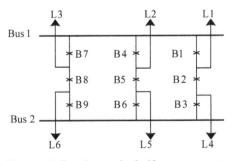

Figure 11. Breaker and a half arrangement.

Table 12. 1.5 breaker arrangement, fault at bus 2.

Case	Place of CLR	Fault current (kA)	Number of CLRs
1	Without CLR	46.31	0
2	Series with B1, B4, B7	46.1	3
3	Series with B2, B5, B8	42.28	3
4	Series with B3, B6, B9	31.18	3
5	Series with B1, B3, B4, B6, B7, B9	31.62	6
6	Series with L1	43.31	1
7	Series with L2	45.67	1
8	Series with L3	45.29	1
9	Series with L4	45.2	1
10	Series with L5	45.73	1
11	Series with L6	43	1
12	Series with L1 + L6	40.1	2
13	Series with L1 + L6 + L4	38.91	3
14	Series with L1 + L6 + L4 + L3	37.94	4
15	Series with L1 + L6 + L4 + L3 + L2	37.38	5
16	Series with all lines	36.84	6

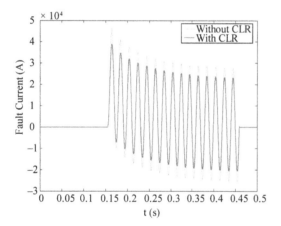

Figure 12. Impact of CLR on the fault current level, 1.5 breaker arrangement.

independent of the fault location. Therefore, installation of CLR in the bus section will be equivalent to the application of 3 CLRs in series with 3 out of 6 feeders.

- It is clear that the shorter the length of the line, the more it contributes to the fault current. Hence, lines number 1, 6 and 4 are the most critical lines respectively. Installation of CLRs in series with these lines is the most effective option, if the CLRs are to be installed in series with the lines. Although 3 CLRs are applied in this case, this option is still less effective, both technically and economically than placing 1 CLR in the bus section.
- In many cases application of 6 CLRs, *i.e.* in series

with all feeders, is not much more effective than one CLR in the bus section.

- From the transient stability and voltage stability point of view, application of CLR in the bus section is more acceptable than in series with lines.
- According to the above discussion, installation of CLR in series with the bus section is recommended for the single bus bar arrangement.

6.2. Double Bus Bar Arrangement

Based on the results of **Tables 4** to **7**, the following points are made:

- Effectiveness of CLR application in the bus section is depended on the fault location. Depending on the fault location, this option may either be much effective or not effective at all. This is due to the fact that in some fault locations, the bus section CLR will not be on the current path of the majority of feeders.
- Similar to the bus section, installation of CLR in series with the bus coupler, will not guarantee that the short circuit current will be restricted for every fault location. Effectiveness of this option is also depended on the fault location.
- Application of two sets of CLR, one in the bus coupler and the other in the bus section, is the most effective option. In some cases their impact on the short circuit level, is approximately identical to application of 6 CLRs, one set in each feeder.
- In some specific cases application of 6 CLRs, *i.e.* in series with all feeders, is much effective than other options. However, this option is not practically acceptable. Since it significantly decreases transient stability and voltage stability margins.
- Based on the above notes, simultaneous application of CLRs in both bus section and bus coupler is recommended for double bus bar arrangement.

6.3. Double Breaker Arrangement

The following points are based on the results of **Tables 8** and **9**:

- In the double breaker arrangement, 3 option are available for CLR placement:
  1) To install adjacent to 1 bus bar, *i.e.* circle or square locations of **Figure 10**.
  2) To install adjacent to both bus bars, *i.e.* both circle and square locations of **Figure 10**.
  3) To install in series with the feeders.
- If the CLR is to be installed adjacent to the bus bars, say bus bar 1, it should be applied to all locations between bus bar 1 and feeders connected to this bus bar. In other words, minimum number of required CLRs is equal to the number of bays. Otherwise, the CLRs will be bypassed by the available parallel paths.

- Installation adjacent to 1 bus bar, will not limit the short circuit current for every fault location. In other words, its effectiveness depends on the fault location.
- Installation adjacent to both bus bars is not much more effective than installation in series with all feeders. However, the former requires twice number of CLRs, compared with the latter.
- Based on the above notes, for the double breaker arrangement, installation of CLR in series with the lines, especially critical lines, is recommended. However, due to the negative impact of this option on the transient stability and voltage stability, application of CLR to the double breaker arrangement requires careful attention.

6.4. Breaker Arrangement

- In 1.5 breaker arrangement, three options are available for CLR installation:
  1) To install adjacent to each bus bar;
  2) To install in series with the intermediate breakers;
  3) To install in series with the lines.
- If CLRs are to be installed adjacent to each bus bar or in series with the intermediate breakers, they should be applied to all bays. If CLR is not installed even in one of the bays, other CLRs will be short circuited. Generally speaking, in the 1.5 breaker arrangement, if CLRs are to be installed between 2 bus bars, there must be at least 1 CLR in each bay. Even if one bay is without CLR, it will bypass all CLRs of other bays.
- If CLRs are installed adjacent to one of the bus bars, their effectiveness in limitation of fault current will depend on the fault location. In this situation, for some fault locations, CLRs will have no impact on the fault current.
- Installation of CLRs in series with the intermediate breakers will reduce fault current for any fault location. However, the degree of reduction is not significant.
- Installation of CLRs adjacent to both bus bars, effectively decrease fault current level. However, this option is not economically justified, since the number of required reactors is equal to the number of lines.
- Installation of CLRs in series with critical lines may significantly restrict the fault current level. Regularly, this is obtained using few CLRs.
- Although installation of CLRs in series with critical lines will pose negative impacts on transient stability and voltage stability of the system, its negative impacts are expected to be less than other mentioned options. As previously mentioned, number of CLRs, in this option, is less than other options.
- Based on the above discussion, it is recommended that, in 1.5 breaker configuration, CLRs be installed in series with critical lines.

7. Conclusion

In this paper application of current limiting reactors, for reduction of fault current, has been analyzed. Four well-known bus bar arrangements in the substation were simulated by EMTP. In each configuration, impact of CLR on the fault current level was evaluated. Numerous CLR placement alternatives along with different fault locations were considered in this analysis. Based on the simulation result and discussions, the most appropriate locations of CLR were recommended for each arrangement. Since the short circuit currents are rising day-to-day, many utilities will have to adopt strategies to limit those high currents. Hence, recommendations of the discussion section will be a useful for utilities on how to apply CLRs.

8. Acknowledgements

The authors really appreciate Gharb Regional Electric Company for its financial support.

REFERENCES

[1] J. F. Amon, P. C. Fernandez, E. H. Rose, A. D'Ajuz and A. Castanheira, "Brazilian Successful Experience in the Usage of Current Limiting Reactors for Short-Circuit Limitation," *International Conference on Power Systems Transients* (*IPST'*05), Montreal, 19-23 June 2005, pp. 215-220.

[2] Z.-X. Geng, X. Lin, J.-Y. Xu and C. Tian, "Effects of Series Reactor on Short-circuit Current and Transient Recovery Voltage," 2008 *International Conference on High Voltage Engineering and Application*, Chongqing, 9-13 November 2008, pp. 524-526.

[3] M. Gilany and W. Al-Hasawi, "Reducing the Short Circuit Levels in Kuwait Transmission Network (A Case Study)," *World Academy of Science, Engineering and Technology*, Vol. 53, 2009, pp. 592-596.

[4] A. Nasiri and H. Barahmandpour, "Fault Current Limitation of Ramin Power Plant," 21st *International Power System Conference* (*PSC*), Tehran, 2006, pp. 1640-1646.

[5] T. Roininen, C. E. Solver, H. Nordli, A. Bosma, P. Jonsson and A. Alfredsson, "ABB Live Tank Circuit Breakers, Application Guide." www.abb.com

[6] D. F. Peelo, G. S. Polovick, J. H. Sawada, P. Diamanti, R. Presta, A. Sarshar and R. Beauchemin, "Mitigation of Circuit Breaker Transient Recovery Voltages Associated with Current Limiting Reactors," *IEEE Transactions on Power Delivery*, Vol. 11, No. 2, 1996, pp. 865-871.

[7] M. Khorrami, M. S. Nader and N. K. Nejhad, "Short Circuit Current Level Control and Its Effects on Circuit Breakers Transient Studies," *Journal of Electrical Engineering: Theory and Application*, Vol. 1, No. 1, 2010, pp. 4-17.

[8] M. M. R. Ahmed, G. A. Putrus, R. Li and L. J. Xiao, "Harmonic Analysis and Improvement of a New Solid-

State Fault Current Limiter," *IEEE Transactions on Industry Applications*, Vol. 40, No. 4, 2004, pp. 1012-1019.

[9] G. G. Karady, "Principles of Fault Current Limitation by a Resonant LC Circuit," *IEEE Proceedings-C*, Vol. 139, No. 1, 1992, pp. 1-6.

[10] B. W. Lee, J. Sim, K. B. Park and I. S. Oh, "Practical Application Issues of Superconducting Fault Current Limiters for Electric Power Systems," *IEEE Transactions on Applied Superconductivity*, Vol. 18, No. 2, 2008, pp. 620-623.

[11] Y. Lin, M. Majoros, T. Coombs and A. M. Campbell, "System Studies of the Superconducting Fault Current Limiter in Electrical Distribution Grids," *IEEE Transactions on Applied Superconductivity*, Vol. 17, No. 2, 2007, pp. 2339-2342.

[12] D. Fedasyuk, P. Serdyuk, Y. Semchyshyn and Lviv Polytechnic National University, "Resistive Superconducting Fault Current Limiter Simulation and Design," *15th International Conference*, Poznan, 19-21 June 2008, pp. 349-353.

[13] M. Noe, A. Kudymow, S. Fink, S. Elschner, F. Breuer, J. Bock, H. Walter, M. Kleimaier, K. H. Weck, C. Neumann, F. Merschel, B. Heyder, U. Schwing, C. Frohne, K. Schippl and M. Stemmle, "Conceptual Design of a 110 kV Resistive Superconducting Fault Current Limiter Using MCP-BSCCO 2212 Bulk Material," *IEEE Transactions on Applied Superconductivity*, Vol. 17, No. 2, 2007, pp. 1784-1787.

[14] T. Janowski, S. Kozak, H. Malinowski, G. Wojtasiewicz, B. Kondratowicz-Kucewicz and J. Kozak, "Properties Comparison of Superconducting Fault Current Limiters with Closed and Open Core," *IEEE Transactions on Applied Superconductivity*, Vol. 13, No. 2, 2003, pp. 851-854.

[15] H. S. Choi and S. H. Lim, "Operating Performance of the Flux-Lock and the Transformer Type Superconducting Fault Current Limiter Using the YBCO Thin Films," *IEEE Transactions on Applied Superconductivity*, Vol. 17, No. 2, 2007, pp. 1823-1826.

[16] H. H. Fahnoe, "Taking Advantage of High-Voltage Fuse Capabilities for System Protection," *IEEE Transactions on Industry and General Applications*, Vol. IGA-6, No. 5, 1970, pp. 463-471.

[17] K. H. Hartung, "I$_s$-limiter, the Solution for High Short-Circuit Current Applications," ABB Calor Emag, 2002. www.abb.com

[18] J. J. Zhang, Q. Liu, C. Rehtan and S. Rudin, "Investigation of Several New Technologies for Mega City Power Grid Issues," *International Conference on Power System Technology*, Chongqing, 22-26 October 2006, pp. 1-6.

10

A Novel High CMRR, Low Power and Low Voltage COS with QFG

Alireza Ghorbani, Ahmad Ghanaatian

Electronics Department, Iran University of Science and Technology, Tehran, Iran

ABSTRACT

A novel high CMRR current output stage (COS) with QFG is presented in this paper. A novel common mode feedback (CMFB) is used to reject the common mode signal in order to achieve high CMRR. The common mode signal is omitted by the technique of adding the main signal and its opposite polarity one. 112 dB of CMRR is obtained in 0.35 μm CMOS technology with ±0.75 v supply voltage and only 182 μw power dissipation which shows good improvement compared to the other work in the literature.

Keywords: CMRR; QFG; Current Mode; Current Operational Amplifier (COA); COS

1. Introduction

Current operational amplifier (COA) have been used as feasible alternative to traditional voltage amplifier (VOA) in order to use in high accuracy closed loop IC configuration [1-3]. Excellent performance feature of current mode blocks, have become main reason to use current mode signal processing instead of voltage mode. Today's, it is well known that high speed and accuracy, low level supply, small size and wide band dynamic range could be achieved by taking advantages of the current mode blocks [1-6]. The current-mode output stage (COS) can be used as the end part of COA, moreover, it could be considered as voltage to current convertor (VIC) which is very significant analog block especially in high frequency applications [7-10]. Many important properties of COA like offset and CMRR is determined by COS which shows great value of this block [7,10-13].

Several COS's have been proposed in literature to improve the parameters like CMRR. [11] fixed the potential at the source of COA transistors by two auxiliary differential amplifier to improve CMRR. But these structures suffer from high power dissipation and high supply voltage. [14] used the same method to achieved high CMRR while it could decrease supply voltages to some extent. [10] used CMFF technique to improve CMRR, but suffer from stability and high supply voltage problem.

The COS's usually constructed in single input, differential output, however the fully differential structure can improve some properties like CMRR, PSRR [13-16]. In this paper a simple fully differential structure of COS is proposed. The CMFB technique is used to remove the common mode signal in the output of COS to improve CMRR. This novel CMFB provide low voltage, low power and much higher CMRR compared to the others in the literature.

QFG transistors are the improved version of MIFG (Multiple Input Floating Gate) transistors [7]. These circuits achieve LV operation by implementing capacitive voltage dividers at the transistor gate. In QFG transistors, similarly to MIFG transistors, inputs are capacitively coupled to the transistor gate, but a very large-valued resistor weakly connects this gate to a *dc* bias voltage. In practice this resistor is implemented by a reverse-biased *p-n* junction of a PMOS transistor in cutoff [7].

The rest of this paper is organized as bellow. Section 2 describes the circuit design procedure. Simulation results are demonstrated in Section 3 and concluding remarks are derived in Section 4.

2. Circuit Design

First, confirm that you have the correct template for your paper size. This template has been tailored for output on the custom paper size (21 cm × 28.5 cm).

The COS is fundamentally transconductance with differential output capability which can be realized by one or two source couple pairs shown in, **Figure 1**. This structure also called floating current source COS [10].

The traditional COS structure was renovated using two auxiliary differential amplifier shown in **Figure 2** to improve CMRR by generating an inverted replica of the input signal, vi [11,12]. The need for high supply voltage of about 5 volt is the main issue of this topology.

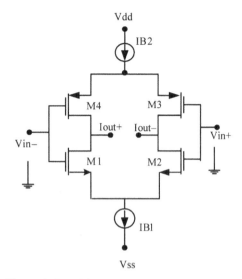

Figure 1. Traditional current output stage [11].

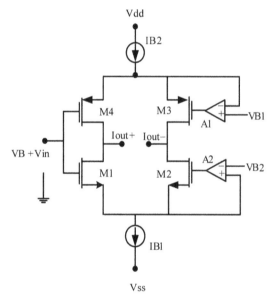

Figure 2. Simplified schematic of the COS in [11].

In traditional COS depicted in **Figure 1**, the differential and common mode transconductance, G_{md} and G_{mc}, can be written as bellow.

$$G_{md} = g_{mp} + g_{mn} \qquad (1)$$

$$G_{mc} = \frac{\left(\dfrac{1}{R_{on}} + \dfrac{1}{R_{op}} \right)}{2} \qquad (2)$$

Considering (1) and (2) CMRR could be expressed as below

$$\text{CMRR} = \frac{G_{md}}{G_{mc}} = 2 \frac{g_{md} + g_{mc}}{\left(1/R_{ON} + 1/R_{OP} \right)} \qquad (3)$$

n and p stand for n type and p type transistor and R_O

represent the output resistance of the IB1, IB2 tail current source.

In the prevalent solution which used in [11], the gate of M2 and M4 are set to constant voltage, which is usually the analog ground. This work Q1-4 shown in **Figure 3** operates like quasi floating gate transistors and is used instead of normal MOS.

An idea based on eliminating common-mode signal is utilized in order to achieve high CMRR. By taking advantage of the quasi floating gate transistor, it is possible to add common-mode signal and it's inverted one to each other. In this case CMRR is expected to improve a lot. M5 and M6 are responsible for applying CMFB which is shown in **Figure 3**.

Using this structure can decrease the differential mode gain inevitably; still omitting the common-mode signal which makes the common-mode gain come near to zero will increase the CMRR finally.

The schematic structure of the proposed COS is shown in **Figure 3** in which M1 - M4 transistors and IB1 - IB2 tail current sources constitute the core structure of proposed COS while A1 is just an inverter with (ideally) unity common mode gain and zero differential gain one. M1 - M4 transistors would be Floating Gate type, although avoid using the expensive technology required to implement double opoly structures, they could be just regular simple MOS Transistors can be simulated/fabricated by regular common CMOS technology. However their inputs are coupled to the rest of the circuit by 10 pF capacitors as is shown in the figure.

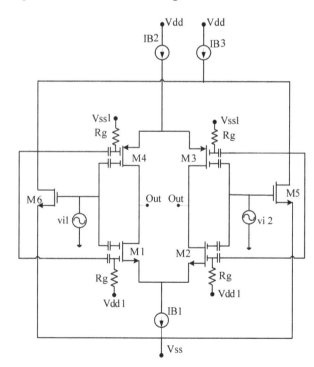

Figure 3. Schematic of the proposed COS.

G_{md} and G_{mc} of proposed COS is obtained as below.

$$G_{mc} = \frac{(1 + A'_c)}{R_{ON2}} \quad (4)$$

$$G_{md} = g_m (1 + A'_d) \quad (5)$$

and so

$$CMRR = \frac{G_{md}}{G_{mc}} = \frac{R_{ON}}{g_{mn}} \frac{1 + A'_c}{1 + A'_d} \quad (6)$$

where

$$A'_c \cong -g_{mn} \left(\frac{2}{R_{ON}} + \frac{1}{R_{O1}} \right) \quad (7)$$

A'_c and A'_d is the common mode and differential transconductance of CMFB circuit and R_{O1} represented the m1 drain-source resistance. To achieve high CMRR the CMFB circuit should have $A_c = -1$ and $A_d \neq -1$, and it is possible if Equation (8) is established.

$$\frac{1}{g_{mn}} = \left(\frac{2}{R_{ON}} + \frac{1}{R_{O1}} \right) \quad (8)$$

3. Simulation

The proposed circuit in **Figure 3** simulated with Hspice using model parameters of 0.35 μ CMOS process while the supply voltage is only ±0.75 v for acceptable comparison. In the following simulation we then compare the simulation result of the proposed COS with traditional one some other which was in other literature to allow fair comparison and emphasize the achievement.

Figure 4 exhibits the common mode transconductance gain of traditional and proposed work. (While the output load is set to 1 kΩ) and the differential gain comparison is derived in **Figure 5**.

CMRR diagrams are demonstrated in **Figure 6** which shows 55 dB improvements in dc value of CMRR. The simulation results confirm what is mentioned before about the improvement in CMRR despite decrement of differential mode gain.

The performance characteristics of simulated COS current output stage are tabulated in **Table 1** and compared with some other structures of COS. The advantage of proposed COS is apparent, especially in power dissipation, voltage supply and CMRR.

Table 1. Complete comparison between several works.

Reference	[3] Traditional COS	[7] Figure 2(c)	[10]	[11]	Proposed
VDD-VSS	2 v	2 v	2 v	5 v	1.5 v
Power	280 μw	900 μw	560 μw	NA[a]	182 μw
CMRR	55 dB	70 dB	105 dB	≤80 dB	112 dB
IB	50 μA	50 μA	35 μA	100 μA	100 μA
PSRR	+: 56 dB −: 57 dB	+: 56 dB −: 57 dB	+: 85 dB −: 90 dB	NA	+: 95 dB −: 98 dB
Tech	0.13 u	0.13 u	0.13 u	0.8 u	0.35 u

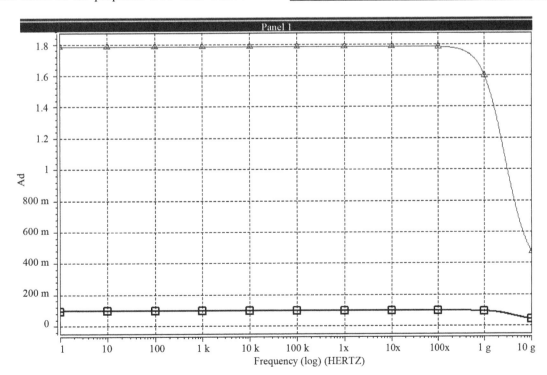

Figure 4. Magnitude of common mode transconductance gain for proposed COS(□) and traditional COS(Δ).

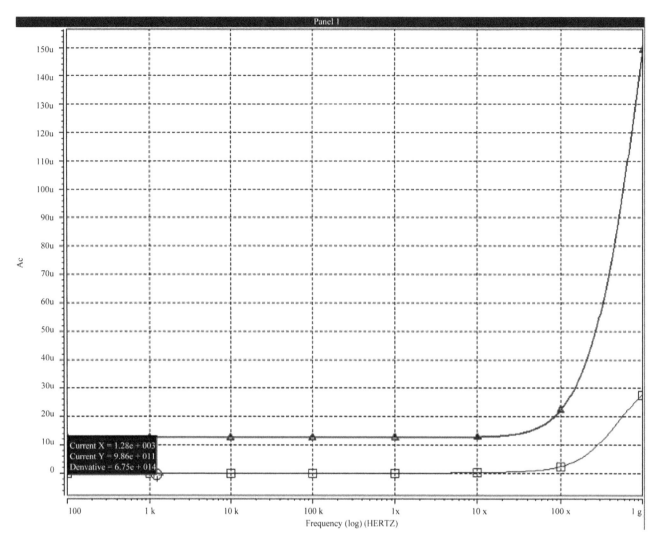

Figure 5. Magnitude of differential transconductance gain for proposed COS(□) and traditional COS(Δ).

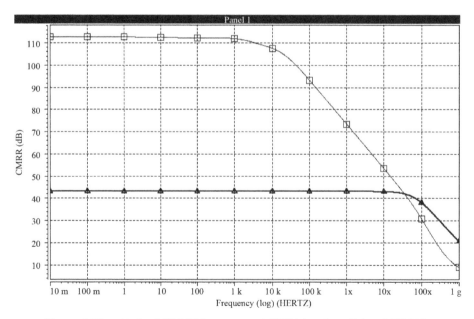

Figure 6. Magnitude of CMRR for proposed COS(□) and traditional COS(Δ).

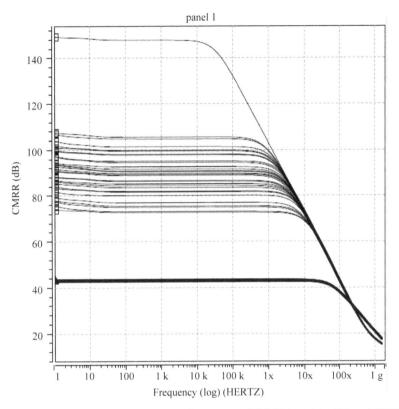

Figure 7. Monte Carlo simulation result for proposed COS(□) and traditional COS(Δ).

To investigate the effect of technology process on performance of the proposed COS, Monte Carlo simulation are performed applying 5% mismatch on 2 important parameters of W/L, V_{th}. The results shown in **Figure 7** indicate good robustness of the proposed COS against those mismatches.

4. Conclusion

A novel simple CMFB is used to remove common mode signal in order to achieve high CMRR in differential COS presented in this paper. It was done by taking advantage of Quasi floating gate (QFG) transistors which add the main signal and it's opposite polarity one. Simulation results show very good improvement in CMRR, compared to others in literature. Also supply voltage and power consumption is decreased in this work.

REFERENCES

[1] E. Allen and M. Terry, "The Use of Current Amplifier in High Performance Voltage Application," *IEEE Journal of Solid State Circuits and Systems*, Vol. 15, No. 2, 1980, pp. 155-162.

[2] C. Toumazou, F. J. Lidgey and D. G. Haigh, Eds., "Analogue IC Design: The Current-Mode Approach," Peter Peregrinus Ltd., London, 1993.

[3] S. Rajput and S. S. Jamuar, "Low Voltage Analog Circuit Design Techniques," *Circuits and Systems Magazine*, Vol.

2, No. 1, 2002, pp. 24-42.

[4] G. Plamisano, C. Palumbo and S. Pennisi, "CMOS Current Amplifiers," Kluwcr Academic Publishers, Boston, 1999.

[5] C. Toumazou, F. Lidgey and D. Haigh, Eds., "Analogue IC Design: The Current-Mode Approach," Peregrinus, London, 1990.

[6] A. F. Arbel, "Output Stage for Current-Mode Feedback Amplifiers, Theory and Applications," *Analog Integrated Circuits and Signal Processing*, Vol. 2, No. 3, 1992, pp. 243-255.

[7] S. Pennisi, M. Piccioni, G. Scotti and A. Trifiletti, "High-CMRR Current Amplifier Architecture and Its CMOS Implementation," *IEEE Transactions on Circuits and Systems II: Express Briefs*, Vol. 53, No. 10, 2006, pp. 1118-1122.

[8] J. A. De Lima and C. Dualibe, "A Linearly Tunable Low-Voltage CMOS Transconductor with Improved Common-Mode Stability and Its Applications to gm-C Filters," *IEEE Transactions on Circuits and Systems II: Express Briefs*, Vol. 48, No. 7, 2001, pp. 649-660.

[9] F. Centurelli, A. D. Grasso, S. Pennisi, G. Scotti and A. Trifiletti, "CMOS High-CMRR Current Output Stages," *IEEE Transactions on Circuits and Systems II: Express Briefs*, Vol. 54, No. 9, 2007, pp. 745-749.

[10] F. Centurelli, S. Pennisi and A. Trifiletti, "Current Output Stage with Improved CMRR," 2003 *IEEE International*

Conference on Circuits and Systems, Vol. 2, 14-17 December 2003, pp. 543-546.

[11] N. Larciprete, F. Loriga, P. Marietti and A. Trifiletti, "A High CMRR GaAs Single-Input to Differential Convertor," *Gallium Arsenide Application Symposium GAAS* 1996, Paris, 5-7 June 1996, pp. 4-9.

[12] M. H. Kashtiban and S. J. Azhari, "A Novel High CMRR Low Voltage Current Output Stage," *Proceedings of* 2009 *IEEE International Symposium on Circuits and Systems*, 9-10 July 2009, pp. 1-4.

[13] F. Centurelli, S. Pennisi and A. Trifiletti, "High-CMRR CMOS Current Output Stage," *Electronics Letters*, Vol. 39, No. 13, 2003, pp. 945-946.

[14] K.-H. Cheng and H.-C. Wang, "Design of Current Mode Operational Amplifier with Differential-Input and Differential-Output," *Proceedings of* 1997 *IEEE International Symposium on Circuits and Systems*, Vol. 1, 9-12 June 1997, pp. 153-156.

[15] I. Mucha, "Current Operational Amplifiers: Basic Architecture, Properties, Exploitation and Future," *Analog Integrated Circuits and Signal Processing*, Vol. 7, No. 3, 1995, pp. 243-255.

[16] E. Bruun, "Bandwidth Optimization of Low Power, High Speed CMOS Current Op Amp," *International Journal of Analog Integrated Circuits and Signal Processing*, Vol. 7, 1995, pp. 11-19.

11

Reactive Compensator Synthesis in Time-Domain as an Alternative to Harmonic Method

Maciej Siwczyński, Marcin Jaraczewski

Electrical and Computer Engineering, Cracow University of Technology, Kraków, Poland

ABSTRACT

The source reactive-current compensation is crucial in energy transmission efficiency. The compensator design in frequency-domain was already widely discussed and examined. This paper presents results of a study on how to design reactive compensators in time-domain. It's the first time the reactive compensator has been designed in time domain. The example of compensator design was presented.

Keywords: Power and Energy Theory; Reactive Power Filters; Reactive Current; Optimization; Harmonic Filter Design

1. Introduction

This article is a discussion on issue raised in the article of L. S. Czarnecki [1] where the author consider if it is possible to make current decomposition into active, reactive and unbalanced current in time domain and basing on it build reactive compensators. The current decomposition in time domain was presented in the previous articles [2, 3] and in this article is presented the reactive compensators design in time-domain.

2. Reactive Current Compensation in Time-Domain

In the article [3] was shown that source-receiver current can be decomposed into active and reactive current in "s" domain *i.e.* for Laplace transform of signals. Reactive current can be compensated with the reactive compensator. The source-receiver current decomposition is given below:

$$I(s) = G^o(s)E(s) + B^o(s)E(s) = I_G^o(s) + I_B^o(s) \quad (1)$$

where:

$$G^o(s) = \frac{1}{2}\left(Y^o(s) + Y^o(-s)\right) \quad (2)$$

$$B^o(s) = \frac{1}{2}\left(Y^o(s) - Y^o(-s)\right) \quad (3)$$

stand for the active and reactive parts of receiver admittance operator $Y^o(s)$.

The $I(s)$ transform for T-periodic signals is derived using the following relation between non-periodic and periodic signals transform [3].

$$\frac{1}{\sigma + s} \rightarrow \frac{e^{-\sigma t}}{1 - e^{-\sigma T}} \qquad \frac{1}{\sigma - s} \rightarrow \frac{e^{\sigma(t-T)}}{1 - e^{-\sigma T}} \quad (4)$$

where $t \in [0, T)$, $\text{Re}(\sigma) > 0$, T-time period.

It can be also calculated directly in time-domain as the T-periodic convolution:

$$i(t) = \left(g^o(t) + b^o(t)\right) \otimes e(t) \quad (5)$$

where $g^o(t)$, $b^o(t)$ stands for T-periodic impulse response of admittance active and reactive part.

Connecting in parallel the compensator (**Figure 1**) the reactive current balance in time-domain states that:

$$b^k(t) + b^o(t) = 0 \quad (6)$$

3. T-Periodic Impulse Response of Compensator and Receiver

Admittance of the elementary RLC compensator branch

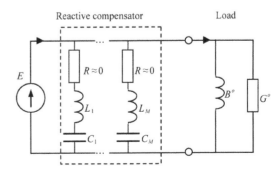

Figure 1. The zero impedance source with receiver and almost lossless compensator connected in parallel.

is:

$$Y^k(s) = \frac{1}{L}\frac{s}{\omega_o^2 + 2\in s + s^2}; \quad \omega_o = \frac{1}{\sqrt{LC}}; \quad \in = \frac{R}{2L}$$

(We assume later that the compensator is composed of almost lossless elementary branches). And its reactive part is then (3)

$$B^k(s) = \frac{1}{2L}\left(\frac{s}{\omega_o^2 + 2\in s + s^2} + \frac{s}{\omega_o^2 - 2\in s + s^2}\right)$$

$$= \frac{1}{2L}\left(\frac{s}{(a+s)(a^*+s)} + \frac{s}{(a-s)(a^*-s)}\right)$$

which leads to general form

$$B(s) = \frac{d(-a)}{a+s} + \frac{d(-a^*)}{a^*+s} + \frac{d(a)}{a-s} + \frac{d(a^*)}{a^*-s} = \frac{L(s)}{M(s)} \quad (7)$$

where $L(s)$, $M(s)$—odd and even polynomials.

The residues meet the relations: if

$$d(-a) = \left[B(s)(a+s)\right]\Big|_{s=-a} = \frac{L(-a)}{M'(-a)} = \frac{L(a)}{M'(a)} \equiv d$$

then:

$$d(a) = -d; \quad d(-a^*) = d^*; \quad d(a^*) = -d^*$$

where:

$M'(s)$ is the derivative of $M(s)$ with respect to s, d—real number.

Thus (7) reduces to

$$B(s) = d\left(\frac{1}{a+s} - \frac{1}{a-s}\right) + d^*\left(\frac{1}{a^*+s} - \frac{1}{a^*-s}\right) \quad (8)$$

and under (4) and trigonometric identity

$$sh(\alpha + j\beta) = sh(\alpha)\cos(\beta) + jch(\alpha)\sin(\beta)$$

where $aT = \alpha + j\beta$.

We get

$$b^k(t) = -2d\,\mathrm{Re}\left\{\frac{sh\left(\alpha\left(\frac{t}{T}-\frac{1}{2}\right)\right)\cos\left(\beta\left(\frac{t}{T}-\frac{1}{2}\right)\right)}{sh\left(\frac{\alpha}{2}\right)\cos\left(\frac{\beta}{2}\right) + jch\left(\frac{\alpha}{2}\right)\sin\left(\frac{\beta}{2}\right)} \right.$$

$$\left. + j\frac{ch\left(\alpha\left(\frac{t}{T}-\frac{1}{2}\right)\right)\sin\left(\beta\left(\frac{t}{T}-\frac{1}{2}\right)\right)}{sh\left(\frac{\alpha}{2}\right)\cos\left(\frac{\beta}{2}\right) + jch\left(\frac{\alpha}{2}\right)\sin\left(\frac{\beta}{2}\right)}\right\}$$

(9)

In the case of almost lossless compensator *i.e.* for $\alpha \rightarrow 0$.

$$b^k(t) = -2d\frac{\sin\left(\beta\left(\frac{t}{T}-\frac{1}{2}\right)\right)}{\sin\left(\frac{\beta}{2}\right)} \qquad t \in (0,T) \quad (10)$$

where:

$$\beta = \omega_o T = 2\pi\sqrt{\frac{X_C}{X_L}}$$

$$X_C = \frac{T}{2\pi C}, \quad X_L = \frac{2\pi L}{T} \text{ —capacitive and inductive}$$

reactance for the main frequency $f = 1/T$.

Residue for $B^k(s)$ in $\alpha = \in + j\omega_o \approx j\omega_o$ can be calculated as

$$d = \left[B^k(s)(a+s)\right]\Big|_{\substack{s=-a \\ \in=0}} = \frac{1}{2L}$$

Thus the T-periodic impulse response of reactive part of the elementary RLC branch (without R) has form

$$b^k(t) = -\frac{1}{L}\frac{\sin\left(2\pi\sqrt{\frac{X_C}{X_L}}\left(\frac{t}{T}-\frac{1}{2}\right)\right)}{\sin\left(\pi\sqrt{\frac{X_C}{X_L}}\right)} \qquad \frac{t}{T} \in [0,1] \quad (11)$$

where:

$$\omega_{om}, \quad W_m = \sqrt{\left(\frac{X_C}{X_L}\right)_m} = \frac{\omega_{on}}{(2\pi)/(T)} \text{ —angular and rela-}$$

tive resonance frequency of m-th branch, and is depicted in **Figure 2**.

Later, in the article, it assumes that the reactive part of receiver $Y^o(s)$ has only real poles, so the receiver is non-oscillatory circuit not as the compensator.

For the single pole receiver e.g. R_L or R_C type the operational admittance is

$$B^o(s) = b\left(\frac{1}{a+s} - \frac{1}{a-s}\right) \qquad a > 0$$

thus its impulse response is

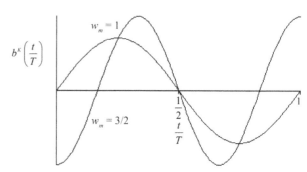

Figure 2. T-periodic impulse response of the compensator elementary branch.

$$b^o\left(\frac{t}{T}\right) = b\frac{e^{-at} - e^{a(t-T)}}{1 - e^{-aT}} = -b\frac{sh\left(A\left(\frac{t}{T} - \frac{1}{2}\right)\right)}{sh\left(\frac{A}{2}\right)} \quad (12)$$

where $A = aT$, $t/T \in [0, 1)$.

The coefficient b can be both positive and negative what is shown below for the RRLC receiver (see **Figure 3**).

Its operator admittance is

$$Y^o(s) = \frac{1}{R + sL} + \frac{1}{R + \frac{1}{sC}} = 2b_L\frac{1}{a_L + s} - 2b_C\frac{1}{a_C + s} + \frac{1}{R}$$

where $a_L = \frac{R}{L}$, $b_C = \frac{1}{RC}$, $b_L = \frac{1}{2L}$, $b_C = \frac{a_C}{2R} = \frac{1}{2R^2C}$.

Then the reactive part of $Y^o(s)$ is

$$B^o(s) = b_L\left(\frac{1}{a_L + s} - \frac{1}{a_L - s}\right) - b_C\left(\frac{1}{a_C + s} - \frac{1}{a_C - s}\right)$$

and its T-periodic impulse response is

$$b^o\left(\frac{t}{T}\right) = -b_L\frac{sh\left(A_L\left(\frac{t}{T} - \frac{1}{2}\right)\right)}{sh\left(\frac{A_L}{2}\right)} + b_C\frac{sh\left(A_C\left(\frac{t}{T} - \frac{1}{2}\right)\right)}{sh\left(\frac{A_C}{2}\right)}$$

where $A_L = a_L T$, $A_C = a_C T$.

For the receiver shown in **Figure 4**, the operational admittance is

$$Y^o(s) = \frac{1}{\frac{1}{sC} + R + sL} = \frac{1}{L}\frac{s}{\omega_0^2 + 2\alpha s + s^2}$$

where $\omega_0 = \frac{1}{\sqrt{LC}}$, $\alpha = \frac{R}{2L}$ and for the positive poles

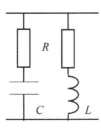

Figure 3. Example of the RRLC load.

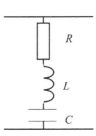

Figure 4. Example of the RRLC load.

$\alpha^2 - \omega^2 > 0$, $Y^o(s)$ takes form

$$Y^o(s) = \frac{1}{L}\frac{s}{(a_1 + s)(a_2 + s)} = 2\left(\frac{b_1}{a_1 + s} + \frac{b_2}{a_2 + s}\right)$$

where $\alpha_1 = \alpha + \sqrt{\alpha^2 - \omega_0^2}$, $\alpha_2 = \alpha - \sqrt{\alpha^2 - \omega_0^2}$ and the coefficients b_1, b_2 are then

$$b_1 = \frac{1}{2}\left[Y(s)(\alpha_1 + s)\right]\Big|_{s=-a_1} = \frac{1}{2L}\frac{a_1}{a_1 - a_2}$$

$$b_2 = \frac{1}{2}\left[Y(s)(\alpha_2 + s)\right]\Big|_{s=-a_2} = -\frac{1}{2L}\frac{a_2}{a_1 - a_2}$$

thus

$$B^o(s) = b_1\left(\frac{1}{a_1 + s} - \frac{1}{a_1 - s}\right) + b_2\left(\frac{1}{a_2 + s} - \frac{1}{a_2 - s}\right)$$

The reactive function $b^o\left(\frac{t}{T}\right)$ (12) is shown in **Figure 5**. It is necessary to distinguish the two cases when $b > 0$ and $b < 0$. When $A/2 \to 0$ the curve become straight line.

$$b^o\left(\frac{t}{T}\right) = -2b\left(\frac{t}{T} - \frac{1}{2}\right) \quad \frac{t}{T} \in [0,1] \quad (13)$$

because $sh(x) \to 0$ for $x \to 0$.

Thus we arrive to the compensatory balance Equation (6) in a new form

$$\sum_{m=1}^{M}\frac{1}{L_m}\frac{\sin\left(2\pi w_m\left(\frac{t}{T} - \frac{1}{2}\right)\right)}{in\left(\pi w_m\right)} = b^o\left(\frac{t}{T}\right) \quad (14)$$

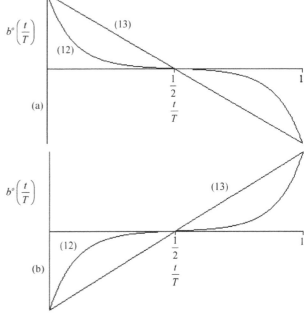

Figure 5. T-periodic single pole reactive operator impulse response of the load (a) *RL* ($b > 0$); (b) *RC* ($b < 0$).

where M—total number of compensator branches.

The solution of (14) (see **Figures 6** and **7**) for the unknowns L_m and C_m, can by find with optimization method. The (14) can be rewritten in respect to D_m and w_m

$$\sum_{m=1}^{M} D_m \sin\left(2\pi w_m\left(\frac{t}{T}-\frac{1}{2}\right)\right) = b^o\left(\frac{t}{T}\right) \quad (15)$$

where

$$D_m = \frac{1}{L_m \sin(\pi w_m)}, \quad w_m = \sqrt{\left(\frac{X_C}{X_L}\right)_m}$$

The relative frequencies of L_C compensator branches have to meet the condition

$$\sin(\pi w_m) \neq 0$$

Thus we must choose relative resonance frequency w_m of compensator branches as not the even numbers $w_m \neq p$; p—even number.

The set of Equations (14) can be then solved for D_m by minimizing δ^2.

$$\delta^2 \to \min \quad (16)$$

where

$$\delta^2 = \int_0^1 \left(\sum_{m=1}^{M} D_m \min\left(2\pi w_m\left(\frac{t}{T}-\frac{1}{2}\right)\right) - b^o\left(\frac{t}{T}\right)\right)^2 d\left(\frac{t}{T}\right)$$

After equate to zero appropriate partial derivatives

$$\frac{\partial\delta}{\partial D_m} = 0$$

and assuming that

$$w_m = m + \alpha, \quad m = 1,2,3,\cdots; \quad 0 < \alpha < 1 \quad (17)$$

we get necessary minimum condition in form of the set of M linear equations for D_m

$$D_m - \sum_{n=1}^{M} D_n \frac{(-1)^{n+m} \sin(2\pi\alpha)}{\pi(m+n+2\alpha)}$$
$$= 2\int_0^1 b^o\left(\frac{t}{T}\right) \sin\left(2\pi w_m\left(\frac{t}{T}-\frac{1}{2}\right)\right) d\left(\frac{t}{T}\right) \quad (18)$$

Then we use relation $D_m = \dfrac{1}{L_m \sin(\pi w_m)}$ as to calculate L_m of compensator branches.

The offset α in (17) must be less then 0.5 as to assure L_p positive.

4. Frequency-Domain Compensator Design

The frequency-domain approach is a well known method (see M. Pasko [4-6]).

The counterpart of (6) in frequency-domain is

$$B_n^k + B_n^o = 0 \quad (19)$$

where:

B_n^k, B_n^o—frequency response of compensator and receiver susceptances,

$n = 1,2,3\cdots$ —harmonic number.

For the elementary compensator branch (L_C in series) the branch elementary susceptance is

$$B_n = \frac{n}{n^2 - \dfrac{X_C}{X_L}} \frac{1}{X_L}$$

Thus the formula of reactances balance (19) (see **Figures 6** and **7**) takes form

$$\sum_{m=1}^{M} \frac{n}{n^2 - w_m^2} \frac{1}{L_m} = \frac{2\pi}{T} B_n^o \quad (20)$$

The Equation (20) is the counterpart of (11) transformed to optimization task (18).

Then in the particular case of the R_L in series receiver we get the set of M linear equations for all L_m of compensator branches

$$\frac{T}{2\pi}\sum_{m=1}^{M} \frac{1}{L_m} \frac{n}{(n^2 - w_m^2)} = -\frac{X_L n}{R^2 + X_L^2 n^2} = B_n^o \quad (21)$$

where
n—harmonic number,
m—branch number.

Comparing (18) with (21) we can see that both formulas are the system of linear equations, but in (18) we have

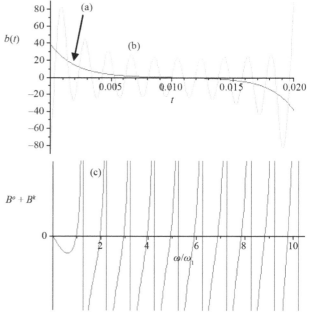

Figure 6. T-periodic time-domain response: (a) Receiver $b^o(t)$; (b) Compensator $(-b^k(t))$ and frequency response; (c) $B^o\left(\omega/\omega_1\right) + B^k\left(\omega/\omega_1\right)$, for $\alpha = 1/4$.

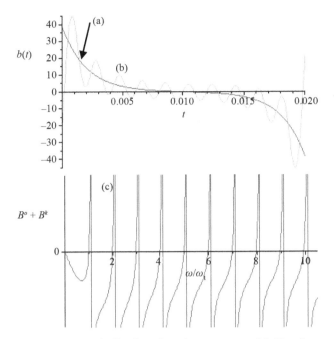

Figure 7. T-periodic time-domain response: (a) Receiver $b^o(t)$**; (b) Compensator (**$-b^k(t)$**) and frequency response; (c)** $B^o\left(\omega/\omega_1\right) + B^k\left(\omega/\omega_1\right)$**, for** $\alpha = 1/10$**.**

the impulse response instead of the frequency response of the receiver.

5. Calculation Example

Let consider the *RL* load in series for which: $P = 500$ [W], $T = 0.02$ [s], $\omega_1 = 314$ [rad/s], $AL = T/\tau = 10$, $L_o = 25.7$ [mH] and $M = 10$, τ—time-constant of the load.

Effective compensation is up to 5-th harmonic (see **Figures 6** and **7**).

The integral in the right side of (18) was calculated numerically using 21 samples and time samples was shifted by $T/21/2$ due to singularity problem.

6. Conclusion

The frequency response method used until now to syn-

thesis L_C compensators and considered the only one [1], has its counterpart in time-domain. In both approaches the L_C parameters can be found with simple optimization techniques for linear system. The only difference is that in (18) we can use directly the impulse response of the load (differentiated step response) instead of harmonic analysis. Moreover it is the first time in literature that the time-domain reactive compensator design is presented.

REFERENCES

[1] L. S. Czarnecki, "Discussion on 'a Uniform Concept of Reactive Power of Nonsinusoidal Currents in a Time-Domain'," *Electrical Review*, Vol. 85 No. 6, 2009, CD-ROM.

[2] M. Siwczyński and M. Jaraczewski, "The L1-Impulse Method as an Alternative to the Fourier Series in the Power Theory of Continues Time Systems," *Bulletin of the Polish Academy of Science, Technical Sciences*, Vol. 57, No 1, 2009, pp. 79-86.

[3] M. Siwczyński, "Decompositions: Active Current, Scattered Current, Reactive Current in Time-Domain—Single-Phase Circuits," *Electrical Review*, Vol. 6, 2010, pp. 11-17.

[4] M. Pasko, "Choice of the Two-Terminal Components, Compensating Reactive Current Component of the Linear Load Fed with Distorted Voltage," *Seminarium z Podstaw Elektrotechniki i Teorii Obwodow*, Gliwice-Wisła, 20-23 May 1992, CD-ROM.

[5] M. Pasko, "Improvement of the Working Conditions of the Real Distorted Voltage Sources Using Two-Terminal LC components," *Scientific Notebook of the Silesium University of Technology Electrotechniques*, Vol. 117, 1991, pp. 45-62.

[6] M. Pasko and J. Walczak, "Optimization of the Power Quality Coefficients of the Electrical Circuits with Nonsinusoidal Periodic Signals," Wydawnictwo Politechniki Śląskiej, Gliwice, 1996.

12

New Integrators and Differentiators Using a MMCC

Palaniandavar Venkateswaran[1], Rabindranath Nandi[1], Sagarika Das[2]
[1]Department of Electronics & Telecommunication Engineering, Jadavpur University, Kolkata, India
[2]B. P. Poddar Institute of Management & Technology, Kolkata, India

ABSTRACT

Using the new building block Multiplication-Mode Current Conveyor (MMCC), some inverting/non-inverting type integrator and differentiator designs are presented, wherein the time constant (τ) is tuned electronically. The MMCC is implemented by a readily available chip-level configuration using a multiplier (ICL 8013) and a current feedback amplifier (AD-844 IC) CFA. Detailed analysis, taking into account the device non-idealities, had been carried out that indicates slight deviations affecting the values of the nominal time constant but the design is practically insensitive to the port mismatch errors (ε). Satisfactory response on wave conversion, for signal frequencies up to 600 kHz had been verified with both hardware circuit test and PSPICE macromodel simulation.

Keywords: Voltage-Controlled Oscillator; Multiplication Mode Current Conveyor (MMCC); Current Feedback Opamp (CFA); Quadrature Oscillator

1. Introduction

Recently a new active building block named as the MMCC [1] is introduced; the element is quite attractive for analog signal conditioning and wave processing applications. Here we present the realization of some simple integrator and differentiator based on the MMCC wherein the time constant (τ) may be tuned electronically by a d.c. control voltage (V_c). The integrators/differentiators find numerous applications in signal processing and filter design [2,3].

The MMCC block here is implemented employing the readily available IC-chips, viz., the ICL-8013 multiplier [4] and a AD-844 CFA [5-7]. Electronic τ-tuning is done by varying V_c of the multiplier and by changing the polarity of V_c, an inverting or non-inverting response may be obtained.

The ICL-8013 device is a four-quadrant analog multiplier whose output is proportional to the electronic product of two input voltage signals with a transmission constant k·volt^{-1} [4]. The high accuracy ($\pm1\%$), relatively wide bandwidth (B = 1 MHz) ad improved versatility make it quite suitable for analog signal conditioning and wave processing applications.

The quality factor (Q) of the circuits is shown to be practically active-insensitive relative to the device port errors (ε) of the multiplier and CFA elements. At relatively higher frequencies, the shunt-RC trans-impedance components across the z-node of the CFA device cause some phase deviations which alter the Q-values slightly; these effects had also been examined. The proposed designs have been tested in time-domain for wave conversion applications up to a signal frequency of 600 KHz and satisfactory response are verified by both hardware test and PSPICE simulation. The Q-value indicates a measure of the idealness of the phase properties of integrator/differentiator in frequency domain. The device non-idealities produce very insignificant effects on these phase properties; hence active-insensitive.

2. Analysis

The MMCC block and its proposed device implementation are shown in **Figures 1(a)** and **(b)**; the nodal equations [1] are $V_x = kV_{y1}V_{y2}$, $I_z = I_x$ and $I_{y1} = 0 = I_{y2}$. In the proposed configuration, the control voltage V_c is used at terminal y_2 with k as the multiplication constant in volt^{-1} wherein the nominal input stimulus V_i is applied to terminal y_1. We could devise either polarity MMCC by changing the sign of (V_c) so as to obtain both inverting/non-inverting functions. The CFA nodal relations are $I_z = aI_x$, $V_x = bV_y$, $V_0 = \delta V_z$ and $I_y = 0$; We thus have design convenience with this implementation that provides an additional voltage source output V_0, which is not usually available with the conventional current conveyor [8] along with the current source output (I_z). The CFA port tracking ratios are postulated in the literature [3,9] in terms of finite but small errors $(|\varepsilon| \ll 1)$ as $a = 1 - \varepsilon_i$, $b = 1 - \varepsilon_y$ and $\delta = 1 - \varepsilon_0$; the error vanish $(\varepsilon = 0)$ for an ideal element,

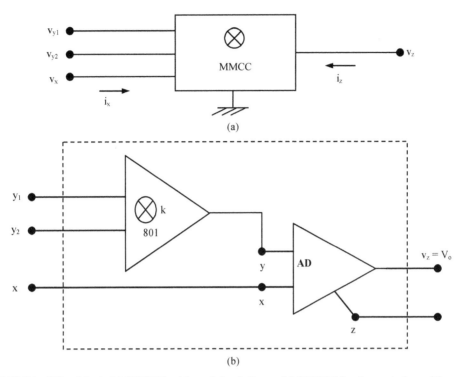

Figure 1. The MMCC building block (a) MMCC with nodal relations; (b) MMCC implementation with commercially available chips.

hence we get in **Figure 1(b)**.

$$V_y = kV_{y1}V_c \qquad (1)$$

$$V_x = V_y; \quad I_z = I_x \qquad (2)$$

and

$$V_0 = V_z \qquad (3)$$

with $\pm V_c$ one gets a $\pm$MMCC.

The proposed integrator/differentiator are obtained after realizing a ratio type (Z_2/Z_1) function as shown in **Figures 2(a)** and **(b)** after incorporating the RC-components in the building block appropriately so that we could implement design within the single MMCC configuration; analysis by Equations (1) to (3) yields in **Figure 2**.

$$G(s) = V_0/V_i = \pm \, kV_c \, Z_2/Z_1 \qquad (4)$$

where $V_{y1} = V_i$ is used as input signal and $V_{y2} = V_c$ is control voltage and $Z_{1,2}$ are passive one-port RC impedances. For **Figure 2(a)** the transfer is non-inverting with positive sign and for **Figure 2(b)** it is inverting. We select $Z_2 = 1/sC$ and $Z_1 = R$, for an ideal integrator so that

$$G_i(s) = \pm 1/s\tau_i \, ; \quad \tau_i = RC/kV_c \qquad (5)$$

Interchanging the components we get the ideal differentiator

$$G_d(s) = \pm s\tau_d \, ; \quad \tau_d = kV_cRC \qquad (6)$$

Thus for a given RC product, $\tau_{i,d}$ are electronically tunable by V_c.

3. Effect of Non-Ideality

The design imperfections of the proposed circuits may be examined in terms of two types device non-idealities, viz., first with respect to parasitic time constant components appearing in shunt at the current source output node-z (r_zC_z) of the AD-844 current amplifier. Effect of these transimpedance components becomes dominant at relatively higher frequency operation of the integrator/differentiator while the parasitic capacitance (C_z) affects the quality factor (Q) due to its excess phase. Analyses show that some upper and lower bounds in the operating frequency ranges of the integrator/differentiator are introduced by the parasitic components, albeit this effect could be minimized with suitable design. The second non-ideality is with respect to the finite device port mismatch errors $(\varepsilon \neq 0)$ which slightly alters the values of the nominal time constant $(\tau_{i,d})$. As per datasheet [5] $r_z \approx 5$ MΩ and 3 pF $\leq C_z \leq$ 6 pF. In the proposed designs we selected $R \ll r_z$ and usually $C_z \ll C$. Also we expressed $k \approx (1 - \varepsilon_m)$ volt^{-1} so that we can essentially write $kV_c = (1 - \varepsilon_m)$ for sensitivity calculation. First we derive the nonideal effects owing to the shunt transimpedance components. The transfer functions for **Figure 2(a)** then modify to

$$G_i'(s) = 1/(s\tau_i' + \lambda) \qquad (7)$$

and $\qquad G'_d(s) = s\tau'_d/(s\tau_z + p + 1)$ (8)

where $\qquad\qquad \tau'_i = (1 + n)\tau_i$ (9)

$p = R/r_z \ll 1$; $\;n = C_z/C \ll 1$; $\;\lambda = p/kV_c$; $\;\tau_z = RC_z$ (10)

Table 1 shows the details of the proposed realizations and the corresponding effects of non-ideality due to the device transimpedance components for both **Figures 2(a)** and **(b)**; here ω_c is the lower bound corner frequency of integrator and ω_z is the upper bound cut-off frequency of differentiator. Above ω_c corner frequency the inte-

grator becomes practically ideal, and below ω_z cut-off frequency the differentiator becomes practically ideal. For example if $r_z \approx 5\ \Omega$, $C \approx 15$ pF, $C_z \approx 5.5$ pF and $R \approx 3$ KΩ, one gets $f_c \approx 2$ kHz and $f_z \approx 10$ MHz.

The port mismatch errors modify the nominal values given by

$$\tau_i = RC/kV_c\,(ab\delta),\;\;f_c \approx kV_c\,RC/(a\delta) \qquad (11)$$

which yields the active sensitivity figures as

$$\tau_i,\;\tau_d,\;\;S \approx -\varepsilon/(1 - \varepsilon_T) \ll 1;\;\;S \approx \varepsilon/(1 - \varepsilon_t) \ll 1$$

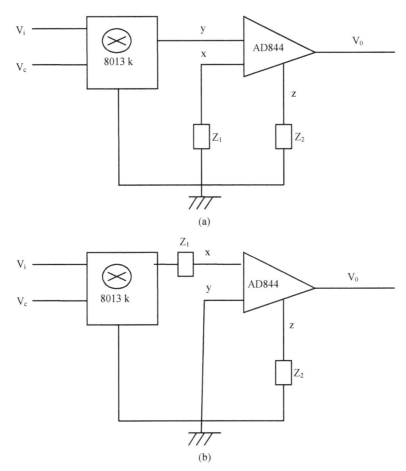

(a)

(b)

Figure 2. Integrator/differentiator design (a) Non-inverting ratio function realization $V_0/V_1 = kV_cZ_2/Z_1$; (b) Inverting ration function realization.

Table 1. Effects of transimpedance non-ideality for Figures 2(a) and (b).

Function	Component Selection	Ideal Transfer	Non-Ideal Transfer	Quality Factor (Q)
Integrator	$Z_1 = R$ $Z_2 = 1/sC$	$G_i = \pm 1/s\tau_i$ $\tau_i = RC/kV_c$	$G'_i = \pm 1/(s\tau'_i + \lambda)$	$Q_i \approx \omega/\omega_c$, $\;\omega_c = 1/r_zC$, $\;Q_i \gg 1$ for $\omega \gg \omega_c$
Differentiator	$Z_1 = 1/sC$ $Z_2 = R$	$G_d = \pm s\tau_d$ $\tau_d = kV_cRC$	$G'_d = \pm s\tau_d/(s\tau_z + p + 1)$, $\;\tau_z = C_zR$	$Q_d \approx \omega_z/\omega$, $\;\omega_z = (1+p)/\tau_z$, $\;Q_d \gg 1$ for $\omega \ll \omega_z$

Transfer G has (+) sign for **Figure 2(a)** and (−) sign for **(b)**.

Table 2. Summary on performance of some recent oscillators.

Ref.	Electronic tunability	Quadrature property	f_o (KHz) tuning range reported	S_f	THD (%)
[11]	No	Yes	20	$\approx 2n(1-\varepsilon) = 2n$	2.50
[12]	Yes	No	145	NI	NI
[13]	No	Yes	986	NI	NI
[14]	No	Yes	15.8	NI	2.47
[15]	Yes	No	73	$2\sqrt{n}/(1-n)$	1.52 - 1.88
Proposed	Yes	Yes	600	$n\sqrt{(1-\varepsilon_T)} \approx n \equiv r_z/R \gg 1$ (assuming equal-value resistors)	1.11

NI: Not indicated.

where $\varepsilon_T \approx \varepsilon_i + \varepsilon_v + \varepsilon_0 + \varepsilon_m$ and $\varepsilon_t \approx \varepsilon_i + \varepsilon_0 + \varepsilon_m$. It may be shown similarly that the active-Q sensitivities are also extremely low.

4. Quadrature Linear VCO Design

We next present the design of a MMCC based Dual Integrator Loop (DIL) sinusoid oscillator (involving one non-inverting and the other inverting type). The feature of four quadrant operation of the multiplier device is utilized here for realizing the opposite polarity ideal integrators by using a bipolar d.c. control voltage $(\pm V_c)$. A linear f_o-tuning law in a range of $40 \text{ KHz} \leq f_o \leq 600 \text{ KHz}$ with satisfactory quadrature signal generation had been measured both by PSPICE macromodel simulation [9] and with hardware circuit implementation. The oscillation frequency is $f_o = kV_c/2\pi\sqrt{(\tau_{i1}\tau_{i2})}$ where τ_{i1} and τ_{i2} denote time constants of the two MMCC-based integrators in loop. The frequency stability factor (S_f) of a sinusoid oscillator is defined as $S_f = (\Delta\theta/\Delta u)|_{u=1}$ where $u = f/f_o$ and θ is the loop phase shift. We evaluated the value of S_f after assuming finite trans-admittance parameters, given by $S_f = (2r_{zp})\sqrt{(1-\varepsilon_T)/R_1 R_2}$ where r_{zp} is the shunt equivalent $\{1/r_{zp} = (1/r_{z1}) + (1/r_{z2})\}$ of the r_z components for the two integrator stages. The stability is quite satisfactory $S_f \gg 1$ since $r_{z1,2} \gg R_{1,2}$. Here both capacitors are grounded [10] and the parasitic capacitances C_z have an additive effect $(C + C_z)$; but since value of C is chosen such that $(C \gg C_z)$ the resulting deviation would be insignificant, or alternatively, the effect of C_z may be pre-absorbed in value of C.

Analysis on the effects of device port mismatch errors (ε) indicate that f_o is practically active insensitive and the effects of the shunt parasitic components of the CFA-device are negligible. The frequency stability (S_f) factor of the proposed oscillator is quite high $(S_f \gg 1)$ at low values of measured THD $(\approx 1.1\%)$. Integrators/dif-ferentiators are useful as filters, phase compensators and delay measuring blocks; double integrator loops are useful as quadrature signal generators which had been proposed here with linear electronic tuning properties.

5. Experimental Results

The proposed circuits were tested for wave conversion application by both hardware test and PSPICE simulation. Some simulation results for square wave to triangular wave conversion by integrator and vice versa for the differentiator are shown in **Figure 3** with inverting/non-inverting polarity. The multiplier constant is set to k = 0.5/volt and the passive components are suitably chosen for the measurement in a frequency range of $50 \text{ KHz} \leq f \leq 600 \text{ KHz}$. Both PSPICE simulation and hardware circuit tests were carried out using AD-844 CFAS Op-amp and ICL 8013 multiplier device; additionally AD-534 multiplier element had also been used to verify the results.

With hardware circuit test, however, a deviation of 2% - 5% in the response had been observed; this may be due to the inter-lead stray capacitance between the chip terminal and the breadboard pin. With sinusoid excitation, the desired phase shift of $\pm\pi/2$ had been verified and a phase error of less than $1°$ had been measured at 900 KHz; expected 6 db/octave attenuation for the integrator and accentuation for the difference in magnitude response had also been measured. It may be mentioned that that the operating range of the circuits concomitant to the bandwidth (=1 MHz) of the ICL-8013 device; embedding the HA 2557 multiplier device [4] with bandwidth equal to 130 MHz is expected to yield an extended frequency range. The error analysis has been carried out here following the model of non-idealities and their subsequent effects on the nominal design as per the relevant recent literature survey cited in **Table 2** [11-15].

6. Conclusion

Some new inverting/non-inverting voltage tunable inte-

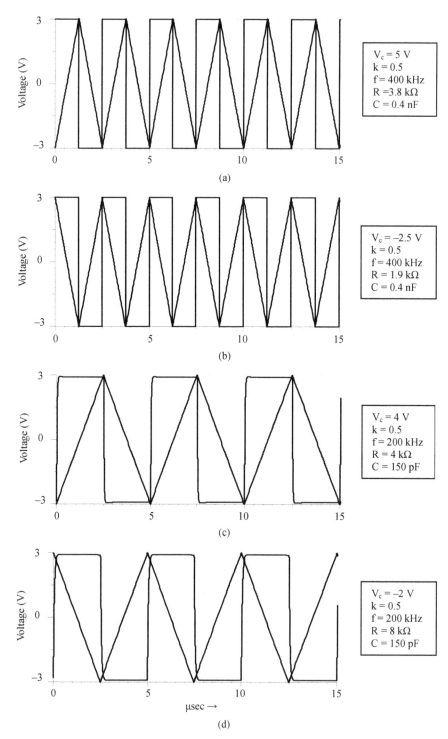

Figure 3. Response of integrator/differentiator, (a) Integrator; (b) Integrator; (c) Differentiator; (d) Differentiator.

grator and differentiator realizations are presented using the recent MMCC device. The chip level design implementation is done by the readily available elements, viz., the ICL-8013 or AD-534 four-quadrant multiplier and the AD-844 CFA unity-gain current amplifier. The quality factor (Q) of the circuits is practically active—insensitive. Satisfactory response had been measured in a range of 50 kHz ≤ f ≤ 600 kHz with suitable design. Measured phase error is less than 1° at 900 kHz. Application to wave conversion had been verified for both the integrator and differentiator function while electronic tuning of $\tau_{i,d}$ with respect to control voltage is obtained satisfactorily. Subsequently a double-integrator loop sine wave quadrature oscillator had been designed and its electronic tuning property is tested in a range of 40 KHz $\leq f_o \leq$ 600 KHz. Experimental results are shown in **Figure 4**. The MMCC is a recently proposed active building block; its application to the design of such integrator/differentiator and linear quadrature VCO had not yet been reported. The VCO is a useful element for PLL or FM discriminator design. The authors are now carrying out further work to extend the functionality of the VCO so as to implement a digitally programmable oscillator wherein a digital code (e.g. BCD word), after being con-

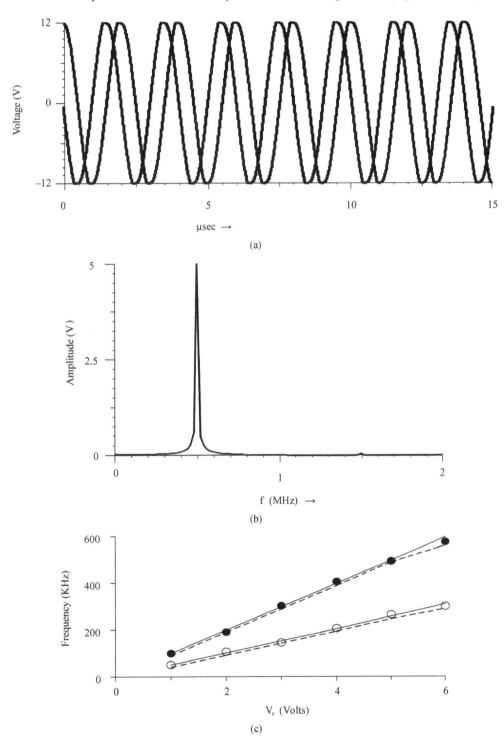

(a)

(b)

(c)

Figure 4. Response of dual-integrator loop quadrature oscillator: (a) Simulated response at f_o = 500 KHz with k = 0.1/volt and V_c = 5 V.d.c.; (b) Spectrum of the generated signal; (c) Linear tuning characteristics with C = 160 pF:R = 1 KΩ (●); R = 2 KΩ (○) (dotted line by hardware test).

verted by a D to A Converter (DAC), would be able to tune and generate a sequence of frequencies leading to FSK/PSK type modulation signal.

REFERENCES

[1]   Y. S. Hwang, W. H. Liu, S. H. Tu and J. J. Chen, "New Building Block: Multiplication-Mode Current Conveyor," *IET Circuits Devices Systems*, Vol. 3, No. 3, 2009, pp. 41-48.

[2]   M. Tanaka, M. Ikeda, H. Ikeda, S. Inata and Y. Fujita, "Monolithic Current Integrator Circuit as a Building Block of Wide Dynamic Range ADC for Calorimetry System," *Conference Record Nuclear Sciences Symposium and Medical Imaging*, Orlando, Vol. 1, 1992, pp. 384-386.

[3]   R. Nandi, S. K. Sanyal and T. K. Bandyopadhyay, "Single CFA Based Integrator, Differentiator, Filter and Sinusoid Oscillator," *IEEE Transactions on Instrumentation and Measurement*, Vol. 58, No. 8, 2009, pp. 2557-2564.

[4]   Intersil Datasheet, File Nos. 2863.4, April 1999, and 2477.5, September 1998.

[5]   Analog Devices, "Linear Products Databook," Analog Devices, Norwood, 1990.

[6]   B. J. Maundy, A. R. Sarkar and S. J. Gift, "A New Design for Low Voltage CMOS Current Feedback Amplifiers," *IEEE Transactions on Circuits Systems (II)*, *Express Briefs*, Vol. 53, No. 1, 2006, pp. 34-38.

[7]   G. Palumbo and S. Pennisi, "Current Feedback Amplifiers versus Voltage Operational Amplifiers," *IEEE Transactions on Circuits Systems (I)*, Vol. 48, 2001, pp. 617-623.

[8]   A. Sedra and K. C. Smith, "A Second Generation Current Conveyor and Its Applications," *IEEE Transactions on Circuit Theory*, Vol. 17, No. 1, 1970, pp. 132-134.

[9]   A. Zeki and H. Kuntman, "Accurate and High Input Impedance Current Mirror Suitable for CMOS Current Output Stages," *Electronics Letters*, Vol. 33, No. 12, 1997, pp. 1042-1043.

[10]   R. Nandi, "High Frequency Q-Compensation of Tunable Summing Integrator and Differentiator," *Freqenz*, Vol. 46, No. 9-10, 1992, pp. 240-244.

[11]   J. W. Horng, "Current Differencing Buffered Amplifier Based Single Resistance Controlled Quadrature Oscillator Employing Grounded Capacitors," *IEICE Transaction*, Vol. E-85(A), No. 6, 2002, pp. 1416-1419.

[12]   N. Pandey and S. K. Paul, "A Novel Electronically Tunable Sinusoidal Oscillator Based on CCCII (-IR)," *Journal of Active & Passive Electronic Devices*, Vol. 3, 2008, pp. 135-141.

[13]   A. Lahiri, "Novel Voltage/Current Mode Quadrature Oscillator Using Current Differencing Transconductance Amplifier," *Analog Integrated Circuits & Signal Processing*, Vol. 61, No. 2, 2009, pp. 199-203.

[14]   W. Tangsrirat and W. Surakampontorn, "Single Resistance Controlled Quadrature Oscillator and Universal Biquad Using CFOAs," *International Journal of Electronics and Communications*, Vol. 63, No. 6, 2009, pp. 1080-1086.

[15]   D. R. Bhaskar, R. Senani, A. K. Singh and S. S. Gupta, "Two Simple Analog Multiplier Based Linear VCOs Using a Single Current Feedback Op-Amp," *Circuits and Systems*, Vol. 1, No. 1, 2010, pp. 1-4.

13

Study of New Planar Resonator's Topologies Little Perceptible in Variations of Substratum's Height

Nizar Zrigui[1], Lahbib Zenkouar[1], Seddik Bri[2]

[1]Laboratory of Electronics and Communication (LEC), Ecole Mohammadia d'Ingénieurs (EMI),
Mohammed V University—Agdal, Rabat, Morocco
[2]Department of Electrical Engineering, Graduate School of Technology, Moulay Ismail University, Meknes, Morocco

ABSTRACT

The mobile communication (radio, mobile, satellite telephony…) insert band filters which are required to comply with stringent pass-band characteristics concerning the selectivity, the group delay, the insertion losses and the mass and volume. The mass and volume of payload electronic equipment is a significant contributor to the overall cost of space systems. Within this framework, many improvements were made in the design of filters and multiplexers which represent a considerable portion of the overall satellite payload. The High Temperature Superconducting (HTS) planar technology permits to realize compact size filtering devices. Moreover, it could also provide a superior performance not attainable by any other technology. However, not controllable parameters in the manufacturing processes (indistinctness of the engraving, the not uniformity of substratum thickness) do not allow to obtain a precision on the echo's frequency and to keep a high quality factor. So, it is necessary to use method to tune the center frequency of filters after the fabrication or to study new resonator topologies which present lower sensitivity to $LAlO_3$ substrate thickness. This last point is the object of this article.

Keywords: Resonator; Planar Technology; Topologies; Echo's Frequency; Substratum's Height; Quality Factor

1. Introduction

At present IMUX microwaves filters of a communications satellite's payload are realized in volume technology, they have an important weight and dimensions; they constitute an important part of the payload and consequently contribute strongly to the launch price of a satellite.

The solution at present studied to obtain a gain of mass of these filters is the use of the planar superconducting technology.

The studies showed that it was not possible to respect the templates imposed because of not controllable parameters. A regulation is then inescapable when we wish to optimize their electric performances. The most current solution is the use of reticule adjusting screws inserted into cases. This technique is mastered well this day but it increases in a significant way the losses the filter insertion of and the size of cases so limiting their mechanical integration. Of more these regulations are expensive and thus it is recommended to aim towards topology of filters less sensitive to the chances of manufacturing and\or adjustable in a single pass.

The simplification of regulation procedures could be a strong argument in favor of the new resonators topology solution in superconducting technology.

The modification of the resonators shape returns their even insensible or less sensitive frequencies of echo to the substratum thickness. Indeed to decrease the effect of the substratum thickness in the structures have try to concentrate the electromagnetic field meadows of the circuit surface between the superconductor and the substratum, what allows to obtain a precision of lower frequency in ±5 MHz with regard to the central frequency (4 GHz) while keeping a raised quality factor.

Indeed we are interested in the improvement of resonator performances in the shape of empty cross used in a communications satellite payload. We show that the shape modification of this resonator allows decreasing the frequency gap.

The resonator studied in this article has the advantage to remedy the problems of dimensions and weight of the volume structures used in the IMUX. Furthermore it is characterized by a good reproducibility, an ease of interconnection with the other active circuits under forms of MMIC (Monolithic Microwave Integrated Circuit), and a low manufacturing cost.

The superconducting technology [1] is interesting because it allows making decrease the metallic losses. Furthermore, superconducting planar filters present very high factors, which can reach 10^7 at 10 GHz and T = 77 K. Consequently, they could replace the volume filters used in IMUX in the satellites payloads. Indeed, the powers received by these are very low and can be supported by a planar technology.

The lanthanate of alumina ($LaAlO_3$) of cubic structure has a perfect agreement of stitch with the YbaCuO deposit [2]. This substratum presents a dielectric constant of 23, 6 and a losses tangent of 7, 6 × 10^{-6} to a frequency of 10 GHz and a temperature of 77 K [3].

The various simulations were realized under ADS Momentum, tool of electromagnetic simulation 2.5 D adapted to the simulation of planar structures.

2. Technologies of Filters

2.1. The Volume Filters

It is filters which allow to support strong powers and to have a very high quality factor a narrow bandwidth, and a high selectivity... they are the reasons for which they are at present used in communications satellites in spite of the inconveniences which they present at the level of the dimensions and of the weight.

The volume filters are realized from generally cylindrical, rectangular status-enhancing metallic cavities, or are built from guides of waves.

2.2. Planar Filters

Planar filters are used to remedy the problems of dimensions and weight of the volume structures. Furthermore they are characterized by a good reproducibility, an ease of interconnection with the other circuits, and a low cost of manufacturing. On the other hand, they cannot support strong powers and their factor of vacuous quality is low in classic technology (microstrip, coplanar, and leak out with localized elements). Planar filters can use superconductive materials to decrease the metallic losses seen that these materials present a surface's resistance very low RS when they are cooled below their critical temperature.

2.3. Microwaves Filters Used in the Payload of a Communications Satellite

In the payload of a communications satellite, there are four types of filters: the filters of reception, the filters of IMUX, the filters of OMUX and the filters of broadcast (**Figure 1**).

2.4. The Multiplexer of Entrance

Has to insure the separation of the band of reception in

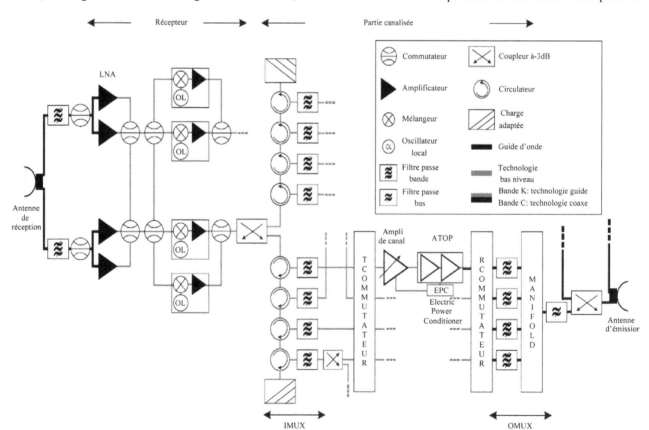

Figure 1. Plan typical block of a reception-broadcast chain of payload of fixed service satellite [4].

several channels. These filters will thus have to have a very low band and be very selective to maximize the number of channels on the useful band.

Furthermore, the undulation in the band has to remain very low to avoid a modulation live as a parasite of the amplitude [5-7]. An IMUX contains so many filters as channels. The increase of the transmission capacity is translated by an increase of the number of channels and thus the number of IMUX filter. This evolution leads naturally to an increase of the weight and the volume of the demultiplexing functions which constitute a not insignificant part of the payload (10% of the mass of the repeater), see of the global satellites load (**Tables 1** and **2**). Where from the interest to realize studies to win on the mass of filters constituting the IMUX.

A possible solution to mitigate these inconveniences is to replace the volume filters by planar filters. However, the use of classic plating leads to too much raised losses of insertion. On the other hand, these losses can be minimized by using superconductive materials.

The first experimental results showed the appearance of a frequency gap with regard to the fixed template. It was shown that variation is bound to the fact, that the thickness of the substratum used during the manufacturing is not perfectly identical to that fixed in the simulations during the conception [8]. To mitigate this problem, new structures of resonators were studied.

3. Results

3.1. Experiment—1

The structure of resonator in empty cross (**Figure 2**) will constitute the reference of our study.

Simulations in Momentum of this topology have allowed us to have an idea on the influence of thickness variation of the substratum on the frequency of echo and the value of the factor quality Q_0. The purpose of the study is to optimize this topology to decrease the effect of these variations.

To calculate the quality factor in load QL we made a simulation in the band of analysis 40,044 GHz - 40,059 GHz. **Figure 3** illustrates the results found for a density of meshing of 120 cells by wavelength (cells/wavelength).

The LaAlO$_3$ substratum of thickness 500 µm possesses

a relative permittivity ε_r of 23, 6 and a losses tangent equal to 1×10^{-5} in 77 K and 4 GHz [9,10].

The precise properties of the superconductive materials will be introduced through an impedance of surface

$$Z_S = (0.095 + 7.290\,j)\,m\Omega .$$

The determination of the quality factor is made in two stages. A first simulation allows determining the quality factor in load Q_L then the second calculation without losses allows determining the outside quality factor Q_e.

3.1.1. Calculation with Losses: Determination of the Quality Factor in Load

The quality factor in load Q_L characterizes at the same time the intrinsic losses of the resonator and coupling systems:

$$Q_L = \frac{f_0}{\Delta f} = 5539$$

or: $\dfrac{1}{Q_L} = \dfrac{1}{Q_0} + \dfrac{1}{Q_{e1}} + \dfrac{1}{Q_{e2}}$

Table 1. Analysis of a typical communications satellite mass.

Payload	28%
Solar panels and batteries	25%
Supports, cables, heat insulations	12%
Structure	14%
Propulsion	10%
Electronics of controls and tests (position)	11%

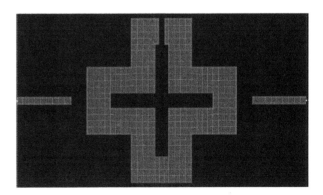

Figure 2. Resonator in cross studied.

Table 2. Analysis of a typical payload mass of communications satellite.

Demultiplexer of entrance (IMUX) and multiplexer release (OMUX)	26%
Antennas	24%
Amplifiers of power	23%
Switches	10%
Receivers and converters in frequency	10%
Miscellaneous	7%

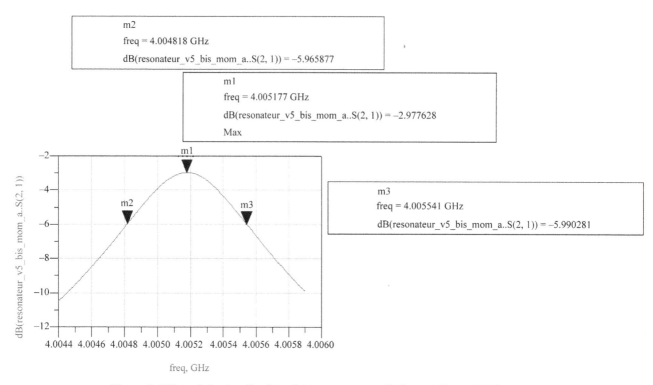

m2
freq = 4.004818 GHz
dB(resonateur_v5_bis_mom_a..S(2, 1)) = –5.965877

m1
freq = 4.005177 GHz
dB(resonateur_v5_bis_mom_a..S(2, 1)) = –2.977628
Max

m3
freq = 4.005541 GHz
dB(resonateur_v5_bis_mom_a..S(2, 1)) = –5.990281

Figure 3. S21 module visualization of the resonator studied according to the frequency.

Q_0 characterizes the intrinsic losses of the resonator and Q_{e1} and Q_{e2} characterizes systems coupling.

The system is symmetric (gaps between the lines of excitation and the resonator are identical) thus $Q_{e1} = Q_{e2} = Q_e$.

3.1.2. Calculation without Losses (Q_0 Aims towards the Infinity): Determination of Q_e

All the drivers (2GND + strip) are perfect drivers and losses tangent of the substratum is equal in zero

$$\frac{1}{Q_L} = \frac{2}{Q_e}$$

$\Rightarrow Q_L = Q_e/2 = 7866$

The knowledge of Q_L and Q_e allows calculating the quality factor Q_0

Thus: $\frac{1}{Q_0} = \frac{1}{Q_L} - \frac{2}{Q_e} = 5.341 \times 10^{-5}$

$\Rightarrow Q_0 = 18723$

This quality factor is thus very high and very sensitive to the errors of measure.

The substratum on which microwaves resonators are engraved can present slightly different thicknesses (**Figure 4**).

Furthermore, when substratums of average thicknesses 500 μm with the lowest tolerances are commanded it is possible that the reserved substratum have an average thickness of 495 μm ± 1 μm. It is for that reason that we

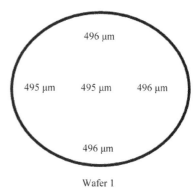

496 μm

495 μm   495 μm   496 μm

496 μm

Wafer 1

Figure 4. Thicknesses of the commanded substratum.

made simulations on various thicknesses to see the effect of the variation of the substratum thickness on the frequency of echo. The following **Table 3** illustrates the found results.

3.2. Experiment—2

To concentrate the electromagnetic field in the surface of the structure, we began by adding a vertical bar in the middle of the opened cross **Figure 5**. We varying the bar dimensions of ±1 μm or look by simulations under ADS for the bar size which approaches most in the value of the echo's frequency while keeping the high quality factor.

By modifying the length and the width of this bar we realized that it was possible to decrease the frequency gap due to the variations of the substratum thickness.

The bar is optimized for a length L = on 2450 μm and a width W = 325 μm and spaced out by 25 μm with regard to the cross.

The obtained results are the following ones (**Table 4**).

We notice that with this topology the obtained gap is 1.09×10^{-3} MHz for a variation of 2 μm of substratum height (between 495 and 497 μm). In the case of the topology in initial cross (of reference), the gap was 2.4×10^{-3} MHz. We thus obtain a 50% decrease.

3.3. Experiment—3

In a second part we were interested in the influence of a horizontal bar superconducting placed inside the resonator (**Figure 6**).

We looked for the minimum of variations by modifying the value of the length and the width. We end in the following results for a length L = 2450 μm and a width

Table 3. Variations of F_0 and Q_0 for a resonator in cross.

T_{sub} (μm)	F_0 (GHz)	Q_0
486	3.99514	15,930
495	4.00517	18,723
496	4.00684	19,040
497	4.00757	20,982
506	4.01106	21,019

Notice: by increasing T_{sub}, we provoke a gap to the right of the frequency of echo, and an increase of quality factor; By decreasing T_{sub}, the gap is this time to the left of the frequency of echo, and the quality factor decreases; For a difference of the thickness T_{sub} of 1 μm, the variation of the frequency of echo is 1.67×10^{-3} MHz. To remedy the problem of the frequency gap we are going to modify the topology of this resonator to have the minimum possible of variations in frequency.

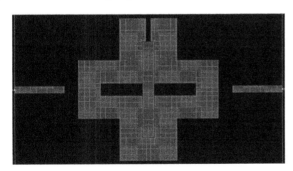

Figure 5. Topology No. 1.

Table 4. Variations of F_0 and Q_0 for the topology No. 1.

T_{sub} (μm)	F_0 (GHz)	Q_0
486	3.98958	12,021
495	3.99418	12,840
496	3.99470	12,842
497	3.99527	13,270
506	3.99987	15,287

W = 285 μm and spaced out of 20 μm with regard to the cross.

The obtained results are presented in the **Table 5**.

With this topology we were able to have a gap of 7.4×10^{-4} MHz for a variation of 2 μm (between 495 and 497 μm). In the case of the topology in initial cross, we had a gap of 2.4×10^{-3} MHz. We thus obtain a 69% decrease.

For this topology we obtain the module of presented S21 represent **Figure 7**.

3.4. Experiment—4

After vertical bar optimization to have the minimum of possible frequency gap, we added a horizontal bar as showed on **Figure 8**.

The bar is optimized for a length L = on 2405 μm and a width W = 290 μm and spaced out by 40 μm with regard to both quoted by the cross.

For this topology we obtain the module of presented S21 represent **Figure 9**.

The obtained results are presented in **Table 6**.

We notice that with this topology we were able to have a gap of 6.5×10^{-4} MHz for a variation of 2 μm (between 495 and 497 μm). This represents a 73% decrease with regard to the initial topology.

The introduction of coplanar structures allows decreasing the variation of the frequency of echo according to the height of the substratum but degrades the quality

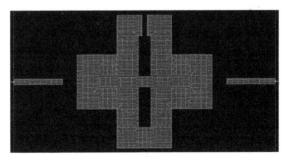

Figure 6. Topology No. 2.

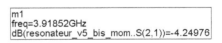
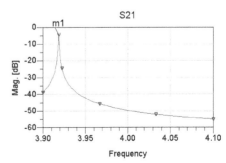

Figure 7. Module of S21 according to the frequency for the topology No. 2.

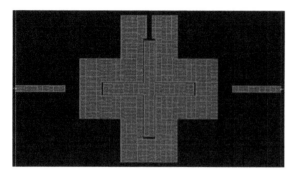

Figure 8. Topology No. 3.

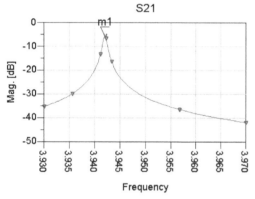

Figure 9. S21 module visualization of according to the frequency of the resonator No. 3.

Notice: the bar dimensions are obtained after several simulations of S21 relative to lengths and heights variations of ± 1 µm. One always looks for the dimensions which present not enough frequency gap with regard to the echo frequency 4 GHz.

Table 5. Variations of F_0 and Q_0 for the topology No. 2.

T_{sub} (µm)	F_0 (GHz)	Q_0
486	3.91444	10,946
495	3.91852	11,489
496	3.91888	11,490
497	3.91926	12,016
506	3.92257	15,570

factor [11].

This various topologies also has the advantage to decrease the dimensions of the resonator because to obtain a frequency of echo of 4 GHz, it would be necessary to decrease the structure dimensions.

Table 7 shows that the final topology (full cross) has allowed to decrease the frequency gap of 73% with regard to the initial structure (empty cross) this topology then present the advantage to be insensible in the sub-

Table 6. Variations of F_0 and Q_0 for the topology No. 3.

T_{sub} (µm)	F_0 (GHz)	Q_0
486	3.93089	10,980
495	3.94199	11,562
496	3.94264	11,563
497	3.94427	11,750
506	3.94625	11,898

Table 7. Comparison of the topology.

Topologie	F_0 (pour 496 µm) (Mhz)	ΔF (pour 2 µm) (Mhz)	Q_0
Empty cross	4.005177	2.4×10^{-3}	19,852
Vertical bar	3.99470	1.09×10^{-3}	13,000
Horizontal bar	3.91888	7.04×10^{-4}	11,750
Full cross	3.94264	6.5×10^{-4}	11,656

stratum height variations.

4. Conclusions

The topology in cross presents the advantage to be little sensitive to the variations of substratum height.

It thus allows freeing himself from regulations systems which increase the dimensions and the weight of filters. The purpose of this article was the improvement of the superconductive planar resonator performances in cross dedicated to the realization of microwaves filters used in the payload of communications satellites, to look for possibility of obtaining a minimum of the echo frequency gap without degrading the quality factor.

The study carried out on this topology consisted in making simulations with the aim of seeing the effect of the addition of a vertical bar, then a horizontal bar inside the initial structure. These modifications allow concentrating the electromagnetic field meadows of the surface of the circuit between the superconductor and the substratum. Our final structure (full cross) has allowed to decrease the effect of the substratum thickness on the echo frequency everything one keeping a high value of quality.

The addition of vertical bar and\or a horizontal bar allows adjusting the frequency gap caused by the manufacturing errors by moving the echo frequency to the left or to the right. This technique allows freeing itself from cumbersome regulation systems.

5. Acknowledgements

This work was realized in the electronics and communications laboratory of the Mohammadia School of engineers in cooperation with Meknes Graduate School of Technology.

REFERENCES

[1] G. Huot, "Cofabrication Monolithique de Capteurs à Supraconducteur $YBa_2Cu_3O_{7\delta}$ et d'une Electronique Supraconductrice sur Même Substrat de Silicium," Ph.D. Thesis, Caen University, Caen, 2004.

[2] Wikipedia. http://fr.wikipedia.org/wiki/Oxyde_mixte_de_baryum_de _cuivre_et_d'yttrium

[3] E. Picard, "Filtres Planaires en Technologies Innovantes Pour des Applications Multimédia," Ph.D. Thesis, Limoges University, Limoges, 2004.

[4] S. Moraud, "Etude et Conception de Nouvelles Technologies de Filtres Destinés à être Intégrés aux Différents Niveaux de la Charge Utile d'un Satellite de Télécommunications," Ph.D. Thesis, Limoges University, Limoges, 1998.

[5] S. B. Cohn, "Microwave Band Pass Filters Containing High Q Dielectric Resonators," *IEEE Transactions on Microwave Theory and Techniques*, Vol. 16, No. 4, 1968, pp. 218-227.

[6] S. J. Fiedziusko, "Dual Mode Dielectrics Resonator Loaded Cavity Filters," *IEEE Transactions on Microwave Theory and Techniques*, Vol. 30, No. 9, 1982, pp. 1311-1316.

[7] D. Baillargeat, "Analyse Globale de Dispositifs Microondes par la Méthode des Eléments Finis. Application aux Filtres à Résonateurs Diélectriques," Ph.D. Thesis, Limoges University, Limoges, 1995.

[8] S. Courreges, "Les Matériaux Ferroélectriques et Supraconducteurs Appliqués à la Conception de Dispositifs Microondes," Ph.D. Thesis, Limoges University, Limoges, 2007.

[9] K. Lascaux, "Analyse, Conception et Réalisation de Dispositifs Microondes Planaires Supraconducteurs en Bande Ka: Applications aux Systèmes de Communication par Satellites," Ph.D. Thesis, Limoges University, Limoges, 2002.

[10] M. V. Jacob, J. Mazierska, N. Savvides, S. Ohshima and S. Oikawa, "Comparison of Microwave Properties of YBCO Films on MgO and $LaAlO_3$ Substrates," *Physica C: Superconductivity*, Vol. 372-376, 2002, pp. 474-477.

[11] H. R. Yi, S. K. Remillard and A. Abdelmonem, "A Novel Ultra-Compact Resonator for Superconducting Thin-Film Filters," *IEEE Transaction on Microwave Theory and Techniques*, Vol. 51, No. 12, 2003, pp. 2290-2296.

14

Influence of Extended Bias Stress on the Electrical Parameters of Mixed Oxide Thin Film Transistors

Winnie P. Mathews[1], Rajitha N. P. Vemuri[2], Terry L. Alford[1,2]
[1]School of Electrical, Computer, and Energy Engineering, Arizona State University, Tempe, USA
[2]School for Engineering of Matter, Transport, and Energy, Arizona State University, Tempe, USA

ABSTRACT

This paper investigates the variation of electrical characteristic of indium gallium zinc oxide (IGZO) thin film transistors (TFTs) under gate bias stress. The devices are subjected to positive and negative gate bias stress for prolonged time periods. The effect of bias stress time and polarity on the transistor current equation is investigated and the underlying effects responsible for these variations are determined. Negative gate stress produces a positive shift in the threshold voltage. This can be noted as a variation from prior studies. Due to variation of power factor (n) from two, the integral method is implemented to extract threshold voltage (v_t) and power factor (n). Effective, mobility (u_{eff}), drain to source resistance (R_{DS}) and constant k' is also extracted from the device characteristics. The unstressed value of n is determined to be 2.5. The power factor increases with gate bias stress time. The distribution of states in the conduction band is revealed by the variation in power factor.

Keywords: Electrical Stress; a-IGZO; Thin Film Transistors; Degradation; Threshold Voltage; Drain to Source Resistance; Power Factor; Equivalent Circuit

1. Introduction

Thin film transistors (TFTs) are used as switching elements in active matrix liquid crystal (LCD) and light emitting diode (LED) displays. Owing to their high mobilities, low temperature fabrication, cost effectiveness and uniformity amorphous IGZO TFTs are a good replacement for a-Si:H TFTs [1,2]. Subjecting TFTs to prolonged bias stress can alter its electrical parameters due to device degradation. Device degradation can adversely affect the threshold voltage and ON current of the device thereby causing unprecedented variations in the pixel brightness of the LCD or LED matrix. There are two possible mechanisms responsible for device degradation. This could be due to trapping of charges in the channel/ dielectric interface due to the creation of defect states in the deep gap states of the channel dielectric interface [3,4]. The analysis of threshold voltage, sub-threshold swing, mobility, power factor and drain to source resistance variation with stress time and stress polarity reveals the underlying phenomenon behind device degradation.

The variation of transistor parameters with stress time and polarity is studied in this paper. The inversion current has a quadratic relation with the overdrive voltage in MOSFETs. However in TFTs they have an nth power relation with the overdrive voltage. This is due to the

variation of the power factor n from 2. The variation of power factor with stress time shows the distribution of states in the conduction band [5]. The variations in the distribution of states will affect the effective mobility of the TFT. The variation in mobility with stress time is extracted from the transfer characteristics of the device. The variation trend in mobility is compared with that of threshold voltage and power factor n to confirm the effect of gate stress on device behavior. An equivalent model of the TFT under study is also presented in this paper.

2. Experiment and Device Fabrication

2.1. Device Fabrication

The n-type enhancement TFTs were fabricated on a 300 mm Si wafer with a thin layer of SiN. Molybdenum was used as the gate, drain and source metal. It was deposited using a sputtering process. The intermetal dielectric is deposited after patterning the gate layer. It consisted of a stack of SiO_x, IGZO and SiO_x. IGZO was sputtered at a temperature between 71°C and 91°C and SiO at 180°C. The mesa passivation layer was formed by SiO_x. The entire wafer was annealed at 200°C for 1 hour after the SiN deposition and over glass etching process.

2.2. Experimental Setup

The devices subjected to electrical stress testing were n-type enhancement TFT with W/L ratio of 9 μm/9 μm. The devices were stressed at positive and negative gate bias of 20 V. The devices were stressed for time periods ranging from 10 s to 100,000 s. The devices were stressed using a HP4451B semiconductor parametric analyzer. The transfer and output characteristics of the devices under test were plotted for different stress times. The drain voltage was maintained at a constant 10 V while recording the transfer characteristics of the device. The gate voltage was swept from −25 V to 20 V. While recording the output characteristics the gate voltage was swept incremented in steps of 5 V from −5 to 20 V while sweeping the drain voltage from 0 to 20 V.

3. Results and Discussion

3.1. Positive Bias Stress

The devices under test were subjected to positive bias gate stress of 20 V for time periods ranging from 10 s to 100,000 s. The transfer and output characteristics of the device were plotted for different stress times and the variations were noted. While recording the transfer characteristics the drain was maintained at a constant voltage of 10 V. A positive shift in the threshold voltage with stress time was observed. This could be due to charge trapping at the channel/dielectric interface or due to the creation of defect states at or near the channel/dielectric interface [6,7]. Variation of subthreshold slope with stress time was negligible. The TFT transfer characteristics in **Figure 1** makes evident that the variation of drain current with gate voltage over different stress times follows a similar pattern. This concluded that no additional defect states were created. Hence, the positive shift in threshold voltage was concluded to be the direct result of trapping of electrons at the channel/dielectric interface.

3.2. Negative Bias Stress

Unlike previous studies done on TFTs, negative gate bias stress resulted in a positive shift in the threshold voltage. The variation in transfer characteristics with stress time is shown in **Figure 2**. The negative shift in threshold voltage can be attributed to the band bending resulting in positively charged donor states [8]. The additional carriers so produced contribute towards conduction. Thereby, increasing the effective channel mobility and decreasing the threshold voltage. The lower threshold voltage results in a higher value of ON current and OFF current. In this study the variation of OFF current magnitude with stress time was negligible.

Injection of electrons into the gate dielectric could be a possible reason behind the positive shift in threshold voltage. The injected charges in the dielectric will attract holes into the channel. An additional voltage has to be applied at the gate terminal to form a channel after repelling the holes, thereby causing a positive shift in threshold voltage. Subthreshold slope variation is not observed for negative bias stress studies either. This confirms that the positive shift in threshold voltage is due to injection of electrons into the gate dielectric rather than due to creation of defect states. The decrease in ON current can be attributed to the deficit in electrons in the channel.

3.3. Variation of V_t with Stress Time

In MOSFETs the threshold voltage is extracted either by extrapolating the $I_{dsat}^{1/2}$ vs V_G curve [9] or by taking the derivative of the drain current with respect to the gate voltage [10]. In TFTs the effective channel mobility increases with gate voltage. This makes it difficult to determine the point on the I_{dsat} vs V_G curve that has to be extrapolated to determine the threshold voltage. The nth power dependence of the drain current on the overdrive voltage further makes the extraction of V_t by conventional

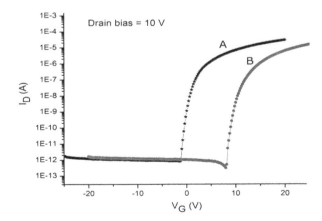

Figure 1. Transfer characteristics for: (A) Unstressed TFT; (B) Positive gate stressed TFT $V_G = 20$ V, $V_D = 0$ V for 100,000 s.

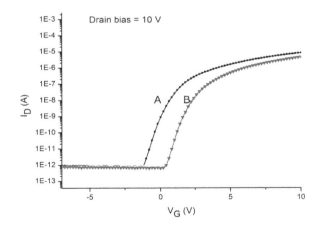

Figure 2. Transfer characteristics for: (A) Unstressed TFT; (B) Negative gate stressed TFT $V_G = -20$ V, $V_D = 0$ V for 100,000 s.

methods difficult. The derivative method is avoided also due to the magnification of experimental error upon taking the derivative.

An integral method [11] is applied here to extract the threshold voltage and the power factor without the limitations posed by experimental errors. The drain current is integrated over the gate voltage. The integral is plotted against the gate voltage. The threshold voltage is extracted from the curve by extrapolation and the power factor is extracted from the slope of the plot. The variation of threshold voltage with stress time and polarity is shown in **Figure 3**. Threshold voltage has a logarithmic relation with stress time as shown in Equation (1).

$$V_t(t) = M \cdot \log(t) \qquad (1)$$

The above equation depicts threshold voltage as a function of stress time. M is a constant; the value of which depends on device properties. The logarithmic variation of threshold voltage with stress time indicates negative charge trapping due to tunneling [12]. The threshold voltage behavior over stress time relates to that observed in previous TFT bias stress studies.

3.4. Drain to Source Resistance and Mobility

The drain to source resistance of the TFTs is the combined effect of the contact resistance at the source and drain, and the channel resistance. The channel resistance increases with degradation of effective channel mobility. **Figure 4** shows the degradation of channel mobility with stress time. The contact resistance depends on the bulk resistance of the semiconductor and the injection of carriers across the metal/semiconductor interface. The drain to source resistance (R_{DS}) is calculated for both positive and negative gate bias stresses. The mobility degradation is more pronounced at positive bias stress. The impact of mobility degradation on the channel resistance is evident from the increase in R_{DS} with stress time as seen in **Figures 5** and **6**.

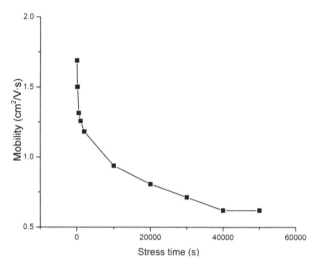

Figure 4. Variation of mobility with stress time at $V_{G\_Stress} = 20$ V and $V_{D\_Stress} = 0$ V.

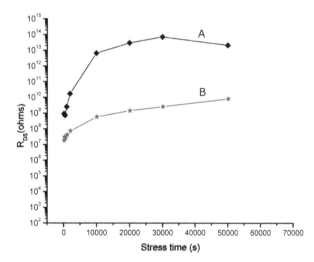

Figure 5. R_{DS} vs Stress time for $V_{G\_Stress} = 20$ V at gate bias of (A) 5 V and (B) 10 V.

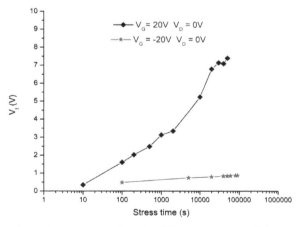

Figure 3. V_t vs stress time for different stress conditions.

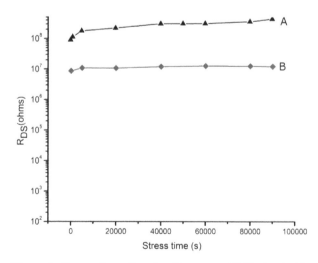

Figure 6. R_{DS} vs stress time for $V_{G\_Stress} = -20$ V at gate bias of (A) 5 V and (B) 10 V.

$$R_{DS} = R_{\text{channel}} + R_{\text{contact}} \qquad (2)$$

$$R_{\text{channel}} \propto \frac{L}{W \cdot k' \cdot \left(V_{GS} - V_t\right)^{n-1}} \qquad (3)$$

The drain to source resistance is extracted from the inverse slope of the extrapolated curve in the output characteristics of the transistor. For positive gate stress bias R_{DS} degrades logarithmically with respect to stress time and for negative gate stress the degradation is negligible. This further confirms the charge trapping at the channel dielectric interface that results in a deficit of mobile charges to carry current in the channel [13].

3.5. Variation of Power Factor with Bias Stress

The drain current in a TFT is proportional to the nth power of the overdrive voltage as shown in Equation (4):

$$I_{\text{dsat}} = k' \cdot \left(V_{GS} - V_t\right)^n \qquad (4)$$

The drain current follows a quadratic relation with the overdrive voltage in the case of MOSFETs. However, in TFTs the power factor n can vary from the usual value of 2.0. Due to this variation conventional extraction techniques cannot be used to extract the threshold voltage and power factor. The drain current is integrated over the gate voltage and the integral is plotted against the gate voltage. A linear fit of this curve is obtained. From the linear fit the threshold voltage and power factor are extracted. The x intercept of the linear fit gives the threshold voltage and the power factor is extracted from the inverse of the slope of the fitted curve.

The density of sub gap states depends on the distribution of tail states near the conduction band and the deep gap states. The power factor reflects on the distribution of tail states near the conduction band. The deep states follow a Gaussian distribution whereas the tail states near conduction band follow an exponential distribution. On increasing the gate bias stress time, the power factor increases. As the power factor increases the density of states will decrease slowly towards the middle of the band gap from the conduction band edge. The turn on voltage of the TFT is dependent on the deep band gap states. However, the ON current and subthreshold behaviors are dependent on the tail states [14]. The relation between effective mobility and power factor can be described as on Equation (5) [5]:

$$\mu_{\text{eff}} = \mu_{\text{band}} \cdot \frac{N_C}{N_O} \cdot \left(\frac{N_O}{N_{tC}}\right)^{\frac{n}{2}} \qquad N_{tC} > N_O \qquad (5)$$

N_O is a reference concentration, N_C is the concentration of free electrons and N_{tC} is the concentration of trapped electrons. The constant k' is directly proportional to the mobility of the device. Under unstressed condition the device has a k' of 1.8×10^{-8} AV$^{-2.5}$, V_t of 0.3 V and n of 2.5. The variation of k', V_t, and n with stress time is shown in **Table 1**.

4. Equivalent Circuit of TFT

The equivalent circuit of the TFT under consideration is shown in **Figure 7**. The variations in current equations that make this device stand out from MOSFETs are incorporated. The inversion current in MOSFETs have a quadratic relation with the gate voltage. For TFT the inversion current varies as the 2.5th power of the gate voltage. Due this variation the transconductance "g_m" differs from that of a MOSFET as shown in Equation (7). The power factor increases as the bias stress time. The significance of power factor is mentioned in section E. The channel resistance degrades with stress time. This adversely affects the drain to source resistance which is the combination of the channel resistance and the contact resistances at the drain and the source. Degradation of R_{DS} and power factor "n" further confirms the mobility degradation with stress time. Transconductance represents the variation of drain current with gate to source voltage.

Table 1. Effect of gate stress on "n", V_t and k'.

Stress voltage	Stress time (s)	n	$V_t(V)$	$k'(A \cdot V^n)$
	100	242	1.59	2.37E−8
	200	2.46	2.02	2.10E−8
$V_G = 20$ V	500	2.53	2.48	1.74E−8
$V_D = 0$ V	1000	2.58	3.13	1.54E−8
	20000	2.52	6.79	1.23E−8
	30000	2.64	7.14	7.37E−9
	40000	2.74	7.09	4.28E−9
	50000	2.78	7.39	3.29E−9
	100	2.59	0.47	1.60E−8
	5000	2.69	0.73	1.18E−8
$V_G = -20$ V	40000	2.76	0.82	9.50E−9
$V_D = 0$ V	50000	2.77	0.83	9.33E−9
	60000	2.79	0.85	8.83E−9
	80000	2.81	0.86	8.40E−9
	90000	2.82	0.87	8.02E−9

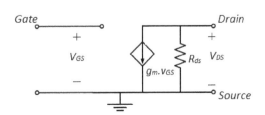

Figure 7. Equivalent circuit of a TFT.

$$g_m @ \left. \frac{\delta I_D}{\delta V_{GS}} \right|_{V_{DS}} \qquad (6)$$

Substituting strong inversion drain current Equations from (4) with (6):

$$g_m = 2.5 \cdot k' \cdot \left(V_{GS} - V_t\right)^{1.5} \qquad (7)$$

5. Conclusion

From this study we determine the effect of bias stress polarity and time on the stability of TFTs by analyzing the device characteristics. The effects of stress time and polarity on ON current, threshold voltage and power factor were determined from the transfer characteristics of the device. The mobility and channel resistance degradation were understood from the output characteristics of the device. The device degradation was dominant for positive bias stress. The impact of device degradation on the ON current was modeled in terms of n, V_t and k'. The model was similar to that of MOSFET except for the variation in the power factor. The increase in power factor with stress time indicated the variation in the distribution of states. This in turn reflected on the mobility degradation in the device. This conclusion was verified by the extracted values of mobility for different stress times. When used as a switching element in LCD and LED displays, TFTs will be exposed continuously to wide wavelengths of light. To understand the effect of prolonged exposure to light and heat illumination and kinetic stress studies can be done.

6. Acknowledgements

This work was partially supported by the National Science Foundation (L. Hess, Grant No. DMR-0902277) to whom the authors are greatly indebted.

REFERENCES

[1] H. Yabuta, M. Sano, K. Abe, T. Aiba, K. Nomura, T. Kamiya and H. Hosono, "High-Mobility Thin-Film Transistor with Amorphous InGaZnO$_4$ Channel Fabricated by Room Temperature rf-Magnetron Sputtering," *Applied Physics Letters*, Vol. 89, No. 11, 2006, Article ID: 112123.

[2] J. K. Jeong, J. H. Jeong, H. W. Yang, J. S. Park, Y. G. Mo and H. D. Kim, "High Performance Thin Film Transistors with Cosputtered Amorphous Indium Gallium Zinc Oxide Channel," *Applied Physics Letters*, Vol. 91, 2007, Article ID: 113505.

[3] K. Sakariya, C. K. M. Ng, P. Servati and A. Nathan, "Accelerated Stress Testing of a-Si:H Pixel Circuits for AMOLED Displays," *IEEE Transactions on Electron Devices*, Vol. 52, No. 12, 2005, pp. 2577-2583.

[4] H. C. Cheng, C. F. Chen and C. C. Lee, "Thin-Film Transistors with Active Layers of Zinc Oxide (ZnO) Fabricated by Low-Temperature Chemical Bath Method," *Thin Solid Films*, Vol. 498, No. 1-2, 2006, pp. 142-145.

[5] P. Servati, D. Striakhilev and A. Nathan, "Above-Threshold Parameter Extraction and Modeling for Amorphous Silicon Thin-Film Transistors," *IEEE Transactions on Electron Devices*, Vol. 50, No. 11, 2003, pp. 2227-2235.

[6] K. Kaftanoglu, S. M. Venugopal, M. Marrs, A. Dey, E. J. Bawolek, D. R. Allee and D. Loy, "Stability of IZO and a-Si:H TFTs Processed at Low Temperature (200°C)," *Journal of Display Technology*, Vol. 7, No. 6, 2011, pp. 339-343.

[7] D. C. Paine, B. Yaglioglu, Z. Beiley and S. Lee, "Amorphous IZO-Based Transparent Thin Film Transistors," *Thin Solid Films*, Vol. 516, No. 17, 2008, pp. 5894-5898.

[8] E. N. Cho, J. H. Kang, C. E. Kim, P. Moon and I. Yun, "Analysis of Bias Stress Instability in Amorphous InGaZnO Thin-Film Transistors," *IEEE Transactions on Device and Materials Reliability*, Vol. 11, No. 1, 2011, pp. 112-117.

[9] D. K. Schroeder, "Semiconductor Material and Device Characterization," 2nd Edition, Wiley, Hoboken, 1998.

[10] L. Dobrescu, M. Petrov, D. Dobrescu and C. Ravariu, "Threshold Voltage Extraction Methods for MOS Transistors," *Proceedings of International Semiconductor Conference*, Vol. 1, 2000, pp. 371-374.

[11] A. Ortiz-Conde, A. Cerdeira, M. Estrada, F. J. Gracia Sanchez and Rodolfo Quintero, "A Simple Procedure to Extract the Threshold Voltage of Amorphous Thin Film MOSFETs in the Saturation Region," *Solid State Electronics*, Vol. 45, No. 5, 2001, pp. 663-667.

[12] S. Sambandan and A. Nathan, "Equivalent Circuit Description of Threshold Voltage Shift in a-Si:H TFTs from a Probabilistic Analysis of Carrier Population Dynamics," *IEEE Transactions on Electron Devices*, Vol. 53, No. 9, 2006, pp. 2306-2311.

[13] T. Richards and H. Sirringhaus, "Bias-Stress Induced Contact and Channel Degradation in Staggered and Coplanar Organic Field-Effect Transistors," *Applied Physics Letters*, Vol. 92, No. 2, 2008, Article ID: 023512.

[14] H.-H. Hsieh, T. Kamiya, K. Nomura, H. Hosono and C.-C. Wu, "Modeling of Amorphous InGaZnO$_4$ Thin Film Transistors and Their Subgap Density of States," *Applied Physics Letters*, Vol. 92, No. 13, 2008, Article ID: 133503.

15

Challenges in Quality Certification of I/O Libraries

Oleg Semenov[*], Dmitry Vasiounin, Victor Spitsyn

Freescale Semiconductor, Moscow, Russia

ABSTRACT

Cooperation between manufacturing and other functional groups is critical to improve the success of new products. However, integrating operations and development methodologies is often challenging due to conflicting priorities and organizational structures. Improving the quality of product development and the transition to manufacturing is not a new venture. Organizations have been incorporating planning and continuous improvement to their product development initiatives for decades. This paper summarizes the experience of I/O libraries quality certification within Freescale Semiconductor and describes the certification flow developed by Corporate Quality and I/O Design teams.

Keywords: I/O Library; Electrostatic Discharge; Quality Certification; Latch-Up; I/O Driver

1. Introduction

The increased power consumption and higher clock frequency compromise ICs reliability and quality. More than ever, Quality has become a primary differentiator in the semiconductor industry, especially in the automotive and high performance microprocessor markets. It is important that each and every one of us understand the challenges and how to contribute to our Quality objectives.

Freescale's goal of world-class quality demands that New Product Introductions (NPIs) are launched successfully in a robust and consistent manner. For each technology, the successful NPI requires that all elements of the technology to be brought up in a concerted manner. The Technology Certification Process (M0 (Maturity Level #0) → M1 (Maturity Level #1) → M2 (Maturity Level #2) → M3 (Maturity Level #3)) offers a method to establish interdependency of the constituent technologies and build in quality up front, thereby promoting risk-free NPI. The requirements for each constituent technology element must be met and maturity levels are granted through the review of detailed checklists generated after the silicon validation of IPs (Intellectual Property).

This paper is focused on the I/O libraries silicon validation steps that are required by the Technology Certification Process for M1, M2 and M3 maturity levels. The list of parameters of I/O cells that should be verified in silicon is common for all technologies. The provided examples are specified for cmos45soi (c45soi) I/O cells used in many Freescale products. The developed test structures are intended to measure the key parameters of I/O cells:

- Leakage current of IO cell.
- DC parameters.
- AC parameters.
- Latch-up testing (not used for SOI technologies).
- Qualification of ESD (electrostatic) protection for Human Body Model (HBM), Machine Model (MM) and Charge Device Model (CDM).

The paper is organized as follows: Section 2 presents an overview of Quality and Validation definitions. The description of concept of Technology Certification process and its major components are given in Section 3. In Section 4, the I/O test structures and measurement techniques are discussed. Section 5 deals with the resources allocation for measurements and cooperation with the test and silicon validation teams. Finally, the successful implementation of quality qualification flow and certification process for c45soi I/O libraries developed for Freescale products are presented in Section 6.

2. Quality and Validation Definitions

As the complexity of the design increases and the required time to market decreases, the need to integrate manufacturing with design becomes even more important. Integration and collaboration among development groups is suggested as one factor that improves the success of new products. Generally, a customer regards a product to be of high quality if the product is meeting their requirements at lowest possible cost. Quality can be expressed as the number of customer returns per million or Parts Per Million (PPM):

---

[*]Corresponding author.

$$\text{Defect level} = \frac{\text{test escapes}}{\text{total number of shipped chips}} (\text{PPM})$$

Or, in another view, quality is related to the population of faulty devices that escape detection at the supplier's plant. The simplest Quality definition that frequently cited by Program Management is "Quality is consistently delivering products that meet customer requirements". Verification, validation and certification are needed to confirm "meeting customer requirements". Repeatable processes ensure "consistent" quality. Appropriate communication in the form of user documentation, training and application support, assist the supplier to deliver their products with a high quality.

When I/O team is tasked with development and delivery of a product, it needs to know how the product will be used and the success criteria before the defining what to develop. Prerequisites of successful development of any I/O library include a good requirements gathering, documentation and verification practices that address how to verify the product quality. I/O teams should put a strong emphasis on validation of all deliverables, both as standalone entities and in conjunction with other IP deliverables. The close cooperation with Corporate Quality team is absolutely needed.

3. Technology Certification Process for I/O Libraries

The term "Technology Certification" as used here includes all major elements required to execute an NPI I/Os, and goes well beyond the traditionally emphasized die processing and packaging aspects. The Technology Certification process determines the maturity/readiness of I/O library according to four maturity levels (M0, M1, M2, & M3), which are awarded after achieving the milestones consistent with the NPI flow from Planning, Prototype, Pilot and Production stages, respectively. These 4 levels (level 0 - 3) reflect the key milestones of readiness from "Technology Specification Defined" through "Ready for Product". The requirements for the entire platform must be satisfied in order to achieve a given certification level for I/O library. Maturity levels are granted through the detailed checklists of intermediate deliverables that are reviewed across all functional areas. The typical checklists for I/O libraries are given below.

1) *Maturity Level 0—Specification Defined*
- Level 0 PDK (Process Development Kit) is available with required components for IP design and implementation.
- Statement of Work (SOW) is complete and under revision control. SOW signed by stakeholders.
- Silicon validation plan is in place.
- All flows and methods have been identified and are aligned with PDK supported tools list.

- Product groups define initial ESD requirements for products including I/O operating specs, voltage ranges, device configurations to be protected, ESD stresses required for qualification, and any special application requirements.

2) *Maturity Level 1—Ready for Design*
- PDK release has passed level 1 Milestone specification.
- I/O library design review sign-off (conformity to SOW specification).
- Front End (FE) and Back End (BE) view validation tests have been implemented in IP environment.
- I/O IP available for test vehicles (TV).
- ESD parameters are characterized based on test vehicles and results are available.
- DFM (Design for Manufacturing rules) score requirements are verified.

3) *Maturity Level 2—Ready for Prototype*
- PDK used for IP development reached M2.
- Actual silicon available for M2 validation with all critical parameters in the following range: typical ± 3 sigma.
- M2 Silicon Validation report completed (Test and Characterization report).
- For all I/O library specifications, actual results within CAD data for WCS (Worst-Case process corner) to BCS (Best-Case process corner) envelop.
- ESD validation report from TV complete and released by the ESD team, product group, and Quality organization (including F/A (Failure Analysis) results for failures).

4) *Maturity Level 3—Ready for Product*
- PDK used for IP development reached M3.
- Actual silicon available for M3 silicon validation with all critical parameters in the following range: targeted process corner ±3 sigma.
- ESD testing and qualification results available from NPI silicon and corrective actions identified on key issues.
- M3 Silicon Validation report completed.

Finally, the Technology Certification Process has a direct impact on reducing defects at customer site, customer quality incidents (CQI) return rate, reduce average CQI cycle time and reduce customer reported PPM.

4. I/O Test Structures and Measurement Techniques

The list of parameters of IO cells that should be verified in silicon is common for all technologies. However, the provided examples in this paper are mostly specified for c45soi IO cells. Test structures are intended to measure the following key parameters of IO cells library:
- Leakage current of IO cell.
- DC parameters.

- AC parameter.
- Latch-up testing (not used for SOI (Silicon-on-Insulator) technologies).
- Qualification of ESD protection for HBM, MM and CDM ESD stresses.

Figure 1 presents the test structures for c45soi LVCMOS I/O library validation, as an example. Similar test structures can be developed for other technologies based on the ESD Integration Guidelines/Rules specified by ESD team. It includes the following functional blocks:

1) The worst case of I/O segment (Pad1 - Pad5) with respect to ESD stress as shown in **Figure 1**, Segment 1. This I/O segment has a minimal number of distributed ESD clamps needed to discharge the required ESD current following the ESD integration rules.

2) I/O cell banks for leakage current measurements: (Pad1 - Pad5) and (Pad6 - Pad14) as shown in **Figure 1** of Segment 1 and Segment 2, respectively.

In **Figure 1**, "Term", "Clamp" and "Trigger" mean the Termination cell, I/O cell with ESD clamp and I/O cell with ESD trigger, respectively.

4.1. ESD testing

ESD protection should be typically sufficient for:
- Human Body Model (HBM)—2 kV.
- Machine Model (MM)—200 V.
- Charge Device Model (CDM)—500 V.

HBM/MM testing is performed in accordance with the ESD association specification:
- Each I/O pin should be stressed against each power supply pin and GND pin.
- Each power supply should be stressed with respect to other power supplies.
- Three repeated ESD zaps in sequence in ESD tester are required, and there should be at least a 300 ms interval between consecutive zaps. It is recommended to run the set of HBM zapping first and then run the set of MM zapping.

The worst case of I/O segment (Pad1 - Pad5) with respect to ESD stress is shown in **Figure 1** (Segment 1).

Item #1 The ESD spec that should be used for ESD testing is the JEDEC standard [1-3].

Item #2 The ESD failure is determined as a significant difference in leakage current between before and after ESD stress on OVDD & IVDD power domains or input leakage current (Iih, Iil) on inputs of IO cells in Segment 1. The ESD failure is occurred if the leakage current difference is exceeded 1mA.

Item #3 The matrix of voltages for ESD testing that should be used is the following:

HBM: 500 V, 1000 V, 1500 V, 2000 V, 2500 V (positive and negative pulses).

CDM: 250 V, 350 V, 500 V, 550 V.

	Cmos45soi_wb_lvcmos_esd_term_ew(ns)	Term	
1	Cmos45soi_wb_lvcmos_io_332518_ew(ns)	Clamp	
2	Cmos45soi_wb_lvcmos_io_332518_ew(ns)	Clamp	
3	Cmos45soi_wb_lvcmos_io_wesdtg_ew(ns)	Trigger	Segment 1
4	Cmos45soi_wb_lvcmos_io_332518_ew(ns)	Clamp	
5	Cmos45soi_wb_lvcmos_io_332518_ew(ns)	Clamp	
	Cmos45soi_wb_lvcmos_esd_term_ew(ns)	Term	

	Cmos45soi_wb_lvcmos_esd_term_ew(ns)	Term	
6	Cmos45soi_wb_lvcmos_io_332518_ew(ns)	Clamp	
7	Cmos45soi_wb_lvcmos_io_332518_ew(ns)	Clamp	
8	Cmos45soi_wb_lvcmos_io_wesdtg_ew(ns)	Trigger	
9	Cmos45soi_wb_lvcmos_io_332518_ew(ns)	Clamp	
10	Cmos45soi_wb_lvcmos_io_332518_ew(ns)	Clamp	Segment 2
11	Cmos45soi_wb_lvcmos_io_332518_ew(ns)	Clamp	
12	Cmos45soi_wb_lvcmos_io_wesdtg_ew(ns)	Trigger	
13	Cmos45soi_wb_lvcmos_io_332518_ew(ns)	Clamp	
14	Cmos45soi_wb_lvcmos_io_332518_ew(ns)	Clamp	
	Cmos45soi_wb_lvcmos_esd_term_ew(ns)	Term	

Figure 1. The test structures for c45soi LVCMOS I/O library validation.

MM: 100 V, 200 V, 250 V.

Item #4 Each of the above mentioned ESD stresses should be applied to each input pad (chip_pad) of I/O cell in I/O segments when GND pad is grounded.

For Segment #1, each of five input pins should be stressed with respect to grounded GND pad and floated OVDD & IVDD.

And, each of five input pins should be stressed with respect to grounded OVDD pad and floated GND & IVDD.

And, each of five input pins should be stressed with respect to grounded IVDD pad and floated GND & OVDD.

Three repeated ESD zaps are required for each test case.

The ESD procedure and pin grouping mentioned above is also defined in JEDEC spec. The pins that are not used in a particular ESD stress should be floated.

Note: It's not necessary to repeat the ESD tests for Segment #2, which is used for leakage current measurements only.

Item #5 Power domain to power domain stresses within Segment 1 should be performed. It includes OVDD to VSS, IVDD to VSS and OVDD to IVDD ESD stresses.

Item #6 The segment to segment power domain ESD stressing is required. It should be OVDD of Segment 1 to OVDD of Segment 2 ESD stressing. It means that ESD stress is applied to OVDD of Segment 1 and OVDD of Segment 2 are grounded and vice versa.

4.2. Measurement of Leakage Current

Figure 1 shows the circuit that should be used for leakage current measurements of IO cell. "Term" cell is the ESD termination cell. This circuit consists on two segments. Segment 1 and Segment 2 should have separated OVDD and IVDD. All IO cells in these segments should be used in the same operating mode "input", "output" or "tri-state".

Measurements of leakage current are performed for OVDD and IVDD supplies.

Ileakage current (for one IO cell)

= (Isegment 2 − Isegment1)/4

4.3. Measurement of DC Parameters

DC parameters include

- VOH and VOL.
- IOH and IOL.
- Tri-state input current.

Generally, DC parameters should be measured for 3 units (packaged chips) for all power supplies (OVDD ±10%) specified in Specification and three temperatures for each OVDD. The details are given in **Table 1** for c45soi 49 μm pitch LVCMOS IO library or GPIO (General Purpose) IO library, as an example. Measurements should be performed for all process corners (Best, Typi-

cal, Worst) available from the Fab.

4.4. Measurement of AC Parameters

Generally, AC parameters for IO libraries are including the operating frequency or delay and Rise & Fall times.

4.4.1. Measurement of Ring Oscillator Frequency of IO Cells

The block diagram to measure the ring oscillator frequency of IO cells is shown in **Figure 2**. The ring oscillator includes twelve IO cells and nand2 cell. The first implementation of ring oscillator (top part) is placed inside of chip to eliminate the parasitic capacitances of wire bonding and packaging. The second implementation of ring oscillator (bottom part) is placed in the IO segment to estimate the impact of package parasitics. The signals "en_osc1" and "en_osc2" are the control signals to switch on/off the ring oscillators: ON (if en_osc<1:2>='0') or OFF (if en_osc<1:2>='1').

Table 1. DC parameters for c45soi LVCMOS IO library.

Test/characterization	GPIO—1.8 V	GPIO—2.5 V	GPIO—3.3 V
	Spec requirement	Spec requirement	Spec requirement
VOH & VOL @IOH = 1 mA	1.65 V, 1.8 V, 1.95 V −40°C, 25°C, 125°C 3 units	2.25 V, 2.5 V, 2.75 V −40°C, 25°C, 125°C 3 units	3.0 V, 3.3 V, 3.6 V −40°C, 25°C, 125°C 3 units
IOH & IOL @VOH = OVDD 0.25 V for IOH & VOL = 0.25 V for IOL	@OVDD = 1.8 V, IVDD = 1 V −40°C, 25°C, 125°C 3 units	@OVDD = 2.5 V, IVDD = 1 V −40°C, 25°C, 125°C 3 units	@OVDD = 3.3 V, IVDD = 1 V −40°C, 25°C, 125°C 3 units
Tri-state input current (no pull-up/ down) on a pad	1.65 V, 1.8 V, 1.95 V, ipp_pue = 0, ipp_ibe = 0 and ipp_obe = 0, IVDD = 1V, −40°C, 25°C, 125°C 3 units	2.25 V, 2.5 V, 2.75 V, ipp_pue = 0, ipp_ibe = 0 and ipp_obe = 0, IVDD = 1 V, −40°C, 25°C, 125°C 3 units	3.0 V, 3.3 V, 3.6 V, ipp_pue = 0, ipp_ibe = 0 and ipp_obe = 0, IVDD = 1 V, −40°C, 25°C, 125°C, 3 units

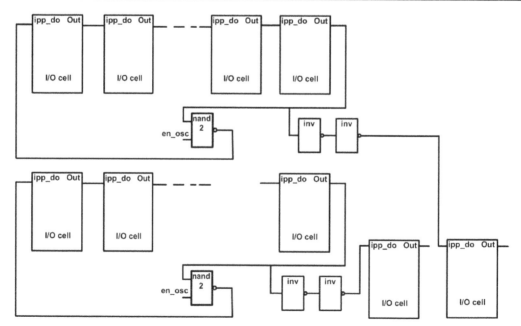

Figure 2. Block diagram to measure frequency of ring oscillator for IO cells.

4.4.2. Measurement of Rise and Fall Times of IO cell

Generally, the Rise and Fall times should be measured for all OVDD and core voltages (IVDD) given in the Specification for IO Library at three temperatures and all process corners available from Fab.

Table 2 presents the example of Rise and Fall times requirement for 49 um pitch LVCMOS IO library. Rise and Fall time measurements should be performed at each OVDD & IVDD = 1 V for three temperatures 125°C, 25°C and –40°C.

4.5. Latch-Up Testing for IOs

Latch-up testing should be performed for IO cells implemented in bulk technologies. Latch-up testing is not required for IO libraries fabricated in SOI technologies.

Latch-up testing of IO cells should include the I-test and Over-voltage latch-up tests for Class I (Level A) performed at room temperature. Note: Class II (high temperature latch-up tests) can be required for some special applications as well.

I-test: A latch-up test that supplies positive and negative current pulses to the pin under test.

Over-voltage test: A latch-up test that supplies over-voltage pulses to the Vsupply pin under test.

4.5.1. I-Test

For I-test, the trigger current should be ±100 mA applied for all pins for product level testing. In case of latch-up testing for Test Vehicle (TV), the IO pins should be grouped by functionality and at least one pin from each group should be tested. IO pins should be tested in all possible operating states or the worst case operating state. IO pins should be tested in the high impedance state or in the valid logic state. After latch-up testing, all devices must pass the functional testing. The equivalent circuits for positive and negative I-test latch-up testing are shown in **Figures 3** and **4**, respectively.

Table 2. Rise and fall times measurement requirements for 49 µm LVCMOS IO library.

Test/characterization	GPIO—1.8 V	GPIO—2.5 V	GPIO—3.3 V
Output Rise and fall times 10% - 90% @Cload = 12 pF, @ 50 MHz	@OVDD = 1.65 V, @OVDD = 1.8 V, @OVDD = 1.95 V, 25°C, –40°C, 125°C 3 units IVDD: 1.00 V	@OVDD = 2.25 V, @OVDD = 2.5 V, @OVDD = 2.75 V, 25°C, –40°C, 125°C 3 units IVDD: 1.00 V	@OVDD = 3 V, @OVDD = 3.3 V, @OVDD = 3.6 V, 25°C, –40°C, 125°C 3 units IVDD: 1.00V

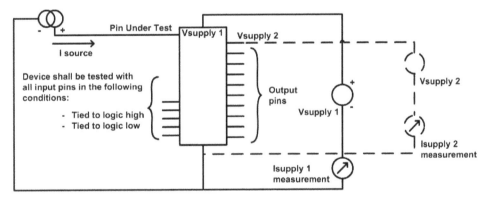

Figure 3. The equivalent circuit for positive I-test latch-up testing [4].

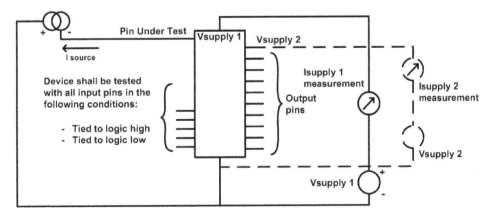

Figure 4. The equivalent circuit for negative I-test latch-up testing [4].

4.5.2. Over-Voltage Latch-Up Test

The Vsupply over-voltage test should be performed on each Vsupply pin or pin group. To provide a true indication of latch-up for the given test conditions, the input pins are configured as logic-high states. They should remain within the valid logic-high region as defined in the device specification. In case of over-voltage latch-up testing, the voltage trigger source equaled to 1.5 × Vsupply max should be applied for each Vsupply pin. In case of over-voltage latch-up testing for Test Vehicle (TV), the Vsupply pins should be grouped by voltage nominal and at least one pin from each group should be tested. The equivalent circuit for over-voltage latch-up testing is given in **Figure 5**. After the trigger source has been removed, return the Vsupply pin under test to the state it was in before the application of the trigger pulse and measure the Isupply for each Vsupply pin (or pin group). If any Isupply is greater than or equal to the failure criteria, the latch-up has occurred and power must be removed from the DUT. The failure criteria is the absolute Isupply after test >1.4 × Inom before test.

5. Execution of Validation Flow— Stakeholders and Communication

The process of the library development has to be aligned with the NPI process. The Quality audit checklist requires validation resource allocation at the very early development phase (*Planning*). During Planning period, the SoW (Statement of Work) has to be created and approved by customer, including scope, schedule, and resources. Resources allocation can be done using RAFT or Primavera tools. Technical specification has to be created, however, at this phase it does not have to be finalized yet. At the end of this phase, the IP validation plan is required. It should include the list of library views and pre-silicon simulation results. In addition, the Initial Silicon validation plan has to be created. It consists of two parts defining What has to be measured, Who has to measure it and When, the list of critical parameters of I/O cells taken from specification, and resource allocation

approved by stakeholders. Usually, at this early phase the NPI roadmap is not finalized yet and the First silicon and NPI certification dates will be determined at the next library validation phase. Each level of Maturity audit assumes Technology, Models, and PDK to be at the same Maturity level, so all collateral plans are mutually dependent. Every one audit must close all the risks identified by the previous audit.

Prototype, followed by the *Pilot*, is a part of *Execution* phase. The gate between Prototype and Pilot is M1 audit and the approval of PSC meeting. When the I/O library development process is completed, the final library is delivered to customer during the Prototype phase. At the time of M1 audit, the silicon data may be or may not be available for the given IP, so the quality assessment of the IP can be done based on simulations and view validation process, which include DRC/LVS checking, unit testing, simple integration tests and other tests. Before M1 audit, the silicon validation plan has to be finalized, approved and committed by the Test engineering team.

For I/O libraries, the Silicon Validation plan usually contains sections for DC, AC and ESD data. If NPI follows the complete lifecycle process, all three groups of parameters can be measured both on Test Vehicle (TV) and product. The TV usage is a good opportunity to get early silicon data with a complete set of measurement structures at different process corners. As opposed to the TV, the measurement of I/O data on product has a limited capability. For example, the packaged products do not allow to measure I/O buffer delay. As a workaround, SGPC ring oscillator can be used for this kind of measurements. Unfortunately, frequently the development program skips the TV phase for some reason, for example limited budget. Usually, DC data measurements are performed using the Automated Test Equipment (ATE). AC data are measured on Lab test bench. ESD tests require special equipment. Hence, different Test engineering teams are involved in the measurement process. The getting validation data on time requires certain communication and coordination efforts from all stakeholders.

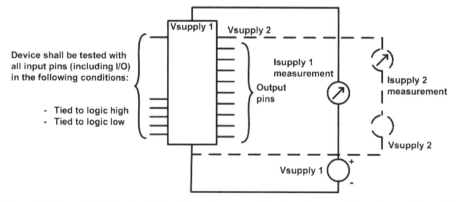

Figure 5. The equivalent circuit for Vsupply over-voltage latch-up testing, adopted from [4].

M2 audit is a gate from *Pilot* to *Certification* phase. For M2 audit, silicon validation data have to be available. The respective checklist requires to have the measurement results within ±10% of typical simulation results. To get a good match, the test environment parameters have to be carefully estimated, such as a load capacitance, tester or oscilloscope parasitics, package and transmission line parameters.

M3 audit completes the Certification step and leads to the *Production* phase. M3 silicon validation deals with the IP performance, functionality and reliability over the process window, so the matrix lot measured data are needed.

There are certain potential difficulties with the practical implementation of described above scheme. 1) They come from the fact that IP is permanently improving during the development process. Every drawback found from any source (simulation data, test vehicle development, or the sample product) is being followed up with IP changes. As a result, the IP versions used on different certification phases are different. The changes in IP have to be tracked down, and their impact on the quality has to be understood and estimated; 2) I/O library re-usage in new products provides more opportunities to get silicon validation data, so the I/O IP may need to be re-validated on every new product.

6. Conclusion

The emphasis of product quality planning is the way to prevent the development and manufacturing problems. There is no way to plan for every possible issue that may happen with a complicated new product development process of semiconductor devices. Maturity qualification flow of semiconductor IPs is not simply a quality planning tool, more importantly it is a philosophy that must be integrated throughout the organization. The maturity qualification methodology described in this paper was successfully applied for different bulk and SOI I/O libraries used in many Freescale products. The silicon validation and quality verification of I/O IPs at early development stages allow us to cut the product costs, to improve the time to market for Freescale products and to reduce the number of engineering re-designs.

REFERENCES

[1] JEDEC CDM, 2012.
http://www.jedec.org/sites/default/files/docs/22C101E.pdf

[2] JEDEC HBM, 2012.
http://www.jedec.org/sites/default/files/docs/js001-2011.pdf

[3] JEDEC MM, 2012.
http://www.jedec.org/sites/default/files/docs/22A115C_0.pdf

[4] JEDEC Latch-Up, 2012.
http://www.jedec.org/sites/default/files/docs/JESD78D.pdf

16

On-Chip Inductor Technique for Improving LNA Performance Operating at 15 GHz

El-Sayed A. M. Hasaneen, Nagwa Okely
Electrical Engineering Department, El-Minia University, El-Minia, Egypt

ABSTRACT

This paper presents a technique for low noise figure reduction of low-noise amplifier (LNA). The proposed LNA is designed in a source degeneration technique that offers lower noise figure. The resistance of the on-chip inductor is reduced by using multilayer that significantly reduces the thermal noise due to spiral inductor. Also, using spiral inductor as a gate inductor reduces the effect of the input parasitic capacitance on the noise figure and provides a good matching at the input and output of the LNA. The results of the LNA using multilayer on-chip inductor compared will off-chip inductor have been illustrated. It shows that the proposed technique reduces significantly the noise figure and improves the matching. The proposed LNA is designed in 0.13 μm process with 1.3 V supply voltage and simulated using Advanced Design System (ADS) software. The simulation results show that the LNA is unconditionally stable and provides a forward gain of 11.087 dB at operating frequency of 15 GHz with 1.784 dB noise figure and input and output impedance matching of −17.93 dB, and −10.04 dB.

Keywords: Low Noise Amplifier; On-Chip Inductor; Noise Figure; Cascade Amplifier; Scattering Matrix

1. Introduction

The communication market has been growing very fast during the last decade especially for mobile communication systems. The low noise amplifier is one of the most essential building blocks in the communication circuits. It can be found in the almost of the commercial and military receivers. The first stage followed the antenna, LNA, is the most critical stage because its noise figure dominates the overall communication systems. The main function of the LNA is to amplify the incoming signal while adding the minimum possible noise and also provides impedance matching. Additional requirement to the LNA is the low power consumption, which is especially important in portable communications systems [1]. Various techniques to improve the LNA performances were proposed [2-5].

In this paper, we propose a new technique for improving LNA performance. The proposed multilayer on-chip spiral inductor technique significantly decreases the value of inductor series resistance that reduces the contribution of the spectral noise current due inductor series resistance and provides a good matching at the LNA input and output. It also reduces the effect of the parasitic capacitance at the input of the LNA which considers one of the biggest problems in the LNA design. In our design, we use inductive source degeneration technique [5].

Source degeneration technique provides no additional noise generation since the real part of the input impedance does not correspond to a physical resistor that offers lower noise figure than the common-gate LNA. Although the distributed amplifiers [6] normally provide wide bandwidth characteristics but it tends to consume a large dc current due to the distribution of multiple amplifying stages, which make them unsuitable for low-power applications. The resistive shunt-feedback-based amplifiers [7] provide good wideband matching and flat gain, but they tend to suffer from poor noise figure (NF) and large power dissipation. It makes the inductive source degeneration technique the best topology for LNA with high gain, low noise figure, good matching and good stability.

This paper is organized as follows. Section 2 describes the proposed LNA circuit and analysis. Section 3 presents modeling of spiral inductor and Section 4 describes the noise analysis. The stability of the LNA is described in Section 5. Results and discussions are illustrated in Section 6 and followed by a conclusion in Section 7.

2. LNA Circuit Description and Analysis

Figure 1(a) shows the schematic circuit diagram of the proposed CMOS LNA with cascoded topology. An inductive source degeneration technique is used to provide no additional noise generation. The cascode topology reduces the influence of the miller capacitance effect which strongly limits the frequency performance and gives a rise to a very poor reverse isolation [8]. It is also used to decouple miller effect from the gain of the circuit and to simplify the design matching network to the antenna. Because LNA directly interfaces with the antenna, a 50 Ω impedance matching is usually required at its input and it is very important to avoid reflections over the transmission line feeding LNA. So, additional tuning components are usually used to match it to the source impedance. The circuit shown in **Figure 1(a)** has purely capacitive input impedance. In order to create a resistive input, a source generation inductor L_S is connected to the source of the input transistor M_1 to provide an effective resistive input without contributing additional noise. The gate inductor L_g is used for input impedance matching which is required to transform upwards the equivalent impedance looking into the gate of M_1 and also it is used to optimize the noise figure.

Figure 1(b) shows the small-signal equivalent circuit for the input transistor M_1 and the overall LNA circuit. The capacitance C_{gs} represents the gate-source capacitance of the input transistor M_1, g_m is the MOS transconductance, and R_s is the source resistance, typically 50 Ω.

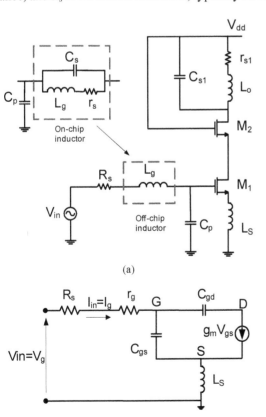

(a)

(b)

Figure 1. (a) Schematic circuit diagram of the proposed CMOS LNA; (b) Small-signal equivalent circuit.

The input impedance can be expressed as:

$$Z_{in} = \frac{V_g}{I_g} = \frac{V_{in}}{I_{in}} = \frac{V_{in}}{j\varpi C_{gs} V_{gs}} \qquad (1)$$

where

$$V_{in} = r_g \left(j\varpi C_{gs} V_{gs} \right) + j\varpi L_g \left(j\varpi C_{gs} V_{gs} \right) + V_{gs} \\ + j\varpi L_s \left(g_m V_{gs} + j\varpi C_{gs} V_{gs} \right) \qquad (2)$$

Substituting (2) into (1) gives:

$$Z_{in} = r_g + \frac{g_m L_s}{C_{gs}} + j\varpi \left[\left(L_s + L_g \right) + \frac{1}{\left(j\varpi \right)^2 C_{gs}} \right] \qquad (3)$$

The real part of Z_{in} is given by:

$$R_e \left(Z_{in} \right) = r_g + \frac{g_m L_s}{C_{gs}}$$

where r_g is the gate resistance of MOS transistor. Neglecting the gate resistance, the real part of the input impedance can be expressed as:

$$R_e \left(Z_{in} \right) = \frac{g_m L_s}{C_{gs}} \qquad (4)$$

For matching purpose, the real part of the input impedance should be equal to the source resistance. It is given by:

$$R_s = \frac{g_m L_s}{C_{gs}} = \varpi_T L_s \qquad (5)$$

where ϖ_T is the unity-current gain angular frequency of the MOS transistor and can be approximated as [8]:

$$\varpi_T = \frac{g_m}{C_{gs} + C_{gd}} = \frac{g_m}{C_{gs}\sqrt{1 + \frac{C_{gd}}{C_{gs}}}} \cong \frac{g_m}{C_{gs}} = \frac{3}{2} \frac{\alpha \mu V_{ov}}{L^2} \qquad (6)$$

The effective transconductance of the matched device of the LNA is defined as the ratio of the input transistor output current to the input voltage and given by:

$$G_m = \frac{I_d}{V_{in}} \qquad (7)$$

In this case, $I_d = g_m V_{gs}$ & $V_{in} = V_{gs}/Q_{in}$, where $Q_{in} = 1/(\omega RC)$ is the quality factor of the input RLC tank which formed from the input matching network and it is given by:

$$Q_{in} = \frac{1}{\varpi \cdot R_s \cdot C_{gs}} = \frac{1}{\varpi \cdot g_m \cdot L_s} \qquad (8)$$

and

$$\varpi = \frac{1}{\sqrt{C_{gs} \left(L_s + L_g \right)}} \qquad (9)$$

Substituting (8) into (7), the input stage transconductance will be:

$$G_m = \frac{1}{\varpi \cdot L_s} \tag{10}$$

The LNA input stage transconductance given by (10) is independent on the actual input device transconductance g_m which considered a merit for LNA circuit.

At output, the output inductance (L_o) of the on-chip inductor is used to resonate with the cascode output capacitance at the resonance frequency. The disadvantage of the on-chip inductor is the series resistance and overlap capacitance between the turns of spiral and the cross-under layer. The series resistance of the spiral decreases the inductor quality factor which has a significant effect on the quality factor of the output tank. In this work, the series resistance is decreased significantly by using multilayer technique as we will discuss in next the sections and the overlap capacitance is used as the output capacitance for LNA circuit. So, on-chip spiral inductor becomes preferable compared to off-chip inductor.

At the resonance frequency, the voltage gain of the LNA shown in **Figure 1(a)** can be expressed as:

$$A_v = G_m \times Z_l\left(\varpi\right) \tag{11}$$

and

$$Z_l\left(\varpi\right) = \left(Q_{ind} \times \left(\varpi L_o\right)\right) // R_{ot} // R_l$$
$$= \left(\frac{\left(\varpi L_o\right)^2}{r_{s1}}\right) // R_{ot} // R_l \tag{12}$$

where R_{ot} is the output resistance of the cascode architecture and R_l is the load resistance. Q_{ind} (ωL_o) is the output inductor parallel resistance. The output resistance is given by:

$$R_{ot} = g_{m2} \times r_{o1} \times r_{o2}$$

where g_{m2}, r_{o1} and r_{o2} are the transconductance of cascode transistor, and output resistance of input and cascode transistors, respectively.

If the load resistance value is small compared with the output resistance of the cascode and parallel resistance of the output inductor, the overall output resistance will be:

$$Z_l\left(\varpi\right) \equiv R_l$$

and

$$A_v = G_m \times R_l = \frac{R_l}{\varpi \times L_s} \tag{13}$$

The voltage gain of the low noise amplifier should be set to maximize the dynamic range of the total receiver. It can be accomplished if the next blocks are very linear but the noise will be increased and vice versa [8].

3. Modeling of Spiral Inductor

A lumped circuit model of on-chip spiral inductor grown on Si substrate is shown in **Figure 2** [9-11]. L_S and r_S are the series inductance and resistance of the spiral respectively. C_S is the overlap capacitance between the turns of spiral and the cross-under layer. C_{OX} is the oxide capacitance between the spiral and the substrate. R_{Si} and C_{Si} are the parameters modeling substrate losses and capacitive effects, respectively. The inductance of a spiral is a complex function of its geometry and includes both self and mutual inductances. The expressions for on-chip spiral inductor parameters are given by [9]:

$$L_s = \frac{\mu l}{2\pi}\left\{ \ln\frac{l}{2N\left(w+t\right)} + 0.5 + \frac{4N\left(w+t\right)}{3l} - 0.47N \right.$$
$$+ \left(N-1\right)\left[\ln\left(\sqrt{1+\left(1/4Nd^+\right)^2} + \frac{l}{4Nd^+} \right) \right.$$
$$\left. \left. - \sqrt{1+\left(4Nd^+/l\right)^2} + \frac{4Nd^+}{l} \right]\right\} \tag{14}$$

$$r_s\left(\omega\right) = \frac{l}{w \cdot \sigma \cdot \delta\left(\omega\right) \cdot \left(1 - e^{\frac{t}{\delta}}\right)} \tag{15}$$

$$C_{OX} = l \cdot w \cdot \frac{\varepsilon_{ox}}{t_{OX}} \tag{16}$$

$$C_s = N \cdot C_{OV} = N \cdot w^2 \cdot \frac{\varepsilon_{ox}}{d} \tag{17}$$

$$R_{Si} = \frac{2}{l \cdot w \cdot G_{sub}} \tag{18}$$

$$C_{Si} = \frac{l \cdot w \cdot C_{sub}}{2} \tag{19}$$

where l is the wire length, w is the width of the metal conductor, and t is the thickness of the metal conductor. The substrate parasitic capacitances and resistances cause

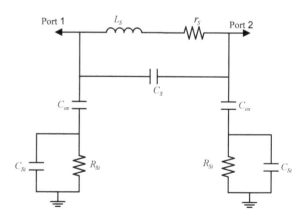

Figure 2. Lumped model of spiral inductor.

high losses in the circuit that present several challenges for implementing monolithic gigahertz circuitry. The placement of a patterned ground shield (PGS) beneath the spiral inductor eliminates the substrate parasites that improve the inductor performance [12]. A patterned ground shield is used in our calculations and simulations in this paper.

4. Noise Analysis

The noise figure of LNA at operation frequency ω can be estimated by analyzing the circuit shown in **Figure 3**. Five noise sources contribute the noise at the output of the low noise amplifier. The MOS transistor M_1 contributes by two of them. The noise sources are as follows:

1) the thermal noise of the channel current ($i_{n,d}$). It has a power spectral density of:

$$\frac{\overline{i_{n,d}^2}}{\Delta F} = 4K \cdot T \cdot \gamma \cdot g_{dso} \qquad (20)$$

where K is the Boltzman constant, T is the absolute temperature, γ is the bias dependent constant, and g_{dso} is the drain-source conductance at $V_{ds} = 0$ and it is defined as:

$$g_{dso} = \frac{g_m}{\alpha}$$

where α equals 1 for long channel and 0.85 for short channel transistors.

2) The gate induced current noise ($i_{n,g}$): It has a power spectral density of:

$$\frac{\overline{i_{n,g}^2}}{\Delta F} = 4KT\delta g_g \qquad (21)$$

and

$$\delta g_g = \frac{\omega^2 C_{gs}^2}{5g_{dso}} = \frac{\alpha \omega^2 C_{gs}^2}{5g_m}$$

Subsituting δg_g in (21) gives:

$$\frac{\overline{i_{n,g}^2}}{\Delta F} = 4KT\frac{\delta \alpha}{5g_m}\omega^2 C_{gs}^2 = \frac{4KT\delta \alpha g_m}{5}\left(\frac{\omega}{\omega_T}\right)^2 \qquad (22)$$

The gate current noise is related to the drain current noise and actually it is partially correlated to it with a correlation coefficient C given by:

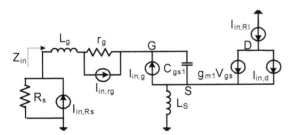

Figure 3. Circuit model for input stage noise analysis.

$$C = \frac{\overline{i_{n,g}i_{n,d}^*}}{\sqrt{\overline{i_{n,g}^2}\,\overline{i_{n,d}^2}}} \qquad (23)$$

where $C = j0.395$ for short channel transistors, and the power spectral density of the gate induced current noise source can be expressed as:

$$\frac{\overline{i_{n,g}^2}}{\Delta F} = \frac{\overline{i_{n,gc}^2}}{\Delta F} + \frac{\overline{i_{n,gu}^2}}{\Delta F}$$

or

$$\frac{\overline{i_{n,g}^2}}{\Delta F} = \frac{4KT\delta \alpha g_m}{5}\left(\frac{\omega}{\omega_T}\right)^2|C^2|$$
$$+ \frac{4KT\delta \alpha g_m}{5}\left(\frac{\omega}{\omega_T}\right)^2\left(1-|C^2|\right) \qquad (24)$$

The first term $i_{n,gc}$ is the correlated term and the second term $i_{n,gu}$ is the uncorrelated term.

3) The distributed gate resistance of CMOS transistor: It is also added noise to the output of the low noise amplifier and has a power spectral density equal to:

$$\frac{\overline{i_{n,rg}^2}}{\Delta F} = 4KTG_m^2 r_g = 4KT\frac{r_g}{\left(\omega_T L_s\right)^2} \qquad (25)$$

where r_g is distributed gate resistance given by:

$$r_g = 1/5g_m$$

where g_m is the input transistor transconductance.

4) The thermal noise due to source resistance: It has a power spectral density of:

$$\frac{\overline{i_{n,Rs}^2}}{\Delta F} = 4KTG_m^2 R_s \qquad (26)$$

5) Thermal noise of the output resistance: The low noise amplifier utilizes an LC resonator circuit at the drain of the output transistor to adjust the output of the LNA at a desired resonance frequency ω. The losses of the LC resonant circuit result from output inductor series resistance R_d. The noise contribution of the series resistance in the LNA in the form of output noise current has a spectral density of:

$$\frac{\overline{i_{n,Rd}^2}}{\Delta F} = \frac{4KT}{R_d} \qquad (27)$$

In this paper, using multilayer on-chip spiral inductor technique significantly decreases the value of the inductor series resistance that reduces the contribution of the spectral noise current due to inductor series resistance. Cascode transistor M_2 has a minor influence on the noise behavior of the LNA and its contribution to the total noise is disregarded in the analysis. Finally, the noise factor F is the ratio between the total output noise power and the noise power due to the source resistance and it is give by:

$$F = 1 + \frac{r_g}{R_s} + \frac{\delta\alpha}{5} g_m R_s \left(\frac{\varpi}{\varpi_T}\right)^2 \left[|C|^2 \left(\frac{\varpi}{\varpi_T}\right)^2\right.$$
$$\left. + \left(1 - |C|^2\right) \left(\frac{\varpi}{\varpi_T}\right)^2\right] + \frac{\gamma}{\alpha} g_m R_s \left(\frac{\varpi}{\varpi_T}\right)^2 + \frac{4R_s}{R_d}\left(\frac{\varpi}{\varpi_T}\right)^2 \quad (28)$$

The above equation describes the noise figure for low noise amplifier without taking the parasitic capacitance C_P effect into consideration. The parasitic capacitance C_P is the total parallel parasitic capacitance due to the ESD protection diodes, QFN package parasitic and bonding pad structure. The value of C_P is a fabrication dependency. If we include the parasitic capacitance effect on the noise figure, the noise factor will be:

$$F = 1 + \frac{r_g}{R_s} + \frac{\delta\alpha}{5} g_m R_s \left(\frac{\varpi\left(C_{gs} + C_p\right)}{g_m}\right)^2 \left[|C|^2 \left(\frac{\varpi}{\varpi_T}\right)^2\right.$$
$$\left. + \left(1 - |C|^2\right)\left(\frac{\varpi}{\varpi_T}\right)^2\right] + \frac{\gamma}{\alpha} g_m R_s \left(\frac{\varpi}{\varpi_T}\right)^2 + \frac{4R_s}{R_d}\left(\frac{\varpi}{\varpi_T}\right)^2 \quad (29)$$

From the above equation, the noise figure of the LNA directly depends on the parallel parasitic capacitance C_P. With off-chip inductor, the value of C_P is very high because the parasitic capacitance dominates the input capacitance of the LNA which considers one of the biggest problems in the LNA design. Therefore, it is difficult to reduce the total noise figure. Our solution for this problem is to use on-chip spiral inductor as a gate inductor. In this case, the parasitic capacitance becomes non-dominat. So, any value for parasitic capacitance, high or low, do not highly effect on the noise figure and LNA gain. It also gives a good matching at input and output of the LNA without using any other matching components. Therefore, we can design a stable LNA circuit that gives the desired performance without taking into consideration C_P and other LNA complemented packaging.

There are many efforts for decreasing the effect of parasitic capacitance in noise figure as follow:

The first one considers a specific value for parasitic capacitance C_p and takes the parasitic capacitance as a part of the circuit and builds the design upon this idea [13] as follow:

$$\text{Re}\left(Z_{in}\right) = R_s = \frac{g_m L_s C_{gs}}{\left(C_P + C_{gs}\right)^2} \quad (30)$$

From the above equation, increasing C_P increases the value of source inductor L_S and lowers the value of gate inductor L_g.

The second effort considers a specific value for C_P and uses matching network at the input [14] and the value of

the matching capacitor is defined from:

$$\text{Re}\left(Z_{in}\right) = R_s = \frac{1}{\left(\varpi * C_m\right)^2} \left(\frac{C_p + C_{gs}}{C_{gs}}\right)^2 \frac{1}{R_s} \quad (31)$$

and

$$L_g = \frac{C_p + C_{gs} + C_m}{C_m \left(C_p + C_{gs}\right)\varpi^2} \quad (32)$$

where C_m is the matching capacitor placed before gate inductor, C_p is parasitic capacitance, and ϖ is the resonance frequency.

5. LNA Stability

The stability of an amplifier is a very important factor which must not be susceptible to unwanted oscillation. The stability factor of an amplifier is a frequency dependent. The amplifier may be stable at its design frequency and unstable at other frequencies. It is highly recommended that the amplifier circuit is made unconditionally stable at all frequencies to ensure that it does not produce unwanted oscillations. For unconditionally stable, the input and output stable circuits should not be clipped the outer edge of the Smith chart. The stability of a two-port network can be determined from its S-parameters and the load and source impedances. The stability is determined by using Rollets factors K and Δ, where K and Δ in terms of S-parameters at frequency of operation is determined as follow [15]:

$$K = \frac{1 - S_{11}^2 - S_{22}^2 + \Delta^2}{2\left|S_{12}S_{21}\right|} \quad (33)$$

$$\Delta = S_{11}S_{22} - S_{12}S_{21} \quad (34)$$

6. Results and Discussions

Cascode low noise amplifier with source degeneration technique shown in **Figure 1(a)** has been designed in 0.13 μm CMOS technology and simulated using ADS software. The value of the source resistance $R_S = 50\ \Omega$ and the input transistor M_1 has W/L ratio of 44.73 μm/ 0.13 μm. It is biased at 1 mA and have a gate-source capacitance of 60 fF. The LNA is optimized at 15 GHz by the proper selection of the on-chip inductor parameters. The inductor has 5-levels, 4.75-turns, and squirrel shape that provides 1.08 nH inductance and its nonidealities series resistance of 2.5 Ω, overlap capacitance of 0.8 fF and the oxide capacitance between the spiral and the substrate of 21 fF with 2 μm width and 1 μm spacing between turns. It is designed to have a very small overlap capacitance and a series resistance to reduce the total LNA noise figure. The effect of the capacitance due to the ESD protection diodes, QFN package parasitic and bonding pad structure is taken in consideration during the design of the LNA circuit. The cascade transistor M_2 is designed to have the same dimensions to decrease the power consumption at output. The output inductor L_o used to resonate with the output cascade capacitance and provide matching with the coupling capacitors C_1 and C_2 at the operating frequency f_o.

In our design, we use on-chip spiral inductor at the output and we include the inductor nonidealities to be part of the circuit. The inductor overlap capacitance is considered a part of the output capacitance and the inductor series resistance a part of the cascade output resistance. The value of L_o used in our simulation is 0.415 nH at an operating frequency of 15 GHz.

Table 1 gives the simulated results of the LNA performance using on-chip spiral inductor compared with off-chip inductor at different values of a parallel parasitic capacitance C_p. From the simulated results, with off-chip inductor, the noise figure (NF) highly increases with increasing C_P. Also, the power gain (A_p), input and output matching decrease to reach no matching when the parasitic capacitance is higher than the gate-source capacitance of input transistor M_1. Since, the parasitic value is undetermined and depends on the fabrication, the off-chip inductor is not effective in LNA design. The LNA with on-chip inductor has a higher power gain (A_p), higher voltage gain (A_v) compared with LNA with off-chip inductor. It also has lower noise figure and better input and output matching compared with LNA with off-chip inductor.

Table 2 gives the simulated results of LNA with different layers of on-chip inductor ($N = 1, 3$ and 5) with a parasitic capacitance of 120 fF. Increasing the number of the metal layers (N) decreases the inductor resistance, increases the power gain, improves the matching and reduces the noise figure. **Figures 4** and **5** show the variation of the LNA noise figure with the frequency for different layers of the on-chip inductor ($N = 1, 3$ and 5) at two different values of the parasitic capacitance C_p ($C_p = 0$ and 120 fF). As illustrated in the figures, increasing the number of the on-chip inductor layers reduces the LNA noise figure due to decrease the inductor resistance. **Figures 6-8** show the simulated LNA gain, input and output matching and noise figure using input matching capacitor and 5-layer on-chip spiral inductor. The results indicate that the maximum gain occurs at 15 GHz. The value of the power gain (A_P), input and output impedances matching (S_{11} and S_{22}), and noise figure are 11.087 dB, −17.93 dB, −10.04 dB, and 1.784 dB, respectively.

Figure 9 shows the stability factor K as a function of frequency. It is clear that K is greater than unity which means the system is stable. **Figures 10** and **11** show the LNA input and output stability circuits. The results illustrate that the LNA is unconditionally stable because the input and output circles locate inside the Smith Chart.

Table 1. Comparison between the simulated results of LNA performance with on-chip spiral and off-chip inductor.

Case	C_P fF	$A_P (S_{21})$ (dB)	A_V (dB)	S_{11} (dB)	S_{22} (dB)	S_{12} (dB)	NF_{min} (dB)	NF (dB)
Results with On-Chip Spiral Inductor								
1	60	11.119	5.09	−20.5	−10.0	−22.2	1.3	1.554
1	90	11.121	5.1	−20.7	−10.2	−22.5	1.3	1.658
3	120	11.087	5.067	−17.9	−10.4	−22.5	1.3	1.784
4	200	10.83	4.8	−11.4	−11.1	−22.8	1.3	2.218
Results with Off-Chip Inductor								
1	60	8.647	2.626	−3.54	−6.78	−24.5	1.229	1.7
2	90	7.064	1.044	−2.13	−6.11	−26.1	1.229	2.487
3	120	5.572	0.449	−1.39	−5.75	−27.57	1.229	3.474
4	200	2.272	−3.75	−0.6	−5.39	−30.9	1.229	6.241

Table 2. Simulated LNA performance with different layers of on-chip inductor.

N	r_S (Ω)	$A_P (S_{21})$ (dB)	A_V (dB)	S_{11} (dB)	S_{22} (dB)	S_{12} (dB)	NF_{min} (dB)	NF (dB)
1	12.6	10.01	3.986	−15.546	−9.656	−23.6	1.807	2.656
3	4.2	10.896	4.875	−17.908	−10.26	−22.7	1.401	1.942
5	2.5	11.087	5.067	−17.931	−10.4	−22.5	1.301	1.784

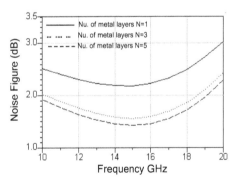

Figure 4. LNA noise figure versus frequency with different layers of on-chip inductor ($N = 1, 2$, and 3) for $C_P = 0$.

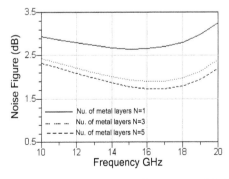

Figure 5. LNA noise figure versus frequency with different layers of on-chip inductor ($N = 1, 3$, and 5) for $C_P = 120$ pF.

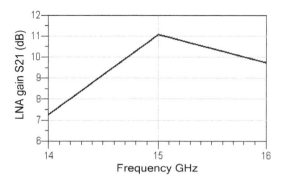

Figure 6. Simulated LNA output gain.

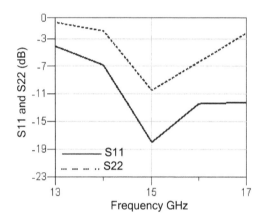

Figure 7. Simulated LNA input and output matching.

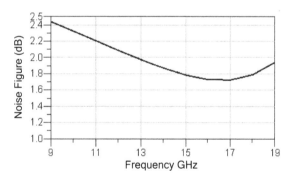

Figure 8. Simulated LNA noise figure.

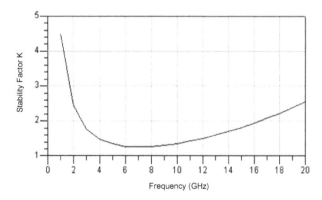

Figure 9. LNA Circuit Stability Factor *K* versus frequency.

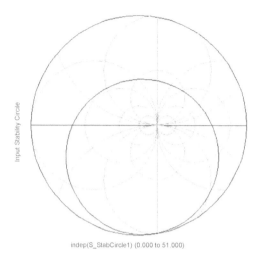

Figure 10. LNA input stability circle.

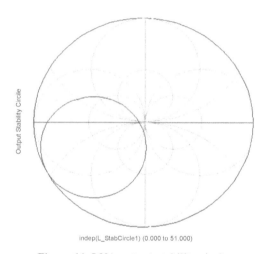

Figure 11. LNA output stability circle.

7. Conclusion

In this paper, a low noise amplifier has been designed using multilayer on-chip inductor to improve the LNA performance. Our results show that the suggested technique improves the noise figure and gives a better matching at the input and output of the LNA. Also, it gives a good power gain. Increasing the on-chip inductor metal layers reduces the spiral resistance and improves the noise figure. The results of our technique are compared with the results of the off-chip inductor technique that show our technique gives a better LNA performance.

REFERENCES

[1] D. K. Shaeffer and T. H. Lee, "A 1.5 V, 1.5 GHz CMOS Low Noise Amplifier," *IEEE Journal of Solid-State Circuits*, Vol. 35, No. 2, 1999, pp. 745-759.

[2] Y.-H. Yu, Y.-S. Yang and Y.-J. Chen, "A Compact Wideband CMOS Low Noise Amplifier with Gain Flatness Enhancement," *IEEE Journal of Solid-State Circuits*, Vol.

45, No. 3, 2010, pp. 502-509.

[3] A. Telli, S. Demir and M. Askar, "CMOS Planar Spiral Inductor Modeling and Low Noise Amplifier Design," *Microelectronics Journal*, Vol. 37, 2006, pp. 71-78.

[4] M. Khanpour, K. W. Tang, P. Garcia and S. P. Voinigescu, "A Wideband W-Band Receiver Front-End in 65-nm CMOS," *IEEE Journal of Solid-State Circuits*, Vol. 43, No. 8, 2008, pp. 1717-1730.

[5] P. Sivonen and A. Pärssinen, "Analysis and Optimization of Packaged Inductively Degenerated Common-Source Low-Noise Amplifiers with ESD Protection," *IEEE Transactions on Microwave Theory*, Vol. 53, No. 4, 2005, pp. 1303-1313.

[6] R.-C. Liu, K.-L. Deng and H. Wang, "A 0.6 - 22 GHz Broadband CMOS Distributed Amplifier," *IEEE Radio Frequency Integrated Circuits Symposium*, Philadelphia, 8-10 June 2003, pp. 103-106.

[7] F. Bruccoleri, E. A. M. Klumperink and B. Nauta, "Noise Canceling in Wideband CMOS LNA's," *IEEE International Solid-State Circuits Conference*, Vol. 1, 2002, pp. 406-407.

[8] D. K. Shaeffer and T. H. Lee, "The Design and Implementation of Low-Power CMOS Radio Receivers," Kluwer, Norwell, 1999.

[9] E. S. Hasaneen, "Modeling of On-Chip Inductor and Transformer for RF Integrated Circuits," *11th Middle-East International Conference on Power Systems*, Vol. 1, 2006, pp. 49-52.

[10] M. Dehan, J.-P. Raskin, I. Huynen and D. Vanhoenacker-Janvier, "An Improved Multiline Analysis for Monolithic Inductors," *IEEE Transactions on Solid-State Circuits*, Vol. 37, No. 1, 2002, pp. 77-80.

[11] C. P. Yue and S. S. Wong, "Physical Modeling of Spiral Inductors on Silicon," *IEEE Transactions on Electronic Devices*, Vol. 47, No. 3, 2000, pp. 560-568.

[12] S. S. Mohan, "Modeling, Design, and Optimization of On-Chip Inductors and Transformers," Ph.D. Thesis, Stanford University, Stanford, 1999.

[13] V. Von, "CMOS Low Noise Amplifier Design for Reconfigurable Mobile Terminals," Ph.D. Thesis, Electrical Elektrotechnik und Informatik der Technishen University, Berlin, 2004.

[14] P. Sivonen, S. Kangasmaa and A. Pärssinen, "Analysis of Packaging Effects and Optimization in Inductively Degenerated Common-Emitter Low-Noise Amplifiers," *IEEE Transactions on Microwave Theory and Techniques*, Vol. 51, No. 4, 2003, pp. 1220-1226.

[15] C. Bowick, "RF Circuit Designs," Howard W. Sams & Co. Inc., Indianapolis, 1982.

17

High-Performance CMOS Current Mirrors: Application to Linear Voltage-to-Current Converter Used for Two-Stage Operational Amplifier

Radwene Laajimi, Mohamed Masmoudi

Department of Electrical Engineering Electronics, Micro-Technology and Communication (EMC) Research Group Sfax (ENIS), University of Sfax, Sfax, Tunisia

ABSTRACT

This paper presents two schemes of high performance CMOS current mirror, one of them is used for operational transconductance amplifier (OTA) in analog VLSI systems. The linearity, output impedance, bandwidth and accuracy are the most parameters to determine the performance of the current mirror. Here a comparison of two architectures based on same architecture of the amplifier is presented. This comparison includes: linearity, output impedance, bandwidth and accuracy. These two circuits are validated with simulation in technology AMS 0.35 μm. An operational amplifier based on the adapted current mirror is proposed. Its frequency analysis with large bandwidth is validated with the same technology.

Keywords: Analog Circuits; Current Source; Current Mirror; Low Voltage; Operational Transconductance Amplifier

1. Introduction

In the last few years, the demand for analog circuits which can operate at low voltage is an established fact and does not need any further justification. In particular structures of current mirrors which have increased rapidly and become one of the most interesting areas of research [1]. Many configurations of current mirror are discussed and used for many applications. Especially cascode current mirror which is one of the main building blocks of analog and mixed-signal integrated circuits. For low voltage design circuit and high speed application, the important parameters to determine high performance current mirror are [2-4]:

- Low input and output voltage.
- Low input impedance.
- High output impedance.
- Minimum error of copying accuracy and settling time.

The four transistors circuit shown in **Figure 1(a)** is a simple cascode current mirror and it is characterized by moderately low input and output voltages.

Equation (1) of input voltage is:

$$V_{in} = 2V_{DSAT} + 2V_T \qquad (1)$$

Equation (2) of output voltage is:

$$V_{out} = 2V_{DSAT} + V_T \qquad (2)$$

(V_{DSAT} and V_T denote is the minimum drain-source saturation voltage and the transistor's threshold voltage.)

This circuit has higher output impedance than the simple current mirror and moderately high input impedance.

Equation (3) of input impedance is:

$$Z_{in} = \frac{1}{gm_{11}} + \frac{1}{gm_{12}} \qquad (3)$$

Equation (4) of output impedance is:

$$Z_{out} = \frac{gm_9}{go_9 \cdot go_{10}} \qquad (4)$$

(where gm and go are the small-signal transconductance gain and the conductance of the MOS transistor, respectively.)

A simple variation of this circuit is shown in **Figure 1(b)** [5]. In this scheme the variable voltage V_{ar} with resistance R1 are added. They are injected between the drain of transistor M12 and the source of transistor M11. The drain source voltage of the mirror transistor M12 is forced to a constant value by means of transistor M11, current I_{in} and variable voltage V_{ar}. Thus, on one hand, a reduction of the input impedance by the gain of M11. On the other hand, it reduces the input voltage requirements. In this case, the input voltage can be set to its minimum value by proper selection of the variable voltage Var. Hence, this scheme achieves low input impedance with low input voltage requirements but with some limitation due to the difference between the current in M11 and M9. This difference causes a mismatch in the drain source

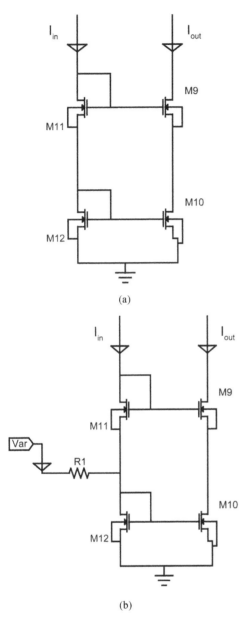

Figure 1. Current mirror configuration. (a) Simple cascode current mirror; (b) Cascode current mirror with regulated voltage.

voltage of M10 and M12 and results in a loss of accuracy, so degraded linearity (due to channel length modulation).

To overcome this limitation, we are proposing two novels structures of current mirror which offers both the low compliance voltage and a minimum error of copying accuracy. The two proposed approaches are based on using a differential amplifier to compare the drain voltages of the input and output mirror transistors, to force the equality between these voltages, thereby improving the accuracy of the current copy, and improving linearity.

The paper is organized as follows. The second section presents the amplifiers structures used for voltage to cur-

rent (V-I) converter. In the third section, the design of proposed version 1 of V-I converter is presented with simulations results. The proposed version 2 of V-I converter is presented in section four. Section 5 presents an application of V-I converter in two-stage operational amplifier. Conclusion is drawn in the last section.

2. Amplifier Structures

In order to achieve high current copy accuracy, it is necessary to use an amplifier between the mirror's input and output transistors.

The amplifier architectures are: simple differential amplifier [6] and amplifier proposed by [5]. As shown in **Figure 2(a)**, this structure is formed by the input differential pair (MP1 and MP2) and the active charge (MN1 and MN2). The **Figure 2(b)** shows a differential amplifier with two MOS transistors (MN1 and MN2) in which MN1 is operated in the weak version region (source gate voltage of MN1 equal to zero). This version can operate either in the linear region or in the saturation region for achieving low voltage and low consumption.

Moreover, the amplifier, which has many transistors, causes the increase of the power dissipation and the chip area. The advantages of the scheme proposed by [7] are low voltage operation, small chip area, high output resistance and no bias current. For this reason we use this structure in our two versions of voltage to current converter which are more described in the following paragraph.

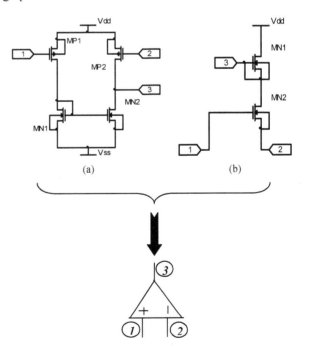

Figure 2. Amplifier configuration. (a) Simple differential amplifier structure [6]; (b) Two-transistor apmlifier structure [7].

3. Proposed Version 1 of Voltage to Current Converter

3.1. Description

According to **Figure 3** the version 1 of V-I converter is composed of three blocks: polarisation, correction and output load.

The polarisation block is formed of four transistors (MP1, MP2, MP3, MP4) with variable input voltage V_{in} and input resistance R_{in}. The correction block is composed of three transistors (M1, M2, MC2). It characterized by minimum error of copying accuracy due to the equality of drain source voltage between M1 and M2. This equality thanks to an amplifier between the mirror's input and output transistors M1 and M2 and causes high accuracy and good linearity. High output impedance is obtained by the output current of amplifier and passes to the gate of transistor MC2. The output load block is a simply resistance (R_{out}).

This scheme offers a comparison between drain source voltage of M1 and M2 by using a differential amplifier to provide higher accuracy of the current copy. The input injection current signal I_{in} is replaced by another source formed by variable input voltage V_{in} with resistance R_{in}. On the one hand, we obtain a reduction of the input impedance which given by this relation:

Equation (5) of input impedance is:

$$Z_{in} = \frac{1}{gm_1 \cdot A_{olinp}} \qquad (5)$$

Equation (6) presents moderate output impedance

$$Z_{out} = ro_2 \cdot A_{olout} = ro_2 \cdot Av_{MC2} \cdot Av_{omp} \qquad (6)$$

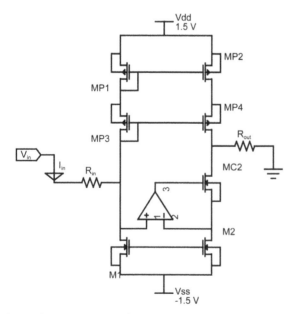

Figure 3. Proposed version 1 of voltage to current converter.

where *gm* and *ro* are the small-signal transconductance gain and the output resistance of the MOS transistors. In this case we assume that the amplifier have an input open-loop gain A_{olinp} and output open-loop gain A_{olout} ($A_{olout} = Av_{MC2} \cdot Av_{omp}$). Av_{MC2} and Av_{omp} denote the voltage gain of the transistor MC2 and amplifier gain respectively.

On the other hand, the drain source voltage of the mirror transistor M1 achieves a small constant value thanks to current source I_{in} and variable voltage source V_{in}. Drain source voltage can be decreasing to a minimum value, by selection of V_{in} and consequently a very low input voltage of the circuit.

3.2. Simulations Results

Different schemes are simulated using Tspice based on BSIM3V3 transistor model for the technology AMS 0.35 μm at ±1.5 V power supply voltage.

Tspice simulations are carried for an input voltage V_{in} varied from −1.1 V to 0 V, **Figure 4** shows the DC characteristic for the V-I converter for different values of resistance (R_{out} = 100 Ω, R_{out} = 1 KΩ, R_{out} = 5 KΩ) in which the full input voltage swing capability is evident with truly linearity.

As shown in **Figure 5**, from DC output characteristics simulations, the output resistance presents a moderate value of 0.18 MΩ.

The **Figure 6** shows the AC characteristic of the proposed V-I converter. For a resistance of 100 Ω, we achieved a common gain bandwidth (GBW) equal to 750 MHz for different values of resistance (R_{out} = 100 Ω, R_{out} = 1 KΩ, R_{out} = 5 KΩ) and variable gain (Av) from 53 dB to 80.2 dB at minimum resistance (R_{out} = 100 Ω).

According to **Figure 7**, the deviation of the DC output current from the ideal characteristic for different values of resistance R_{out}. The large error is reached for the lowest input voltage V_{in} of −1.1 V. On the other hand the variation of V_{in} between −0.9 V to 0 V provide a small current error under 0.1% for different values of resistance (R_{out} = 100 Ω, R_{out} = 1 KΩ, R_{out} = 5 KΩ). Moreover for the maximum current error of 0.5%, V_{in} varied from −1.1 V to −0.95 V in particular for output resistance R_{out} = 5 KΩ.

4. Proposed Version 2 of Voltage to Current Converter

4.1. Description

The version 2 of V-I converter is presented in **Figure 8**. It is like the structure of version 1 shown in **Figure 3** and composed of three blocks: polarisation, correction and output load. The main difference is in the correction block. In which there are three transistors (M1, M2, MC2)

High-Performance CMOS Current Mirrors: Application to Linear Voltage-to-Current Converter Used for Two-Stage Operational Amplifier

115

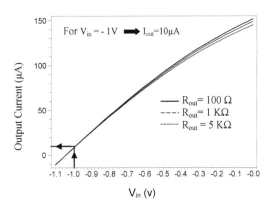

Figure 4. DC characteristics of V-I converter for different values of resistance R_{out}.

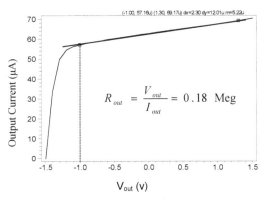

Figure 5. Output current vs output voltage variation of proposed V-I converter.

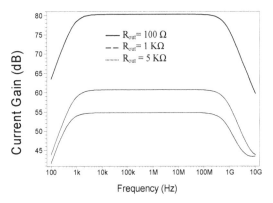

Figure 6. Frequency response of proposed V-I converter.

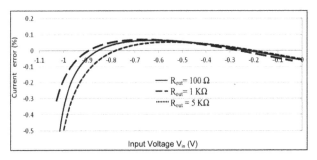

Figure 7. Current error of V-I converter.

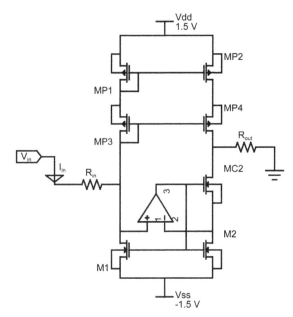

Figure 8. Proposed version 2 of voltage to current converter.

with an amplifier between M1 and M2 in order to minimise error of copying accuracy.

In this case of structure an approach is used to increase the output impedance without sacrificing the equality between input and output of drain source voltage (M1 and M2), consists in integrating a connection between the gate of transistor MC2 and the gate of transistor M2. We achieved very high output impedance due to the output current of amplifier. This current is passed through each gate of transistors MC2 and M2. Equation (8) shows the value of output impedance which is:

$$Z_{out} = ro_2 \cdot A_{olout} = ro_2 \cdot Av_{MC2} \cdot Av_{M2} \cdot Av_{omp} \quad (8)$$

ro_2 denote the output resistance of the MOS transistor M2. The amplifier has an output open-loop gain A_{olout}. Equation (9) give this relation:

$$A_{olout} = Av_{MC2} \cdot Av_{M2} \cdot Av_{omp} \quad (9)$$

We assume that Av_{MC2}, Av_{M2} and Av_{omp} denote the voltage gain of the transistor MC2, M2 and amplifier gain respectively.

4.2. Simulations Results

From Tspice simulations, an input voltage V_{in} varied from −1 V to 0 V, the DC characteristic for the V-I converter for different values of resistance ($R_{out} = 100$ Ω, $R_{out} = 1$ KΩ, $R_{out} = 5$ KΩ) is shown in **Figure 9**. We find that the linearity is evident for each value of resistance.

To confirm the high output resistance given by the proposed version 2 of V-I converter, **Figure 10** shows the DC output characteristics simulations. The value of the output resistance in this case is equal to 0.34 MΩ.

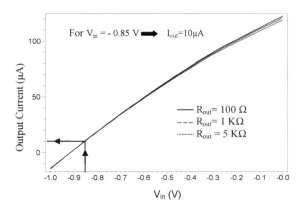

Figure 9. DC characteristics of V-I converter for different values of resistance R_{out}.

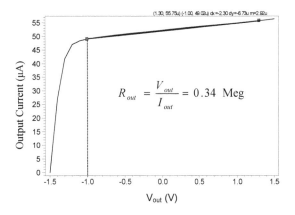

Figure 10. Output current vs output voltage variation of proposed V-I converter.

From AC characteristic, we note an improvement of the gain (Av). Its maximum value is 73 dB but it is 80.2 dB for the proposed version 1 of V-I converter. The bandwidth responses for different values of resistance are presented in **Figure 11**.

From **Figure 12**, we present a current error of V-I converter for different values of resistance R_{out}. On the one hand, the variation of V_{in} from −0.9 V to 0 V give the same characteristic of error for different values of resistance ($R_{out} = 100$ Ω, $R_{out} = 1$ KΩ, $R_{out} = 5$ KΩ). On the other hand for the maximum current error of 0.35%, V_{in} is lower than −0.95 V.

5. Application of V-I Converter in Two-Stage Operational Amplifier

Voltage to current V-I converter becomes the most interesting element of interface measurement in the field of mixed signal systems [8].

The most important parameters to determine high performance of current V-I converters are:
- High linear range.
- Large bandwidth and gain.

Because the large bandwidth and gain of the proposed

version 1 of V-I converter, it is possible to use this approach for Operational amplifier [9,10]. The **Figure 13** shows a practical implementation of the two-stage Operational amplifier.

The simulated output frequency response of our application is shown in **Figure 14**. The bode diagram gives an open loop gain of 60 dB with a large GBW of 82 MHz, a 97 KHz of cut-off frequency and a phase margin of 62°. We note that the input current passes through M8 using for polarisation is equal to 10 µA and this corresponds to an input voltage V_{in} of −1 V.

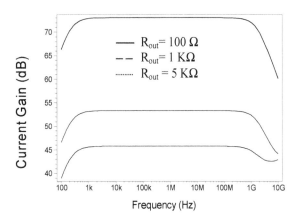

Figure 11. Frequency response of proposed V-I converter

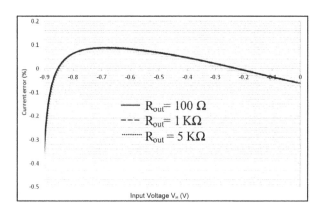

Figure 12. Current error of V-I converter.

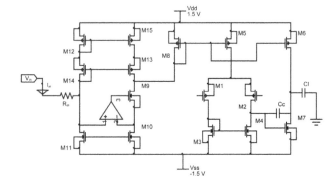

Figure 13. Proposed two-stage operational amplifier with proposed version 1 of V-I converter.

High-Performance CMOS Current Mirrors: Application to Linear Voltage-to-Current Converter Used for
Two-Stage Operational Amplifier

117

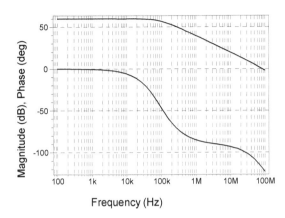

Figure 14. Frequency response of proposed V-I converter.

6. Conclusion

Current mirror play an important role in analog circuits used for V-I converter. This work presents two novels design of V-I converter. The version 1 of V-I converter is implemented in Two-Stage Operational Amplifier. However the version 2 gives high output impedance. The use of version 1 due to its large bandwidth of 750 MHz and gain of 80.2 dB. Simulations results of application of V-I converter in two-stage operational amplifier indicated that phase margin is 62° to ensure a good stability, gain of 60 dB for ±1.5 V, and GBW of 82 MHz.

REFERENCES

[1] M. H. Li and H. L. Kwork, "The Application of Current-Mode Circuits in the Design of an A/D Converter," *IEEE Canadian Conference on Electrical and Computer Engineering*, Vol. 1, 1998, pp. 41-44.

[2] K.-H. Cheng, C.-C. Chen and C.-F. Chung, "Accurate Current Mirror with High Output Impedance," *8th IEEE International Conference Electronics on Circuits and Systems*, Vol. 2, 2001, pp. 565-568.

[3] K.-H. Cheng, T.-S. Chen and C.-W. Kuo, "High Accuracy Current Mirror with Low Settling Time," *Proceedings of the 46th IEEE International Midwest Symposium on Circuits and Systems*, Vol. 1, 2003, pp. 189-192.

[4] M. S. Sawant, J. Ramirez-Angulo, A. J. Lopez-Martin and R. G. Carvajal, "New Compact Implementation of a Very High Performance CMOS Current Mirror," *48th Midwest Symposium on Circuits and Systems*, Vol. 1, 2005, pp. 840-842.

[5] J. Ramirez-Angulo, R. G. Carvajal and A. Torralba, "Low Supply Voltage High Performance CMOS Current Mirror with Low Input and Output Voltage Requirements," *IEEE Transactions on Circuits and Systems-II Express Briefs*, Vol. 51, No. 3, 2004, pp. 124-129.

[6] A. N. Mohieldin, E. Sánchez-Sinencio and J. Silva-Martínez, "Nonlinear Effects in Pseudo Differential OTAs with CMFB," *IEEE Transactions on Circuits and Systems-II: Analog and Digital Signal Processing*, Vol. 50, No. 10, 2003, pp. 762-770.

[7] K. tanno, O. Ishizuka and Z. Tang, "Low Voltage and Low Frequency Current Mirror Using a Two-MOS Sub-threshold op-amp," *Electronics Letters*, Vol. 32, No. 7, 1996, pp. 605-606.

[8] V. Srinivasan, R. Chawla and P. Haster, "Linear Current to Voltage and Voltage to Current Converters," *48th Midwest Symposium on Circuits and Systems*, Vol. 1, 2005, pp. 675-678.

[9] B. H. Soni and R. N. Dhavse, "Design of Operational Transconductance Amplifier Using 0.35 μm Technology," *International Journal of Wisdom Based Computing*, Vol. 1, No. 2, 2011, pp. 28-31.

[10] M. M. Amourach and R. L. Geiger, "Gain and Bandwidth Boosting Techniques for High-Speed Operational Amplifiers," *IEEE International Symposium on Circuits and Systems*, Vol. 1, 2001, pp. 232-235.

18

An Analytical Approach for Fast Automatic Sizing of Narrow-Band RF CMOS LNAs with a Capacitive Load[*]

Jin Young Choi

Electronic & Electrical Engineering Department, Hongik University, Jochiwon, South Korea

ABSTRACT

We introduce a fast automatic sizing algorithm for a single-ended narrow-band CMOS cascode LNA with a capacitive load based on an analytical approach without any optimization procedure. Analytical expressions for principle parameters are derived based on an ac equivalent circuit. Based on the analytical expressions and the power-constrained noise optimization criteria, the automatic sizing algorithm is developed. The algorithm is coded using Matlab, which is shown capable of providing a set of design variable values within seconds. One-time Spectre simulations assuming usage of a commercial 90 nm CMOS process are performed to confirm that the algorithm can provide the aimed first-cut design with a reasonable accuracy for the frequency ranging up to 5 GHz.

Keywords: Automatic Synthesis; Analytical Approach; CMOS LNA; Narrow Band; Cascode

1. Introduction

In the field of RF transceiver design, there is a strong demand to digitalize even RF analog parts to mount a transceiver on a single chip [1,2] to utilize the capability of automatic synthesis in digital circuit design. However, the low noise amplifier (LNA), which is a critical building block in any RF front-end, is not ready for digitalization yet. Many efforts have been done for design automation of LNA beforehand since the design of LNA is a time-consuming task that typically relies heavily on the experience of RF designers. LNA design automation can significantly simplify the design task, and also opens a possibility towards digitalization.

There are two basic methods for LNA design automation: simulation based or equation based. Although the simulation-based methods [3,4] are more accurate, they are time consuming due to optimization procedures. On the other hand, equation-based methods [5-7] are faster, but are dependent on the accuracy of the models used. To overcome the disadvantages in some extent, advanced methods using both of equation-based and simulation-based approaches [8-10] have been also suggested.

The difficulties in design automation of LNA lie in several aspects. It is topology dependent, and the design itself is difficult involving trade-offs among critical figures of merits such as *NF*, power gain, impedance matching, power consumption, linearity, and stability. It is desirable if the first-cut design synthesis can be done automatically and fast with an acceptable accuracy.

A methodology for providing a set of first-cut design variables with a reasonable accuracy for a narrow-band LNA with a resistive load was previously suggested [11].

The purpose of this work is to extend the above methodology to a narrow-band LNA with a capacitive load, which is frequently encountered in front-end design.

In this paper, based on an analytical approach without any optimization procedure, we introduce a speedy automatic sizing algorithm for a single-ended narrow-band cascode LNA adopting inductive source degeneration with a capacitive load. In Section 2, design assumptions are discussed. In Section 3, analytical expressions for principle parameters are derived based on an ac equivalent circuit assuming a capacitive output termination. In Section 4, the developed automatic sizing algorithm is explained. In Section 5, verifications are given to check the accuracy of the automatic sizing results.

2. Design Assumptions

The cascode structure with an inductive source degeneration shown in **Figure 1** is chosen as the objective circuit for automatic sizing.

To avoid any confusion, we show the assumptions made in this work, which are same with those in [11].

1) Narrow-band LC matching networks are used for input and output as shown in **Figure 1**. R_1 is used to provide capability for adjusting power gain. As the output termination, two cases are considered: resistive or capacitive termination.

[*]This work was supported by 2012 Hongik University Research Fund.

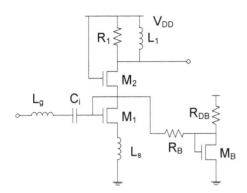

Figure 1. Assumed cascode LNA circuit.

2) For sizing of the MOS transistors M_1 and M_2, the power-constrained noise optimization (PCNO) criteria [12] is adopted to trade off noise performance against power consumption.

3) Ideal inductors and capacitors are used by assuming usage of off-chip components.

4) A current-mirror biasing is adopted as shown in **Figure 1**.

5) The widths of M_1 and M_2 are set as same.

6) The design specifications include operating frequency, input and output terminations, power consumption, power gain, and sufficiently low input and output reflection coefficients S_{11} and S_{22}.

7) The design variables include L_g, L_s, L_1, C_i, R_1, R_{DB}, and R_B including the widths of M_1, M_2, and M_B in **Figure 1**.

3. Derivation of Analytic Expressions for Principal Parameters

3.1. Input Impedance

Figure 2 is the whole ac equivalent circuit for the cascode LNA shown in **Figure 1** including the input signal source and the output capacitive termination C_t. We note

that, compared to the complete equivalent circuit of the BSIM4 NMOS transistor in SPICE, only the back-gate transconductance g_{mb} and the gate-body capacitance C_{gb} in the transistor model are ignored to simplify the analysis. The distributed resistances including R_s, R_d, R_g, and R_{sub}, which are included in the BSIM 4 transistor model, are also ignored since they are negligible in large transistors.

In **Figure 2**, g_{m1} and g_{m2} denote the transconductances of M_1 and M_2, respectively. C_{gs}, C_{gd}, and C_{ds} denote the gate-source, gate-drain, and drain-source capacitances of the NMOS transistors, respectively. C_{js} and C_{jd} denote the source-body and drain-body junction capacitances, and C_L is equal to the sum of C_{dg2} and C_{jd2}, which are the capacitances present at the drain node of M_2 in **Figure 1**.

The impedances Z_{in}, Z_{in1}, Z_{in2}, Z_o, Z_{out}, Z_{out1}, and Z_{out2} are self-defined in the circuit. We note that C_{gs}, C_{gd}, and C_{ds} are replaced by C_{sg}, C_{dg}, and C_{sd}, respectively, in some part of our derivations for input and output impedances considering the non-reciprocal nature of gate-oxide capacitances in the BSIM4 MOSFET capacitance model [13].

First, we derive Z_{in} by deriving Z_o, Z_{in2}, and Z_{in1} in order. We note that, we use s and $j\omega$ without differentiation since we are dealing with ac response only.

$Y_o = 1/Z_o$ is simply expressed as

$$Y_o = \frac{1}{sL_1} + sC_t \qquad (1)$$

Following the same procedure in deriving $Y_{in2} = 1/Z_{in2}$ in [11], we get the same Y_{in2} expression as

$$Y_{in2} = Y_{in21} + s\left(C_{sg2} + C_{js2}\right), \qquad (2)$$

where $Y_{in21} = \dfrac{\left(g_{m2} + g_{ds2} + sC_{sd2}\right)}{1 + \left(g_{ds2} + sC_{sd2}\right)Z_p}$

and $Z_p = (1/sC_L)//R_1//Z_o$.

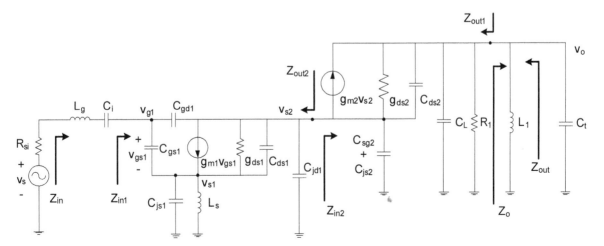

Figure 2. AC equivalent circuit of the cascode LNA in Figure 1.

Following the same procedure in deriving $Y_{in1} = 1/Z_{in1}$ in [11] again, we get the same Y_{in1} expression as

$$Y_{in1} = Y_{in11} + Y_{in12} + Y_{in13} , \qquad (3)$$

where $\quad Y_{in11} = \left(sC_{gs1} + sC_{gd1} \right)$,

$$Y_{in12} = \frac{\left[\begin{array}{l} \left(sC_{gs1} + g_{m1} \right)\left(g_{m1} + g_{ds1} + sC_{ds1} \right) \\ + \left(sC_{gd1} - g_{m1} \right)e_1 \end{array} \right] \cdot sC_{gd1}}{\left(g_{ds1} + sC_{ds1} \right)\left(g_{m1} + g_{ds1} + sC_{ds1} \right) - e_1 e_2} ,$$

$$Y_{in13} = \frac{\left[\begin{array}{l} \left(sC_{gs1} + g_{m1} \right)e_2 + \\ \left(sC_{gd1} - g_{m1} \right)\left(g_{ds1} + sC_{ds1} \right) \end{array} \right] \cdot sC_{gs1}}{\left(g_{ds1} + sC_{ds1} \right)\left(g_{m1} + g_{ds1} + sC_{ds1} \right) - e_1 e_2} ,$$

$$e_1 = \frac{1}{sL_s \; // \; \dfrac{1}{sC_{js1}}} + sC_{gs1} + g_{m1} + g_{ds1} + sC_{ds1} ,$$

$$Y_{out22} = \frac{\left[sC_{sg1}\left(g_{ds1} + sC_{ds1} \right) + sC_{dg1}d_1 \right] \cdot \left(g_{m1} - sC_{dg1} \right)}{d_1 d_2 - sC_{sg1}\left(sC_{sg1} + g_{m1} \right)} ,$$

$$Y_{out23} = -\frac{\left[\left(g_{ds1} + sC_{ds1} \right)d_2 + sC_{dg1}\left(sC_{sg1} + g_{m1} \right) \right]\left(g_{m1} + g_{ds1} + sC_{ds1} \right)}{d_1 d_2 - sC_{sg1}\left(sC_{sg1} + g_{m1} \right)} ,$$

$Y_{out24} = sC_{jd1}$,

$$d_1 = \frac{1}{\dfrac{1}{sC_{js1}} \; // \; sL_s} + sC_{sg1} + g_{m1} + \left(g_{ds1} + sC_{ds1} \right) ,$$

$$d_2 = \frac{1}{Z_i} + sC_{dg1} + sC_{sg1} ,$$

and $\quad Z_i = R_{si} + sL_g + \dfrac{1}{sC_i}$.

$Y_{out1} = 1/Z_{out1}$ is expressed as

$$Y_{out1} = \frac{1}{Z_2} + sC_L + \frac{1}{R_1} , \qquad (6)$$

where $\quad Z_2 = \dfrac{1}{g_{ds2} + sC_{ds2}} + Z_1\left(1 + \dfrac{g_{m2}}{g_{ds2} + sC_{ds2}} \right)$

and $\quad Z_1 = Z_{out2} \; // \; \dfrac{1}{s\left(C_{sg2} + C_{js2} \right)}$.

Then Z_{out} is expressed as

$$Z_{out} = Z_{out1} \; // \; sL_1 . \qquad (7)$$

3.3. Power Gain

To derive the LNA voltage gain, the equivalent circuit in **Figure 2** is simplified into the one shown in **Figure 3**, where the whole circuit is expressed as a 3-stage cas-

$$e_2 = \frac{1}{Z_L} + sC_{gd1} + g_{ds1} + sC_{ds1} ,$$

and $Z_L = (1/(sC_{jd1}))//Z_{in2}$.

Then Z_{in} is expressed as

$$Z_{in} = Z_{in1} + sL_g + \frac{1}{sC_i} . \qquad (4)$$

3.2. Output Impedance

Z_{out} derivation can be done similarly as the Z_{in} derivation using the equivalent circuit in **Figure 2** assuming R_{si} input termination. We present the results here, which are same with those presented in [11].

$Y_{out2} = 1/Z_{out2}$ is expressed as

$$Y_{out2} = Y_{out21} + Y_{out22} + Y_{out23} + Y_{out24} , \qquad (5)$$

where $\quad Y_{out21} = g_{ds1} + sC_{ds1} + sC_{dg1}$,

caded amplifier.

Z_{in1}, Z_{in2} and Z_o in **Figure 3** are already derived in (3), (2) and (1), respectively. Notice that $A_1 v_{g1}$, gZ_{out2}, $A_2 v_{s2}$, and gZ_{out1} are the Thevenin equivalent voltages and impedances of the 2nd and 3rd gain stages in **Figure 2**.

The derivation procedures and the expressions are exactly same with those in [11]. Here we show the expressions.

$$gY_{out2} = \frac{1}{gZ_{out2}} = gY_{out21} + s\left(C_{dg1} + C_{jd1} \right) \qquad (8)$$

$$A_1 = -\frac{\left(sC_{gs1} + g_{m1} \right)\left(g_{m1} + g_{ds1} + sC_{ds1} \right) + \left(sC_{gd1} - g_{m1} \right)f_1}{\left(g_{ds1} + sC_{ds1} \right)\left(g_{m1} + g_{ds1} + sC_{ds1} \right) - f_1 f_2} \qquad (9)$$

where $\quad f_1 = \dfrac{1}{sL_s \; // \; \dfrac{1}{sC_{js1}}} + sC_{gs1} + g_{m1} + g_{ds1} + sC_{ds1}$

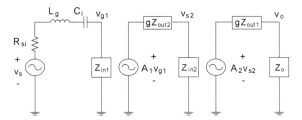

Figure 3. Equivalent circuit to find the voltage gain.

and $f_2 = sC_{jd1} + sC_{gd1} + g_{ds1} + sC_{ds1}$.

$$gZ_{out1} = g_{ds2} + sC_{ds2} + sC_L + \frac{1}{R_1} \qquad (10)$$

$$A_2 \equiv \frac{v_{oo}}{v_{s2}} = \frac{g_{m2} + g_{ds2} + sC_{sd2}}{g_{ds2} + sC_{sd2} + 1 \Big/ \left(\frac{1}{sC_L} // R_1\right)} \qquad (11)$$

In **Figure 2**, the available input power P_i, which is supplied to the LNA when impedance matched, is defined as

$$P_i = \frac{v_s^2}{4R_{si}} . \qquad (12)$$

In a capacitive load case, we can derive the available power gain by assuming an additional imaginary load Z_L connected to the v_o node in **Figure 3**. In this situation, the impedence Z_{pp} seen by Z_L is equal to $gZ_{out1}//Z_o$. When $Z_L = Z_{pp}^*$, the maximum power P_o can be transferred to the load. If we define R_L and R_{pp} are the real parts of Z_L and Z_{pp}, respectively, then P_o can be expressed as

$$P_o = \frac{v_{RL}^2}{R_L} = \frac{v_o^2}{4R_{pp}} . \qquad (13)$$

Then the available power gain G is expressed as

$$G = \frac{P_o}{P_i} = \frac{R_{si}}{R_{pp}} \left(\frac{v_o}{v_s}\right)^2 \qquad (14)$$
$$= \frac{R_{si}}{R_{pp}} \left(\frac{v_{g1}}{v_s} \frac{v_{s2}}{v_{g1}} \frac{v_o}{v_{s2}}\right)^2 \equiv \frac{R_{si}}{R_{pp}} A_{v1}^2 A_{v2}^2 A_{v3}^2,$$

where A_{v1}, A_{v2}, and A_{v3} can be easily derived from **Figure 3** as follows.

$$A_{v1} \equiv \frac{v_{g1}}{v_s} = Z_{in1} \Big/ \left(R_{si} + sL_g + \frac{1}{sC_i} + Z_{in1}\right) \qquad (15)$$

$$A_{v2} \equiv \frac{v_{s2}}{v_{g1}} = A_1 Z_{in2} \Big/ \left(gZ_{out2} + Z_{in2}\right) \qquad (16)$$

$$A_{v3} \equiv \frac{v_o}{v_{s2}} = A_2 Z_o \Big/ \left(gZ_{out1} + Z_o\right) \qquad (17)$$

4. Automatic Sizing Algorithm

Figure 4 shows the automatic sizing algorithm developed in this work. Here, we explain the procedures from top to bottom.

4.1. 1st Step: Entering Design and Process Specifications

The 1st step in the automatic sizing is to enter the design and process specifications. The design specifications

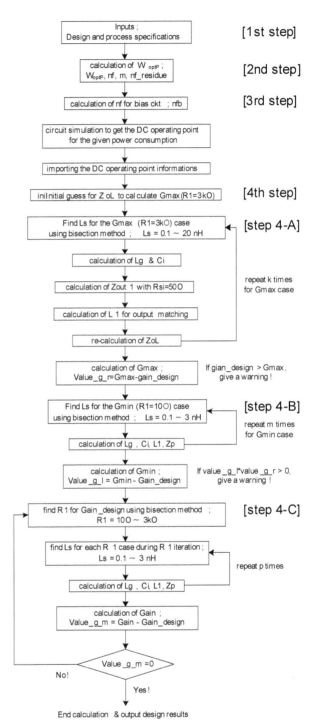

Figure 4. Automatic sizing algorithm.

include the operating frequency f, the input output terminations R_{si} and R_{so}, the supply current I_{DD}, the desired power gain Gain_design. Instead of I_{DD}, the power consumption PWR and the supply voltage V_{DD} can be entered to calculate I_{DD} by PWR/V_{DD}. The process specifications include the transistor channel length L, the transistor channel width per finger WF, and the maximum finger number nf_max defined for one unit of transistors.

4.2. 2nd Step: Calculation of Optimum Transistor Width

The next step is to calculate the transistor channel width W for optimum noise performance. The power-constrained noise optimization device width W_{optP} [12] is adopted as W in this work. W_{optP} is calculated according to the last rough equation in (18).

$$W_{optP} = \frac{3}{2} \frac{1}{\omega L C_{ox} R_{si} Q_{sp}} \approx \frac{1}{3\omega L C_{ox} R_{si}} \qquad (18)$$

As shown in (18), W_{optP} increases continuously as the frequency decreases. Therefore it may be necessary to define a maximum value for W considering lower frequency design. We suggest to limit W below 1000 μm.

If W_F and nf_max are defined, the finger number nf is first calculated as W/W_F, and the number of the maximum-fingered units m is calculated as the integer value of nf/nf_max, and the residual finger number nf_residue is determined as the residue to give an information for the transistor layout. Then the final W is determined by $W = W_F \times (m \times$ nf_max + nf_residue$)$. We note that W_F and nf_max are usually defined in most of recent processes.

4.3. 3rd Step: Calculation of Bias Circuit Design Variables and Getting DC Operating Point

The next step is to determine the bias circuit variable values and to get the dc operating point information.

The finger number for the bias transistor nfb and the drain bias resistance R_{DB} in **Figure 1** should be determined. By limiting the bias circuit current around 100 μA, for example, we can determine nfb by nfb = (100 μA/I_{DD}) × nf. For the decoupling resistor R_B, we can simply use 5 kΩ, which is a reasonable value.

The next procedure is to determine R_{DB}, which, however, is very difficult to determine by calculation. Since I_{DD} is sensitive to the value of R_{DB}, it should be manually determined to give the specified I_{DD} value by dc circuit simulations. This procedure is one obstacle against full design automation in this work. However, it is an essential procedure since it provides the accurate operating point information to proceed with the remaining part of the design automation. The needed operating point information include the values of g_m, g_{ds}, C_{gs}, C_{sg}, C_{gd}, C_{dg}, C_{ds}, C_{sd}, C_{js}, and C_{jd} of M_1 and M_2 in **Figure 1**, which should be imported into the automatic sizing algorithm.

4.4. 4th Step: Iterations to Determine Design Variable Values

There are three main iteration loops in the automatic sizing algorithm as shown in **Figure 4**. The 1st loop finds G_{max}, which corresponds to the case with the upper limit of R_1, which is chosen arbitrarily large enough as 3 kΩ in this work. We note that this value is smaller than 10 kΩ compared to the 50 Ω resistive load case in [11] since it is easier to get a higher gain in the capacitive load case. To find G_{max}, we need to find all the design variable values for the G_{max} case simultaneously. Iteration is needed since the input and output matching designs affect each other. The 2nd loop finds G_{min}, which corresponds to the case with the lower limit of R_1, which is arbitrarily chosen small as 10 Ω in this work to allow a larger allowable gain range. This iteration is also needed for the same reason explained for the G_{max} case. The 3rd loop finds the proper R_1 value for the desired gain Gain_design by the bisection method, which lies within the lower and upper boundaries G_{min} and G_{max}, and its inner loop finds the corresponding design variable values for the present gain value during iteration similarly as in the 1st and 2nd iteration loops.

A. Iterations to Solve for the G_{max} Case

As explained above, Z_{in1} is affected by output matching design, and Z_{out} is affected by input matching design. Therefore we need some iteration to determine L_s. Since Z_{in2} is affected by Z_o, which is unknown yet, we need an initial guess for Z_o to find the 1st L_s value. As shown in **Figure 4**, an initial guess for $Z_{oL} = Z_o//(1/sC_L)$ is given as $200/g_{m2}$, which is shown to be large enough for all possible situations in the procedure, to solve for Z_{in2} by (2). We note that the initial guess is much larger than that for the resistive load case, which is due to the larger magnitude of the output node impedance.

The impedance seen at the gate of M_1 is equal to Z_{in1}, which is derived in (3). By setting the real part of Z_{in1} Re(Z_{in1}) equal to R_{si} for input impedance matching, we can find L_s. However this equation Re(Z_{in1}) = R_{si} is too complicated to get the solution directly with the other present design variables values given, and therefore L_s is solicited numerically within the lower and upper boundaries of 0.1 nH and 20 nH. We use the bisection method for this purpose.

The next procedure is to calculate L_g and C_i, which nullify the imaginary part of Z_{in1} Im(Z_{in1}) in **Figure 2**. Z_{in1} is usually capacitive to give a negative value for Im(Z_{in1}), and therefore L_g can be calculated using the equation Im(Z_{in1}) $- 1/(\omega C_i) + \omega L_g = 0$, where C_i is simply a large dc blocking capacitor. We first calculate L_{g1}, which nullifies Im(Z_{in1}) using Im(Z_{in1}) $+ \omega L_{g1} = 0$. Although C_i is larger the better, considering the layout size, $1/(\omega C_i) = \omega L_{g1}/10$ is used to determine C_i. L_g is then recalculated using Im(Z_{in1}) $- 1/(\omega C_i) + \omega L_g = 0$.

Depending on to the operating frequency and the desired gain, Z_{in1} may happen to be inductive, or this situation can happen in the middle of the iterations. For this case, a nominal single bond wire inductance of 1 nH is assumed for L_g and $\text{Im}(Z_{in1}) - 1/\omega C_i + \omega L_g = 0$ is used to calculate the required C_i value.

In the next procedure, the design variable L_1 should be determined, which gives rise to a maximum gain.

The total admittance YY at the output (v_o) node in **Figure 2** is equal to $Y_{out1} + 1/(sL_1) + sC_t$. By recognizing a maximum voltage output is obtained at the output resonance condition, the required L_1 value is the one which gives rise to a zero imaginary value of YY. This ends up with the L_1 expression as

$$L_1 = \frac{1}{\omega\left[\text{Im}\left(Y_{out1}\right) + C_t\right]}. \tag{19}$$

Now the 1st set of the design variable values are ready to update Z_{oL} and the remaining iterations are performed to find the final design variable values for the G_{max} case. It was found that the iteration number for this loop should be larger than 10.

Right after the iteration loop, A_1, gZ_{out2}, A_2, and gZ_{out1} are calculated using (9), (8), (11), and (10), respectively, and G_{max} is calculated using (14).

If the G_{max} value is smaller than the desired gain, the routine gives a warning and stops.

B. Iterations to Solve for the G_{min} Case

The 2nd loop finds the design variable values for the G_{min} case. The same iteration as above with the last Z_{oL} value as an initial guess is performed to find G_{min} using (14) again.

C. Iterations to Solve for the Gain_design Case

The 3rd loop finds the proper R_1 value for the desired gain Gain_design using the bisection method while the inner loop finds the corresponding design variable values for the present gain value. This inner iteration loop is exactly same as the 1st and 2nd loops. After all the design variables are determined for the present gain value, the gain is calculated using (25) again. If the calculated gain is equal to Gain_design within the allowed tolerance, the calculation stops to output the final set of the design variable values, which include W, nf, m, nf_residue, nfb, L_s, L_g, C_i, R_1, and L_1.

5. Verifications

The automatic sizing algorithm explained in Section 4 was coded using Matlab (Version 7.9.0.529) assuming usage of a 90 nm commercial CMOS process. The design variable sets for seven different operating frequencies ranging from 0.5 GHz to 5 GHz were synthesized, and verifications were done by one-time Spectre circuit simulations with the corresponding BSIM4.5.0 MOSFET model [13] for the assumed process.

The process specifications include $L = 75$ nm, $W_F = 3$

µm, and nf_max = 64, where 75 nm for L is the effective channel length in this process. The maximum transistor width was set as W_{max} = nf_max × m × W_F = 64 × 5 × 3 µm = 960 µm, which is below 1000 µm as we suggested.

When the output is terminated by a capacitor, we encounter a difficulty to monitor the output matching and power gain in measurement. Therefore it is customary to connect a dummy source follower output stage for measurement purpose as shown in **Figure 5**. We note that the situation of the output node of M_2 in this case is similar to the one in an LNA connected directly to a mixer in a same chip, which is the capacitive load case we are discussing here. Therefore, for the simulation setup for verification, we also added the source follower to monitor the output matching and power gain as shown in **Figure 5**. The output impedance of the source follower was adjusted to around 50 Ω regardless of the operating frequency, which is same with the assumed value of R_{so}. The dc blocking capacitor at the output was set very large as 1000 pF to eliminate any effect on the circuit in simulations.

To select the design specification value for C_t, we monitored the admittance Y_{11} seen at the input of the source follower in **Figure 5** by circuit simulations, which were done separately but maintaining the same bias point setup and the same output termination as those in the whole circuit simulation. **Table 1** shows the calculated parallel resistance and capacitance values calculated from the simulated Y_{11} values for the frequency range from 0.3 GHz to 5 GHz. From the results in **Table 1**, we concluded that the equivalent circuit of the source follower can be approximated by a simple capacitor of 93 fF since the parallel R_p values are large enough with fortune.

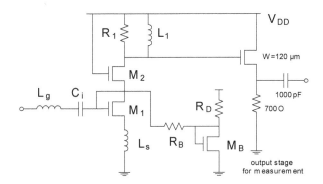

Figure 5. LNA circuit for verification in case of the capacitive output termination.

Table 1. Equivalent parallel R and C values of the source follower stage in Figure 5 as a function of frequency.

f [GHz]	0.3	1	2	3	4	5
C_p [fF]	92.9	93.2	93.0	92.9	92.8	92.7
R_p [kΩ]	11,400	253	59.8	26.3	14.8	9.4

This situation coincides with the design objective we are focusing on here, which is the design of LNA with a capacitive load.

Verifications were done with the same automatic sizing algorithm explained in Section 4.

Design specifications include I_D = 5 mA, V_{DD} = 1.2 V, Gain_design = 25 dB, R_{si} = 50 Ω, and C_t = 93 fF. We ignored the loss in the source follower stage to regard S_{21} of the whole circuit as the power gain of the LNA without the source follower. Therefore we can expect the power gain will be slightly larger than the simulated S_{21} values.

We did not include the power consumed in the source follower stage as the total power consumption since it is used only for measurement purpose.

As an example of the verifications, **Figure 6** shows the simulated LNA characteristics without any tuning for the operating frequency of 2 GHz, when the corresponding set of the design variable values obtained using the automatic sizing algorithm are used for the simulation. The synthesized design variable values are R_{DB} = 9.9 kΩ, W = 576 μm (m = 3, nf_residue = 0), nfb = 4, L_s = 1.4693 nH,

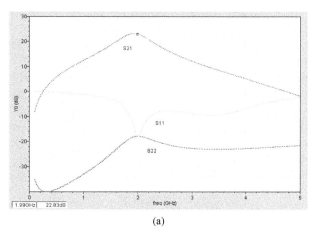

(a)

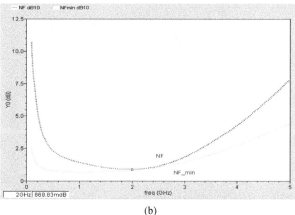

(b)

Figure 6. Simulated (a) S parameter and (b) Noise characteristics for f = 2 GHz and Gain_design = 25dB: S_{21} = 22.74 dB, NF = 0.870 dB, NF_{min} = 0.790 dB, S_{11} = −17.8 dB, S_{22} = −18.0 dB.

L_g = 6.868 nH, C_i = 10.14 pF, R_1 = 631.4 Ω, and L_1 = 11.713 nH. As expected with the source follower output stage adopted, S_{22} stays low for the whole frequency range.

Table 2 summarizes the simulated results of the designs for for Gain_design of 25dB for the frequency range from 0.5 GHz to 5 GHz.

In **Table 2**, the loss in the source follower seems negligible as desired, which is evident from the result for the 0.8 GHz design. We can see that the input and output matchings are reasonably good in the lower frequencies, but is not good enough in the higher frequencies, especially in the output matching. This may be caused by approximating the equivalent circuit of the source follower by a single capacitor of 93 fF in the syntheses by neglecting the smaller parallel resistance in higher frequencies shown in **Table 1**. If this is the case, we can say this discrepancy is caused by assigning the load improperly, which is not related to the adequacy of the synthesis algorithm. The S_{21} values in **Table 2** are smaller than the desired gain of 25 dB in the higher frequency range. However we believe that the result is pretty good for the first-cut quick design.

Table 3 summarizes the synthesized available gain ranges with the corresponding R_1 values for each design. For the operating frequency below 1 GHz, the synthesized device width is constrained as 960 μm, which is set as maximum, and decreases with frequency as expected.

Table 2. Simulation summary for the desired gain Gain_design of 25 dB.

f [GHz]	W [μm]	S_{21} [dB]	S_{11} [dB]	S_{22} [dB]	NF [dB]	NF_{min} [dB]
0.5	960	22.6	−19.0	−55.1	1.13	0.564
0.7	960	24.30	−21.1	−35.4	0.792	0.562
0.8	960	24.76	−21.1	−30.5	0.727	0.569
1	960	24.51	−19.6	−24.9	0.698	0.610
2	576	22.74	−17.8	−18.0	0.870	0.790
3	384	22.20	−16.5	−14.2	1.040	0.931
4	291	21.56	−14.9	−11.3	1.160	1.040
5	231	20.96	−13.9	−9.5	1.340	1.180

Table 3. Synthesis summary for the available gain ranges with the corresponding R_1 values.

f [GHz]	W [μm]	S_{21} [dB]	R_1 [Ω]
0.5	960	13.8 - 30.0	10.1 - 735
0.7	960	11.0 - 27.3	10.2 - 632
0.8	960	9.8 - 26.8	10.1 - 734
1	960	8.0 - 28.3	10.2 - 2.72 k
2	576	5.9 - 27.8	10.2 - 1.54 k
3	384	5.2 - 27.7	10.4 - 1.90 k
4	291	4.3 - 27.4	10.4 - 2.17 k
5	231	4.1 - 27.3	10.4 - 2.41 k

6. Conclusions

The analytical expressions for the principle parameters were derived using the ac equivalent circuit of the single-ended narrow-band cascode CMOS LNA with a capacitive load. Based on the expressions, the automatic sizing algorithm was developed by adopting the power-constrained noise optimization criteria. The algorithm was coded using Matlab, and could provide a set of design variable values within seconds. One-time Spectre simulations without any tuning assuming usage of a commercial 90 nm CMOS process were performed to confirm that the automatic sizing program can synthesize the aimed first-cut design with a reasonable accuracy for the frequency range reaching up to 5 GHz.

This work showed in detail how the accurate automatic sizing can be done in an analytical approach. The approach can be applied to a common source LNA more easily since the derivation of principal parameters will be simpler with a fewer gain stages. It can be also applied to a differential LNA easily since the derivation will be basically same.

REFERENCES

[1] K. Muhammad, R. B. Staszewski and D. Leipold, "Digital RF Processing: Toward Low-Cost Reconfigurable Radios," *IEEE Communications Magazine*, Vol. 43, No. 8, 2005, pp. 105-113.

[2] A. A. Abidi, "The Path to the Software-Defined Radio Receiver," *IEEE Journal of Solid-State Circuits*, Vol. 42, No. 5, 2007, pp. 954-966.

[3] G. Zhang, A. Dengi and L. R. Carley, "Automatic Synthesis of A 2.1 GHz SiGe Low Noise Amplifier," *Proceedings of IEEE Rado Frequency Integrated Circuits Symposium*, Seattle, 2-4 June 2002, pp. 125-128.

[4] M. Chu and D. J. Allstot, "An Elitist Distributed Particle Swarm Algorithm for RF IC Optimization," *Proceedings of Asia South Pacific Design Automation Conference*, Shanghai, 18-21 January 2005, pp. 671-674.

[5] P. Vancorenland, C. De Ranter, M. Steyaert and G. Gielen, "Optimal RF Design Using Smart Evolutionary Algorithms," *Proceedings of Design Automation Conference*, Los Angeles, 4-8 June 2000, pp. 7-10.

[6] G. Tulunay and S. Balkır, "A Compact Optimization Methodology for Single-Ended LNA," *Proceedings of IEEE International Symposium Circuits and Systems*, Geneva, 23-26 May 2004, pp. 273-276.

[7] T.-K. Nguyen, C.-H. Kim, G.-J. Ihm, M.-S. Yang and S.-G. Lee, "CMOS Low-Noise Amplifier Design Optimization Techniques," *IEEE Transactions on Microwave Theory and Technique*, Vol. 52, No. 5, 2004, pp. 1433-1442.

[8] G. Tulunay and S. Balkir, "Automatic Synthesis of CMOS RF Front-Ends," *Proceedings of IEEE International Symposium Circuits and Systems*, Island of Kos, 21-24 May 2006, pp. 625-628.

[9] A. Nieuwoudt, T. Ragheb and Y. Massoud, "SOC-NLNA: Synthesis and Optimization for Fully Integrated Narrow-Band CMOS Low Noise Amplifiers," *Proceedings of Design Automation Conference*, San Francisco, 24-28 July 2006, pp. 879-884.

[10] W. Cheng, A. J. Annema and B. Nauta, "A Multi-Step P-Cell for LNA Design Automation," *Proceedings of IEEE International Symposium Circuits and Systems*, Seattle, 18-21 May 2008, pp. 2550-2553.

[11] J. Y. Choi, "An Aanalytical Approach for Fast Automatic Sizing of Narrow-Band RF CMOS LNAs," *Circuits and Systems*, Vol. 3, No. 2, 2012, pp. 136-145.

[12] T. H. Lee, "The Design of CMOS Radio-Frequency Integrated Circuits," 2nd Edition, Cambridge University Press, Cambridge, 2004.

[13] "BSIM4.5.0 MOSFET Model, User's Manual," University of California, Berkeley, 2004.

19

A Power Grid Optimization Algorithm by Direct Observation of Manufacturing Cost Reduction

Takayuki Hayashi[1], Yoshiyuki Kawakami[1], Masahiro Fukui[2]
[1]Graduate School of Science and Engineering, Ritsumeikan University, Kusatsu, Japan
[2]Department of VLSI System Design, Ritsumeikan University, Kusatsu, Japan

ABSTRACT

With the recent advances of the VLSI technologies, stabilizing the physical behavior of VLSI chips is becoming a very complicated problem. Power grid optimization is required to minimize the risks of timing error by IR drop, defects by electro migration (EM), and manufacturing cost by the chip size. This problem includes complicated tradeoff relationships. We propose a new approach by observing the direct objectives of manufacturing cost, and timing error risk caused by IR drop and EM. The manufacturing cost is based on yield for LSI chip. The optimization is executed in early phase of the physical design, and the purpose is to find the rough budget of decoupling capacitors that may cause block size increase. Rough budgeting of the power wire width is also determined simultaneously. The experimental result shows that our approach enables selection of a cost sensitive result or a performance sensitive result in early physical design phase.

Keywords: Power Grid Optimization; Manufacturing Cost; Timing Violation; Decoupling Capacitor

1. Introduction

With the advent of super deep submicron technologies, designing stable and dependable physical behavior of LSIs is becoming very difficult and serious problems, due to the IR-drop and the EM. Insertion of decupling capacitances and making wider the power grid wires are most effective for this purpose, but we must pay area penalty which causes cost increase. Conventional approaches [1,2] deal with the chip area or the IR drop as their design constraint or objective function. However, no designer can say adequate goal of the chip area without detailed statistical data about the relations between the chip area and the manufacturing cost. Similarly, no designer can say adequate value of the IR drop constraint without detailed statistical data about the relations between the IR drop and timing error risks. Only experienced manager can indicate those goals and suitable values. Without considering that the manufacturing cost increases exponentially as the chip area increase, it is difficult to develop effective optimization system. Furthermore, there is another aspect of the design optimization. Many conventional power grid optimization algorithms have been proposed [1-5]. But most of them select one metric from IR-drop, EM, wiring congestion, or area. Then it is used for their objective function of the optimization, and other metrics are selected as their constraint

function. We introduced in [6] a new concept of a risk function to deal with those different characteristics of metrics at the natural process of the optimization schedule. Furthermore, we introduced a timing error risk as a direct metrics for optimization instead of IR drop in [7].

In this paper we propose a new efficient and effective power optimization algorithm, appropriate for current large scale chips. It deals directly with the manufacturing cost, which is calculated by the chip area increase caused by inserting the decoupling capacitors. The main design steps of VLSI are composed of system level design, function/logic design, and physical design. The area and timing can be dealt with the physical design phase. Especially, the manufacturing cost information is more effectively optimized in the early physical design phase called floor planning because there is more freedom of shape and size selection of the functional blocks. To reduce the design turnaround time, the power grid optimization is usually divided into two steps, high-level power grid optimization and detailed power grid optimization. The insertion of decoupling capacitors is executed in the high-level optimization to abstracted power grids. After the area of each block is fixed, the detailed power grid optimization makes detailed power grid physical patterns.

Our target is "power grid resource budgeting" in early physical design phase. The power grid resource includes both of power supply/ground lines and decoupling capacitors. The advantage of our approach is to optimize power/ground supply lines roughly and to insert decoupling capacitors analyzing trade-off between the yield for LSI chip and a manufacturing cost. Since the ground wiring can be treated as well as the power wiring, in the following description, we will explain using only the power supply wiring. As a result, the unnecessary cost can be eliminated from early design phase, and LSI's design becomes more sophisticated. That is to say, not only the cost of a chip but also IR-drop, EM and wiring congestion are considered simultaneously in this optimization.

The rest of this paper is organized as follows. We discuss the layout model which enables the design exploration in high-level floor-plan in Section 2. In Section 3, we briefly summarize the optimization flow that enables simultaneous optimization of multi-objective optimization. In Section 4, we explain an important concept of risk function which is introduced in the optimization algorithm. The risk function is defined for each objective, the wiring congestion, the EM, the timing error due to IR drop, and the chip cost. Most of these are already proposed in other papers [6,7]. Thus, we spend more space to the chip cost risk. It represents the manufacturing cost characteristic which is associated with the chip area. In Section 5, experimental results are showed and the effectiveness of our proposed algorithm is discussed. The conclusion is stated in Section 6.

2. Layout Model

A power grid model and block layer model are shown in **Figure 1**. The power grid formed the mesh has two-layer structure, the horizontal and the vertical layer. These layers are connected with vias. The power grid optimization is performed by not only changing power wiring width [4] but also insertion of decoupling capacitors. Insertion of decoupling capacitors is effective for reducing IR-drop and inductor noise. Decoupling capacitors are placed in spare area in the block layer [3]. Block layer is mainly covered with standard cells. The ratio of the spare area is preset as the limitation which is able to place decoupling capacitors. The chip area is not increased by insertion of the capacitors if they were placed in the spare area. However the optimization algorithm may require additional decoupling capacitors by increasing the block size. It is necessary to consider resulting in manufacturing cost increase.

3. Multi-Objective Optimization Flow

Power grid optimization is a multi-objective optimization problem. We want to optimize many objectives, IR drop, EM, chip area, wiring congestion and so on simultane-

ously. It is, generally, a very difficult problem. One reason is that each objective has different dimension. Second reason is that each of them has a different characteristic curve. We have introduced a new concept of risk functions to deal with those different characteristics at the natural process of the optimization schedule [6,7]. The risk function represents dangerous condition of LSI implementation by using 0% to 100%. Each objective is converted into the same dimension of risk using the risk function. The shape of the risk function should be carefully defined. The combination of IR drop risk, EM, and wiring congestion risk is defined for each grid. Detail definition of the risk functions are stated in [7]. The risk value of the chip area is stated in this paper. The effectiveness is also shown in the section of experimental results.

Figure 2 shows a flow of the power grid optimization. The optimization is scheduled with the gradient method. First, the power grid circuit is constructed with an RC network and initial values of the circuit elements are given (STEP 1). The dynamic current consumption of each functional block is pre-determined by an RTL power simulation. It is represented as current sources connecting the power grid nodes of the corresponding area. Then, voltage and current of each nodes and edges are calculated by dynamic circuit simulation (STEP 2). Next, a risk value of each grid is calculated (STEP 3). And the worst and four random grids are selected as the candidates of that they may be improved (STPE 4). Then for each candidate grid, the improvement operation *i.e.*, change of power wiring width or insertion of decoupling capacitors, is examined (STEP 5). And a combination of selection of grids which has the highest value of the evaluation function is selected. If the value of the evaluation

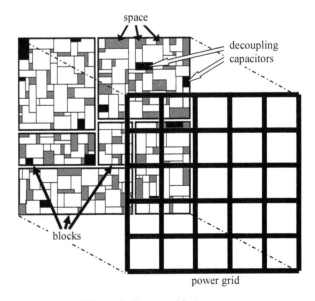

Figure 1. Power grid structure.

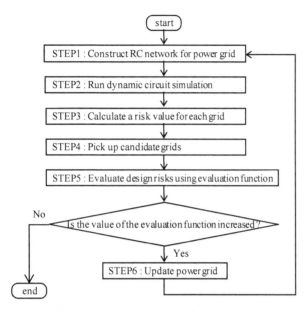

Figure 2. Power grid optimization flow.

function is increased, the power grid by change of power wiring width and insertion of decoupling capacitors is updated (STEP 6). These operations are repeated as long as the value of the evaluation function is improved.

4. Risk Functions

4.1. Manufacturing Cost Risk Function

This chapter explains the relation between chip area and manufacturing cost. We begin with the definition of yield and critical area, and then we discuss about the manufacturing cost risk. The calculation accuracy of manufacturing cost has been increased by using exact critical area and by revealing the relation between critical area and chip area.

4.1.1. Yield

When chip area size increases, the number of chips produced from one slice of wafer decreases. In addition, defective chips due to dust increase. Therefore, we consider a ratio of the number of the good chips which is produced by one slice of wafer. This ratio is called "yield". The yield equation for LSI chip refers to [8,9]. Equation (1) is the yield function and **Figure 3** shows the yield curve. The D_0 is the average value of defect density in a unit area and the A_{cr} in the Equation (1) is size of critical area. We explain in detail by the following chapter.

$$Y = e^{-D_0 A_{cr}} \tag{1}$$

4.1.2. Critical Area

Critical area [9] is a layout area which has functional defects caused by particle contamination. Refer to Chapter 2 of [9] for a detailed account of the critical area. The

size of critical area is expressed by Equation (2).

$$A_{cr} = \int_{x_{\min}}^{x_{\max}} A_c(x) f(x) \, dx \tag{2}$$

The A_{cr} is average value of the total of critical area, and it is calculated in critical area for all defect sizes. The $A_c(x)$ is calculated in a critical area for defect size x. The $f(x)$ is the defect size distribution function, and it is defined by Equation (3). The x_0 is defined as a minimum spacing in the design rule of LSI chip.

$$f(x) = \begin{cases} \dfrac{x}{x_0^2} & if \ \ 0 < x \le x_0 \\[2mm] \dfrac{x_0^2}{x^3} & if \ \ x_0 \le x \le x_{\max} \end{cases} \tag{3}$$

Critical area is defined by the sum of short critical area A_{short} and open critical area A_{open}, and is shown in Equation (4).

$$A_c(x) = A_{\text{short}}(x) + A_{\text{open}}(x) \tag{4}$$

The $A_c(x)$ of each defect size is calculated. **Figure 4** shows a short and an open critical area. The functional failure by the short happens when defect size x exceeds the wiring spacing. And the functional failure by the open happens when defect size exceeds the wiring width. They are defined as Equations (5) and (6).

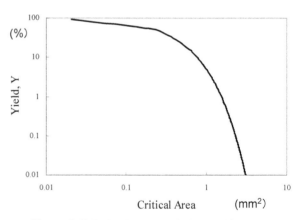

Figure 3. Relation between yield and chip area.

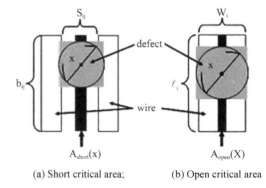

(a) Short critical area;　　　(b) Open critical area

Figure 4. Short and open critical areas.

$$A_{\text{short}} = \begin{cases} 0 & \text{if } x < S_{ij} \\ (x - S_{ij}) \times b_{ij} & \text{if } x \geq S_{ij} \end{cases} \quad (5)$$

$$A_{\text{open}} = \begin{cases} 0 & \text{if } \quad x < W_i \\ (x - W_i) \times \ell_i & \text{if } W_i \leq x \leq x_{\max} \end{cases} \quad (6)$$

An actual signal wire's width and spacing are not uniform. However, this paper's purpose is the power grid optimization in consideration of manufacturing chip cost. Therefore, we define signal wires are arranged at equal interval, and the number of them is defined depending on the wire congestion in an area. **Figure 5** shows the relation between the chip area and the critical area calculated from signal wires that we defined temporarily. $x_{\max}$ of Equation (2) used in this paper defined as a clean level of 0.12 μm.

Generally, if the chip area is only increased without re-design, spacing between the wires will be increased. Thus, critical area does not increase as same ratio as the area increase. It is observed from **Figure 5** that if the chip area is increased three times, the critical area increases about two times. Thus, it is possible to more accurately estimate the chip area, and we can accurately estimate the manufacturing cost described in the next section.

4.1.3. Manufacturing Cost vs Chip Area

The more the chip area increases, the more the yield decreases. The chip cost (=manufacturing cost) function can be represented by the Equation (7).

$$\text{Cost}(A) = \frac{W_{\text{Cost}}}{\dfrac{W_s}{A} \times Y} + a \quad (7)$$

In this Equation, A is a chip area, Y is a yield, W_S is a wafer area, and W_{Cost} is a cost per one wafer. Here, the Y is given by Equation (1). This is influenced by the critical area A_{cr}. Also the A_{cr} is influenced by the chip area A as shown in **Figure 5**. Thus, the Y is a function of A. The term $W_S/A \times Y$ indicates the number of the good quality chips that can be manufactured from one wafer.

The basic cost of the chip is obtained by dividing the W_{Cost} by the term. The parameter a is a cost that does not depends on the chip area. For example, the cost for testing and packaging are included in a. This cost value should be assigned depending on the circuit size and power consumption. The value is not so important for the discussions in this paper, and we set a relatively low cost 25 for a by assuming a low-power and low cost package for our experiment. Consequently the graph of the Equation (7) is shown in **Figure 6**.

We understand that chip costs increase at the same time when chip areas increase, and the area of the chip doesn't necessarily increase because it may be arranged

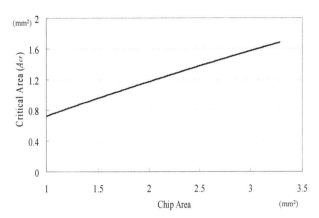

Figure 5. Relation between chip area and critical area.

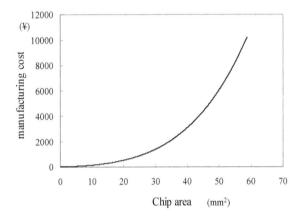

Figure 6. Manufacturing cost and chip area.

in the space margin of the block, even if many decoupling capacitors are arranged. However the chip area increases when more decoupling capacitors are arranged than a certain number. Thus, the chip area is able to be represented by Equation (8).

$$A = S + S_{DC} \times (C_D - C_{D_0}) \quad (8)$$

The S_{DC} is the size of a piece of decoupling capacitor, e.g., 0.05 mm × 0.05 mm, C_D is the total number of decoupling capacitors. The C_{D_0} is the number of decoupling capacitors filled into the space area. No area penalty is paid if the placed decoupling capacitors are less than C_{D_0}. The S is initial chip area without decoupling capacitors.

4.1.4. Manufacturing Cost Risk Definition

Chip area increases depending on a total number of decoupling capacitors. Chip cost is proportional to number of decoupling capacitors. Therefore the manufacturing cost risk function becomes a function to change depending on the number of decoupling capacitors arranged to a chip area. The borderline of whether there is a profitable chip or not depends on the quality of chip design. Thus we define the cost risk R_{cost} by the Equation (9), where-

MAX_{cost} is the border value.

$$R_{cost} = \frac{Cost(A)}{MAX_{cost}} \times 100 \qquad (9)$$

4.2. Timing Error Risk Function

We have used the IR-drop risk function to eliminate the timing error caused by IR-drop. LSI's functional blocks are constructed by a lot of transistors. To supply enough electrical power to the transistors is essential for desirable operation of LSI because their operational speed degradation is caused by significant IR-drop. The low operational speed causes the timing error of the LSI. Hence, we have used "timing error risk function caused by IR drop" such as in **Figure 7**. This risk function defines the value of IR-drop in the horizontal axis and this risk value is defined as R_{ir}. Details are explained in [7].

4.3. EM Risk Function

EM risk represents the danger of EM [6,7]. In super deep submicron technology, wire width of power grid becomes more complicated and narrower, and power consumption of LSI becomes larger due to increased transistors. The narrow wire tends to cut off by high current density so that larger current flows in the power grid. To design a chip which has high reliability, it is essential to eliminate the danger of EM, and so we have formulated EM risk function.

The EM risk function is defined the current density in a horizontal axis and the EM risk value is defined as R_{em} in the vertical axis. The EM risk is defined with the maximum current density, σ_{max}. The value of R_{em} is 100% when current density is σ_{max}. The value of R_{em} is defined 0% when the current density is less than σ_p. The σ_p is shown in the Equation (10). The risk value between σ_{max} and σ_p is used a linear function proportional to current density.

$$\sigma_P = \sigma_{max} \times \gamma \qquad (10)$$

4.4. Wiring Risk Function

Wiring risk represents the danger of unwired failure on power grid. To optimize the power grid, we need to change wire width and insert decoupling capacitors. If the changed wire width is too wide, the LSI chip cannot be designed in desired chip area, and the power grid may become an unfeasible circuit [9]. Thus we have defined wiring risk function to get feasible power grid.

Each grid area includes power supply wires and signal wires. If a ratio of the total wiring area to the grid area increases, unconnected wire may occur. S_g is a grid area, S_p is an area that the power supply wires occupy, S_w is an area of the signal wires, and W_c formulated by Equation (11) represents a ratio of wiring area. The risk value is defined as R_{rw}. When the value of W_c is 0.2 or less, the risk value of R_{rw} is 0. When the value of W_c is 0.6 or more, this risk value of R_{rw} is defined as 100%. The risk value of R_{rw} between 0.2 and 0.6 is represented in shape similar to the EM risk. This function has been obtained by many experimental results.

$$W_c = \frac{S_p + S_w}{S_g} \qquad (11)$$

4.5. Evaluation Function

We define new evaluation function which timing error due to IR-drop, EM, wiring congestion and chip cost are able to be all optimized simultaneously. If one of three risks, timing error, EM and wiring risks, becomes 100%, it is clear not to achieve feasible power grid. Hence we have defined a safety which a risk value is subtracted from 100. We have got a safe function by multiplication of three safeties from timing error, EM and wiring congestion. However, a safety value of manufacturing cost is changed by number of decoupling capacitors arranged in the entire chip. So we have not used manufacturing cost safety to evaluate each grid area. The safety function Safe(B) of a grid area B is shown as follows.

$$\text{Safe}(B) = \frac{(100 - R_{ir})(100 - R_{em})(100 - R_{rw})}{100^2} \qquad (12)$$

Since R_{ir}, R_{em} and R_{rw} are within 0% and 100%, Safe(B) is within 0% and 100%.

We define the evaluation function by a minimum safety value, the sum of safety value of all grids and safety value of manufacturing cost risk. A value of manufacturing cost risk is decided by the number of decoupling capacitors arranged in the whole chip. And a value of cost risk is not derived in each grid. So the manufacturing cost element is not added in the safety function. Instead, we can add a safe degree of manufacturing cost risk to the evaluation function because the evaluation function represents a safety of entire grid area.

Our evaluation function $F(B)$ is defined as follows.

$$F(B) = M \times \min_{B} \text{Safe}(B)$$
$$+ \sum_{B} \text{Safe}(B) + N \times (100 - R_{cost}) \qquad (13)$$

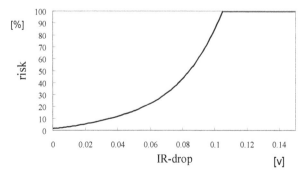

Figure 7. IR-drop Risk Function.

The evaluation function $F(B)$ consists of three of safeties. It is necessary to raise the minimum value of the safety of each grid in order to lead more safely for the entire power grid. The first term (1st safety) is the lowest safety in the entire power grid. The second term (2nd safety) is the total sum of the safety of each grid. A good solution cannot be obtained only by the 2nd safety. The 2nd safety is a role for preceding the optimization schedule smoothly. The reason why M is multiplied to the minimum $Safe(B)$ is to improve a worst evaluated grid preferentially. Thus the M should be a big value to make the 1st safety bigger enough than the 2nd safety. The third tern (3rd safety) is the safety value of the manufacturing cost risk.

The 1st safety and the 3rd safety decide the quality of optimization. That is, by controlling the M and N, it is possible to change the quality of the solution. When N is small enough compared with M, the safe value of the manufacturing cost reached almost to 0, and stop at the manufacturing cost limit. When N is gradually increased, the constraint of the manufacturing cost increases, and the safety of the electric and physical constraints (=1st safety) is slightly lower. **Figure 8** shows a transition of each safety to M/N. The data used is 1.3 mm × 1.3 mm sized circuit data described in the next section.

As shown in **Figure 8**, $N/M = 0.02$ - 0.05 is the range which electrical and physical constraints are dominant because the manufacturing cost does not almost change. On the contrary, $N/M = 0.12$ is the range which the manufacturing cost constraints are dominant. When the adequate values of M and N are selected, tradeoff analysis is performed well, and it is considered to be able to reach better manufacturing cost result still keeping the good electric and physical conditions.

Figures 9-11 show transition of each safety to each M/N. **Figure 10** shows an example when the tradeoff analysis is performed well. When the N is larger enough, only the cost optimization is performed as shown in **Figure 11**. This is the case that we do not expect. We rather expect the case of **Figure 9** or **Figure 10** in general. These can be performed with less computation time of optimization. We may expect the case of **Figure 10** optimally. But it requires try and errors for selection of adequate M and N values to each LSI chip, and takes large computation time.

5. Experimental Results

We have applied to three different sized circuits to show the effectiveness of our proposal technique. $N/M = 0.07$ has used in Equation (13). The experiments are performed on P-4 processor with a speed of 3.4 GHz and 4 GB RAM. The program uses C language.

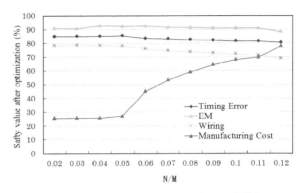

Figure 8. Transition of each safety to M/N.

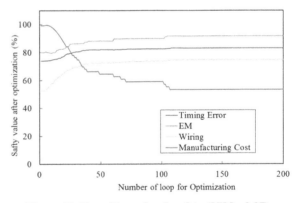

Figure 9. Transition of each safety (N/M = 0.05).

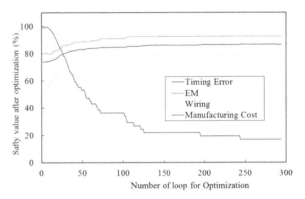

Figure 10. Transition of each safety (N/M = 0.07).

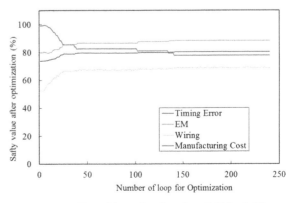

Figure 11. Transition of each safety (N/M = 0.12).

The effects of safety improvement are shown in **Table 1**. In the table, "Average safety" is the average safety in the entire chip. IR-drop, EM, wiring and manufacturing cost have been all optimized in this experimentation.

For example, Transition of each safety for CHIP 1 is shown in **Figure 10**. Safety of the manufacturing cost has deteriorated from start to about ten times optimization because the priorities of IR-drop, EM and wiring are higher than the manufacturing cost. However, the safety of manufacturing cost is improved later and finally stabilized on about 100 times in this case. As a result, manufacturing cost is slightly higher, but electrical constraints, IR-drop and EM are satisfied with all. The reason with sufficient electric constraints is an effect of insertion of decoupling capacitors. The distribution of decoupling capacitors placed on chip after the optimization of power grid is shown in **Figure 12**.

Although the processing time of CHIP 1 is 104 sec in **Table 1**, CHIP 3 reaches about 38 times longer than CHIP 1. There is room for improvement for the chip size.

Risk distributions of the whole circuit before and after optimization for CHIP 1 are shown in **Figure 13**. From **Figure 9**, safe degree of EM comes up to the upper limit value soon after the optimization starts. IR-drop and EM risk values are noticeable at grids of both (1,1) and (6,6) in **Figures 13(a)** and **(b)**. Because two power supply resources are connected to the points. They have no voltage drop due to the power supply connections, but EM risk is high because a large current density flows there. The placement of decoupling capacitors has also the same tendency as EM in **Figure 13(b)**. Not so many decoupling capacitors are placed around the power supply resources, and the number of the capacitors increases on the area far away from the power sources.

Table 1. Result of power grid optimization for 3 chips.

Name	Size (mm²)	IR-drop		EM		Wiring		Manufacturing cost	Runtime (sec)
		Average Safety	Improvement (%)	Average Safety	Improvement (%)	Average Safety	Improvement (%)	Increased cost ratio (%)	
CHIP 1	1.3 × 1.3	83.1	9.1	91.7	11.6	74.6	22.1	11.5	104
CHIP 2	5 × 5	79.8	3.6	99.5	0.1	43.2	6.8	3.5	2322
CHIP 3	10 × 10	79.5	5.5	99.9	0.1	39.8	5.7	5.5	38,403

Figure 12. Placement distribution of decoupling capacitors for CHIP 1.

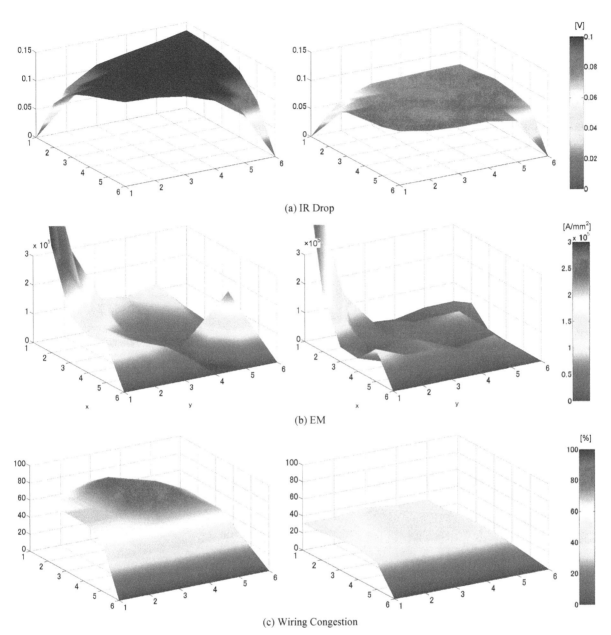

(a) IR Drop

(b) EM

(c) Wiring Congestion

Figure 13. Optimization results for CHIP 1.

6. Conclusion

We have proposed a methodology to optimize a power grid system in the floor plan for the physical design phase. Our approach can consider the risk of physical constraints and timing errors simultaneously, such as IR drop, EM and manufacturing cost. In particular, the manufacturing cost is calculated based on chip yield. In addition, since considering placement of decoupling capacitance at the same time in the chip, power wiring strong against EM noise can be constructed. The experimental results have shown that power wiring optimization can be done while taking the balance of chip reliability and manufacturing cost. However, relatively large chip such as the 10×10 mm^2 will require longer processing time. A key issue for the future is speed up.

REFERENCES

[1] H. Su, K. H. Gala and S. S. Sapatnekar, "Fast Analysis and Optimization of Power/Ground Networks," *International Conference on Computer Aided Design*, San Jose, 5-9 November 2000, pp. 477-480.

[2] K. Wang and M. M. Sadowska, "On-Chip Power Supply Network Optimization Using Multigrid-Based Technique," *IEEE Transactions on Computer-Aided Design of Integrated Circuits and Systems*, Vol. 24, No. 3, 2005, pp. 407-417.

[3]   J. Fu, Z. Luo, X. Hong, Y. Cai, S. X.-D. Tan and Z. Pan, "A Fast Decoupling Capacitor Budgeting Algorithm for Robust On-Chip Power Delivery," *Proceedings of the Asia and South Pacific Design Automation Conference*, Yokohama, 27-30 January 2004, pp. 505-510.

[4]   T.-Y. Wang and C. C.-P. Chen, "Optimization of the Power/Ground Network Wire-Sizing and Spacing Based on Sequential Network Simplex Algorithm," *Proceedings of International Symposium on Quality Electronic Design*, San Jose, 21 March 2002, pp. 157-162.

[5]   X. Wu, X. Hon, Y. Ca, C. K. Cheng, J. Gu and W. Dai, "Area Minimization of Power Distribution Network Using Efficient Nonlinear Programming Techniques," *International Conference on Computer Aided Design*, San Jose, 4-8 November 2001, pp. 153-157.

[6]   H. Ishijima, K. Kusano, T. Harada, Y. Kawakami and M. Fukui, "An Algorithm for Power Grid Optimization Based on Dynamic Current Consumption," *International Association of Science and Technology for Development on Circuits, Signals and Systems*, Vol. 531, 2006, pp. 114-119.

[7]   Y. Kawakami, M. Terao, M. Fukui and S. Tsukiyama, "A Power Grid Optimization Algorithm by Observing Timing Error Risk by IR Drop," *The IEICE Transactions on Fundamentals of Electronics, Communications and Computer Sciences*, Vol. E91-A, No. 12, 2008, pp. 3423-3430.

[8]   The Institute of Electronics and Communication Engineers, "LSI Handbook," Ohmsha, 1984.

[9]   C.-C. Chiang and J. Kawa, "Design for Manufacturability and Yield for Nano-Scale CMOS," Springer, Berlin, 2007.

20

Grounded and Floating Inductance Simulation Circuits Using VDTAs

Dinesh Prasad[*], D. R. Bhaskar

Department of Electronics and Communication Engineering, Faculty of Engineering and Technology,
Jamia Millia Islamia, New Delhi, India

ABSTRACT

New electronically-controllable lossless grounded and floating inductance simulation circuits have been proposed employing Voltage Differencing Transconductance Amplifiers (VDTA). The proposed grounded inductance (GI) circuit employs a single VDTA and one grounded capacitor whereas the floating inductance (FI) circuit employs two VDTAs and one grounded capacitor. The workability of the new circuits has been verified using SPICE simulation with TSMC CMOS 0.18 μm process parameters.

Keywords: VDTA; Inductance Simulation; Filters

1. Introduction

Several circuits and techniques for the simulation of grounded and floating inductance employing different active elements such as operational amplifiers, current conveyors, current controlled conveyors, current feedback operational amplifiers, operational mirrored amplifiers, differential voltage current conveyors, current differencing buffered amplifiers, current differencing transconductance amplifiers, operational transconductance amplifiers (OTAs) have been reported in the literature see [1-33] and the references cited therein. Many active elements have been introduced by Biolek, Senani, Biolkova and Kolka in [34], VDTA is one of them. A CMOS realization of VDTA and its filter application have also been reported in [35]. The purpose of this pa- per is, to propose new electronically-controllable VDTA- based lossless GI and FI circuits employing a grounded capacitor. The GI uses only one VDTA along with a grounded capacitor and does not require any matching condition whereas FI employs two VDTAs, a grounded capacitor and requires matching conditions. The worka- bility of the proposed new circuits has been verified us- ing SPICE simulation with TSMC CMOS 0.18 μm proc- ess parameters.

2. The Proposed New Configurations

The symbolic notation of the VDTA is shown in **Figure 1**, where V_P and V_N are input terminals and Z, X^+ and X^-

are output terminals. All terminals of VDTA exhibit high impedance values [35]. The VDTA can be described by the following set of equations:

$$\begin{bmatrix} I_Z \\ I_{X^+} \\ I_{X^-} \end{bmatrix} = \begin{bmatrix} g_{m_1} & -g_{m_1} & 0 \\ 0 & 0 & g_{m_2} \\ 0 & 0 & -g_{m_2} \end{bmatrix} \begin{bmatrix} V_{V_P} \\ V_{V_N} \\ V_Z \end{bmatrix} \qquad (1)$$

The proposed grounded and floating inductance circuits are shown in **Figures 2** and **3** respectively.

A routine circuit analysis of the circuit shown in **Figure 2** results in the following expression for the input impedance

$$Z_{\text{in}}(s) = \frac{V_{\text{in}}(s)}{I_{\text{in}}(s)} = s\left(\frac{C}{g_{m_1} g_{m_2}}\right) \qquad (2)$$

The circuit, thus, simulates a grounded inductance with the inductance value given by

$$L_{eq} = \frac{C}{g_{m_1} g_{m_2}} \qquad (3)$$

which is electronically controllable by either g_{m_1} or g_{m_2}.

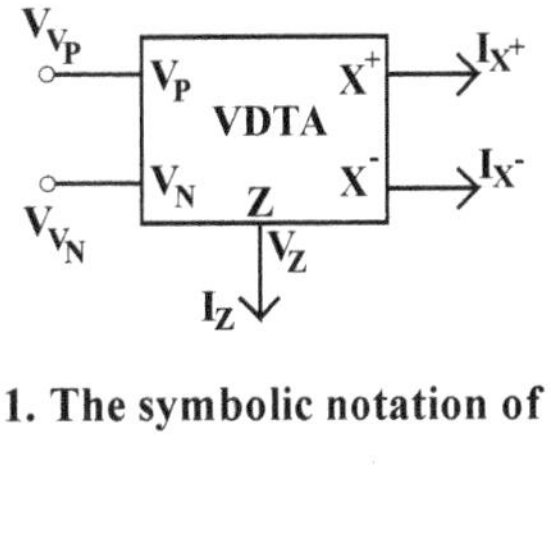

Figure 1. The symbolic notation of VDTA.

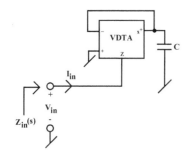

Figure 2. Proposed grounded inductance simulation configuration.

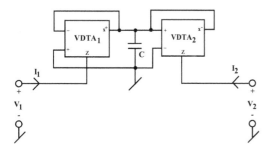

Figure 3. Proposed floating inductance simulation configuration.

On the other hand, analysis of the new FI circuit shown in **Figure 3** yields $\begin{bmatrix} I_1 \\ I_2 \end{bmatrix} = \dfrac{g_{m_1} g_{m_2}}{sC} \begin{bmatrix} +1 & -1 \\ -1 & +1 \end{bmatrix} \begin{bmatrix} V_1 \\ V_2 \end{bmatrix}$, with $g_{m_1} = g_{m_3}$ and

$$g_{m_2} = g_{m_4} \tag{4}$$

which proves that the circuit simulates a floating lossless electronically-controllable inductance with the inductance value given by

$$L_{eq} = \frac{C}{g_{m_1} g_{m_2}} \tag{5}$$

3. Non-Ideal Analysis and Sensitivity Performance

Considering the various VDTA non-ideal parasitics *i.e.*, the finite X-terminal parasitic impedance consisting of a resistance R_X in parallel with capacitance C_X and the parasitic impedance at the Z-terminal consisting of a resistance R_Z in parallel with capacitance C_Z.

The non-ideal input impedance for the circuit shown in **Figure 2** is given by

$$Z_{in}(s) = \frac{\left\{ s(C+C_x) + \dfrac{1}{R_x} \right\}}{\left\{ s^2 C_z (C+C_x) + s\left\{ \dfrac{(C+C_x)}{R_z} + \dfrac{C_z}{R_x} \right\} + \dfrac{1}{R_x R_z} + g_{m_1} g_{m_2} \right\}} \tag{6}$$

From Equation (6) a non-ideal equivalent circuit of the grounded inductor is derivable which is shown in **Figure 4**.

Where $L_{GI} = \dfrac{(C+C_x)R_x R_z}{(1+g_{m_1} g_{m_2} R_x R_z)}$, $R' = \dfrac{(C+C_x)R_x R_z}{R_x(C+C_x)+R_z C_z}$,

$C' = \dfrac{(C+C_x)R_x + C_z R_z}{R_z}$, $R'' = \dfrac{R_z}{(1+g_{m_1} g_{m_2} R_x R_z)}$ and

$D = R_x R_z (C+C_x)$

From the above, the sensitivities of L_{GI} with respect to various active and passive elements are found to be

$$S_C^{L_{GI}} = \frac{C}{(C+C_x)}, \quad S_{C_x}^{L_{GI}} = \frac{C_x}{(C+C_x)}, \quad S_{R_x}^{L_{GI}} = \frac{1}{(1+g_{m_1} g_{m_2} R_x R_z)} = S_{R_z}^{L_{GI}}, \quad S_{g_{m_1}}^{L_{GI}} = -\frac{g_{m_1} g_{m_2} R_x R_z}{(1+g_{m_1} g_{m_2} R_x R_z)} = S_{g_{m_2}}^{L_{GI}} \tag{7}$$

Similarly, for the circuit shown in **Figure 3**, the input-output current and voltage relationships are given by:

$$\begin{bmatrix} I_1 \\ I_2 \end{bmatrix} = \frac{g_{m_1} g_{m_2}}{\left\{ s(C+2C_x) + \dfrac{2}{R_x} \right\}} \begin{bmatrix} 1 + \left\{ s(C+2C_x) + \dfrac{2}{R_x} \right\}\left(sC_z + \dfrac{1}{R_z} \right) & -1 \\ -1 & 1 + \left\{ s(C+2C_x) + \dfrac{2}{R_x} \right\}\left(sC_z + \dfrac{1}{R_z} \right) \end{bmatrix} \begin{bmatrix} V_1 \\ V_2 \end{bmatrix}$$

with $\quad g_{m_1} = g_{m_3}$ and $g_{m_2} = g_{m_4}$ (8)

The non-ideal equivalent circuit of floating inductor of **Figure 3** is derivable from Equation (8) and is shown in **Figure 5**.

where $\quad L_{FI} = \dfrac{(C+2C_x)}{g_{m_1} g_{m_2}}$ and $R = \dfrac{2}{R_x g_{m_1} g_{m_2}}$

The various sensitivities of L_{FI} with respect to active and passive elements are:

$$S_C^{L_{FI}} = \frac{C}{(C+2C_x)}, \quad S_{C_x}^{L_{FI}} = \frac{C_x}{(C+2C_x)},$$

$$S_{g_{m_1}}^{L_{FI}} = -1, \quad S_{g_{m_2}}^{L_{FI}} = -1 \tag{9}$$

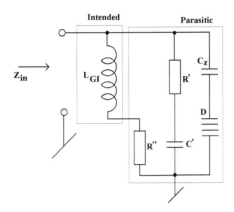

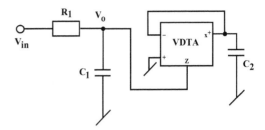

Figure 6. Band pass filter realized by the new grounded simulated inductor.

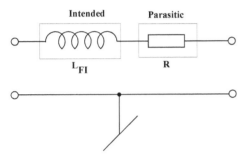

Figure 4. Non-ideal equivalent circuit of Figure 2.

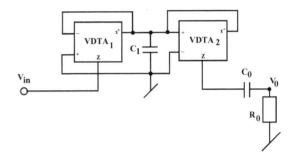

Figure 7. Band pass filter realized by the new floating simulated inductor of Figure 3.

Figure 5. Non-ideal equivalent circuit of Figure 3.

$$\frac{V_0}{V_{in}} = \frac{s\left(\dfrac{R_0 g_{m_1} g_{m_2}}{C_1}\right)}{s^2 + s\left(\dfrac{R_0 g_{m_1} g_{m_2}}{C_1}\right) + \dfrac{g_{m_1} g_{m_2}}{C_0 C_1}} \quad \text{with} \quad g_{m_1} = g_{m_3}$$

and $\qquad g_{m_2} = g_{m_4}$ $\qquad\qquad$ (11)

Taking $g_{m1} = g_{m2} = 631.702\ \mu A/V$, $C_z = C_Z = 0$, $R_x = R_z = \infty$ and $C = 0.01nF$, these sensitivities are found to be (1, 0, 0, 0, 1, 1) and (1, 0, –1, –1) for Equations (7) and (9) respectively. Thus, all the passive and active sensitivities of both grounded and floating inductance circuits are low.

4. Simulation Results of the New Proposed Grounded/Floating Inductance Configurations

The workability of the proposed simulated inductors has been verified by realizing a band pass filter (BPF) as shown in **Figures 6** and **7**.

The transfer function realized by this configuration is given by

$$\frac{V_0}{V_{in}} = \frac{s\left(\dfrac{1}{R_1 C_1}\right)}{s^2 + s\left(\dfrac{1}{R_1 C_1}\right) + \left(\dfrac{g_{m_1} g_{m_2}}{C_1 C_2}\right)} \qquad (10)$$

from where it is seen that bandwidth and centre frequency both are independently tunable, the former by R_1 and the latter by any of the transconductances g_{m1}, g_{m2} and C_2.

The transfer function realized by the configuration shown in **Figure 7** is given by

In this case, bandwidth is tunable by R_0 whereas centre frequency can be tuned by C_0.

Performance of the new simulated inductors was verified by SPICE simulations. CMOS-based VDTA from [35] was used to determine the frequency responses of the grounded and floating simulated inductors. The following values were used for grounded as well as floating inductor: $C = 0.01$ nF, $g_{m1} = g_{m2} = 631.7\ \mu A/V$. From the frequency response of the simulated grounded inductor (**Figure 8**) it has been observed that the inductance value remains constant upto 10 MHz. Similarly, from the frequency response of the simulated floating inductor (**Figure 9**) the inductance value also remains constant up to 10 MHz.

To verify the theoretical analysis of the application circuits shown in **Figures 6** and **7**, these configurations have also been simulated using CMOS VDTAs. The component values used were for **Figure 6**: $C_1 = 5$ pF, $C_2 = 0.01$ nF, $R_1 = 1.58$ kΩ and for **Figure 7**: $C_0 = 0.01$ nF, $C_1 = 5$ pF, $R_0 = 1.58$ kΩ. The VDTAs were biased with ± 0.9 volts D.C. power supplies with $I_{B1} = I_{B2} = I_{B3} = I_{B4} = 150\ \mu A$. **Figures 10** and **11** show the simulated filter responses of the BP filters. A comparison of the other

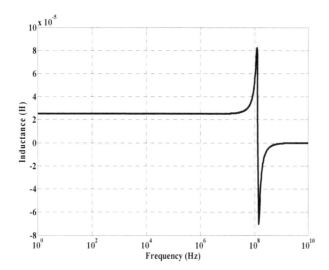

Figure 8. Frequency response of the simulated grounded inductor.

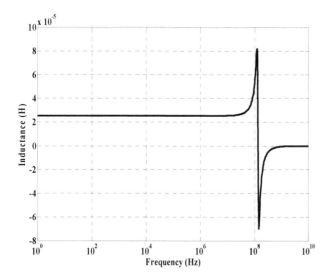

Figure 9. Frequency response of the simulated floating inductor.

previously known grounded and floating inductance simulators has been presented in **Table 1**.

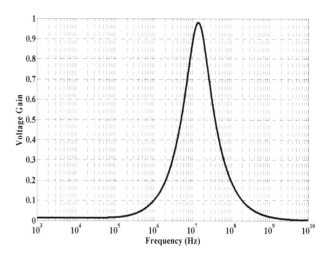

Figure 10. Frequency response of BPF using the proposed simulated GI.

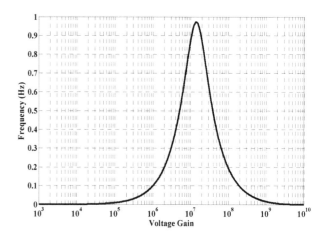

Figure 11. Frequency response of BPF using the proposed simulated FI.

Table 1. Comparison with other previously known grounded and floating simulators.

Reference	Inductance type+	Number of active devices	Number of resistors	Number of capacitors	Required Matching condition	Electronic Tunable Inductance
[4]	F	3	3	1	YES	NO
[7]	G	2	0	1	NO	YES
[10]	F	3	0	1	YES	YES
	F	4	4	1	YES	NO
[11]	F	4	3	1	YES	NO
[12]	F	4	2	1	NO	NO
[14]	G	2	2	1	NO	NO
[15]	F	3	2	1	NO	NO
[16]	F	3	2	1	NO	NO
[17]	F	4	2	1	NO	NO
[18]	F	2	2	1	NO	NO
[22]	F	3	0	1	YES	YES

Continued

[23]	F	3/4	4	1	YES	YES
[24]	G	1	2	1	YES	NO
[25]	F	3	0	1	YES	YES
[26]	F	4/3	3	1	NO	NO
[27]	G	2	0	1	NO	YES
[28]	G	3	3	1	NO	NO
[29]	G	3	4	1	NO	NO
[30]	F	3	4	1	NO	NO
	G	2	0	1	NO	YES
[32]	F	3	0	1	YES	YES
	G	2	0	1	NO	YES
[33]	F	3	0	1	YES	YES
	F	2	3	2	YES	NO
Proposed	G	1	0	1	NO	YES
	F	2	0	1	YES	YES

G = Grounded, F = Floating.

The above results, thus, confirm the validity of the applications of the proposed grounded and floating simulated inductance circuits.

5. Conclusion

New electronically-controllable circuits of lossless grounded and floating inductance have been proposed employing VDTAs. The proposed grounded inductance circuit employs only one VDTA and one grounded capacitor. On the other hand, the floating inductance configuration uses two VDTAs and one grounded capacitor, requires realization conditions for floatation. A comparison of the other previously known grounded and floating inductance simulators has been presented in **Table 1**. The SPICE simulation results have confirmed the workability of the new proposed circuits.

REFERENCES

[1] R. Senani, "New Single-Capacitor Simulations of Floating Inductors," *ElectroComponent Science and Technology*, Vol. 10, No. 1, 1982, pp. 7-10.

[2] A. Antoniou, "Gyrators Using Operational Amplifiers," *Electronics Letters*, Vol. 3, No. 8, 1967, pp. 350-352.

[3] A. Antoniou, "Realization of Gyrators Using Op-Amps and Their Use in RC Active Network Synthesis," *Proceedings of the IEEE*, Vol. 116, 1969, pp. 1838-1850.

[4] R. Senani, "Realization of Single Resistance-Controlled Lossless Floating Inductance," *Electronics Letters*, Vol. 14, No. 25, 1978, pp. 828-829.

[5] R. Senani, "New Tunable Synthetic Floating Inductors," *Electronics Letters*, Vol. 16, No. 10, 1980, pp. 382-383.

[6] T. S. Rathore and B. M. Singhi, "Active RC Synthesis of Floating Immittances," *International Journal of Circuit Theory and Applications*, Vol. 8, No. 2, 1980, pp. 184-188.

[7] R. Nandi, "Lossless Inductor Simulation: Novel Configurations Using DVCCs," *Electronics Letters*, Vol. 16, No. 17, 1980, pp. 666-667.

[8] R. Senani, "Some New Synthetic Floating Inductance Circuits," *International Journal of Electronic and Communications*, Vol. 35, 1981, pp. 307-310.

[9] R. Senani, "Canonic Synthetic Floating-Inductance Circuits Employing Only a Single Component-Matching Condition," *Journal of IETE*, Vol. 27, No. 6, 1981, pp. 201-204.

[10] K. Pal, "Novel Floating Inductance Using Current Conveyors," *Electronics Letters*, Vol. 17, No. 18, 1981, p. 638.

[11] V. Singh, "Active RC Single-Resistance-Controlled Lossless Floating Inductance Simulation Using Single Grounded Capacitor," *Electronics Letters*, Vol. 17, No. 24, 1981, pp. 920-921.

[12] R. Senani, "Novel Lossless Synthetic Floating Inductor Employing a Grounded Capacitor," *Electronics Letters*, Vol. 18, No. 10, 1982, pp. 413-414.

[13] R. Senani, "Three Op-Amp Floating Immittance Simulators: A Retrospection," *IEEE Transactions on Circuits and Systems*, Vol. 36, No. 11, 1989, pp. 1463-1465.

[14] A. Fabre, "Gyrator Implementation from Commercially Available Trans Impedance Operational Amplifiers," *Electronics Letters*, Vol. 28, No. 3, 1992, pp. 263-264.

[15] R. Senani and J. Malhotra, "Minimal Realizations of a Class of Operational Mirrored Amplifier Based Floating Impedance," *Electronics Letters*, Vol. 30, No. 14, 1994, pp. 1113-1114.

[16] S. A. Al-Walaie and M. A. Alturaigi, "Current Mode

Simulation of Lossless Floating Inductance," *International Journal of Electronics*, Vol. 83, No. 6, 1997, pp. 825-830.

[17] W. Kiranon and P. Pawarangkoon, "Floating Inductance Simulation Based on Current Conveyors," *Electronics Letters*, Vol. 33, 1997, pp. 1748-1749.

[18] P. V. Anand Mohan, "Grounded Capacitor Based Grounded and Floating Inductance Simulation Using Current Conveyors," *Electronics Letters*, Vol. 34, No. 11, 1998, pp. 1037-1038.

[19] O. Cicekoglu, "Active Simulation of Grounded Inductors with CCII+s and Grounded Passive Elements," *International Journal of Electronics*, Vol. 85, No. 4, 1998, pp. 455-462.

[20] M. T. Abuelma'atti, M. H. Khan and H. A. Al-Zaher, "Simulation of Active-Only Floating Inductance," *Journal of RF-Engineering and Telecommunications*, Vol. 52, 1998, pp. 161-164.

[21] H. Sedef and C. Acar, "A New Floating Inductor Circuit Using Differential Voltage Current Conveyors," *Journal of RF-Engineering and Telecommunications*, Vol. 54, 2000, pp. 123-125.

[22] D. Biolek and V. Biolkova, "Tunable Ladder CDTA-Based Filters," 4*th Multiconference WSEAS*, Spain, 2003, pp. 1-3.

[23] A. U. Keskin and H. Erhan, "CDBA-Based Synthetic Floating Inductance Circuits with Electronic Tuning Properties," *ETRI Journal*, Vol. 27, No. 2, 2005, pp. 239-242.

[24] E. Yuce, S. Minaei and O. Cicekoglu, "A Novel Grounded Inductor Realization Using a Minimum Number of Active and Passive Components," *ETRI Journal*, Vol. 27, No. 4, 2005, pp. 427-432.

[25] W. Tangsrirat and W. Surakampontorn, "Electronically Tunable Floating Inductance Simulation Based on Current-Controlled Current Differencing Buffered Amplifiers," *Thammasat International Journal of Science and Technology*, Vol. 11, No. 1, 2006, pp. 60-65.

[26] E. Yuce, "On the Realization of the Floating Simulators Using Only Grounded Passive Components," *Analog Integrated Circuits and Signal Processing*, Vol. 49, 2006,

pp. 161-166.

[27] T. Parveen and M. T. Ahmed, "Simulation of Ideal Grounded Tunable Inductor and Its Application in High Quality Multifunctional Filter," *Microelectronics Journal*, Vol. 23, No. 3, 2006, pp. 9-13.

[28] E. Yuce, "Grounded Inductor Simulators with Improved Low Frequency Performances," *IEEE Transactions on Instrumentation and Measurement*, Vol. 57, No. 5, 2008, pp. 1079-1084.

[29] K. Pal and M. J. Nigam, "Novel Active Impedances Using Current Conveyors," *Journal of Active and Passive Electronic Devices*, Vol. 3, 2008, pp. 29-34.

[30] D. Prasad, D. R. Bhaskar and A. K. Singh, "New Grounded and Floating Simulated Inductance Circuits using Current Differencing Transconductance Amplifiers," *Radioengineering*, Vol. 19, No. 1, 2010, pp. 194-198.

[31] D. Biolek and V. Biolkova, "First-Order Voltage-Mode All-Pass Filter Employing One Active Element and One Grounded Capacitor," *Analog Integrated Circuits and Signal Processing*, Vol. 65, No. 1, 2010, pp. 123-129.

[32] D. Prasad, D. R. Bhaskar and K. L. Pushkar, "Realization of New Electronically Controllable Grounded and Floating Simulated Inductance Circuits Using Voltage Differencing Differential Input Buffered Amplifiers," *Active and Passive Electronic Components*, Vol. 2011, 2011, Article ID: 101432.

[33] R. Senani and D. R. Bhaskar, "New Lossy/Loss-Less Synthetic Floating Inductance Configuration Realized with Only two CFOAs," *Analog Integrated Circuits and Signal Processing*, 2012.

[34] D. Biolek, R. Senani, V. Biolkova and Z. Kolka, "Active Elements for Analog Signal Processing; Classification, Review and New Proposals," *Radioengineering*, Vol. 17, No. 4, 2008, pp. 15-32.

[35] A. Yesil, F. Kacar and H. Kuntman, "New Simple CMOS Realization of Voltage Differencing Transconductance Amplifier and Its RF Filter Application," *Radioengineering*, Vol. 20, No. 3, 2011, pp. 632-637.

21

A Novel Responsivity Model for Stripe-Shaped Ultraviolet Photodiode

Yongjia Zhao[1], Xiaoya Zhou[1], Xiangliang Jin[1*], Kehan Zhu[2]

[1]Faculty of Materials, Optoelectronics and Physics, Xiangtan University, Xiangtan, China
[2]Electrical and Computer Engineering Department, Boise State University, Boise, USA

ABSTRACT

A novel responsivity model, which is based on the solution of transport and continuity equation of carriers generated both in vertical and lateral PN junctions, is proposed for optical properties of stripe-shaped silicon ultraviolet (UV) photodiodes. With this model, the responsivity of the UV photodiode can be estimated. Fabricated in a standard 0.5 μm CMOS process, the measured spectral responsivity of the stripe-shaped UV photodiode shows a good match with the numerical simulation result of the responsivity model at the spectral of UV range. It means that the responsivity model, which is used for stripe-shaped UV photodiode, is reliable.

Keywords: Responsivity; Model; Lateral PN Junction; Stripe-Shaped; Silicon; Ultraviolet (UV) Photodiode; CMOS

1. Introduction

UV detectors which is invented after infrared and laser detection technology, are widely used in many application areas such as biology, medicine and environmental monitoring [1]; flame detection [2]; space ionizing radiation detection [3], personal radiation protection, semiconductor process control [4]; optical storage system [5]; ultraviolet warning, ultraviolet communication, UV/infrared composite guidance and missile detection.

As UV detectors being developed toward high responsivity and high selectivity, numerical model acts as a design guide to better realization of the performances becomes an essential. UV detectors usually have striped-shaped anode structure; carrier generated in this region can travel vertically and laterally. Although different models for detectors have been presented, most of them only consider carriers transfer vertically, and ignore the transmission in lateral. Dead space effects on gain and noise have been studied in [6-8], but optical characteristic is not considered. UV responsivity models proposed by Pauchard [9,10] showed a good selectivity, but it ignored the influence of lateral PN junction. A two dimensional model proposed in [11] took transverse diffusion into consideration, but longitudinal diffusion is ignored in this model.

In this work, a two dimensional responsivity model for stripe-shaped UV photodiodes is presented. As there is no similar model, silicon test results are used to verify the

validity of the this work, so simulation results and test results are all needed in this paper. In the next section, the structure and its characteristics are introduced and analyzed. The responsivity model of the stripe-shaped UV photodiode is given in Section 3. The numerical simulation result and silicon test result are presented and discussed in Sections 4 and 5, respectively. Test devices are fabricated in standard 0.5 μm CMOS process.

2. Structure and Characteristics of Stripe-Shaped UV Photodiode

The device consists of several P^+-type anodes, which are implemented by boron implantation in N-well, the P^+ anodes are connected by metal outside of the photosensitive region. The substrate is P-type; its electrode is connected with N^+ electrode and leads to restrained photon absorption in N-well/P-sub junction. The width W of the stripes is 3.8 μm. The distance D between two adjacent stripes is 7.7 μm. The total sensor area is about 103 × 103 μm². The upper P^+N junctions are at a depth of 140 nm. When the device is biased at its breakdown voltage, the photosensitive region of the photodiode is bounded by the structure surface and the potential barrier x_b (x_b = 800 nm).

When the photodiode is under illumination, UV photons are absorbed at the silicon surface, and these photo-generated carriers are separated by upper P^+N junction. The photons in visible and infrared range absorbed in deeper junction, but as the N-well-P-substrate junction is short circuited, these photo-generated carriers recom-

---

*Corresponding author.

bined and won't contribute to total photocurrent. Thus, the influence of deeper junction can be ignored.

3. Responsivity Model of the Stripe-Shaped UV Photodiode

The exposed part of the stripe-shaped photodiode features a periodic distribution, so that it is adequate to investigate the section within the dashed rectangular area as indicated in **Figure 1** to present the whole photodiode structure. Presuming the credibility of the depletion-approximation, there can define two quasi-neutral regions I, II and one space charge region A within the dashed rectangular area, as shown in **Figure 2**. Otherwise, the space between two adjacent anodes is assumed entirely depleted.

Assuming the minority carrier in region I, II is totally generated by diffusion. The contribution of the current in quasi-region to the total photocurrent of the photodiode is elicited by solving the following diffusion equation:

$$\frac{d^2\Delta n(x,y)}{dx^2} + \frac{d^2\Delta n(x,y)}{dy^2} - \frac{\Delta n(x,y)}{L_n^2} = -\frac{\tau}{L_n^2}g(x,\lambda) \quad (1)$$

As the carriers in quasi-neural region-I have two-dimensional distribution. To simplify the complexity of carrier distribution, assuming $\Delta n(x,y) = \Delta n(x) \cdot \Delta n(y)$, that is to say carrier diffusion current in x-axis and y-axis is independent. Then, Equation (1) can be given

$$\Delta n(y) \cdot \frac{d^2\Delta n(x)}{dx^2} + \Delta n(x) \cdot \frac{d^2\Delta n(y)}{dy^2} - \frac{\Delta n(x) \cdot \Delta n(y)}{L_n^2} = -\frac{\tau}{L_n^2}g(x,\lambda) \quad (4)$$

It can be written as

$$\frac{d^2\Delta n(y)}{dy^2} + \frac{\Delta n(y)}{\Delta n(x)}\left(\frac{d^2\Delta n(x)}{dx^2} - \frac{\Delta n(x)}{L_n^2}\right) = -\frac{\tau}{\Delta n(x)L_n^2}g(x,\lambda) \quad (5)$$

If only considered electron diffusion current in x direction, i.e. $\Delta n(y) = 1$. Then, with boundary conditions $\left(\frac{d}{dx}\Delta n\right)_{x=0} = 0$ and $\Delta n(x_j) = 0$, solving the diffusion equation

where $\Delta n(x,y)$ indicates the excess minority carrier density, τ and $L_n = \sqrt{D_n\tau}$ refers to its lifetime and diffusion length, respectively; see **Table 1** $g(x,\lambda)$ is photogeneration rate within silicon material, it is given as below:

$$g(x,\lambda) = P\eta\left[1-R(\lambda)\right]a(\lambda)\exp\left[-a(\lambda)x\right]/(hv) \quad (2)$$

where P is the optical power, η is the quantum efficiency, $R(\lambda)$ is the surface reflection rate, $\alpha(\lambda)$ the optical absorption coefficient, h and v is the Planck's constant and optical frequency, respectively. The absorption coefficient [12] is related via:

$$\alpha(\lambda) = \frac{g_1 hc}{\lambda}\exp\left(\frac{b_2 hc}{\lambda}\right) \quad (3)$$

where $g_1 = 1.23 \times 10^{-3} \, \mu m^{-1} \cdot ev^{-1}$, $b_2 = 2.42 \, ev^{-1}$. **Figure 3** shows the curve of wavelength vs absorption coefficient.

As the carriers in quasi-neural region-I have two-dimensional distribution. To simplify the complexity of carrier distribution, assuming $\Delta n(x,y) = \Delta n(x) \cdot \Delta n(y)$, that is to say carrier diffusion current in x-axis and y-axis is independent. Then, Equation (1) can be given

$$\frac{d^2\Delta n(x)}{dx^2} - \frac{\Delta n(x)}{L_n^2} = -\frac{\tau}{L_n^2}g(x,\lambda) \quad (6)$$

The y-dependency of electron distribution density can be concluded

$$\Delta n(x) = \frac{\alpha(\lambda)P\left[1-R(\lambda)\right]\tau\left[e^{\frac{x_j[1-\alpha(\lambda)L_n]-x}{L_n}} - e^{-\alpha(\lambda)x} + e^{\frac{x_j[1-\alpha(\lambda)L_n]+x}{L_n}} - e^{\frac{2x_j}{L_n}-\alpha(\lambda)x} + \alpha(\lambda)e^{\frac{2x_j-x}{L_n}} - \alpha(\lambda)L_n e^{\frac{x}{L_n}}\right]}{\left(1+e^{\frac{2x_j}{L_n}}\right)\left[-1+\alpha^2(\lambda)L_n^2\right](hv)} \quad (7)$$

If considering diffusion current in both x-axis and y-axis. Comparing Equations (5) and (6) leads to

$$\frac{d^2\Delta n(y)}{dy^2} - \frac{\tau g(x,\lambda)}{\Delta n(x)L_n^2}\Delta n(y) = -\frac{\tau g(x,\lambda)}{\Delta n(x)L_n^2} \quad (8)$$

To solving Equation (8), the boundary conditions are assumed to be $\Delta n(x,0) = 0$ and $\Delta n(x,w) = 0$, then

$$\Delta n(y) = \frac{1}{e^{2\sqrt{H}w}-1}e^{\sqrt{H}y} - \frac{1}{e^{2\sqrt{H}w}-1}e^{-\sqrt{H}y} + 1 \quad (9)$$

where

$$H = \frac{\tau_n}{L_n^2}\frac{\int_0^{x_j}Pg(x,\lambda)dx}{\int_0^{x_j}\Delta n(x)dx} \quad (10)$$

As the minority carrier distribution $\Delta n(x,y) = \Delta n(x) \cdot \Delta n(y)$ in region I is known, the components of diffusion current density can be calculated

$$I_{x_j} = qD_n\int_0^w \frac{d\Delta n(x,y)}{dx}\bigg|_{x=x_j} dy \quad (11)$$

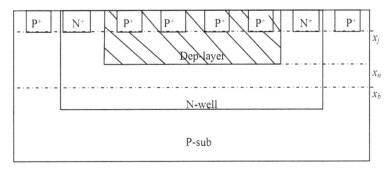

Figure 1. Cross-section view of the stripe-shaped UV photodiode.

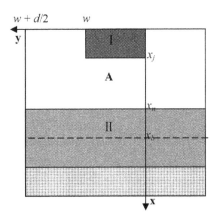

Figure 2. The section within the dashed rectangular area.

Table 1. Some parameters used in this paper.

Parameter	Name	Parameter	Name
w	with of P$^+$ anode	d	distance of two adjcent anode
$\Delta n(x, y)$	the excess minority carrier density	τ	minority carrier lifetime
L_n	diffusion length	$\Delta n(x)$	carrier diffusion in x-axis
$g(x, \lambda)$	photo-generation rate within silicon material	$\Delta n(x)$	carrier diffusion in y-axis
P	the optical power	η	the quantum efficiency
$R(\lambda)$	the surface reflection rate	$\alpha(\lambda)$	optical absorption coefficient
h	the Planck's constant	v	optical frequency

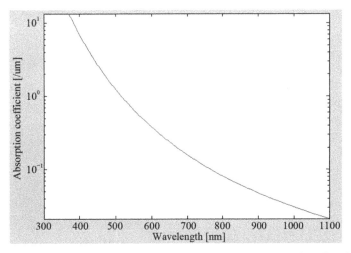

Figure 3. Calculated wavelength vs absorption coefficient based Equation (3) using Matlab.

$$I_{I,\text{left}} = qD_n \int_0^{x_j} \frac{d\Delta n(x,y)}{dy}\bigg|_{y=w} dx \qquad (12)$$

$$I_{I,\text{right}} = qD_n \int_0^{x_j} \frac{d\Delta n(x,y)}{dy}\bigg|_{y=0} dx \qquad (13)$$

The drift current in region A is obtained by integration of generation rate of electron-hole pairs $g(x,\lambda)$ over the whole depletion region

$$I_A = qd \int_0^{x_n} g(x,\lambda) dx + qw \int_{x_j}^{x_n} g(x,\lambda) dx \qquad (14)$$

Assuming the distance between x_n and x_b is much smaller than diffusion length of electrons, which are a few microns. Thus, all carriers generated by photon absorption in region II diffuse toward region A. The electron diffusion current in region II can be expressed using

$$I_{\Pi} = q(w+d) \int_{x_n}^{x_b} g(x,\lambda) dx \qquad (15)$$

Adding all the current generated in region I, II and A, then multiplying the number of fingers, we conclude the total photocurrent of the photodiode

$$
\begin{aligned}
I_{ph} &= 4\left(I_{x_j} + I_{I,\text{left}} + I_{I,\text{right}} + I_A + I_{\Pi}\right) \\
&= 4\Bigg(qD_n\Bigg(\int_0^w \frac{d\Delta n(x,y)}{dx}\bigg|_{x=x_j} dy + \int_0^{x_j} \frac{d\Delta n(x,y)}{dy}\bigg|_{y=w} dx \\
&\quad + \int_0^{x_j} \frac{d\Delta n(x,y)}{dy}\bigg|_{y=0} dx\Bigg) + qd\int_0^{x_n} g(x,\lambda) dx \\
&\quad + qw\int_{x_j}^{x_n} g(x,\lambda) dx + q(w+d)\int_{x_n}^{x_b} g(x,\lambda) dx\Bigg)
\end{aligned}
$$
$$(16)$$

4. Numerical Simulation Result

The spectral responsivity of the model is simulated by Matlab. **Figure 4** shows the simulation result of this structure for a standard 0.5 μm CMOS technology. As expected, there is an excellent UV responsivity and UV selectivity, as UV photons are absorbed near the surface of the structure and all the generated carriers are absorbed by the device, while the photo-generated carriers of longer wavelength are recombined at the short-circuited deeper junction. The maximal photocurrent is 1.38×10^{-7} A at the wavelength of 460 nm, corresponding a responsivity of 0.42 A/W; the photocurrent at longer wavelength is weak, it meets the properties of UV photodiode mainly well.

5. Silicon Test Result

The UV photodiode device under test is fabricated in a standard 0.5 μm CMOS process, the microphotograph is

shown in **Figure 5**. It concludes stripe-shaped anode, and short-circuited substrate electrode and cathode electrode. Two pads are connected with anode and cathode, respectively.

The responsivity is tested using the configuration as shown in **Figure 6**. The anode of the stripe-shaped UV photodiode is connected to a high precision amperemeter (with the accuracy of 1 fA), the cathode is connected with power source (V_{DD}). The high precision amperemeter is connected with a resistance of 200 KΩ.

Placing the UV photodiode in a dark environment, external power supplies $V_{DD} = 18$ V, incident optical wavelength is 400 nm, 460 nm, 520 nm, 585 nm, 605 nm and 630 nm, respectively.

The measured curve of photo-current vs wavelength is shown in **Figure 7**. It has relatively high photo-current in UV spectral range; the maximal photo-current is 1.34×10^{-7} A at the wavelength of 460 nm. If translate photo-current into responsivity, that is to say, the maximal responsivity is 0.42 A/W at the wavelength of 460 nm. Comparing with simulation results, it's easy to see that silicon test results are agree with simulation results at the spectral range of UV.

6. Conclusion

In this work, a novel responsivity model is established

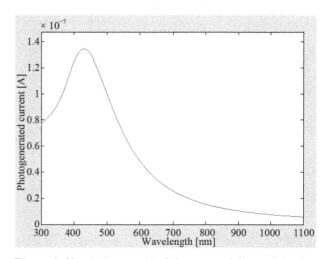

Figure 4. Simulation result of the responsivity model using Matlab.

Figure 5. Microphotograph of stripe-shaped UV photodiode fabricated in a standard 0.5 μm CMOS process.

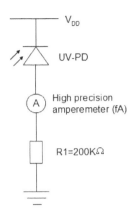

Figure 6. Configuration of test circuit for UV photodiode.

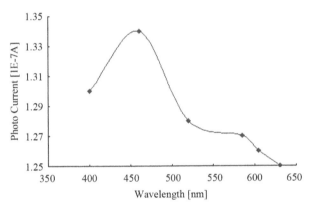

Figure 7. Measured photo-current vs wavelength.

for stripe-shaped UV photodiode. The structure is taped-out by 0.5 μm CMOS process. Simulation results and silicon test results are both have maximal UV responsivity at UV spectral range. The mainly agreement between them demonstrate that this work can be used to analysis the optical properties of stripe-shaped UV photodiode.

7. Acknowledgements

This paper is supported by Scientific Research Fund of Hunan Provincial Education Department (11A116), by Key Project of Chinese Ministry of Education of China (212125) and by Hunan Provincial Natural Science Foundation of China (11JJ2036).

REFERENCES

[1]   E. Charbon, "Towards Large Scale CMOS Single-Photon Detector Arrays for Lab-on-Chip Applications," *Journal of Physics D*: *Applied Physics*, Vol. 41, No. 9, 2008, Article ID: 094010.

[2]   Z. Djuric, K. Radulovic, N. Trbojevic and Z. Lazic, "Silicon Resonant Cavity Enhanced UV Flame Detector," *International Conference on Microelectronics*, Vol. 1, 2002, pp. 239-242.

[3]   M. P. Ulmer, "A Review of UV Detectors for Astrophysics: Past, Present, and Future," *Proceedings of SPIE*, Vol. 7222, 2009, Article ID: 722210.

[4]   G. K. Li, P. Feng and N. J. Wu, "A Novel Monolithic Ultraviolet Image Sensor Based on a Standard CMOS Process," *Journal of Semiconductors*, Vol. 32, No. 10, 2011, Article ID: 105008.

[5]   A. Ghazi, H. Zimmermann and P. Seegebrecht, "CMOS Photodiode with Enhanced Responsivity for the UV/Blue Spectral Range," *IEEE Transactions on Electron Devices*, Vol. 49, No. 7, 2002, pp. 1124-1128.

[6]   B. A. Saleh, M. M. Hayat and M. C. Teich, "Effect of Dead Space on the Excess Noise Factor and Time Response of Avalanche Photodiodes," *IEEE Transactions on Electron Devices*, Vol. 37, No. 9, 1990, pp. 1976-1984.

[7]   M. M. Hayat, W. L. Sargeant and B. E. A. Saleh, "Effect of Dead Space on Gain and Noise in Si and GaAs Avalanche Photodiodes," *IEEE Journal of Quantum Electronics*, Vol. 28, No. 5, 1992. pp. 1360-1365.

[8]   M. M. Hayat, B. E. A. Saleh and M. C. Teich, "Effect of Dead Space on Gain and Noise of Double-Carrier-Multiplication Avalanche Photodiodes," *IEEE Transactions on Electron Devices*, Vol. 39, No. 3, 1992, pp. 546-552.

[9]   A. Pauchard, P.-A. Besse and R. S. Popovic, "A Silicon Blue/UV Selective Stripe-Shaped Photodiode," *Sensors and Actuators A*: *Physical*, Vol. 76, No. 1-3, 1999, pp. 172-177.

[10] A. Pauchard, P.-A. Besse and R. S. Popovic, "Dead Space Effect on the Wavelength Dependence of Gain and Noise in Avalanche Photodiodes," *IEEE Transactions on Electron Devices*, Vol. 47, No. 9, 2000, pp. 1685-1693.

[11] A. Alexandre, F. Dadouche and P. Garda, "Two Dimensional Model for Lateral Photodiode," *International Conference on Design and Test of Integrated Systems in Nanoscale*, Tunis, 5-7 September 2006, pp. 294-298.

[12] I. R. Rawlings, "Optical Absorption in Silicon Monoxide," *Journal of Physics D*: *Applied Physics*, Vol. 1, No. 6, 1733, p. 733.

22

Low Phase Noise and Wide Tuning Range VCO Using the MOS Differential Amplifier with Active Load

Cher-Shiung Tsai[1], Kwang-Jow Gan[2*], Ming-Shin Lin[1]

[1]Department of Electronic Engineering, Kun Shan University, Yongkang, Chinese Taipei
[2]Department of Electrical Engineering, National Chiayi University, Chiayi, Chinese Taipei

ABSTRACT

We demonstrate the design of a novel voltage-controlled oscillator (VCO), which is based on a metal-oxide-semiconductor field-effect transistor (MOS) differential amplifier with active load. This VCO achieves low phase noise and wide tuning range. The phase noise is –120 dBc/Hz at 600 KHz offset from a 1.216 GHz carrier frequency. This value is comparable to that of a LC-based integrated oscillator. The operating frequency can be tuned from 117 MHz to 1.216 GHz with the supply voltage varying from 1.3 V to 3.3 V. Therefore, the tuning range is about 90.38% which is larger than most of the LC and ring oscillator. The VCO circuit, which is constructed using a standard 0.35 μm CMOS technology, occupies only 26.25×7.52 μm^2 die area and dissipated 10.56 mW under a 3.3 V supply voltage.

Keywords: Voltage-Controlled Oscillator (VCO); Differential Amplifier; Phase Noise; Tuning Range

1. Introduction

Wireless communication systems contain low-noise amplifiers, mixers, power amplifiers, and phase-locked loops (PLLs). In particular, the PLL, which provides the function of frequency synthesis, is very important in designing such systems. The voltage-controlled oscillator (VCO) often plays the key element in PLL circuit. Designing VCO for the monolithic integration is always desirable but most challenging. In general, there are two main structures of designing the VCO in monolithic integration. One is the LC-based integrated oscillator and the other is the ring oscillator. The low phase noise, wide tuning range, and low power dissipation and are the most important factors of the basic design of a VCO. The operations of the LC oscillators are excellent in phase-noise performance but their tuning ranges are only about 10% to 20% [1-3]. Besides, they often require extra processes and occupy a large area of chip size due to the existence of inductor and capacitor. However, the ring oscillators have wide tuning range but they are poor in phase-noise performance.

In order to depress the phase noise, the differential pairs (or amplifiers) could be used in designing a VCO [3-5]. In this work, we design a novel VCO, which is designed based on a metal-oxide-semiconductor field-effect transistor (MOS) differential amplifier with active load. Its whole structure is like a ring oscillator. We can

obtain low phase noise and wide tuning range in this VCO. The phase noise is –120 dBc/Hz at 600 KHz offset from a 1.216 GHz carrier frequency. The operating frequency is tuned from 117 MHz to 1.216 GHz with the supply voltage varying from 1.3 V to 3.3 V. Therefore, the tuning range is as high as 90.38%. Wide tuning range is required in VCO for supporting broadband and multiband RF transceivers. This VCO circuit, which is fabricated using a standard 0.35 μm CMOS technology provided by the Taiwan Semiconductor Manufacturing Company (TSMC) foundry, occupies 26.25×7.52 μm^2 die area and dissipated 10.56 mW under 3.3 V supply.

2. Circuit Design

The VCO demonstrated in this work is shown in **Figure 1**. This circuit is composed of a MOS-based differential amplifier, two standard CMOS inverters, and a buffer. It is an asymmetric structure and is similar to a ring oscillator. The differential amplifier is designed using two PMOS devices as the active load. This differential amplifier can achieve high voltage gain and output resistance. We use a NMOS device to act as a constant current source. Therefore, two NMOS devices (M1 and M2) can not be turned of simultaneously. When the M1 or M2 device is turned on, it is designed to be operated in the saturation state. The parameters of M1 device is designed as the same as those of M2 device. After the operation of this VCO circuit is stable, one of two NMOS devices should be turned on, and the other device should be turned off.

---

*Corresponding author.

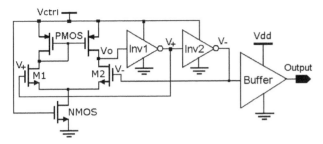

Figure 1. Circuit configuration of our proposed VCO structure.

The possible operation states of the V_+, V_- and Vo are all listed in **Table 1**. V_+, V_- are inputs and Vo is output of the differential amplifier with active load. There might be four possible states during the operation of this VCO circuit. The state 1 and state 2 will be only existed in the initial conditions. If the circuit is operated at the state 1 firstly, yet the next state will be changed to state 3 after the propagation of Vo. Then the operation of circuit will be transferred to state 4. Finally, the operation state will be back to state 3 again. As a result, the operation state will be alternately switched between state 3 and state 4. For the other possible condition, if the circuit is operated at the state 2 firstly, yet the following states will be changed to state 4 and state 3 in order. Therefore, the operation state will be located at state 4 and state 3 back and forth. Based on the discussion above, we can obtain the oscillation waveform. The buffer stage is composed of four cascaded CMOS inverters. The functions of the first and second stages are used as a wave-shaping modulator. However, the third and fourth stages are designed to amplify the amplitude of the output waveform and also to isolate the oscillator core from large capacitive load.

This VCO structure is a phase control operation circuit. The oscillation period will be the sum of time delays of the differential amplifier, inverter 1, inverter 2, and the buffer. The supply voltage of the differential amplifier, inverter 1, and inverter 2 is Vctrl. The output oscillation frequency is proportional to the magnitude of the voltage Vctrl. However, the bias Vdd for the buffer is fixed at 3.3 V in this design.

3. Measured Results

The VCO is implemented in a 0.35-μm N-well one-poly three-metal CMOS process provided by the TSMC foundry. The chip area is 26.25×7.52 μm^2. The measured output spectrum is shown in **Figure 2**. The center frequency is 1.216 GHz under a 3.3 V supply voltage, the resolution bandwidth is 100 KHz, and the output power peak is –2.72 dBm. The measured phase noise is shown in **Figure 3**. We can realize that the phase noise is –108.34 dBc/Hz at 100 KHz offset, –120 dBc/Hz at 600

Table 1. Possible operation states of the V_+, V_- and Vo for the VCO circuit.

	V_+	V_-	Vo
State 1	H	H	L
State 2	L	L	H
State 3	H	L	H
State 4	L	H	L

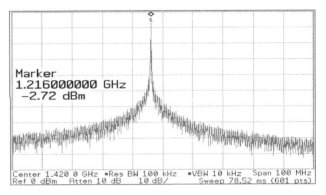

Figure 2. Measured output spectrum of the VCO circuit.

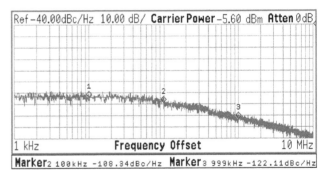

Figure 3. Measured phase noise of the VCO circuit at 1.216 GHz.

KHz offset, and –122.11 dBc/Hz at 1 MHz offset from a 1.216 GHz carrier frequency. Notice that the phase noise at 600 KHz offset is comparable with the LC-based integrated oscillators published in Refs. [1-3].

Figure 4 shows the comparison of the post-layout simulation and measured results of operating frequency with different supply voltages Vctrl. The linearity of two curves is good. The frequency can be tuned from 117 MHz to 1.216 GHz with the supply voltage varying from 1.3 V to 3.3 V. The frequency is ranged from very high frequency (VHF) to ultra high frequency (UHF) bands. As shown, the tuning range is about 90.38%. It is much wider than that of the LC-based integrated oscillators [1-3]. **Figure 5** shows the comparison of the post-layout simulation and measured results of power dissipation with different supply voltages Vctrl. The maximum dissipation power is about 10.56 mW under supply voltage 3.3 V. This value is reasonable in comparison with those

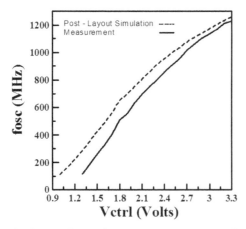

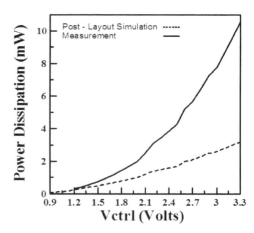

Figure 4. Comparison of the post-layout simulation and measured results of operating frequency with different supply voltages Vctrl.

Figure 5. Comparison of the post-layout simulation and measured results of power dissipation with different supply voltages Vctrl.

Table 2. Comparisons of our VCO circuit with the other oscillators.

Design	Process (μm)	Frequency Range (GHz)	Tuning Range (%)	Phase Noise (dBc/Hz @1MHz)	Power Dissipation (mW)	Type
This Work	0.35	0.117 - 1.216	90.4	−120	10.56	Ring
H. Wang, *et al.* [6]	0.25	1.99 - 2.73	27.10	−102	10	Ring
L. S. de Paula, *et al.* [7]	0.18	0.39 - 1.41	72.34	−89.79	16	Ring
J. Kim, *et al.* [8]	0.18	0.924 - 1.85	50.05	−127.1	10.8	LC
C. Shi, *et al.* [9]	0.18	1.71 - 2.19	21.91	−132	34	LC
G. Huang, *et al.* [10]	0.18	1.86 - 2.2	15.45	−134	36	LC

shown in Refs. [4,5]. The dissipation power is proportional to the $f \times CL \times Vdd^2$. The deviation between the simulated and measured curves might be resulted from the output parasitic loading capacitance.

Compared to the recently published papers [6-10], we have shown the relative VCO characteristics listed in **Table 2**. The phase noise of the circuits shown in Refs. [6-10] has been recalculated to an equivalent offset frequency of 1 MHz by assuming a dependence of 20 dB per decade. As shown, the phase noise is better than the ring oscillator [6,7], and is slightly larger than the complicated LC oscillators [8-10]. But the tuning range of our VCO circuit is the widest. Although the supply voltage of our proposed VCO circuit is 3.3 V, yet the power dissipation is competitive to the ring oscillator in Refs. [6,7] and better than the LC oscillators in Refs. [8-10]. This power dissipation could be decreased, if we implement this VCO circuit using a further scaled-down CMOS technique. Based on the above analysis, our VCO circuit possesses low phase noise, wide tuning range, and low power dissipation.

4. Conclusion

We present a novel VCO circuit, which is mainly con-

structed by a MOS-based differential amplifier with active load. This VCO can achieve low phase noise as the LC-based integrated oscillator and possess wide operating frequency range as the ring oscillator. The phase noise is −120 dBc/Hz at 600 KHz offset from a 1.216 GHz carrier frequency. The operating frequency can be tuned from 117 MHz to 1.216 GHz with the supply voltage varying from 1.3 V to 3.3 V. The tuning range is about 90.38%. This VCO circuit is fabricated using a standard 0.35 μm CMOS technology, occupies 26.25 × 7.52 μm² die area and dissipated 10.56 mW under 3.3 V supply. A prototype PLL (Phase-Locked Loop) uses the same VCO and will be implemented in the future.

5. Acknowledgements

This work was financially supported by the National Science Council of Taiwan under the contract no. NSC 97-2221-E-168-046. The authors would like to thank the Chip Implementation Center (CIC) of Taiwan for their great assistance in arranging the fabrication of this chip.

REFERENCES

[1] P. Andreani and H. Sjoland, "A 2.2 GHz CMOS VCO with Inductive Degeneration Noise Suppression," *Pro-

ceedings of the IEEE Conference on Custom Integrated Circuits, San Diego, 6-9 May 2001, pp. 197-200.

[2] M. Tiebout, "Low-Power Low-Phase-Noise Differentially Tuned Quadrature VCO Design in Standard CMOS," *IEEE Journal of Solid-State Circuits*, Vol. 36, No. 7, 2001, pp. 1018-1024.

[3] P. Andreani, A. Bonfanti, L. Romano and C. Samori, "Analysis and Design of a 1.8-GHz CMOS LC Quadrature VCO," *IEEE Journal of Solid-State Circuits*, Vol. 37, No. 12, 2002, pp. 1737-1747.

[4] C. H. Park and B. Kim, "A Low Noise, 900-MHz VCO in 0.6-μm CMOS," *IEEE Journal of Solid-State Circuits*, Vol. 34, No. 5, 1999, pp. 586-591.

[5] W. S. T. Yan and H. C. Luong, "A 900-MHz CMOS Low-Phase-Noise Voltage-Controlled Ring Oscillator," *IEEE Transactions on Circuits and Systems II: Analog and Digital Signal Processing*, Vol. 48, No. 2, 2001, pp. 216-221.

[6] H. Wang, N. Wu and G. Shou, "A Novel CMOS Low-Phase-Noise VCO with Enlarged Tuning Range," *Proceedings of the International Conference on Microwave and Millimeter Wave Technology*, Nanjing, 21-24 April 2008, pp. 570-573.

[7] L. S. de Paula, S. Bampi, E. Fabris and A. A. Susin, "A Wide Band CMOS Differential Voltage-Controlled Ring Oscillator," *Proceedings of the International IEEE Northeast Workshop on Circuits and Systems and TAISA Conference*, Montreal, 22-25 June 2008, pp. 9-12.

[8] J. Kim, J. Shin, S. Kim and H. Shin, "A Wide-Band CMOS LC VCO with Linearized Coarse Tuning Characteristics," *IEEE Transactions on Circuits and Systems II: Express Briefs*, Vol. 55, No. 5, 2008, pp. 399-403.

[9] C. Shi, R. Zhang, L. Chen, Z. Chen and Z. Lai, "A Low Noise VCO with Quadrature Prescaler for UHF RFID Reader," *Proceedings of the International Conference on Wireless Communications and Trusted Computing*, Wuhan, 25-26 April 2009, pp. 357-360.

[10] G. Huang and B. S. Kim, "Low Phase Noise Self-Switched Biasing CMOS LC Quadrature VCO," *IEEE Transactions on Microwave Theory and Techniques*, Vol. 57, No. 2, 2009, pp. 344-351.

23

High Accurate Howland Current Source: Output Constraints Analysis

Pedro Bertemes-Filho[*]**, Alexandre Felipe, Volney C. Vincence**
Department of Electrical Engineering, State University of Santa Catarina (UDESC), Joinville, Brazil

ABSTRACT

Howland circuits have been widely used as powerful source for exciting tissue over a wide frequency range. When a Howland source is designed, the components are chosen so that the designed source has the desired characteristics. However, the operational amplifier limitations and resistor tolerances cause undesired behaviors. This work proposes to take into account the influence of the random distribution of the resistors in the modified Howland circuit over the frequency range of 10 Hz to 10 MHz. Both output current and impedance of the circuit are deduced either considering or the operational amplifiers parameters. The probability density function due to small changes in the resistors of the circuit was calculated by using the analytical modeling. Results showed that both output current and impedance are very sensitive to the resistors variations. In order to get higher output impedances, high operational amplifier gains are required. The operational amplifier open-loop gain increases as increasing the sensitivity of the output impedance. The analysis done in this work can be used as a powerful co-adjuvant tool when projecting this type of circuit in Spice simulators. This might improve the implementations of practical current sources used in electrical bioimpedance.

Keywords: Howland Current Source; Electrical Bioimpedance; Probability Density Function; Resistors Mismatching

1. Introduction

Because of its simplicity, stability and other advantages, the voltage controlled current source (VCCS) has been widely used in many applications, such as in neuron-stimulation systems [1-3], single-electrode capacitive sensors [4], electrical impedance tomography (EIT) systems both for industrial and medical applications [5,6] and bioimpedance analysis (BIA) for tissue characterization [7,8]. It is also been used for exciting tissue for cancer characterization in electrical impedance spectroscopy [9-11]. Most VCCS circuits in BIA use the Howland current source (HCS) [12]. The first HCS circuit was proposed by Howland in 1962 [13] for converting a voltage into a current. However, it suffers from output voltage compliance [7]. Therefore, the modified version of the circuit has been proposed and widely used [14,15].

The most important requirement in EIS systems is to assure that the injecting current, also called source current, has constant amplitude over a wide frequency range, which should be obtained by a high output impedance circuit [7]. However, stray capacitances [4] and non-

idealities of the operational amplifiers used for the design [15] reduce the current amplitude and introduce phase shift errors at higher frequencies. However, some of these requirements are essentially in conflict with each other. For example, the frequency of the current source is practically limited to 100 kHz when the output impedance is required to be sufficiently larger, say larger than 1 MΩ [1]. In most publications, the analysis of the circuit is based on either simplified ideal opamp circuits or using simulation tools, e.g. PSpice or Multisim from NI [12,16]. In many cases, however, the formulas they used are not suitable because the calculation errors are too large with a high-frequency current source [16]. Furthermore, the formulas do not take into account the mismatch between the resistors used to design such a current source. The HCS circuit is sensitive upon this mismatching [7].

The objective of this work is to investigate the probability density function for the analysis of the Howland circuit. It also investigates the sensibility of the Howland current source over the frequency range of 10 Hz to 10 MHz due to value mismatching between resistors.

---
[*]Corresponding author.

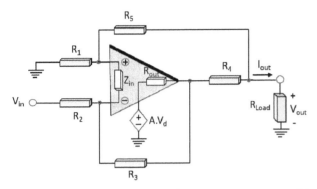

Figure 1. Schematic diagram of the current source with grounded load [17], where V_d is the differential voltage across the input terminals.

2. Howland Current Source

Figure 1 shows the modified Howland current source (HCS) circuit used for modeling the output characteristics taking into account the effects of the resistors tolerances. If all resistors are perfectly matched and the operational amplifier (opamp) has got a large gain, then the output current is given by $-V_{in}/r$ (assuming $R_2 = R_3 = R_5 = R$, $R_4 = r$ and $R_1 = R + r$). This approximation yields a good result if the Opamp gain is sufficiently high and the load impedance is small.

In order to get good Common Mode Rejection Ratio (CMRR) and high output impedance it is necessary to trim the resistors and choose FET inputs amplifiers. On the other hand, the non-ideal characteristics of the operational amplifiers (*i.e.*, input impedance Z_{in}, output resistance R_o and open-loop gain A) reduce frequency bandwidth of both output current and impedance.

2.1. Circuit Nodal Equations

The circuit can be characterized by the nodal Equations (1)-(4), where V_1 is the voltage at non-inverting input of the Opamp, V_2 is the inverting input of the Opamp and V_3 is the voltage at the output of the Opamp. After determining the voltages the output current is calculated by Equation (4). The transconductance gain is calculated by I_{out}/V_{in} with Vout grounded. On the other hand, the output impedance Z_{out} is calculated by I_{out}/V_{out} with V_{in} grounded.

$$\frac{V_1 - V_{out}}{R_5} + \frac{V_1}{R_1} + \frac{V_1 - V_2}{Z_{in}} = 0 \tag{1}$$

$$\frac{V_2 - V_{in}}{R_2} + \frac{V_2 - V_1}{Z_{in}} + \frac{V_2 - V_3}{R_3} = 0 \tag{2}$$

$$\frac{V_3 - V_2}{R_3} + \frac{V_3 - V_{out}}{R_4} + \frac{V_3 - (V_1 - V_2)A}{R_o} = 0 \tag{3}$$

$$I_{out} = \frac{V_3 - V_{out}}{R_4} + \frac{V_1 - V_{out}}{R_5} \tag{4}$$

$$A = A(j\omega) = \frac{A_o}{1 + j\omega/\omega_{co}} \tag{5}$$

where A_o and ω_{co} are the open-loop gain modulus at zero frequency and the open-loop gain corner frequency, respectively.

$$Z_{in}(j\omega) = \frac{1}{1/R_{in} + j\omega C_{in}} \tag{6}$$

where R_{in} and C_{in} are both input resistance and capacitance of the opamp, respectively.

The Norton theorem can be applied to the circuit shown in **Figure 1** then the shunt impedance Z_N of the circuit can be calculated by Equation (7) and the transconductance gain G_N can be calculated by Equation (8).

$$Z_N = \left(-I_{out}/V_{out}\right)\big|_{V_{in}=0} \tag{7}$$

$$G_N = \left(I_{out}/V_{in}\right)\big|_{V_{out}=0} \tag{8}$$

3. Probability Distribution Function

The probability distribution functions (PDF) of the source parameters are calculated by classifying and counting the elements falling in each class. It is expected that any combination of resistors of ±1% tolerance (δ) may produce either significant reduction in the output impedance or a large variation in the transconductance gain (I_{out}/V_{in}).

The box below shows the pseudo-code program developed in a very high level for the determination of some statistics of the circuit, which was projected by using resistors whose values distribution are known.

```
Begin
H = empty list
for the desired number of samples
- R1 = random resistor(R + r, tolerance of R1)
- R2 = random resistor(R, tolerance of R2)
- R3 = random resistor(R, tolerance of R3)
- R4 = random resistor(r, tolerance of R4)
- R5 = random resistor(R, tolerance of R5)
- H.append(Howland Circuit(R1, R2, R3, R4, R5, selected OPA))
repeat
Estimate Zout distribution of H[]
Estimate Iout distribution of H[]
Calculate other parameters of H[]
End
```

This program was implemented in R scripting language, which is a language and environment for statistical computing and graphics. In this work the resistors were distributed uniformly by using the run if R function, and the estimation of probability density functions was made with the density R function. More detailed information can be seen in the link http://www.r-project.org.

A Howland current source is designed by using $R = 100$ kΩ, $r = 1$ kΩ and it is assumed that each resistor has a tolerance δ of ±1% with no correlation to each other.

It was investigated the effect of the tolerance of the resistors in the transconductance gain when designing a Howland current source, Equation (4) was used by assuming a tolerance of ±1% for each discrete frequency over the range 10 Hz to 1 MHz. It was used the operational amplifier OPA655 from Texas Instruments, where the technical specifications are shown in **Table 1**.

The result is shown in **Figure 2**, where the probability density is represented by a gray scale. The white points represent the values where the transconductance might not be achieved at that frequency. It can also be seen that the frequency dependency mater is much more relevant than the tolerance of the resistors.

The transconductance gain G_N can be approximately calculated by the ratio $-R_3/(R_2R_4)$, thus if the tolerance of the resistors are equal to δ, the tolerance of the transconductance gain will have a tolerance of approximately 3δ. It implies that the use of a wideband operational amplifier will produce a very stable transconductance gain. On the other hand, the output impedance Z_{out} will be significantly changed by the tolerance of the resistors.

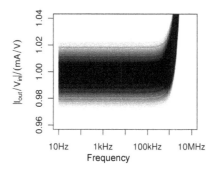

Figure 2. Probability distribution of the transconductance gain, using the OPA655 and resistors of ±1% tolerance.

Table 1. The main technical specifications of the operational amplifiers used in this work.

	R_{in} (MΩ)	C_{in} (pF)	R_0 (Ω)	A_0 (dB)	ω_{c0} (πHz)
OPA657	1000	0.7	0.02	75	600,000
OPA656	1000	0.7	0.01	66	200,000
OPA655	1000	1.2	0.04	58	400,000
LMH6654	4	1.8	0.08	80	50,000
OP07C	50	NF	60	115	4
TL081	1000	3.0	10	105	50
uA741	2	1.4	75	97	30

Note that A_0 of the opamp has been extracted from the plots of the open-loop gain versus frequency presented in the datasheet.

4. Output Impedance Modeling

4.1. Model 1: Infinite Open-Loop Gain

By solving Equation (4) and consider a suficiently high open-loop gain A, the output impedance can be briefly calculated by Equation (9)

$$Z_{\text{out}}\big|_{A=\infty} = \frac{R_2R_4R_5 + R_1R_2R_4}{R_2R_5 + R_2R_4 - R_1R_3} \tag{9}$$

It can be seen in Equation (9) that the relative error of the numerator is approximately three times larger than the resistor tolerances. The denominator of the equation would be zero if the resistors were perfectly matched. Therefore, the output would be very dependent on their values. By assuming equal tolerances for all resistors with a fraction nominal value of each reritor, and also using an operational amplifier with high open-loop gain A, the minimum ouput impedance can be calculated by Equation (10).

$$Z_{\text{out,min}}(\delta) = \frac{rR}{2\delta(R+r)} \tag{10}$$

where $R = R_2 = R_3 = R_5$, $r = R_4$ and $R + r = R_1$.

It can be seen in Equation (10) that if R is much greater than r and assuming equal tolerances for all resistors, then variations on the resistor R_4 ($=r$) become much less signicant for the output impedance compared to the variations on other resistors.

4.2. Model 2: Finite Open-Loop Gain

By sampling randomly the resistors to fall next to theirs nominal values and calculating Z_{out}, it would imply that we are assigning to Z_{out} randomly values which are selected near by a pole of a function. It means that high values can be obtained as well as the small ones, which, in turns, are much more difficult to happen. Furthermore, as it can be seen in **Figure 3**, the output impedance has a finite upper limit.

Both V_{out} and I_{out} can be written by two polynomial functions, which are both related to A, Z_{in}, R_o and the resistors. Considering Z_{in} sufficiently large and R_o sufficiently small, Z_{out} can be calculated according to Equation (11) as a function of the open-loop gain A.

$$Z_{\text{out}}(A) = \frac{R_2R_{E1}A + R_{E1}(R_2 + R_3)}{A(R_{E2} - R_1R_3) + (R_2 + R_3)(R_1 + R_{E2}/R_2)} \tag{11}$$

where $R_{E2} = R_2(R_4 + R_5)$ and $R_{E1} = R_4(R_1 + R_5)$.

Perturbations in the coefficients of the gain A in both numerator and denominator of Equation (11) may lead it to negative values and then to instability. Therefore, they are much more important than the independent terms. The numerator can be approximately bounded by $r(A + 2)R(2R + r)(1 \pm 3\delta)$, by assuming $R = R_2 = R_3 = R_5$, $r = R_4$ and $R + r = R_1$. On the other hand, the coefficient of the

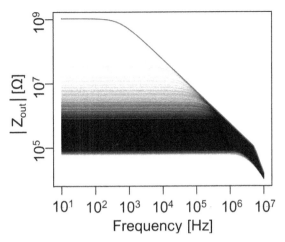

Figure 3. Probability distribution of the output impedance, using the OPA655 and resistor tolerances of ±1%.

gain A in the denominator of Equation (11) may assume both positive and negative values in the range of $-2\delta R(R + r)$ to $+2\delta R(R + r)$, and the independent term is $4R(R + r)(1 + 2\delta)$.

By considering small perturbations, Z_{out} can be approximated by $A/(a_1 A + a_0)$, where the denominator of this expression in the complex plane is a straight line crossing a_0 with an angle $\theta(A)$. Therefore, it can be calculated that the modulus of Z_{out} is inversely proportional to the distance from a point in that line to the origin and the phase is the difference between the arguments of such a point and the gain A. As a result, the modulus of Z_{out} can be written as a function of its phase, as shown in Equation (12).

$$|Z_{out}| \cong \frac{rR(r + 2R)}{a_1 + a_0/A} \qquad (12)$$

where

$$a_0 = 2R(r + R)\left[2 + \frac{r + 2R}{Z_{in}}\right] \qquad (13)$$

$$a_1 = R_2(R_5 + R_4) - R_1 R_3 \qquad (14)$$

$$|A| = A_0 \cdot \cos(\theta(A)) \qquad (15)$$

By doing a simple geometric analysis in Equation (12), it can be observed that the distribution of Z_{out} in the complex plane results into a circle centered at the imaginary axis with one of its vertices at the origin. It can be concluded that small Z_{out} has a phase near zero or -180 degrees, as the resistors are combined to give a higher Z_{out} and then the phase tends to -90 degrees, as shown in Equation (16) by assuming that the Equation (17) is satisfied.

$$|Z_{out,max}| = \frac{rR(r + 2R)}{|Im(a_0/A)|} \qquad (16)$$

$$R_2(R_5 + R_4) - R_1 R_3 + Re(a_0/A) = 0 \qquad (17)$$

By considering negligible variations in the denominator of Equation (12) and also assuming only real values for the coefficient a_0 (see Equation 13), the Z_{out} phase can be given by "$-\theta(a_1 + a_0/A)$" and the modulus by "$rR(2R + r)/|a_1 + a_0|$". The term "$a_1 + a_0/A$" represents a horizontal line in the complex plane, so that the product between "$|a_1 + a_0/A|$" and "$\sin[\theta(a_1 + a_0/A)]$" is always constant. Therefore, Z_{out} can be approximated by a circumference of radius $|Z_{out,max}|/2$ according to Equation (18).

$$|Z_{out}| = |Z_{out,max}|\left|\sin\left[-\theta(Z_{out})\right]\right| \qquad (18)$$

Figure 4 shows both real and imaginary parts of Z_{out} calculated by using a set of random resistors ($r = 1$ k$\Omega \pm$ 0.1% and $R = 100$ k$\Omega \pm$ 0.1%) and the operational amplifiers TL081 (graphics 1, 2 and 3), uA741 (graphics 4, 5 and 6) and OPA655 (graphics 7, 8 and 9), according to the parameters shown in **Table 1**. Simulations were made with and without the output resistance R_0. The red points were calculated values by using randomly values for the resistors in the range +0.1% and −0.1%. The blue circle represents the geometric space in the complex plan which contains the calculated points according to Equation 12. The simulations show the results at three different frequencies: 10 KHz (first column); 100 kHz (second column); and 1 MHz (third column). It can be seen that the MMHCS circuit designed by using the OPA655 has the highest output impedance, which is approximately 1.02 MΩ at 10 kHz. It can also be seen that the probability of getting the maximum output impedance does depend on the frequency and opamp used which, in turns, depends on the open-loop gain corner frequency. The graphic 6 shows that Z_{out} is equal to zero at 1 MHz when using the opamp uA741.

Figure 5 shows the output impedance of the MMHCS designed by the operational amplifiers TL081 (first column) and OPA655 (second column) at 10 kHz, using resistor tolerances of 0.1% (graphics "a" and "b"), 1% (graphics "c" and "d") and 10% (graphics "e" and "f"). It can be calculated that the maximum Z_{out} is approximately 213.6 kΩ when using the opamp TL081 whereas 1.06 MΩ for the OPA655 one, considering resistor tolerances of 0.1%. However, the probability of getting such a value is much smaller for the OPA655 case. It can also be seen that the probability density on getting maximum Zout increases significantly as increasing the resistor tolerances.

5. Mirrored Howland Current Source: Modeling

In order to improve the stability of the circuit, two single-ended Howland circuits can be set together in order to have a differential output current, which is also called

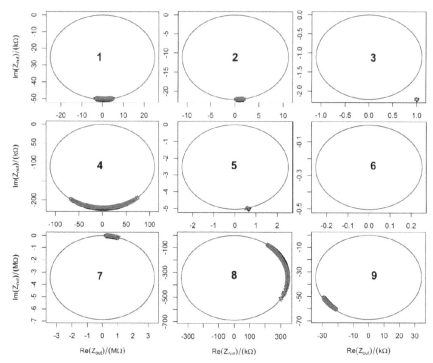

Figure 4. The real and imaginary part of the output impedance by using resistor tolerance of 0.1%.

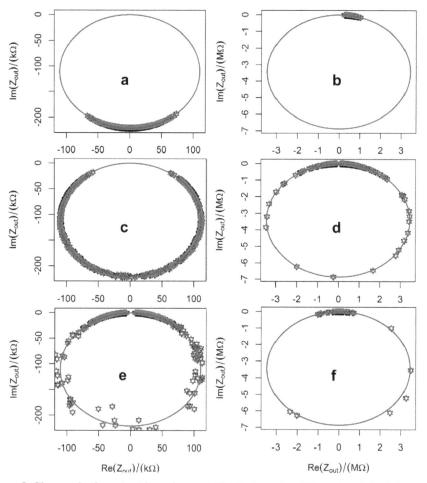

Figure 5. Changes in the output impedance at 10 kHz by using different resistor tolerances.

as Mirrored Modified Howland Current Source (MMHCS) and it is shown in **Figure 6** [17]. This type of current source uses two equal input voltages with 180 degrees phase shift from each other but also has a unique reference for both sides of the circuit, which, in turns, reduce the feed-through capacitance between output and input. This topology may significantly reduce the even harmonics of the output current, and then improving its linearity and reducing the amount of output voltage level at each side of this current source.

The MMHCS can be represented by its Norton equivalent circuit, as shown in **Figure 7**. The output voltage at each side of the load can then be calculated according to Equations (19) and (20), where I_{N1} and I_{N2} are the short-circuit currents and Z_{N1} and Z_{N2} are the output impedance of each side of the circuit.

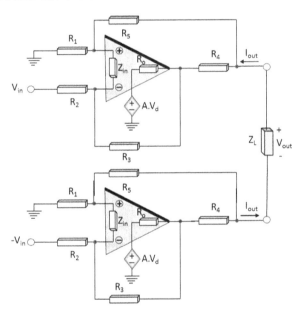

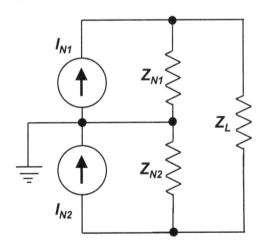

Figure 6. Schematic diagram of the mirrored modified Howland current source.

Figure 7. Equivalent Norton circuit for the mirrored modified Howland current source.

$$V_{\text{out1}} = \frac{I_{N1} \cdot Z_{N2} \cdot Z_{N2} - I_{N2} \cdot Z_{N2} \cdot (Z_L + Z_{N1})}{Z_L + Z_{N1} + Z_{N2}} \quad (19)$$

$$V_{\text{out2}} = \frac{I_{N1} \cdot Z_{N1} \cdot (Z_L + Z_{N2}) - I_{N2} \cdot Z_{N2} \cdot Z_{N1}}{Z_L + Z_{N1} + Z_{N2}} \quad (20)$$

The output current in the load impedance Z_L can then be calculated according to Equation (21). As a result, the differential output voltage V_{diff} can be calculated by Equation (22).

$$I_L = \frac{I_{N1} \cdot Z_{N1} + I_{N2} \cdot Z_{N2}}{Z_L + Z_{N1} + Z_{N2}} \quad (21)$$

$$V_{\text{diff}} = \frac{(I_{N1} - I_{N2}) \cdot Z_{N1} \cdot Z_{N2} + (V_{N1} - V_{N2}) \cdot Z_L/2}{Z_L + Z_{N1} + Z_{N2}} \quad (22)$$

where $V_{N1} = Z_{N1}I_{N1}$ and $V_{N2} = Z_{N2}I_{N2}$.

It is important to note that if the output impedances Z_{N1} and Z_{N2} have got similar high values, then it is expected that the difference $Z_{N1} - Z_{N2}$ be very small whereas the sum $Z_{N1} + Z_{N2}$ be very high. It can be seen in (22) that the differential voltage V_{diff} reduces to the product between $(I_{N1} - I_{N2})$ and $Z_{N1,2}$, for example if the output impedances of the current source are hundred times larger than the load impedance. A difference of 1% in I_{N1} or I_{N2} can duplicate the voltage in one of the load terminals. The difference at the output which is seeing by each terminal leads to a common mode voltage, which is dependent of the load charge. This results from the fact that each side of the current source tries to fix the output current to a different value.

6. Discussions

6.1. Output Impedance

It is predicted by Equation (12) that if the open-loop gain A is large, then it is very difficult to set the output impedance to its optimal value. It was showed that as decreasing the gain A the size of the impedance circle is also decreased and then the region away from the origin become more statistically populated, as shown in **Figure 3**.

Researches have been using the differential (mirrored) output current sources for getting a more stable circuit and higher output impedance. The output impedance of this type of current source can be calculated by sum of the output impedances from both single-ended circuits (*i.e.* $Z_{N1} + Z_{N2}$). It is thought having only advantage reasons for doing that but it also suffers from high open-loop gain of the operational amplifiers. The real part of Z_{out} can be either positive or negative and its imaginary part very small, then leading to a differential Z_{out} even smaller than the single-ended output impedances.

6.2. Operational Amplifier Limitations

As discussed before, from (22) it can be seen that small current differences at each side of the mirrored current source can increase the common mode voltage at the load terminals. In order to preserve those differences in the output current, the operational amplifiers have to supply the differential voltage as well as the common mode voltage.

The output impedance of the current source must be high otherwise the load current varies as varying the load impedance. By designing a high output impedance current source, the transconductance gains have to be precisely matched for preventing the operational amplifiers to work one against each other. This might be explained by the fact that they are connected in series, and then both circuits are designed to reject any variation in its output current.

6.3. Tuning the Mirrored Current Source

Tuning the mirrored Howland current source is not a simple task as it has to be done in both side of the circuit at the same time.

It was shown that the transconductance gain can be approximately given by the ratio between the resistor $-R_3$ and the product "R_2R_4". Consequently, it can be interpreted as a current gain, where instead of having an input voltage it has an input current ($=V_{in}/R_2$). As a result, both branches of the circuit which contains the resistors R_2 (see **Figure 6**) should be connected in series in order to prevent input current differences at each side of the current source. Therefore, it can be used only one resistor R_2 for both source sides.

In order to have equal output characteristics at both sides of the mirrored modified Howland current source, both sides have to have an equal ratio of R_3/R_4. This might be solved by adding a potentiometer in series with one of R_4 for tuning the differential output current. In practice, this can be done by short-circuiting the output and measuring the output voltage while tuning the potentiometer to have a null output voltage. It might be necessary to connect a resistor at each side of the short-circuit in order to prevent saturation by the operational amplifiers.

By the fact that the resistor R_4 has a very small influence in the output impedance, this last can be tuned by varying either the resistor R_5 or R_1. The resistor R_1 of both sides can also be connected in series in order to reduce imbalances from these circuit sides, thus one of the resistors R_5 becomes the natural tuning element for controlling the output impedance of the mirrored modified Howland current source.

6.4. Limitations

The analytical analyses and the equations related to the output of the Howland current source have not considered any stray capacitances which might be found in practical circuits. Also, the numerical solutions for both output current and impedance of the circuit have not considered the common-mode input impedance of the operational amplifiers, as well as the common-mode rejection ratio (CMRR). It has to be pointed out that the probability density function was used by assuming that the resistor variations behave as a normal distribution. Therefore, care should be taken when analyzing the results obtained in this work, especially when they are related to practical circuits.

7. Conclusions

It was fully described the modeling of both output current and impedance of the Howland current source by considering the operational amplifier parameters and the mismatching between electrodes. It was shown that the output resistance of the operational amplifier does not play a role in the output characteristic of the Howland circuit whereas the open-loop gain causes a great impact on it.

It was also shown that the higher the gain, the most sensitive is the output impedance in respect to the resistors tolerances, as illustrated in **Figures 4** and **5**. In order to operate at high frequency, the open-loop gain of the opamp has to be very high. This explain why the resistors have to be precisely matched in order to obtain a MMHCS circuit which can deliver a constant differential output current into the load over a wide frequency range.

It can be concluded from this work that both side of the MMHCS should be very symmetrical if high output impedance from this type of circuit is desired. This is a very significant achievement found in this work for the design of high output impedance Howland current sources used in bioimpedance measurements. This may lead to empirical distribution of important characteristics of the MMCHS during the design and it might save time and money when this type of circuit is put in production scale. Furthermore, the error estimation provided here can guide researchers, who have no previous knowledge in Howland current source, to design a high quality circuit in terms of both output current and impedance spectra according to the application requirements.

8. Acknowledgements

This work was supported by the State University of Santa Catarina and the National Council for Scientific and Technological Development (grant 237931/2012-5).

REFERENCES

[1]   P. Pouliquen, J. Vogelstein and R. Etienne-Cummings,

"Practical Considerations for the Use of a Howland Current Source for Neuron-Stimulation," *Proceedings of the IEEE Biomedical Circuits and Systems Conference*, Baltimore, 20-22 November 2008, pp. 33-36.

[2]   E. Basham, Z. Yang and W. Liu, "Circuit and Coil DE-SIGN for *in-Vitro* Magnetic Neural Stimulation Systems," *IEEE Transactions on Biomedical Circuits and Systems*, Vol. 3, No. 5, 2009, pp. 321-331.

[3]   K. Sooksood, T. Stieglitz and M. Ortmanns, "An Active Approach for Charge Balancing in Functional Electrical Stimulation," *IEEE Transactions on Biomedical Circuits and Systems*, Vol. 4, No. 3, 2010, pp. 162-170.

[4]   D. X. Chen, X. Deng and W. Q. Yang, "Comparison of Three Current Sources for Single-Electrode Capacitance Measurement," *Review of Scientific Instruments*, Vol. 81, No. 3, 2010, pp. 1-3.

[5]   R. A. Pease, "A Comprehensive Study of the Howland Current Pump," 2008. http://www.ti.com/lit/an/snoa474a/snoa474a.pdf

[6]   J. Frounchi, F. Dehkhoda and M. H. Zarifi, "A Low-Distortion Wideband Integrated Current Source for Tomography Applications," *European Journal of Scientific Research*, Vol. 27, No. 1, 2009, pp. 56-65.

[7]   P. Bertemes-Filho, "Tissue Characterization Using an Impedance Spectroscopy Probe," Ph.D. Thesis, University of Sheffield, Sheffield, 2002.

[8]   S. Grimnes and O. G. Martinsen, "Bioimpedance and Bioelectricity Basics," 2nd Edition, Elsevier Ltd, Amsterdam, 2008.

[9]   A. Keshtkar, Z. Salehnia and B. Shokouhi, "Bladder Cancer Detection Using Electrical Impedance Technique (Tabriz Mark 1)," Pathology Research International, Vol. 2012, 2012, pp. 1-5.

[10] P. Aberg, I. Nicander and S. Ollmar, "Minimally Invasive Electrical Impedance Spectroscopy of Skin Exemplified by Skin Cancer Assessments," *Proceeding of the 25th Annual International Conference of the IEEE Engineering in Medicine and Biology Society*, Cancun, 17-21 September 2003, pp. 3211-3214.

[11] P. Åberg, I. Nicander, J. Hansson, P. Geladi, U. Holmgren and S. Ollmar, "Skin Cancer Identification Using Multifrequency Electrical Impedance-A Potential Screening Tool," *IEEE Transactions on Biomedical Engineering*, Vol. 51, No. 12, 2004, pp. 2097-2102.

[12] D. H. Sheingold, "Impedance & Admittance Transformations Using Operational Amplifiers," Lightning Empiricist, Vol. 12, No. 1, 1964, pp. 1-8. http://www.philbrickar-chive.org/1964-1_v12_no1_the_lightning_empiricist.htm

[13] P. Bertemes-Filho, R. G. Lima, M. B. P. Amato and H. Tanaka, "Performance of an Adaptive Multiplexed Current Source Used in Electrical Impedance Tomography," *Proceeding of the 20th Brazilian Congress on Biomedical Engineering*, São Pedro, 22-26 October 2006, pp. 1167-1170.

[14] F. Seoane, R. Bragós and K. Lindecranz, "Current Source for Multifrequency Broadband Electrical Bioimpedance Spectroscopy Systems. A Novel Approach," *Proceedings of the 28th Annual International Conference of the IEEE Engineering in Medicine and Biology Society*, New York, 31 August-3 September 2006, pp. 5121-5125.

[15] F Seoane, R Macías, R Bragos and K Lindecrantz, "Simple Voltage-Controlled Current Source for Wideband Electrical Bioimpedance Spectroscopy: Circuit Dependences and Limitations," *Measurement Science and Technology*, Vol. 22, No. 11, 2011, pp. 1-11.

[16] P. Bertemes-Filho, B. H. Brown and A. J. Wilson, "A Comparison of Modified Howland Circuits as Current Generators with Current Mirror Type Circuits," *Physiological Measurement*, Vol. 21, No. 1, 2000, pp. 1-6.

[17] P. Bertemes-Filho, L. H. Negri, A. Felipe and V. C. Vincence, "Mirrored Modified Howland Circuit for Bioimpedance Applications: Analytical Analysis," *Journal of Physics: Conference Series*, Vol. 407, No. 1, 2012, pp. 1-8.

24

A Robust Denoising Algorithm for Sounds of Musical Instruments Using Wavelet Packet Transform

Raghavendra Sharma, Vuppuluri Prem Pyara
Department of Electrical Engineering, Dayalbagh Educational Institute, Agra, India

ABSTRACT

In this paper, a robust DWPT based adaptive bock algorithm with modified threshold for denoising the sounds of musical instruments shehnai, dafli and flute is proposed. The signal is first segmented into multiple blocks depending upon the minimum mean square criteria in each block, and then thresholding methods are used for each block. All the blocks obtained after denoising the individual block are concatenated to get the final denoised signal. The discrete wavelet packet transform provides more coefficients than the conventional discrete wavelet transform (DWT), representing additional subtle detail of the signal but decision of optimal decomposition level is very important. When the sound signal corrupted with additive white Gaussian noise is passed through this algorithm, the obtained peak signal to noise ratio (PSNR) depends upon the level of decomposition along with shape of the wavelet. Hence, the optimal wavelet and level of decomposition may be different for each signal. The obtained denoised signal with this algorithm is close to the original signal.

Keywords: DWPT; Adaptive Block Denoising; Peak Signal to Noise Ratio; Wavelet Thresholding

1. Introduction

In the field of denoising the sounds of musical instruments, time frequency based transforms play an important role. They allow us to work with a sound signal from both time and frequency perspectives simultaneously. Such transforms have traditionally been useful in studying the nature of the sound signal, noise, and in facilitating the application of aesthetically interesting and novel modification to specific sound signals [1]. We are interested in a transform that is useful in working with musical instrument sound signals, and we look at the application of the discrete wavelet packet transform (DWPT) to remove the additive white Gaussian noise. There are several reasons for choosing the DWPT, it is inherently multi-resolution, making it more suited to human psychoacoustics than fixed resolution transforms as short time Fourier transform (STFT) [2]. It is easily reconfigured to allocate time frequency resolution in different ways through various basis selection approaches. Furthermore, efficient discrete time algorithms are available, and the transform basis function is inherently time localized without the introduction of a separate window function.

Signals may be transformed, modified and re-synthesized using DWPT without affecting the quality of the signal [3].

Noise has been a major problem for all signal processing applications. An unwanted signal gets superimposed over clean undisturbed signal. Noise exists in high frequency, but the sound signal is primarily low frequency. Since the wavelet transform decomposes the signal into approximation (low frequency) and detail (high frequency) coefficients [4,5], much of the noise is concentrated in detail coefficients. This suggests a method to denoise the signal, simply reducing the size of the detail coefficients before using them to reconstruct the signal, which is called thresholding or shrinkage rule [6]. We cannot eliminate the detail coefficients entirely, because they contain some important information of the signal. Various kinds of thresholding have been proposed in literature [7], but the choice depends upon the application at hand. The two important types of thresholing, hard and soft have been used to denoise the signal. In hard thresholding the wavelet coefficients below the given threshold are set to zero, but in soft thresholding the wavelet coefficients are reduced by a quantity equal to the threshold value. The extension of discrete wavelet transform is discrete wavelet packet transform in which we split both low pass and high pass filters at all scales in filter bank implementation to obtain flexible and detail analysis transform for denoising the sound signals [8]. In [9], wavelet packet approach which deals with heterogeneous noise for preprocessing of mass spectrometry data is discussed which incorporate a variance change point detection method in thresholding. Wavelet packet method has been used to reduce the Additive White Gaussian Noise from the speech signal which shows significant SNR improvement [10]. The rest of the article is organized as follows: In Section 2, brief theory of discrete wavelet packet transform (DWPT) is given. Wavelet packet adaptive block denoising scheme is discussed in Section 3, which is preceded by block denoising algorithm based on DWPT in Section 4. The various experimental results are discussed in Section 5. Section 6 gives the concluding remarks based on the experimental results.

2. Discrete Wavelet Packet Transform (DWPT)

Discrete wavelet packet transforms are used to get the advantage of better frequency resolution representation. When the wavelet transform is generalized to wavelet packet transform, not only the low pass filter output is decomposed through further filtering, but the high pass filter output decomposed as well. The ability to decompose the high pass filter outputs means that the wavelet packet allows for more than one basis function at a given scale, versus the wavelet transform which has one basis function at each scale other than the deepest level, where it has two.

The set of wavelet packets collectively make up the complete family of possible basis, and many potential basis can be constructed from them. If only the low pass filter is decomposed, the result is wavelet basis. If all low pass and high pass filters are decomposed, the complete tree basis results. This basis has the time frequency partitioning like STFT. Between these two extremes lie a large number of possible basis and their associated sub trees. Nodes can be merged or split based on the requirement of application. In all cases, the leaves of each connected sub tree of the complete wavelet packet tree from the basis of initial space; they span the space in linearly independent fashion. The tree diagram of a depth-3 complete tree basis is shown in the **Figure 1**.

As with the wavelet transform tree diagram in [11], denotes the depth within the transform and k the position of each node (j,k), but now the position index conveys more information, specifically which wavelet packet it corresponds to a given scale. We refer to the associate wavelet packet as $w_{j,k,p}$ analogus to the

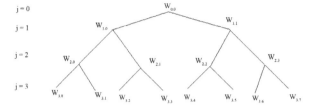

Figure 1. Depth-3 discrete wavelet packet transform tree.

wavelet $w_{k,p}$. The tree diagram does not convey time domain information, so the index p is not used in node naming. Hence in wavelet packet, if all the packets are at the same scale, we may simply refer to them as w_k as shown in the **Figure 1**.

Furthermore, $w_{j,k}$ is either the scaling function, or derived from the scaling function. DWPT does not require the explicit definition of wavelet, only filter definitions are enough. To see the wavelet packet at given level of decomposition, we can do a recursion of them at each node moving down the tree, to get the wavelet at next level. Specifically, if we split a wavelet packet node at level j and position k into two nodes at level $j+1$ and locations $2k$ and $2k+1$, we get the following two packets:

$$w_{j+1,2k}(n) = \sum_{m=0}^{M-1} h_0[m] w_{j,k}(2n-m) \qquad (1)$$

and

$$w_{j+1,2k+1}(n) = \sum_{m=0}^{M-1} h_1[m] w_{j,k}(2n-m) \qquad (2)$$

Then the wavelet packet transform coefficients $c_{j,k,p}$ are given by:

$$c_{j,k,p} = \sum_{m=0}^{M-1} s[m] w_{j,k,p}(m) \qquad (3)$$

And the original signal can be expressed in terms of these coefficients and the corresponding wavelet packets as:

$$s[m] = \sum_{j,k,p} c_{j,k,p} w_{j,k,p}[m], \qquad (4)$$

$(j,k) \in$ all leaf nodes of basis.
where p ranges over all time offsets at scale j for which signal s is defined.

3. Wavelet Packet Adaptive Block Denoising

The wavelet packet based denoising technique employs the decomposition concept in adaptive base of wavelets. This technique is efficient in denoising the musical sound signal corrupted with additive white Gaussian noise (AWGN), which is evenly distributed over the entire signal, and removal of AWGN from noisy signal is difficult task. Donoho and Johnstone pioneered the work of filtering the additive white Gaussian noise using wavelet thresholding [12]. The block denoising is explained in the following sub sections:

3.1. Thresholding Based Denoising

A noise reduction technique developed by donoho, uses the wavelet coefficients contraction and its principle consists of three steps;

1) Apply discrete wavelet transform to noisy signal:

$$W \cdot y = W \cdot s + W \cdot z \qquad (5)$$

where y, s, z and W are the noisy musical instrument sound, original clean sound signal, noise signal and the matrix associated to the discrete wavelet transform respectively.

2) Threshold the obtained wavelet coefficients.

3) Reconstruct the desired signal by applying the inverse wavelet transform to the thresholded wavelet coefficients.

The thresholding function which is also known as wavelet shrinkage function is categorized as hard thresholding and soft thresholding function. The hard thresholdingfunction retains the wavelet coefficients which are greater than the threshold λ and sets all other to zero. The hard thresholding is defined as:

$$f_h(x) = \begin{cases} x, & \text{if } |x| \geq \lambda \\ 0, & \text{otherwise} \end{cases} \qquad (6)$$

The threshold λ is chosen according to the signal energy and the standard deviation σ of the noise. If the wavelet coefficient is greater than λ, then it is assumed that it is significant and contributes to the original signal. Otherwise it is due to the noise and discarded. The soft thresholding function shrinks the wavelet coefficients by λ towards zero. Hence this function is also called as shrinkage function. The soft thresholding function is defined as:

$$f_s(x) = \begin{cases} x - \lambda, & \text{if } |x| \geq \lambda \\ 0, & \text{if } |x| < \lambda \\ x + \lambda, & \text{if } |x| \leq \lambda \end{cases} \qquad (7)$$

In [13], we see that the soft thresholding gives lesser mean square error. Due to this reason soft thresholding is preferred over hard thresholding, but in case of some signals, we could see that hard thresholding results in lesser amount of mean square error.

3.2. Block Selection

Most of the musical instrument sound signals are far too long to be processed in their entirety; for example a 10 second sarangi sound signal sampled at 44.1 KHz will contain 441,000 samples. Thus, as with spectral methods of noise reduction, it is necessary to divide the time domain signal in multiple blocks and process the each block individually. The block formation of the signal is shown in the **Figure 2**. The important task is to choose the block length. Berger *et al.* [14] shows that, blocks which are too shorts fail to pick important time structures of the signal. Conversely, blocks which are too long miss cause the algorithm to miss the important transient details in the musical instrument sound signal. Due to the binary splitting nature of the tree bases in wavelet analysis to decompose the signal, it is better to choose the length of each block with a number of samples to a power of two.

As discussed previously, the block size chosen must strike a balance between being able to pick up important transient detail in the sound signal, as well as recognizing longer duration, sustained events. **Tables 1** and **2** shows the PSNR values which are quality measures, obtained for various block sizes and for different signals.

Tables 1 and **2** show that the PSNR values for different wavelets are varying with the block size. Hence the optimum block is that for which we have maximum PSNR or minimum mean square error. The optimal block

Table 1. PSNR values obtained for different block length on shehnai sound with different wavelets.

Samples/block length (ms)	haar	db10	sym3	coif5	dmey
1024/23	23.06	33.99	30.99	36.42	36.41
2048/46	23.37	34.82	30.27	36.07	36.57
4096/92	23.96	36.45	31.73	36.9	39.62
8192/185	22.50	34.06	30.73	36.81	38.37
16,384/371	23.12	35.85	30.86	34.59	36.31
32,768/743	23.60	34.64	31.28	35.38	35.76
65,536/1486	22.50	33.21	30.95	35.25	36.25

Table 2. PSNR values obtained for different block length on dafli sound with different wavelets.

Samples/block length (ms)	haar	db10	sym3	coif5	dmey
1024/23	07.39	13.20	09.22	08.91	08.84
2048/46	32.74	34.84	23.43	34.15	37.22
4096/92	35.78	35.42	36.96	37.66	37.28
8192/185	37.17	44.95	43.17	46.76	42.57
16,384/371	43.77	50.17	45.63	49.68	47.20
32,768/743	41.89	44.79	42.88	42.58	39.49
65,536/1486	40.84	45.29	44.32	45.37	38.54

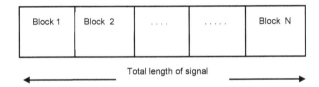

Figure 2. Block formation of signal

size for shehnai sound is 4096 samples and for dafli 16,384 samples. The informal listening test agree with this statement in a general sense, hence the block size is variable for musical instrument sound signals.

3.3. Threshold Selection

Donoho and Johnstone derived a general optimal universal threshold for the Gaussian white noise under a mean square error (MSE) criterion described in [12]. However this threshold is not ideal for musical instrument sound signals due to poor correlation between the MSE and subjective quality and the more realistic presence of correlated noise. Here we use a new time frequency dependent threshold estimation method. In this method first of all the standard deviation of the noise, σ is calculated for each block. For given σ, we calculate the threshold for each block. Noise component removal by thresholding the wavelet coefficients is based on the observation that in musical instrument sound signal, energy is mostly concentrated in small number of wavelet dimensions. The coefficients of these dimensions are relatively very large compared to other dimensions or to any other signal like noise that has its energy spread over a large number of coefficients. Hence by setting smaller coefficients to be zero, we can optimally eliminate noise while preserving important information of the signal. In wavelet domain noise is characterized by smaller coefficients, while signal energy is concentrated in larger coefficients. This feature is useful for eliminating noise from signal by choosing the appropriate threshold. Generally the selected threshold is multiplied by the median value of the detail coefficients at some specified level which is called threshold processing.

At each level of decomposition, the standard deviation of the noisy signal is calculated. The standard deviation is calculated by Equation (8):

$$\sigma_j = \frac{\text{median}\left(\left|c_j\right|\right)}{0.6745} \tag{8}$$

where c_j are high frequency wavelet coefficients at j^{th} level of decomposition, which are used to identify the noise components and σ_j is Median Absolute Deviation (MAD) at this level. This standard deviation can be further used to set the threshold value based on the noise energy at that level. The modified threshold value [15] can be obtained by the equation (9):

$$T_h = k \cdot \sigma_j \sqrt{2\log\left(L_j \log_2 L_j\right)} \tag{9}$$

where T_h is threshold value, L_j is the length of each block of noisy signal and k is the constant whose value is varying between 0 - 1. For determining the optimum threshold, value of k should be estimated.

4. Denoising Algorithm

The proposed wavelet packet based block denoising algorithm for reduction of white Gaussian noise is explained in the following steps:
1) Take a musical instrument sound signal of suitable length.
2) Add White Gaussian Noise to the original signal depending upon the standard deviation σ.
3) Divide the noisy signal into blocks of different length depending upon the length of the signal in time domain, and the number of samples should be to a power of two.
4) Determine the optimal block size based on minimum mean square error criteria.
5) Compute the discrete wavelet packet transform (DWPT) of one block of the noisy signal at level 1.
6) Estimate the standard deviation of the noise using Equation (8) and determine the threshold value using Equation (9), then apply the different thresholding techniques for time and level dependent wavelet co-

efficients using Equations (6) and (7).

7) Take inverse discrete wavelet packet transform (IDWPT) of the coefficients obtained through step 6, which has reduced noise.

8) Calculate mean square error (MSE), peak signal to noise ratio (PSNR) for denoised signal.

9) Repeat steps 4 to step 7 for other level of decomposition 2 - 5.

10) Concatenate all the blocks of the denoised signals obtained through step 8 and do averaging operation for MSE and PSNR of the musical instrument sound signal.

The complete DWPT based denoising algorithm is shown graphically in **Figure 3**.

5. Results and Discussions

The denoising algorithm developed in the previous section is applied to the sound samples of the various Indian musical instruments sampled at 44.1 K samples per second. For experimental purpose the sounds of three musical instruments shehnai, dafli and flute are taken. For comparing the performance of the various wavelets for musical instrument sound signals, six wavelets haar, db10, sym3, coif5, dmey and bior 2.2 are taken. Besides observing the performance of the wavelets, the effect of decomposition is also discussed.

For comparing the performance and measurement of quality of denoising, the peak signal to noise ratio (PSNR) is determined between the original signal S_i and the signal denoised S_d, by our algorithm.

$$PSNR = 10\log_{10}\left(\frac{S_{\max}^2}{MSE}\right) \quad (10)$$

where $S_{\max}$ is the maximum value of the signal and is given by,

$$S_{\max} = \max\left(\max\left(S_i\right), \max\left(S_d\right)\right) \quad (11)$$

And MSE is mean square error, given by:

$$MSE = \frac{1}{N}\sum_{l=1}^{N}\left[S_d\left(l\right) - S_i\left(l\right)\right]^2 \quad (12)$$

where N is the length of the signal. The PSNR vaues obtained for different wavelets applied on shehnai, dafli and flute signals at different level of decomposition are shown in **Tables 3-5**. The additive white Gaussian noise is taken at $\sigma = 0.1$, which is approximately 50% of the signal value.

It is observed from **Tables 3-5** that the PSNR values are dependent upon the shape of the wavelet, type of thresholding and the level of decomposition. Hard thresholds are better than soft thresholds for denoising the musical instrument sound signals. The selection of level of decomposition plays a significant role, and should be optimal for best denoising results. Hence, the shehnai sound will give best results when denoised with db 10 wavelet at level 5, dafli sound with dmey at level 5 and flute sound with db10 at level 4, respectively. The different signals denoised with optimal wavelet and level of decomposition are shown in the **Figures 4-6**.

6. Conclusion

Adaptive wavelet packet transform has been widely used in denoising the sounds of musical instruments and

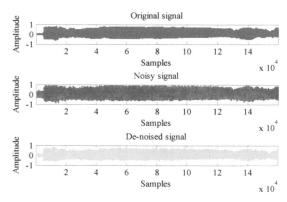

Figure 4. Original, noisy and denoised shehnai signal with db 10 at level 5.

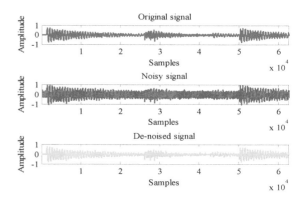

Figure 5. Original, noisy and denoised dafli signal with dmey at level 5.

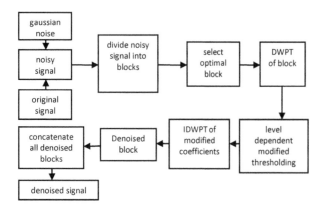

Figure 3. DWPT based block denoising algorithm with modified threshold.

Table 3. PSNR values of shehnai sound after decompostion at different levels.

Wavelet	Level 2		Level 3		Level 4		Level 5	
	soft	hard	soft	hard	soft	hard	soft	hard
haar	26.02	31.33	18.57	18.72	23.09	27.65	16.89	25.32
db10	23.95	23.43	18.53	18.55	20.14	27.23	16.52	31.62
sym3	26.44	25.68	18.56	18.56	19.65	27.21	14.85	30.39
coif5	24.02	23.71	18.68	19.65	21.05	27.22	18.13	29.65
dmey	23.92	23.78	18.57	18.76	23.34	23.48	22.76	23.43
bior2.2	31.06	26.27	18.44	18.54	25.26	25.75	20.61	26.93

Table 4. PSNR values of dafli sound after decomposition at different levels.

Wavelet	Level 2		Level 3		Level 4		Level 5	
	soft	hard	soft	hard	soft	hard	soft	hard
haar	20.07	19.88	17.56	17.72	27.76	27.58	26.08	27.48
db10	20.14	19.56	17.66	17.75	24.30	24.56	26.05	27.67
sym3	20.12	19.86	17.46	17.56	26.12	25.24	26.92	26.93
coif5	19.65	20.05	17.50	17.59	25.88	24.88	27.05	26.79
dmey	20.05	19.78	17.44	17.65	24.47	25.18	27.05	27.97
bior2.2	20.00	19.77	17.35	17.53	23.58	21.73	24.21	23.11

Table 5. PSNR values of flute sound after decomposition at different levels.

Wavelet	Level 2		Level 3		Level 4		Level 5	
	soft	hard	soft	hard	soft	hard	soft	hard
haar	21.83	22.99	19.55	19.21	16.16	18.82	9.07	18.97
db10	23.73	24.02	19.09	19.40	13.65	35.71	11.31	33.00
sym3	24.50	24.64	19.36	19.52	16.49	28.64	11.48	30.47
coif5	23.98	24.10	19.40	19.63	13.75	33.98	11.42	29.68
dmey	23.75	24.37	19.25	19.53	13.74	34.53	11.76	30.26
bior2.2	28.80	27.72	19.41	19.48	13.46	18.94	10.87	19.70

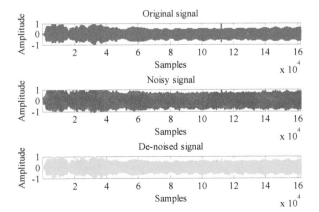

Figure 6. Original, noisy and denoised flute signal with db10 at level 4.

Providing better performance in terms of PSNR values than the other denoising techniques. In this paper, discrete wavelet packet transform is used for denoising-shehnai, dafli and flute sound signal corrupted with additive white Gaussian noise, 50% of the signal strength. First, sound signal is divided into multiple blocks depending upon the optimal block size for each signal. Denoising of signal is performed with these optimal block sizes in wavelet packet domain by thresholding the wavelet coefficients at different level of decomposition. It is observed that hard thresholding gives better PSNR than soft thresholding at all the decomposition levels. The choice of the optimal level of decomposition is important, and different for each sound signal. If the level of decomposition is not optimal then the PSNR value will not be maximum, hence denoising will not be the best. Maximum PSNR value for shehnai sound is at level 5 with db10 wavelet, dafli at level 5 with dmey and flute at level 4 with db10 respectively. When each block is denoised, all the blocks are concatenated to form the final denoised signal. It is also observed that when modified threshold with is used, the PSNR values are increased. Higher thresholds remove the noise well but some parts of the original signal are also removed because it is not possible to remove the noise without affecting the original signal.

REFERENCES

[1] M. Lang, H. Guo, J. E. Odegard, C. S. Burrus and R. O. Wells, "Noise Reduction Using an Undecimated Discrete Wavelet Transform," *IEEE Signal Processing Letters*, Vol. 3, No. 1, 1996, pp. 10-12.

[2] J. Yang, Y. Wang, W. Xu and Q. Dai, "Image and Video Denoising Using Adaptive Dual Tree Discrete Wavelet Packets," *IEEE Transaction on Circuit and Systems for Video Technology*, Vol. 19, No. 5, 2009, pp. 642-655.

[3] B. J. Shankar and K. Duariswamy, "Wavelet Based Block Matching Process: An efficient Audio Denoising Technique," *European Journal of Scientific Research*, Vol. 48, No. 1, 2010, p. 16.

[4] R. Sharma and V. P. Pyara, "A Novel Approach to Synthesize Sounds of Some Indian Musical Instruments Using DWT," *International Journal of Computer Applications*, Vol. 45, No. 13, 2012, pp. 19-22.

[5] R. Sharma and V. P. Pyara, "A Comparative Analysis of Mean Square Error Adaptive Filter Algorithms for Generation of Modified Scaling and Wavelet Function," *International Journal of Engineering Science and Technology*, Vol. 4, No. 4, 2012, pp. 1396-1401.

[6] J. Yu and D. C. Liu, "Thresholding Based Wavelet Packet Methods for Doppler Ultrasound Signal Denoising," *IF-MBE Proceedings Springer Verlag Berlin Heidelberg*, Vol. 19, No. 9, 2008, pp. 408-412.

[7] T. Mourad, S. Lotfi and C. Adnen, "Spectral Entropy Employment in Speech Enhancement Based on Wavelet Packet," *International Journal of Computer and Information Engineering*, Vol. 1, No. 7, 2007, pp. 404-411.

[8] N. S. Nehe and R. S. Holambe, "DWT and LPC Based Feature Extraction Methods for Isolated Word Recognition," *EURASIP Journal of Audio, Speech and Music Processing*, Vol. 7, No. 1, 2012, pp. 1-7.#

[9] D. Kwon, M. Vannucci, J. J. Song, J. Jeong and R. M. Pfeiffer, "A Novel Wavelet Based Thresholding Method for the Pre-Processing of Mass Spectrometry Data That Accounts for Heterogeneous Noise," *Proteomics*, Vol. 8, No. 15, 2008, pp. 3019-3029.

[10] Y. Ren, M. T. Johnson and J. Tao, "Perceptually Motivated Wavelet Packet Transform for Bio-Acoustic Signal Enhancement," *Journal of Acoustic Society of America*, Vol. 124, No. 1, 2008, pp. 316-327.

[11] K. Ramchandran and M. Vetterli, "Best Wavelet Packet Bases in a Rate-distortion Sense," *IEEE Transaction on Image Processing*, Vol. 2, No. 2, 1993, pp. 160-175.

[12] D. L. Donoho and I. M. Johnstone, "Adapting to Unknown Smoothness via Wavelet Shrinkage," *Journal of the American Statistical Association*, Vol. 90, No. 432, 1995, pp. 1200-1224.

[13] S. G. Chang, B. Yu and M. Vetterli, "Adaptive Wavelet Thresholding for Image Denoising and Compression," *IEEE Transaction on Image Processing*, Vol. 9, No. 9, 2000, pp. 1532-1546.

[14] J. Berger, R. R. Coifman and J. G Maxim, "Removing Noise from Music Using Local Trigonometric Bases and Wavelet Packets," *Journal of The Audio Engineering Society*, Vol. 42, No. 10, 1994, pp. 808-818.

[15] M. T. Johnson, X. Yuan and Y. Ren, "Speech Signal Enhancement through Adaptive Wavelet Thresholding," *Speech Communication*, Vol. 49, No. 2, 2007, pp. 123-133.

25

Two Analytical Methods for Detection and Elimination of the Static Hazard in Combinational Logic Circuits

Mihai Grigore Timis, Alexandru Valachi, Alexandru Barleanu, Andrei Stan

Automatic Control and Computer Engineering Faculty, Technical University Gh.Asachi, Iasi, Romania

ABSTRACT

In this paper, the authors continue the researches described in [1], that consists in a comparative study of two methods to eliminate the static hazard from logical functions, by using the form of Product of Sums (POS), static hazard "0". In the first method, it used the consensus theorem to determine the cover term that is equal with the product of the two residual implicants, and in the second method it resolved a Boolean equation system. The authors observed that in the second method the digital hazard can be earlier detected. If the Boolean equation system is incompatible (doesn't have solutions), the considered logical function doesn't have the static 1 hazard regarding the coupled variable. Using the logical computations, this method permits to determine the needed transitions to eliminate the digital hazard.

Keywords: Combinational Circuits; Static Hazard; Logic Design; Boolean Functions

1. Introduction

Under certain conditions, on the output of the logical signals may occur unwanted transitions. These transitions are known as glitches. The logic glitch is a kind of unwanted noise presenting inthe output signal that can initiate an uncontrollable process. In the next level there is an input signal [2].

We can distinguish three types of noise that is introduced in CLC (Combinational Logic Circuits), called hazards (Static, Dynamic and Function Hazards).

In the following we consider only the static hazard problem in combinational logic systems, called static hazard "0".

- Static 1 hazard, also called SOP (Sum of Products) hazard—a glitch that occurs in otherwise steady-state 1 output signal from SOP logic;
- Static 0 hazard, also called POS (Product of Sums) hazard—a glitch that occurs in otherwise steady-state 0 output signal from POS logic.

Static Hazards in Two-Level Combinational Logic Circuits (Consensus Method [2]).

We will initially define:

- Coupled variable; a variable input is complemented within a term of function and uncomplemented in another term of the same function.

- Coupled term; one of two terms containing only one coupled variable.
- Residue; the part of a coupled term that remains after removing the coupled variable.
- Hazard cover (or consensus term).

The RPI (Redundant Prime Implicant) required to eliminate the static hazards:

AND the residues of coupled p-term to obtain the SOP hazard cover,

OR the residues of coupled s-term to obtain the POS hazard cover.

POS example: any logic function can be described as:

$$y = (e_0 + x_i)(e_1 + \overline{x_i})$$

where

$$e_0 = y(x_{n-1}, x_{n-2}, \cdots, x_{i+1}, 0, x_{i-1}, \cdots, x_0)$$
$$e_1 = y(x_{n-1}, x_{n-2}, \cdots, x_{i+1}, 1, x_{i-1}, \cdots, x_0) \tag{1}$$

Sometimes, the same function can be describes as:

$$y = (a + x_i)(b + \overline{x_i})c \tag{2}$$

Using the (1) form, we can say:

$$e_0 = ac$$
$$e_1 = bc \tag{2.1}$$

Using the algorithm described in [3], if $c \le a + b$, the expression from (2), (2.1) doesn't present static hazard in relation with the x_i input, and if $a = b = 0$, then results $c = 0$.

The condition to have static hazard in relation with the x_i input, is when $a = b = 0$ and $c = 1$.

The consensus method [4] consists of determination of coupled terms, then by removing the coupled variables we obtain residual values.

That meaning the (2) equation can be written like:

$$y = (a + x_i)(b + \overline{x_i})c(a + b) \quad (3)$$

It can be observed that the expression of the function is multiplied by the sum of residual values, the new expression presents static hazard in relation with the x_i input.

We proposed as example the 4 inputs logic function:

$$y = y(x_4, x_3, x_2, x_1, x_0)$$
$$= R_0(1, 3, 6, 7, 9, 11, 14, 17, 19, 20, 25, 27, 28) \quad (4)$$
$$+ R_\Phi(0, 5, 10, 16, 23, 24, 29, 31)$$

Using the Quine-McCluskey minimization method we obtain the equation from (5) and also the residual values determined by x_0 input:

$$y = (x_4 + x_3 + \overline{x_2} + \overline{x_1})(\overline{x_4} + x_1 + x_0)(x_2 + \overline{x_0})$$
$$\cdot (x_4 + + \overline{x_2} + \overline{x_1} + x_0)$$

$$a = (\overline{x_4} + x_1)(x_4 + \overline{x_2} + \overline{x_1}x_0)$$
$$b = x_2 \quad (5)$$
$$a + b = x_2 + \overline{x_4 x_2} + \overline{x_4 x_1}x_0 + x_4 x_1 + \overline{x_2}x_1 = x_2 + \overline{x_4} + x_1$$

The expression of no static hazard in relation with x_0 input:

$$y = (x_4 + x_3 + \overline{x_2} + \overline{x_1})(\overline{x_4} + x_1 + x_0)(x_2 + \overline{x_0})$$
$$\cdot (x_4 + \overline{x_2} + + \overline{x_1} + x_0)(\overline{x_4} + x_2 + x_1) \quad (6)$$

2. Method of Resolving of Boolean Equations [5]

In this paragraph we apply the consensus method [5] and the method of solving some specific Boolean equations.

If $y = (a + x_i)(b + \overline{x_i})c$, by resolving the next system equations it can be determined the vectors input values which presents static hazard.

$$a = 0$$
$$b = 0 \quad (7)$$
$$c = 1$$

If the (7) system has no solution, the function doesn't presents static hazard in relation with x_i.

Therefore, the expression of the function becomes:

$$a = (\overline{x_4} + x_1)(x_4 + \overline{x_2} + \overline{x_1} + x_0) = 0$$
$$b = x_2 = 0 \quad (8)$$
$$c = x_4 + x_3 + \overline{x_2} + \overline{x_1} = 1$$

Therefore, $x_2 = 0$ imposes the reduction of the system to: $\overline{x_4} + x_1 = 0$ or $\overline{x_4 x_1} = 1$

So, the solution is:

$$x_4 = 1$$
$$x_3 = \Phi$$
$$x_2 = 0 \quad (8.1)$$
$$x_1 = 0$$

So, the function will have hazard at commutation

$$x_4 x_3 x_2 x_1 x_0$$
$$1\,0\,0\,0\,0 \leftrightarrow 1\,0\,0\,0\,1 \quad (16 - 17)$$
$$1\,1\,0\,0\,0 \leftrightarrow 1\,1\,0\,0\,1 \quad (24 - 25)$$

So, in the POS_relation will be added the multiplied prime implicant $\overline{x_4} + x_2 + x_1$.

The function will have the same expression like in (7).

3. Static Hazards in Two-Level Combinational Logic Circuits

We will consider two analytical methods to detect and eliminate this type of hazard:

(A) Consensus method [1]

We will initially define:

- Coupled variable; a variable input is complemented within a term of function and uncomplemented in another term of the same function.
- Coupled term; one of two terms containing only one coupled variable.
- Residue; the part of a coupled term that remains after removing the coupled variable.
- Hazard cover (or consensus term).

The RPI (Redundant Prime Implicant) required to eliminate the static hazards:

- AND the residues of coupled p-term to obtain the SOP hazard cover,
- OR the residues of coupled s-term to obtain the POS hazard cover.

Example 1. Lets consider the logic function $f(x_2 x_1 x_0) = R_1(2, 3, 5, 7)$.

a) *SOP example*: will be determined the prime implicants using Veitch-Karnaugh or Quine-McCluskey methods, as:

$$A = \overline{x_2} \cdot x_1 \quad (2, 3)$$
$$B = x_1 \cdot x_0 \quad (3, 7) \quad (9)$$
$$C = x_2 \cdot x_0 \quad (5, 7)$$

One of the minimal equations is:

$$y = A + C = \overline{x_2} \cdot x_1 + x_2 \cdot x_0 \qquad (10)$$

where we have:
- coupled variable: x_2
- coupled terms: $\overline{x_2} \cdot x_1, x_2 \cdot x_0$
- residues: x_1, x_0
- consensus term: $x_1 \cdot x_0$

Therefore, the logic expression that has no static hazard in relation to x_2 variable is:

$$y = \overline{x_2} \cdot x_1 + x_2 \cdot x_0 + x_1 \cdot x_0 \qquad (11)$$

b) *POS example*: will be determined the prime implicants using Veitch-Karnaugh or Quine-Mc Cluskey methods, as:

$$a = x_2 + x_1 \quad (0,1)$$
$$b = x_1 + x_0 \quad (0,4) \qquad (12)$$
$$c = \overline{x_2} + x_0 \quad (4,6)$$

One of the minimal equations is:

$$y = (x_2 + x_1) \cdot (\overline{x_2} + x_0) \cdot (x_1 + x_0) \qquad (13)$$

where we have:
- coupled variable: x_2
- coupled terms: $x_2 + x_0, \overline{x_2} + x_1$
- residues: x_1, x_0
- consensus term: $x_1 + x_0$

The equation (13) shows no static 0 hazard.

Example 2. Let's consider the function of four variables $y = f(x_3 x_2 x_1 x_0) = R_1(0,1,2,5,6,7,8,9,10,14)$.

SOP hazard: will be determined the prime implicants using Quine-McCluskey method, as:

$$A = \overline{x_3} \cdot \overline{x_1} \cdot x_0 \quad (1,5)$$
$$B = \overline{x_3} \cdot x_1 \cdot \overline{x_0} \quad (2,6)$$
$$C = \overline{x_3} \cdot x_2 \cdot x_0 \quad (5,7)$$
$$D = \overline{x_3} \cdot x_2 \cdot x_1 \quad (6,7)$$
$$E = x_3 \cdot x_1 \cdot \overline{x_0} \quad (10,14) \qquad (14)$$
$$F = \overline{x_2} \cdot \overline{x_1} \quad (0,1,8,9)$$
$$G = \overline{x_2} \cdot \overline{x_0} \quad (0,2,8,10)$$
$$H = x_1 \cdot \overline{x_0} \quad (2,6,10,14)$$

Applying the Patrick method [6], going from prime implicants table will be determined all SOP solutions.

Let's consider the logical p_i variables attached to the prime implicants as follows: $p_0 \leftrightarrow A$, if $p_0 = 1$, the A prime implicant is present in the logical function expression, otherwise $p_0 = 0$ (A prime implicant is not present in the logical function expression), etc.

Therefore, considering the correspondence $p_1 \leftrightarrow B$, $p_2 \leftrightarrow C$, $p_3 \leftrightarrow D$, $p_4 \leftrightarrow E$, $p_5 \leftrightarrow F$, $p_6 \leftrightarrow G$, $p_7 \leftrightarrow H$, in the table illustrated in **Table 1** is shown the

Table 1. The SOP coverage table.

dec. equiv.	0	1	2	5	6	7	8	9	10	14
p_i										
p_0		1		1						
p_1			1		1					
p_2				1		1				
p_3					1	1				
p_4									1	1
p_5	1	1					1	1		
p_6	1		1				1		1	
p_7			1		1				1	1

Patrick coverage:
It writes the coverage equation:

$$(p_5 + p_6) \cdot (p_0 + p_5) \cdot (p_1 + p_6 + p_7)$$
$$\cdot (p_0 + p_2) \cdot (p_1 + p_3 + p_7) \cdot (p_2 + p_3) \qquad (15)$$
$$\cdot (p_5 + p_6) \cdot p_5 \cdot (p_4 + p_6 + p_7) \cdot (p_4 + p_7) \equiv 1$$

Simplifications are made by using the laws of Boolean algebra: the redundance law, the identity law and the distributive law.

$$p_5 \cdot (p_1 + p_6 + p_7) \cdot (p_1 + p_3 + p_7)$$
$$\cdot (p_4 + p_7) \cdot (p_2 + p_0) \cdot (p_2 + p_3) = 1$$
$$\text{or } p_5 \cdot (p_7 + p_1 + p_3 \cdot p_6) \cdot (p_7 + p_4)$$
$$\cdot (p_2 + p_0 \cdot p_3) = 1 \qquad (16)$$
$$\text{or } p_5 \cdot (p_7 + p_1 \cdot p_4 + p_3 \cdot p_4 \cdot p_6)$$
$$\cdot (p_2 + p_0 \cdot p_3) = 1$$
$$\text{or } (p_5 \cdot p_7 + p_1 \cdot p_4 \cdot p_5 + p_3 \cdot p_4 \cdot p_5 \cdot p_6)$$
$$\cdot (p_2 + p_0 \cdot p_3) = 1$$

A version of the optimal solution corresponds to $p_5 \cdot p_7 \cdot p_2$ triplet, *i.e.*

$$y = f(x_3, x_2, x_1, x_0) = F + H + C$$
$$= \overline{x_2} \cdot \overline{x_1} + x_1 \cdot \overline{x_0} + \overline{x_3} \cdot x_2 \cdot x_0 \qquad (17)$$

The cost of this function in SOP implementation is:

$$C(y) = C(\overline{x_2} \cdot \overline{x_1}) + C(x_1 \cdot \overline{x_0}) + C(\overline{x_3} \cdot x_2 \cdot x_0) + 3 = 10$$

(It was considered the variables $x_i, \overline{x_i}$, available at input).

It can verify that any other coverage has a higher cost. For example, the coverage $p_5 \cdot p_7 \cdot p_0 \cdot p_3$ which corresponds to

$$y = F + H + A + D$$
$$= \overline{x_2} \cdot \overline{x_1} + x_1 \cdot \overline{x_0} + \overline{x_3} \cdot \overline{x_1} \cdot x_0 + \overline{x_3} \cdot x_2 \cdot x_1 \qquad (18)$$

has the cost $C_1(y) = 14$.

4. The Static Hazard Elimination

(B) The consensus method

We apply the same method as in [7], only that it has a strong computing nature. Any logic function can be written as:

$$y = e_0 \cdot \overline{x_i} + e_1 \cdot x_i \quad (11),$$

where

$$e_0 = y(x_{n-1}, x_{n-2}, \cdots, x_{i+1}, 0, x_{i-1}, \cdots, x_0),$$

$$e_1 = y(x_{n-1}, x_{n-2}, \cdots, x_{i+1}, 1, x_{i-1}, \cdots, x_0).$$

Obviously, if $y = a \cdot \overline{x_i} + b \cdot x_i + c$ (12), then $e_0 = a + c$, $e_1 = b + c$.

If we add the term $e_0 \cdot e_1$ to relation (11), the function presents no hazard towards x_i.

In terms of the consensus method, the term that covers the static 1 hazard is

$$e_0 \cdot e_1 = (a + c) \cdot (b + c) = c + a \cdot b \quad (19),$$

therefore for the form (11) will be $e_0 \cdot e_1$, and for the form (12), $a \cdot b$.

Considering the second example, we will have: hazard in relation to the input x_0:

$$y = F + H + C = \overline{x_2} \cdot \overline{x_1} + x_1 \cdot \overline{x_0} + \overline{x_3} \cdot x_2 \cdot x_0 \quad (20),$$

where

$$e_0 = x_1 + \overline{x_2} \cdot \overline{x_1} = x_1 + \overline{x_2},$$
$$e_1 = \overline{x_3} \cdot x_2 + \overline{x_2} \cdot \overline{x_1} = \overline{x_3} \cdot x_2 + \overline{x_2} \cdot \overline{x_1},$$
$$e_0 \cdot e_1 = (x_1 + \overline{x_2}) \cdot (\overline{x_3} \cdot x_2 + \overline{x_2} \cdot \overline{x_1}) \quad (21)$$
$$= \overline{x_3} \cdot x_2 \cdot x_1 + \overline{x_2} \cdot \overline{x_1} = F + D$$

By adding $F + D$ term to relation (14), it obtains:

$$y = F + H + C + (F + D)$$
$$= \overline{x_2} \cdot \overline{x_1} + x_1 \cdot \overline{x_0} + \overline{x_3} \cdot x_2 \cdot x_0 + \overline{x_3} \cdot x_2 \cdot x_1 \quad (22)$$

hazard in relation to the input x_1:

$$e_0 = \overline{x_2} + \overline{x_3} \cdot x_2 \cdot x_0 = \overline{x_2} + \overline{x_3} \cdot x_0$$
$$e_1 = \overline{x_0} + \overline{x_3} \cdot x_2 + \overline{x_3} \cdot x_2 \cdot x_0 = \overline{x_0} + \overline{x_3} \cdot x_2 \quad (23)$$
$$e_0 \cdot e_1 = (\overline{x_2} + \overline{x_3} \cdot x_0) \cdot (\overline{x_0} + \overline{x_3} \cdot x_2) = \overline{x_2} \cdot \overline{x_0} = G$$

Therefore, the expression of the function becomes:

$$y = F + H + C + D + G$$
$$= \overline{x_2} \cdot \overline{x_1} + x_1 \cdot \overline{x_0} + \overline{x_3} \cdot x_2 \cdot x_0 \quad (24)$$
$$+ \overline{x_3} \cdot x_2 \cdot x_1 + \overline{x_2} \cdot \overline{x_0}$$

hazard in relation to the input x_2:

$$e_0 = \overline{x_1} + \overline{x_0} + x_1 \cdot \overline{x_0} = \overline{x_1} + \overline{x_0}$$
$$e_1 = \overline{x_3} \cdot x_0 + \overline{x_3} \cdot x_1 + x_1 \cdot \overline{x_0}$$

Therefore,

$$e_0 \cdot e_1 = (\overline{x_1} + \overline{x_0}) \cdot (\overline{x_3} \cdot x_0 + \overline{x_3} \cdot x_1 + x_1 \cdot \overline{x_0})$$
$$= \overline{x_3} \cdot \overline{x_1} \cdot x_0 + \overline{x_3} \cdot x_1 \cdot \overline{x_0} + x_1 \cdot \overline{x_0} \quad (25)$$
$$= x_1 \cdot \overline{x_0} + \overline{x_3} \cdot \overline{x_1} \cdot x_0 = H + A$$

The expression of the function becomes:

$$y = F + H + C + D + G + A$$
$$= \overline{x_2} \cdot \overline{x_1} + x_1 \cdot \overline{x_0} + \overline{x_3} \cdot x_2 \cdot x_0$$
$$+ \overline{x_3} \cdot x_2 \cdot x_1 + \overline{x_2} \cdot \overline{x_0} + \overline{x_3} \cdot \overline{x_1} \cdot x_0 \quad (26)$$
$$= \overline{x_3} \cdot x_2 \cdot x_0 + \overline{x_3} \cdot x_2 \cdot x_1 + x_1 \cdot \overline{x_0} + t$$

hazard in relation to the input x_3:

$$e_0 = x_2 \cdot x_0 + x_2 \cdot x_1 + x_1 \cdot \overline{x_0} + t,$$

where

$$t = \overline{x_2} \cdot \overline{x_1} + x_1 \cdot \overline{x_0} + \overline{x_2} \cdot \overline{x_0} + \overline{x_3} \cdot \overline{x_1} \cdot x_0$$

$$e_1 = t$$

$$e_0 \cdot e_1 = (x_2 \cdot x_0 + x_2 \cdot x_1 + x_1 \cdot \overline{x_0} + t) \cdot t = t \quad (27)$$

so that remains the same expression (20), which has no hazards in relation to x_3.

From the relation (20), it sees that the expression of the function without SOP hazards contains all prime implicants without B and E.

(C) The method of solving of some Boolean equations [8]

A logic function can be written as:

$$y = a \cdot \overline{x_i} + b \cdot x_i + c \quad (28)$$

where

$$a + c = f(x_{n-1}, x_{n-2}, \cdots, x_{i+1}, 0, x_{i-1}, \cdots, x_0),$$
$$b + c = f(x_{n-1}, x_{n-2}, \cdots, x_{i+1}, 1, x_{i-1}, \cdots, x_0).$$

According to a theorem from [8], a logic function expressed as SOP, presents a static hazard in the situation $x_i + \overline{x_i} = 1$, a situation deducted by solving the following system of logical equations:

$$a = 1$$
$$b = 1 \quad (29)$$
$$c = 0$$

We return to the same function, (14):

$$y = F + H + C = \overline{x_2} \cdot \overline{x_1} + x_1 \cdot \overline{x_0} + \overline{x_3} \cdot x_2 \cdot x_0.$$

hazard in relation to the input x_0:

$$y = (x_1) \cdot \overline{x_0} + (\overline{x_3} \cdot x_2) \cdot x_0 + \overline{x_2} \cdot \overline{x_1} \quad (30)$$

The function will present SOP hazard, if

$$x_1 = 1$$
$$\overline{x_3} \cdot x_2 = 1 \qquad (31)$$
$$\overline{x_2} \cdot \overline{x_1} = 0$$

Therefore, $x_3 = 0$, $x_2 = 1$, $x_1 = 1$, which imposes a hazard at commutation

$$x_3 x_2 x_1 x_0$$
$$0\,1\,1\,0 \leftrightarrow 0\,1\,1\,1,$$

which imposes the adding of the prime implicant $D = (6,7)$ to function.

The function becomes

$$y = F + H + C + D$$
$$= \overline{x_2} \cdot \overline{x_1} + x_1 \cdot \overline{x_0} + \overline{x_3} \cdot x_2 \cdot x_0 + \overline{x_3} \cdot x_2 \cdot x_1 \qquad (32)$$

hazard in relation to the input x_1:

$$a = \overline{x_2} = 1$$
$$x_2 = 0$$
$$b = \overline{x_0} + \overline{x_3} \cdot x_2 = 1 \qquad (33)$$
$$\text{or } x_0 = 0$$
$$c = \overline{x_3} \cdot x_2 \cdot x_0 = 0$$
$$x_3 = \phi$$

Therefore, we will have hazards in the following cases:

$$x_3 x_2 x_1 x_0$$
$$0\,0\,0\,0 \leftrightarrow 0\,0\,1\,0 \quad (0,2)$$
$$1\,0\,0\,0 \leftrightarrow 1\,0\,1\,0 \quad (8,10)$$

The previous commutations are equivalent to the implicant $G = (0,2,8,10)$.

The function becomes

$$y = F + H + C + D + G$$
$$= \overline{x_2} \cdot \overline{x_1} + x_1 \cdot \overline{x_0} + \overline{x_3} \cdot x_2 \cdot x_0 \qquad (34)$$
$$+ \overline{x_3} \cdot x_2 \cdot x_1 + \overline{x_2} \cdot \overline{x_0}$$

hazard in relation to the input x_2:

$$a = \overline{x_1} + \overline{x_0} = 1$$
$$x_3 = 0$$
$$b = \overline{x_3} \cdot x_0 + \overline{x_3} \cdot x_1 = 1 \qquad (35)$$
$$\Rightarrow \text{and } c = x_1 \cdot \overline{x_0} = 0, x_0 + x_1 = 1$$

We will have the solution:

$$x_3 = 0$$
$$x_1 = 0 \qquad (35.1)$$
$$x_0 = 1$$

The corresponding commutation is:

$$x_3 x_2 x_1 x_0$$
$$0\,0\,0\,1 \leftrightarrow 0\,1\,0\,1 \quad (1,5)$$

Therefore, the term $A = (1,5)$ is added to the function.

And therefore:

$$y = F + H + C + D + G + A \qquad (36)$$

hazard in relation to the input x_3:

$$y = \overline{x_2} \cdot \overline{x_1} + x_1 \cdot \overline{x_0} + \overline{x_3} \cdot x_2 \cdot x_0$$
$$+ \overline{x_3} \cdot x_2 \cdot x_1 + \overline{x_2} \cdot \overline{x_0} + \overline{x_3} \cdot \overline{x_1} \cdot x_0 \qquad (37)$$

$$a = x_2 \cdot x_0 + x_2 \cdot x_1 + \overline{x_1} \cdot x_0 = 1$$
$$b = 0 \qquad (38)$$
$$c = \overline{x_2} \cdot \overline{x_1} + x_1 \cdot \overline{x_0} + \overline{x_2} \cdot \overline{x_0} = 0$$

Because one of the terms (a,b) is zero, we have no hazards in relation to that variable.

5. Conclusions

The contribution of the authors consists in that by analysis of two methods of detection/elimination of the static hazard, insisting of the POS method for the logic function which wasn't analyzed in [1].

The boolean equation [2,3], presents some advantages instead the consensus methods, the most important to determine the transactions which causes static hazard.

It concludes that the classical method of the 70s, the method of solving some specific Boolean equations [4], presents some advantages compared to consensus method [5], which has a strong heuristic nature.

In the first method it used the consensus theorem to determine the cover term that is equal with the product of the two residual implicants [6], and in the second method it resolved a Boolean equation system [7]. The authors observed that in the second method the digital hazard can be earlier detected. If the Boolean equation system is incompatible (doesn't have solutions), the considered logical function doesn't have the static 1 hazard regarding the coupled variable. Using the logical computations, this method permits to determine the needed transitions to eliminate the digital hazard.

From the both methods, we can observe that static 1 hazard can be removed by adding the prime implicants step by step.

The same method with the same conclusions was applied to the static 0 hazard (POS), using the duality theorem [8,9].

The authors observed that in the second method the digital hazard can be earlier detected. If the Boolean equation system is incompatible (doesn't have solutions), the considered logical function doesn't have the static 1 hazard regarding the coupled variable. Using the logical computations, this method permits to determine the needed transitions to eliminate the digital hazard.

REFERENCES

[1]   "The Comparative Study of Two Analytical Methods for Detection and Elimination of the Static Hazard in Combinational Logic Circuits," 2011 15*th International Conference on System Theory, Control and Computing* (*ICSTCC*), Sinaia, 14-16 October 2011, pp. 1-4.

[2]   R. F. Tinder, "Engineering Digital Design," Academic Press, Waltham, 2010.

[3]   Ch. Roth, "Fundamentals of Logic Design," West Publishing Company, Eagan, 1999.

[4]   J. P. Perrin, M. Denouette and E. Daclin, "Systems Logiques," Tome 1 Dunord, Paris, 1997.

[5]   E. T. Ringkjob, "A Method for Detection and Elimination of Static Hazards in Factored Combinational Switching Circuits," Syracuse University, New York, 2013.

[6]   J. A. McCormick, "Detection and Elimination of Static Hazards in Multilevel XOR-SOP/EQV-POS Functions," Washington State University, Pullman, 2013.

[7]   K. Raj, "Digital Systems Principles and Design," Pearson Education India, Upper Saddle River, 2013.

[8]   Al. Valachi, R. Silion, V. Onofrei and Fl. Hoza, "Analysis, Synthesis and Verification of Digital Logic Systems," Ed. Nord-Est, Iasi, 1993.

[9]   O. Ursaru and C. Aghion, "Multilevel Inverters with Imbricated Switching Cells, PWM and DPWM-Controlled," Electronics and Electrical Engineering, Kaunas, 2010.

26

Effective Task Scheduling for Embedded Systems Using Iterative Cluster Slack Optimization

Jongdae Kim, Sungchul Lee, Hyunchul Shin

Electrical and Computer Engineering, Hanyang University, Ansan Kyeonggi-do, South Korea

ABSTRACT

To solve computationally expensive problems, multiple processor SoCs (MPSoCs) are frequently used. Mapping of applications to MPSoC architectures and scheduling of tasks are key problems in system level design of embedded systems. In this paper, a cluster slack optimization algorithm is described, in which the tasks in a cluster are simultaneously mapped and scheduled for heterogeneous MPSoC architectures. In our approach, the tasks are iteratively clustered and each cluster is optimized by using the branch and bound technique to capitalize on slack distribution. The proposed static task mapping and scheduling method is applied to pipelined data stream processing as well as for batch processing. In pipelined processing, the tradeoff between throughput and memory cost can be exploited by adjusting a weighting parameter. Furthermore, an energy-aware task mapping and scheduling algorithm based on our cluster slack optimization is developed. Experimental results show improvement in latency, throughput and energy.

Keywords: Multi-Processor; Mapping; Scheduling

1. Introduction

As many systems in communication and multi-media become more and more complex and require a large amount of computation, a single processor can't frequently satisfy the performance criteria. Since designing a high performance custom integrated circuit requires great cost and a long design period, using multiple processors (or multi-cores) is increasingly seen as an alternative approach. However, mapping of applications to MPSoC architectures and scheduling of tasks are key problems in high-level design of embedded systems.

System performance or throughput can be improved by using parallel processing or pipelining. In parallel processing, multiple functions can be executed in parallel or a single function can be executed for multiple data sets. In pipelining, consecutive data streams are processed with overlaps in processing time for larger throughput. Data streams of audio and video signals should be processed within appropriate interval between consecutive inputs to provide the correct information for users. The most important factor to decide the performance of a pipeline is the interval between the consecutive inputs, and

this interval can be fixed or varied. A small interval means a higher throughput.

Mapping and scheduling problems for multiple processors belong to the class of NP-hard problems [1]. Research has been carried out in solving task mapping and scheduling problems. Different tools and models have been developed to address the problems above.

The branch and bound algorithm can be used to map an application to architecture so that the total execution time is minimized. This algorithm checks all possible cases of assignments of n tasks to m processors leading to huge search space and minimizes the search area by using bounding procedure to reach an optimum solution in less time [2]. However, due to the worst-case exponential complexity, this method can only be used for "small" sized problems.

2. Related Works

Mapping and scheduling problems for multi processors belong to the class of NP-hard problems [1]. We consider Problem Model like the one described in [2] where n tasks are to be allocated to m heterogeneous processing elements (PEs). The mapping has to be found under constraints where all tasks are assigned to PEs and every task is assigned to only one PE. The task scheduling problem is the problem of assigning the order of tasks in the system to optimize the overall performance for the given application.

A very popular heuristic method to schedule tasks is list scheduling [3]. Tasks are scheduled from a prespecified list and the task with the highest priority is removed from the priority list and then scheduled, one by one.

For scheduling heterogeneous processing elements, the Heterogeneous Earliest Finish Time (HEFT) algorithm [4] is used. This algorithm uses upward rank value which represents the longest path from each task to set the priority of each task. The task list is ordered by decreasing value of upward rank. Based on this list, tasks are scheduled onto the processors that have the earliest finish time. Another scheduling algorithm based on list scheduling is the Critical-Path-On a Processor (CPOP) algorithm [4]. In contrast to the HEFT algorithm, this algorithm uses upward ranking and downward ranking to set the priority of each task. The downward ranking is computed by adding the average execution time of the task and maximum downward rank value of the predecessors. The task with highest priority is selected for execution. If the selected task is on a critical path, then it is scheduled for the critical path processor. A critical processor is one that minimizes the cumulative computation cost of the tasks on the critical path. Otherwise, the task is assigned to the processor which has the minimum execution finish time of the task.

Similarly, Performance Effective Task Scheduling (PETS) algorithm [5] consists of three stages, Level sorting, Task prioritization, and Processor selection. In Level sorting, each task is sorted at each level in order to group the tasks. Because of this, tasks in the same level could be executed in parallel. In Task prioritization, the priority of each task is computed by using average computation cost, data transfer cost, and highest rank of the predecessors. In Processor selection, task is assigned to the processor which gives the minimum finish time. Compared to the Heft and CPOP algorithm, PETS algorithm shows good performance.

The force-directed scheduling algorithm [6] prioritizes and schedules the subtasks based on the resource utilization probability in each step. Recently, other techniques, such as simulated evolution based method [7], were reported. The genetic algorithm [8,9] is a widely researched random search technique. This algorithm executes in generations, producing better solutions using crossover and mutation operators. In the genetic algorithm, candidate solutions are represented by sequences of symbols called chromosomes. Evolutionary algorithms (EAs) operate on a population of potential solutions, applying the principle of survival of the fittest to produce successively better approximations to a solution. At each generation of the EAs, a new set of approximations is created by the process of selecting individuals according to their level of fitness in the problem domain and reproducing them using variation operators. This process may lead to the evolution of populations of individuals that are better suited to their environment than the individuals from which they were created, just as in natural adaptation. EAs are characterized by the representation of the individual, the evaluation function representing the fitness level of the individuals, and the population dynamics such as population size, variation operators, parent selection, reproduction and inheritance, survival competition method, etc. To have a good balance between exploration and exploitation, those components should be designed properly [10].

Like all other EAs, a quantum-inspired evolutionary algorithm (QEA) also consists of the representation of individuals, the evaluation function, and the population dynamics. The only difference is that it uses quantum bits as probabilistic representation for individuals instead of binary representation of genes [7].

In [11], energy aware scheduling that uses task ordering and voltage scaling in an integrated manner is presented, and the voltage level instead of the speed level was considered in the cost function for each processor. Dynamic voltage scaling (DVS) is one of the most powerful techniques to reduce energy consumption [12,13]. All these methods are heuristic approaches.

3. Mapping and Scheduling for Batch Processing Systems

By using the branch and bound algorithm [2], one can obtain an optimum solution for "small" mapping problems. However, one cannot afford run-time (CPU time) for large problems due to the exponential worst case run-time. To solve the complex mapping problems in a reasonable time, we propose a cluster slack optimization algorithm. In this algorithm, we divide all tasks in a task flow graph by a given number of clusters. Each cluster is optimized to find a best solution capitalizing on the slack distribution. The algorithm to minimize the execution (finish) time can be written as in **Algorithm 1**.

The cluster slack optimization algorithm consists of five major steps, which are initialization, As Late As Possible (ALAP) scheduling, making clusters, cluster selection, and slack optimization for the selected cluster.

In the initialization step, we find an initial solution by using a greedy list scheduling method. In the ALAP scheduling step, we reschedule all tasks by using ALAP scheduling to maximize the slacks in the optimization zone to capitalize the slacks during optimization. By

Algorithm 1. Cluster slack optimization algorithm for task mapping and scheduling.

Input : task flow graph, execution time table, processors
Output : mapped and scheduled tasks

Find an initial greedy solution;
   while (solution can be improved) do
      ALAP scheduling for slack maximization;
      Make clusters;
      while (not completed) do
         Select a cluster to optimize;
         Find the task optimization zone for the selected cluster;
         Optimize the tasks in the selected cluster within the task optimization zone;
      end
   end
Output the solution;

clustering the given tasks into several clusters in making cluster step, only a small number of tasks in a cluster are remapped and re-scheduled, and thus the run-time can be controlled by adjusting the cluster size. In the cluster selection step, an un-processed task cluster is selected in order of execution start times. In the optimization step, we optimally remap and reschedule the tasks in the selected cluster within the task optimization zone. The task optimization zone is defined by two boundaries called floor and ceiling. When the optimization of the current cluster is finished, the floor and the ceiling will be updated and thus the task optimization zone is moved. The optimization is repeated when the new solution is better than the previous best solution.

Figure 1 shows an example from [5], in which 10 tasks are to be mapped to 3 heterogeneous processors. **Figure 1(a)** shows the task flow graph and **Figure 1(b)** shows the execution time table from [5]. For example, the execution of task T1 by processor P1 takes 14 cycles. The communication time to transfer the output of task 1 to the input of task 2 takes 18 cycles as shown by the edge weight. Different processors may take different number of cycles to finish a given task. **Figures 1(c)-(e)** show the scheduling results by using the HEFT, CPOP and PETS algorithm respectively [5]. The produced solutions use 80, 86, and 79 cycles, respectively.

Now we explain our method by using the same example. **Figure 2(a)** shows the initial solution by using greedy list scheduling and **Figure 2(b)** shows the solution after the ALAP scheduling step. The produced initial solution used 82 cycles.

After the ALAP scheduling step, all tasks are clustered in the order of execution start time, and each cluster is re-mapped and re-scheduled. We perform the branch and bound by evaluating the slacks of all possible mappings and schedules for tasks in the current cluster. The objective of slack optimization is to maximize the minimum slack for each processor. Slack optimization tries to achieve a near global optimum solution by solving iterative local optimization problems. **Figure 3** shows an example process of slack calculation. Let ST_i be starting time of task i and FT_i be finishing time of task i. Let $C_{a,b}$ be communication time from n_a to n_b and $E_{i,j}$ be execution time of task i on processor j. Since n_a, n_i, and n_d are executed on P1, the communication times $C_{a,i}$ and $C_{i,d}$ can be 0. Now, we define the slack when the task n_i is mapped to P1, as follows.

$$\text{Slack}_i = \min \begin{bmatrix} ST_d - \{\max\left(FT_a + C_{a,i}, FT_b + C_{b,i}\right) + ET_{i,1} + C_{i,d}\}, \\ ST_f - \{\max\left(FT_a + C_{a,i}, FT_b + C_{b,i}\right) + ET_{i,1} + C_{i,f}\} \end{bmatrix}$$

The goal of the optimization is to remap/re-schedule to maximize the slack, since the minimum slack of all output tasks in the current cluster is the gain of the optimization. In other words, the latency can be reduced by the minimum slack.

Figure 4 shows the process of our algorithm for the example shown in **Figure 1**. After ALAP scheduling, all tasks are clustered to form 3 clusters as shown in **Figure 4(a)**. In this case, 1st_cluster = {n1, n2, n4, n5}, 2nd_cluster = {n3, n6, n7}, and 3rd_cluster = {n8, n9, n10}. **Figures 4(b)-(d)** show optimized results after optimization of each cluster. In **Figure 4(b)**, the slacks of each processor are 13, 19, and 7 cycles, respectively. So we can reduce 7 cycles after the 1st cluster optimization. In **Figure 4(c)**, there is no change during the 2nd cluster optimization. In the same way, we can reduce 1 cycle after the 3rd cluster optimization. Finally, the solution is

reduced to 74 cycles, and 8 cycles are reduced when compared to the initial solution. This is really the optimum solution, as verified by using the branch and bound algorithm. Compared to the three previous algorithms shown in **Figure 1**, our new iterative slack optimization algorithm produced a significantly better solution (the latency has been reduced to 74 cycles from 79 cycles or more), which is the optimum solution in this case.

4. Mapping and Scheduling of Pipelined Systems for Data Stream Processing

4.1. Throughput Increase by Pipelining

Figure 5(a) shows the task flow graph with 15 tasks, and **Figure 5(b)** shows the execution time table for three processors (P1, P2, P3). For example, execution of task T1 by processor P1 takes 5 cycles. The edge weights

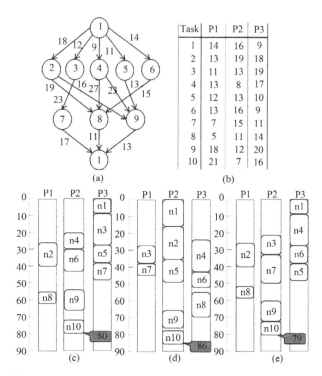

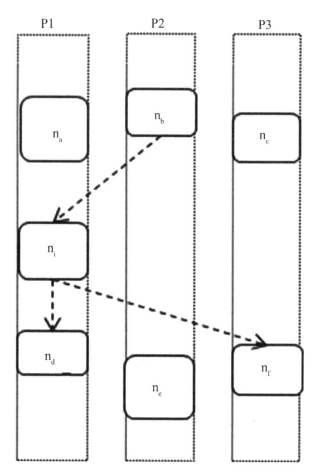

Figure 1. An example and scheduling results. (a) Task flow graph; (b) Execution time table; (c) The HEFT algorithm [4]; (d) The CPOP algorithm [4] (e) The PETS algorithm [5].

Figure 3. Calculation of the slack.

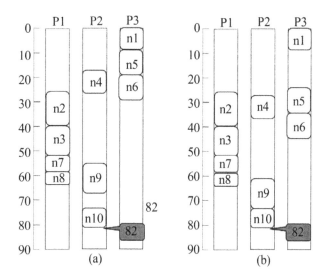

Figure 2. (a) Initial solution by using list scheduling; (b) Solution after the ALAP scheduling.

show the data communication times. Different processors may take different numbers of cycles to finish a given task.

In batch-mode task parallel execution, the goal is to minimize latency. However, continuous data stream processing is needed to process audio and video signals. Therefore, the most important factor of scheduling for data stream processing is to reduce the interval between

consecutive data inputs for larger throughput. A small interval means higher throughput. To reduce data input interval (DII), we divide all tasks into several stages and use pipelining. For example, three candidate schedule positions of task 5 (T5) of the task flow graph shown in **Figure 5(a)** are shown in **Figure 6(a)** for the batch-mode task parallel execution. For pipelined execution, data can be processed by forming several stages. When the first stage processes i-th input data, the second stage process (i-1)-th input data. This pipelined scheduling allows 7 candidates schedule positions for T5, as shown in **Figure 6(b)**.

4.2. Optimization Using a Cost Function

Usually, the throughput can be increased by increasing the number of stages. However, this may increase the latency and memory cost. To optimize the trade-off, we define the following cost function.

$$\text{Total\_Cost} = \alpha \text{DII\_cost} + (1-\alpha)\text{Memory\_cost} \quad (1)$$

DII_cost is inversely proportional to the throughput and Memory_cost represents the cost of memory to store intermediate data among stages. The Memory_cost can

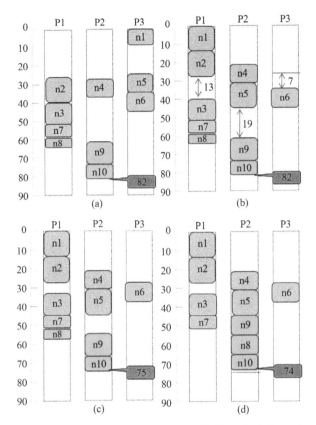

Figure 4. (a) Task clustering after ALAP scheduling; (b) Result after 1st cluster optimization; (c) Result after 2nd cluster optimization; (d) Result after 3rd cluster optimization.

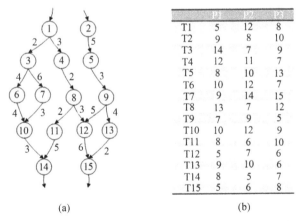

Figure 5. (a) Task flow graph with 15 tasks; (b) Execution time table for 3 processors (P1, P2, P3).

be computed as follows.

$$\text{Memory\_cost} = \sum_{i=1}^{N}\left(M_i \times S_i\right) \qquad (2)$$

where N is the number of stages, Mi is the amount of memory for i-th stage, and Si is the number of pipeline stages to store the data of i-th stage.

Figure 7 shows the pipelined schedule results of the

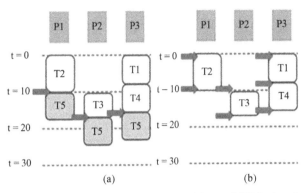

Figure 6. (a) Candidate schedule positions of T5 in batch-mode execution; (b) Candidate schedule positions of T5 in pipelined execution.

task flow graph given in **Figure 5**. The clustering results are shown in **Figures 7(b)** and **(c)** when $\alpha = 0.7$ and $\alpha = 0.3$, respectively. Five stages (A, B, C, D, E) are used when $\alpha = 0.7$ as shown in **Figure 7(b)** and four stages (A, B, C, D) are used when $\alpha = 0.3$ as shown in **Figure 7(c)**. The result of batch processing is shown in **Figure 7(d)**, in which the data input interval (DII) is 49. **Figure 7(e)** shows the pipelined schedule using 5 stages with DII of 34.

When the number of stages is 5, the latency can be up to 5× DII (5 × 34 = 170 cycles), even though one set of input data can be processed every 34 cycles. **Figure 7(f)** shows the pipelined schedule using 4 stages with DII of 37. When the number of stages is 4, the latency can be up to 4× DII (4 × 37 = 148 cycles). Memory_cost is 44 and 28 when α is 0.7 and 0.3, respectively. When α is small then the weight of Memory_cost in (1) is large and thus memory cost is reduced even though DII can be increased. This shows that α can be used to optimize the trade-off between DII and memory cost. **Figure 8** shows how the data streams flow through the pipelining stages.

5. Energy Aware Mapping and Scheduling

Over the last decade, manufacturers have competed to advance the performance of processors by raising the clock frequency. However, recent computer systems are focused on battery-driven devices such as portable handheld devices, sensors, and robots, rather than traditional large devices and desktops. Therefore, technical issues are miniaturization and low energy consumption. Specially, low power is extremely important for many real-time embedded systems. To apply our iterative slack optimization algorithm for energy aware mapping and scheduling, we only need to modify the cost function in slack optimization. The modified cost we used is shown in (3).The energy-aware cluster slack optimization algorithm is shown in **Figure 9**.

$$\text{Cost}_E = \beta\text{latency} + \left(1-\beta\right)K \times \text{energy} \qquad (3)$$

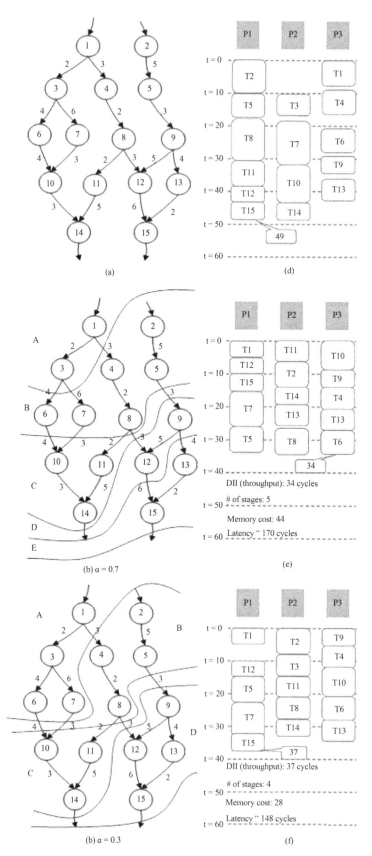

Figure 7. (a) Task flow graph; (b) Pipeline stage ($\alpha = 0.7$); (c) Pipeline stage ($\alpha = 0.3$); (d) Scheduling result for non-pipeline system; (e) Scheduling result for pipeline system ($\alpha = 0.7$); (f) Scheduling result for pipeline system ($\alpha = 0.3$).

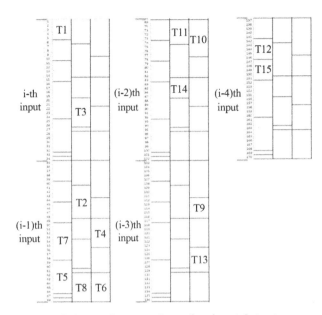

Figure 8. Processing procedure of an input data stream.

where β is the weighting factor and K is the scaling constant.

6. Experimental Results

We implemented the cluster slack optimization algorithm by using the "C" programming language under the Windows operation system. The experiments were performed by using both real applications and randomly generated task flow graphs with 20 to 100 tasks. The parallel Gaussian elimination, LU decomposition [9] and molecular dynamics [14] are used as real applications. The tasks are mapped and scheduled by our method and by branch and bound, HEFT [4], CPOP [4] and PETS [5] algorithms for comparisons.

Table 1 shows the solution comparisons for real applications. A base algorithm for comparisons is the branch and bound algorithm which can find an optimum solution by spending much more time than other algorithms.

However, in molecular dynamics applications, we use our algorithm as a base algorithm because the branch and bound algorithm cannot obtain the solution within 24 hours.

Table 2 shows the solution comparisons for the randomly generated task flow graphs. In experiments, we used 5 randomly generated task graphs for each number of tasks (# tasks). The results of our algorithm are obtained by taking up to 20 tasks in a cluster.

Randomly generated task graphs with 20 to 50 tasks are used for experiments in pipelined systems. The results are compared with those of a recent method, QEA [7]. **Table 3** shows DII_cost and Memory cost for QEA and our method. In Equation (1), $\alpha = 0.7$ was used. On

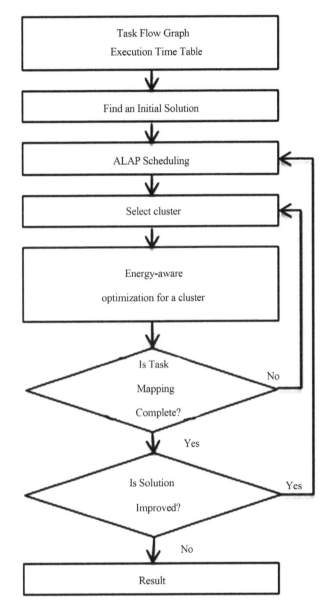

Figure 9. Energy aware cluster optimization algorithm.

the average, our method shows better results. DII_cost is improved by 2% and Memory_cost is improved by 23%.

Table 4 shows tradeoff between DII_cost and Memory_cost by changing the weight α. As α gets smaller, DII increases and Memory_cost decreases.

Energy aware mapping and scheduling experiments are processed by using randomly generated task flow graphs with 20 to 50 tasks. We use three commercial processor power models consisting of XScale, PowerPC, and DSP [15] for power estimation. The tasks are mapped and scheduled by using our method and the results are compared with those of Energy Gradient-based Multiprocessor Scheduling (EGMS) [11].

Tables 5 and **6** show the energy consumption comparisons when β is 0.3 and 0.7, respectively. In experi-

Table 1. Solution comparisons for real applications.

#tasks	CPOP	HEFT	PETS	Ours	Branch and Bound
Parallel Gaussian elimination (15 tasks)	120.7%	112.2%	109.7%	100%	100%
LU decomposition (14 tasks)	113.1%	111.9%	103.5%	100%	100%
Molecular dynamics (40 tasks)	120.4%	117.6%	109.6%	100%	N.A.

Table 2. Solution comparisons for randomly generated task flow graphs with 20 to 100 tasks.

#tasks	CPOP	HEFT	PETS	Ours	Branch and Bound
20	94.8 (108%)	91.6 (104.5%)	90.6 (103.4%)	87.6 (100%)	87.6 (100%)
30	142.8 (111.9%)	137 (107.3%)	132 (103.4%)	127.6 (100%)	N.A.
40	174.6 (114.0%)	169 (110.3%)	163.2 (106.5%)	153.2 (100%)	N.A.
50	196.6 (110.5%)	194.4 (109.3%)	189.6 (106.6%)	177.8 (100%)	N.A.
60	228.6 (113.3%)	226 (112.0%)	221.8 (109.9%)	201.8 (100%)	N.A.
70	245.8 (113.6%)	246 (113.7%)	242.2 (111.9%)	216.4 (100%)	N.A.
80	270.6 (115.0%)	269.4 (114.4%)	267 (113.4%)	235.4 (100%)	N.A.
90	291.6 (113.0%)	289 (112.0%)	287.8 (111.6%)	258 (100%)	N.A.
100	329.8 (111.3%)	328.4 (110.9%)	326.2 (110.1%)	296.2 (100%)	N.A.
Average	219.5 (112.6%)	216.8 (111.2%)	213.4 (109.5%)	194.9 (100%)	N.A.

Table 3. DII and memory cost comparisons in pipelined systems.

#tasks	DII cost		Memory cost	
	QEA	Ours	QEA	Ours
20	425 101.9%)	417 (100%)	8910 (128.7%)	6920 (100%)
30	831 (101.3%)	820 (100%)	15,353 (122.1%)	12,568 (100%)
40	1241 (102.8%)	1207 (100%)	19,181 (122.9%)	15,599 (100%)
50	1616 (102.3%)	1579 (100%)	23,926 (123.1%)	19,434 (100%)
Total	4113 (102.2%)	4023 (100%)	67,370 (123.6%)	54,521 (100%)

Table 4. Trade off between DII and memory.

#tasks	$\alpha = 0.7$		$\alpha = 0.5$		$\alpha = 0.3$	
	DII	Memory	DII	Memory	DII	Memory
20	417	6920	459	6327	489	5967
30	820	12,568	907	11,397	967	10,994
40	1207	15,599	1331	13,151	1481	11,831
50	1579	19,434	1781	17,924	1861	15,984
Total	4023 (100%)	54,521 (100%)	4478 (111.3%)	48,799 (89.5%)	4798 (119.3%)	44,776 (82.1%)

Table 5. Energy consumption and latency comparisons ($\beta = 0.3$).

#tasks	Energy consumption		Latency	
	EGMS	Ours	EGMS	Ours
20	67.746 (100%)	64.974 (95.9%)	86.8 (100%)	91.2 (105.1%)
30	95.442 (100%)	90.238 (94.5%)	127.2 (100%)	131.8 (103.6%)
40	131.246 (100%)	127.344 (97.0%)	153.8 (100%)	161.2 (104.8%)
50	179.134 (100%)	163.128 (91.1%)	173.2 (100%)	179.4 (103.6%)
Average	118.392 (100%)	111.421 (94.1%)	135.25 (100%)	140.90 (104.2)

Table 6. Energy consumption and latency comparisons ($\beta = 0.7$).

#tasks	Energy consumption		Latency	
	EGMS	Ours	EGMS	Ours
20	67.746 (100%)	66.464 (98.1 %)	86.8 (100%)	88.2 (101.6%)
30	95.442 (100%)	93.768 (98.2%)	127.2 (100%)	130.4 (102.5%)
40	131.246 (100%%)	128.524 (97.9%)	153.8 (100%)	160.4 (104.3%)
50	179.134 (100%%)	171.642 (95.8%)	173.2 (100%)	176.8 (102.1%)
Average	118.392 (100%)	115.100 (97.2%)	135.25 (100%)	138.95 (102.7%)

ments, we used 5 randomly generated task graphs for each task.

The results of our algorithm are obtained by taking up to 20 tasks in a cluster for simultaneous optimization.

7. Conclusions

We developed an effective algorithm to map and schedule tasks simultaneously for heterogeneous processors. By partitioning all tasks into several clusters, only a small number of tasks in a cluster are re-mapped and re-scheduled at the same time. Therefore, the run-time can be controlled by adjusting the cluster size and can increase linearly with the number of tasks. Experimental results show that our algorithm can obtain 9.5%, 11.2% and 12.6% better solutions compared to PETS, HEFT and CPOP algorithms, respectively, in batch-mode systems. Furthermore, our method can improve the DII_cost by 2% and Memory_cost by 23% when compared to [7] in pipelined systems. Finally, energy-aware cluster slack optimization results show that our algorithm can effectively perform the trade-off between the latency and the energy consumption.

The techniques described in this paper can be applied to static scheduling for multiple processors, to optimize latency, throughput and energy. Future works include developing dynamic scheduling techniques, optimization for networks on chip and consideration of memory bandwidth.

8. Acknowledgement

This work was supported by the Ministry of Science, ICT & Future Planning and IDEC Platform center (IPC) in Korea.

REFERENCES

[1]   P. Luh, D. Hoitomt, E. Max and K. Pattipati, "Schedule Generation and Reconfiguration for Parallel Machines," *Robotics and Automation*, Vol. 6, No. 6, 1990, pp. 687-696.

[2]   K. Vivekanandarajah and S. Pilakkat, "Task Mapping in Heterogeneous MPSoCs for System Level Design," 13*th IEEE International Conference on Engineering of Complex Computer Systems*, Belfast, 31 March 2008-3 April 2008, pp. 56-65.

[3]   T. Adams, K. Chandy and J. Dickson, "A Comparison of List Schedules for Parallel Processing Systems," *Communications of the ACM*, Vol. 17, No. 12, 1974, pp. 685-690.

[4]   H. Topcuoglu, S. Hariri and M. Wu, "Performance-Effective and Low-Complexity Task Scheduling for Heterogeneous Computing," *IEEE Transactions on Parallel and Distributed Systems*, Vol. 13, No. 3, 2002, pp. 260-274.

[5]   E. Ilavarasan and P. Thambidurai, "Low Complexity Performance Effective Task Scheduling Algorithm for Heterogeneous Computing Environments," *Journal of Computer Sciences*, Vol. 3, 2007, pp. 94-103.

[6]   P. Paulin and J. Knight, "Scheduling and Binding Algo-

rithms for High-Level Synthesis," *26th Conference on Design Automation*, 25-29 June 1989, pp. 1-6.

[7]   H. Yang and S. Ha, "Pipelined Data Parallel Task Mapping/Scheduling Technique for MPSoC," *Proceedings of Design, Automation & Test in Europe Conference & Exhibition*, Nice, 20-24 April 2009, pp. 69-74.

[8]   A. Wu, H. Yu, S. Jin, L. Kuo-Chi and G. Schiavone, "An Incremental Genetic Algorithm Approach to Multiprocessor Scheduling," *IEEE Transactions on Parallel and Distributed Systems*, Vol. 15, No. 9, 2004, pp. 824-834.

[9]   T. Tsuchiya, T. Osada and T. Kikuno, "Genetic-Based Multiprocessor Scheduling Using Task Duplication," *Microprocessors and Microsystems*, Vol. 22, 1998, pp. 197-207.

[10]   K. Han and J. Kim, "Quantum-Inspired Evolutionary Algorithm for a Class of Combinatorial Optimization," *IEEE Transactions on Evolutionary Computation*, Vol. 6, No. 6, 2002, pp. 580-593.

[11]   L. Goh, B. Veeravalli and S. Viswanathan, "Design of Fast and Efficient Energy-Aware Gradient-Based Scheduling Algorithms Heterogeneous Embedded Multiprocessor Systems," *IEEE Transactions on Parallel and Distributed Systems*, Vol. 20, No. 1, 2009, pp. 1-12.

[12]   Y. Yu and V. Prasanna, "Energy-Balanced Task Allocation for Collaborative Processing in Wireless Sensor Networks," *Mobile Networks and Applications*, Vol. 10, 2005, pp. 115-131.

[13]   A. Andrei, M. Schmitz, P. Eles, Z. Peng, B. M. Al-Hashimi, "Overhead-Conscious Voltage Selection for Dynamic and Leakage Energy Reduction of Time-Constrained Systems," *IEE Proceedings on Computers and Digital Techniques*, Vol. 152, No. 1, 2005, pp. 28-38.

[14]   S. Kim and J. Browne, "A General Approach to Mapping of Parallel Computation upon Multiprocessor Architectures," *Proceedings of the International Conference on Parallel Processing*, 1988, pp. 1-8.

[15]   G. Zeng, T. Yokoyama, H. Tomiyama and H. Takada, "Practical Energy-Aware Scheduling for Real-Time Multiprocessor Systems," *15th IEEE International Conference on Embedded and Real-Time Computing Systems and Applications*, Beijing, 24-26 August 2009, pp. 383-392.

27

Design and Digital Implementation of Controller for PMSM Using Extended Kalman Filter

Mamatha Gowda, Warsame H. Ali, Penrose Cofie, John Fuller

Department of Electrical and Computer Engineering, Prairie View A&M University, Prairie View, USA

ABSTRACT

A novel digital implementation of speed controller for a Permanent Magnet Synchronous Motor (PMSM) with disturbance rejection using conventional observer combined with Extended Kalman Filter (EKF) is proposed. First, the EKF is constructed to achieve a precise estimation of the speed and current from the noisy measurement. Second, a proportional integral derivative (PID) controller is developed based on Linear Quadratic Regulator (LQR) to achieve speed command tracking performance. Then, an observer is designed and its error is utilized to provide load disturbance compensation. The proposed method greatly enhances the PMSM performance by reducing the control signal variation as well as the disturbance. The speed control performance is significantly improved compared to the case when we have an observer acting alone. The simulation results for the speed response and variation of the states when the PMSM is subjected to the load disturbance are presented. The results verify the effectiveness of the proposed method.

Keywords: Permanent Magnet Synchronous Motor; Extended Kalman Filter; PID; Vector Control; Observer

1. Introduction

Permanent Magnet synchronous Motor (PMSM) has a high torque/inertia ratio, high speed, high efficiency as well as high reliability and is of compact size. These qualities render PMSM as one of the most applicable AC machines for servo control applications and PMSM is therefore gaining extensive research attention in recent years [1-3]. PMSM weighs less and is of low maintenance; it offers many advantages in the high performance application areas such as in robotics, aerospace, navigation and many more. The modeling and control of the PMSM is complex because of two main reasons: 1) the multi-input nature of the motor, 2) the coupling between the stator current and rotor speed are non-linear. For high performance of PMSM that drives the vector control theory is applied, in which 3-φ stationary frame transforms into 2-φ synchronously rotating rotor reference frame; thus the flux and torque can be controlled independently, similar to the DC motor [4-6]. Though, the vector control is a complex control technique, the progress in the development of fast semiconductors switches and cost efficiency micro-controller has made the vector control fea-

sible. PMSM uses known rotor shaft position as well as the inverter to control the armature currents, and is usually employed in direct drive system. The direct drive systems are more prone to load variations and these variations directly impact the motor shaft; this deteriorates the performance of the system. In order to mitigate these defects, the disturbance rejection control technique is used.

In this paper a vector control method is developed and implemented by means of a conventional observer combined with Extended Kalman Filter algorithm to provide the speed control and disturbance rejection. In the vector control method, to achieve better control performance, it is important to know the information of the rotor speed and position. Here, state space representation of the model and observer is obtained. Utilizing the state space model, a PID controller is designed using Linear Quadratic Regulator (LQR) approach [7]. Commonly, the aim of the observer design is to reduce the observation error, but it is used to serve as feed forward compensation for the load disturbance in the proposed method [8].

Many research works have been done in speed and position estimation of PMSM using sliding mode, high frequency signal injection method, adaptive control theory, fuzzy control, state observer, EKF [9-16]. In all, EKF is more attractive as well as popular and is continuously being used in research and applications because it delivers rapid, precise, and accurate estimation. In many applications EKF is implemented because of its low-pass filter characteristics [17,18]. The feedback gain used in EKF achieves quick convergence and provides stability for the observer.

In this article, the conventional observer combined with the Extended Kalman Filter is presented. The accurate estimation of states is very essential to achieve better control and performance of the PMSM drives. Here the EKF is utilized for the precise estimation of the rotor speed and stator q-axis current. Since the drive speed and drive current are measured directly from the machine terminals contain noise, they are not precise for speed control. In the proposed approach, the speed and q-axis current are estimated accurately by introducing EKF algorithm theory. The estimated current acts as an input to the state observer while the estimated speed is compared with the reference speed. The proposed method yields a smooth and quick speed tracking, reduction in the disturbance applied to the system, and better control of the control signal variation. The overall system performance is greatly enhanced with the proposed method.

2. Model of PMSM

The stator voltage and stator flux linkages equations in the rotor references frame are [4]:

$$v_{sd} = R_s i_{sd} + L_s \frac{\mathrm{d}}{\mathrm{d}t} i_{sd} - \omega_m L_s i_{sq},$$ (1)

$$v_{sq} = R_s i_{sq} + L_s \frac{\mathrm{d}}{\mathrm{d}t} i_{sq} + \omega_m \left(L_s i_{sd} + \lambda_{fd} \right),$$ (2)

$$\lambda_{sd} = L_s i_{sd} + \lambda_{fd},$$ (3)

$$\lambda_{sq} = L_s i_{sq}$$ (4)

where v_{sd}, v_{sq}, i_{sd}, i_{sq}, λ_{sd}, λ_{sq} are d-axis and q-axis voltages, currents and flux linkages respectively. R_s, L_s are the stator winding resistance and inductance.

The electromagnetic torque generated and the acceleration is given by:

$$T_{em} = \frac{p}{2} \lambda_{fd} \cdot i_{sq},$$ (5)

$$\frac{\mathrm{d}}{\mathrm{d}t} \omega_{mech} = \frac{T_{em} - T_L}{J} - \frac{B}{J} \omega_{mech},$$ (6)

$$\omega_m = \frac{p}{2} \omega_{mech}$$ (7)

where ω_{mech} is the speed of the motor and p is the number of poles.

Since the torque developed by the motor is directly proportional to the motor drive current, it is difficult to control the drive current directly. Therefore the drive current is indirectly controlled through the input voltage. The simplified model of the PMSM q-axis subsystem is shown in **Figure 1**.

In vector control, assuming $i_{ds} = 0$, the state-space model of the PMSM q-axis subsystem is derived as [8]:

$$\begin{bmatrix} \dot{i}_{sq} \\ \dot{\omega}_{mech} \end{bmatrix} = \begin{bmatrix} -\dfrac{R_s}{L_s} & -\left(\dfrac{\lambda_{fd}}{L_s} \cdot \dfrac{p}{2} \right) \\ \left(\dfrac{p}{2} \cdot \dfrac{\lambda_{fd}}{J} \right) & -\dfrac{B}{J} \end{bmatrix} \begin{bmatrix} i_{sq} \\ \omega_{mech} \end{bmatrix} + \begin{bmatrix} \dfrac{1}{L_s} \\ 0 \end{bmatrix} \begin{bmatrix} v_{sq} \end{bmatrix}$$ (8)

For the speed controller design, the system output is

$$[y] = \begin{bmatrix} 0 & 1 \end{bmatrix} \begin{bmatrix} i_{sq} \\ \omega_{mech} \end{bmatrix}$$ (9)

If the motor output is considered as the drive current, then the motor output is given by:

$$[y'] = \begin{bmatrix} 1 & 0 \end{bmatrix} \begin{bmatrix} i_{sq} \\ \omega_{mech} \end{bmatrix}$$ (10)

3. PID Parameters Tuning with State-Feedback and State-Feed forward LQR

The controller is designed as a single-input—single-output (SISO) system. The following discussion is based on the

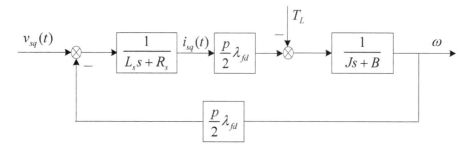

Figure 1. Q-axis subsystem of a simplified PMSM.

q-axis controller/observer design [8].

The state space model of the simplified PMSM, $G1(s)$, with reference to the q-axis is:

$$\dot{x}_1(t) = A_1 x_1(t) + B_1 u_1(t), \quad x_1(0) = x_{10} \quad (11a)$$

$$y_1(t) = C_1 x_1(t) \quad (11b)$$

where, $x_1(t) \in R^{2\times1}$, $u_1(t) \in R^{1\times1}$, $y_2(t) \in R^{1\times1}$, and A_1, B_1 and C_1 are constant matrices.

The entire system output is the sum of the motor output and load disturbance and is given by:

$$y(t) = y_1(t) + d(t) \quad (12)$$

where $y(t) \in R^{1\times1}$, $d(t) \in R^{1\times1}$

The state space model of the speed controller, $G_2(s)$, can be written as:

$$\dot{x}_2(t) = A_2 x_2(t) + B_2 u_2(t), \quad x_2(0) = x_{20}, \quad (13a)$$

$$y_2(t) = C_2 x_2(t) = u_1(t), \quad (13b)$$

$$u_2(t) = -y(t) + E_c r(t) \quad (13c)$$

where $x_2(t) \in R^{2\times1}$, $u_2(t) \in R^{1\times1}$, $y_2(t) \in R^{1\times1}$, $r(t) \in R^{1\times1}$, and A_2, B_2, C_2, E_c are constant matrices.

In order to convert the PID tuning problem to an optimal design, we modify the closed loop cascade system into an augmented system with $d(t) = 0$. The result is the following equation:

$$\dot{x}_e(t) = A_e x_e(t) + B_e u_1(t) + E_e r(t) \quad (14a)$$

$$y_e(t) = y_1(t) = C_e x_e(t) \quad (14b)$$

where

$$A_e = \begin{bmatrix} A_1 & 0 \\ -B_2 C_1 & A_2 \end{bmatrix}, \quad B_e = \begin{bmatrix} B_1 \\ 0 \end{bmatrix}, \quad E_e = \begin{bmatrix} 0 \\ B_2 E_c \end{bmatrix},$$

$$x_e = \begin{bmatrix} x_1(t) \\ x_2(t) \end{bmatrix}, \quad C_e = \begin{bmatrix} C_1 & 0 \end{bmatrix}$$

The resulting state-feedback LQR for the augmented system is:

$$u_1(t) = -K_e x_e(t) = -K_1 x_1(t) - K_2 x_2(t) \quad (15)$$

where $K_1 \in R^{1\times2}$, $K_2 \in R^{1\times2}$.

The quadratic cost function for the system J, is given as:

$$J = \int_0^\infty \left[x_e^T(t) Q x_e(t) + u_1^T(t) R u_1(t) \right] dt \quad (16)$$

where $Q \geq 0$, $R > 0$, which represent the states variation and control energy consumption, respectively.

The optimal state-feedback control gain which minimizes the performance index is given by:

$$K_e = R^{-1} B_e^T P. \quad (17)$$

The solution of the revised Riccati equation is given by:

$$P(A_e + hI) + (A_e + hI)^T P - PB_e R^{-1} B_e^T P + Q = 0 \quad (18)$$

where $P > 0$, $h > 0$.

The motor states feedback actually act as the proportional and derivative controller $\{K_1 x_1(t)\}$ respectively and the controller act as an integral only. Then K_2 is a gain for the integral controller. Hence, the total control law is equivalent to a PID controller. By choosing the desired values of h and the weighting matrices Q and R, the control gain can be determined. The block diagram of the designed augmented system including the controller is shown in the **Figure 2**.

The calculated control gains are given by:

$$K_1 = \begin{bmatrix} 0.2241 & 0.0030 \end{bmatrix}, \quad (19a)$$

$$K_2 = \begin{bmatrix} -0.1333 \end{bmatrix}. \quad (19b)$$

4. Design of Observer

A state observer is constructed mainly to achieve the speed control and disturbance rejection. The observation error and properly adjusted observer gain can provide feed-forward compensation for the output disturbance.

Suppose the state space model of the PMSM $G_1(s)$ is:

$$\dot{x}_1(t) = A_1 x_1(t) + B_1 u_1(t), \quad (20a)$$

$$y_1(t) = C_1 x_1(t) \quad (20b)$$

with the entire system output being the sum of the motor output and load disturbance as :

$$y(t) = y_1(t) + d(t). \quad (21)$$

The design of an observer, whose dynamic function is the same as that of the motor is as follows (see Equation (22)):

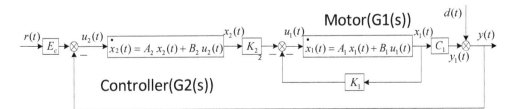

Figure 2. PID controller system.

$$\dot{\hat{x}}_1(t) = A_1\hat{x}_1(t) + B_1 u_1(t) - J_o\left[C_1\hat{x}_1(t) - y(t)\right] \quad (22)$$

where $\hat{x}_1(t)$ is an observed state and $x_1(t)$ is the real state.

Then

$$\dot{\hat{x}}_1(t) = A_1\hat{x}_1(t) + B_1 u_1(t) - J_o\left[C_1\hat{x}_1(t) - C_1 x_1(t) - d(t)\right] \quad (23)$$

The observation error is expressed as:

$$e(t) = \hat{x}_1(t) - x_1(t). \quad (24)$$

The observation error dynamic function is then given by:

$$\dot{e}(t) = (A_1 - J_o C_1)e(t) + J_o d(t) \quad (25)$$

Applying the Laplace transform, we get

$$e(s) = \left[sI - (A_1 - J_o C_1)\right]^{-1} J_o \cdot d(s). \quad (26)$$

From the above equation it is clear that the observation error will inevitably exist due to the load disturbance, and then the observed-state feedback can be regarded as:

$$K_1\hat{x}_1(t) = K_1 x_1(t) + K_1 e(t) \quad (27)$$

where, the term $K_1 x_1(t)$ is the exact motor state feedback, while the term $K_1 e(t)$ comes from the observation error. The PID controller system including the observer structure is shown in the **Figure 3**.

The feedback of the observation error actually acts as feed forward compensation for the load disturbance. Also the proper adjustment of the observer gain makes sure that the system is less affected by the load disturbance and provides additional feed forward compensation.

The speed signal differentiated through the position output of the encoder is very noisy. Thus i_{sd} instead of ω_{mech} can be regarded as the system output in the following observer design. Selecting appropriate values for h, Q and R, the revised Riccati equation is solved as follows [8]:

$$P(A_d + hI) + (A_d + hI)^T P - PB_d R^{-1}B_d^T P + Q = 0 \quad (28)$$

yields the desired optimal observer gain given as:

$$J_o = \left(R^{-1}B_d^T P\right)^T = \begin{bmatrix} 118.1727 \\ -120.6678 \end{bmatrix} \quad (29)$$

where $A_d = A_1^T$, $B_d = C_1^T$, $C_d = B_1^T$.

5. State Observer Based Extended Kalman Filter

The Extended Kalman Filter is a set of mathematical equations which produces the optimal estimation of the state system based on least square method. The EKF estimates the process by using a feedback control. The EKF provides considerable good tolerance for the mathematical model error and noises in the measurement inaccuracy [19].

The state space model of the simplified PMSM given by "(11a)" and "(11b)" is the non-linear system. To apply the EKF algorithm, the system needs be discretized and linearized [20].

The discrete approximated equation is given by:

$$x_k = (I + AT)x_{k-1} + BTu_k, \quad (30a)$$

$$y_k = cx_k. \quad (30b)$$

The nonlinear stochastic equation is:

$$x_k = f(x_{k-1}, u_k) \quad (31)$$

$$f(x_{k-1}, u_k) = \begin{bmatrix} \left(1 - \dfrac{TR_s}{L_s}\right)i_{sq} - \left(\dfrac{T\lambda_{fd}}{L_s} \cdot \dfrac{p}{2}\right)\omega_{mech} + \dfrac{T}{L_s}\left[v_{sq}\right] \\ \left(\dfrac{Tp}{2} \cdot \dfrac{\lambda_{fd}}{J}\right)i_{sq} + \left(1 - \dfrac{B}{J}\right)\omega_{mech} \end{bmatrix} \quad (32)$$

The Jacobian matrices of the partial derivative of f and h with respect to x are:

$$A_k = \left.\frac{\partial f(x_k, u_k)}{\partial x}\right|_{x_k = \hat{x}_k}, \quad (33a)$$

$$H_k = \left.\frac{\partial h(x_k)}{\partial x}\right|_{x_k = \hat{x}_k} \quad (33b)$$

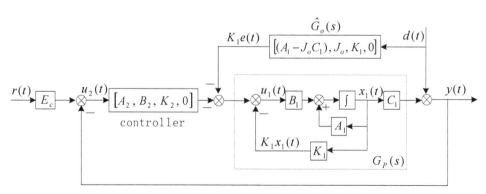

Figure 3. Observer structure.

The motor nonlinear state equations given in the discretized form is as follows:

$$x_k = f(x_{k-1}, u_k) + w_k,$$ (34a)

$$y_k = h(x_k) + v_k$$ (34b)

where w_k and v_k are zero-mean White Gaussian noise process and measurement noise with covariance Q and R. Mainly, there are two states in the Extended Kalman Filter, namely the prediction state and the correction state.

In the prediction state also called the time update, the optimal state estimate $\hat{x}$ and state covariance P are predicted.

$$\left. \begin{array}{l} \hat{x}_{pk} = f(\hat{x}_{k-1}, u, 0) \\ \hat{P}_{pk} = A_k \hat{P}_{k-1} A_k^T + Q \end{array} \right\} \text{ Time update}$$ (35)

In the correction state also called the measurement update, the predicted state estimate $\hat{x}$ and covariance matrix P are corrected as follows:

$$\left. \begin{array}{l} K_k = \hat{P}_{pk} H_k^T \left(H_k \hat{P}_{pk} H_k^T + R \right)^{-1} \\ \hat{x}_{ck} = \hat{x}_{pk} + K_k \left(y_k - H_k(\hat{x}_{pk}) \right) \\ \hat{P}_{ck} = (I - K_k H_k) \hat{P}_{pk} \end{array} \right\} \text{ Measurement update}$$

(36)

The important and difficult part in the design of the EKF is choosing the proper values for the covariance matrices Q and R [21,22]. The change of values of co-variance matrices affects both the dynamic and steady-state. By using trial and error method, a suitable set of values of Q and R are selected to insure better stability and convergence time.

The chosen values of Q, R and P are:

$$Q = \begin{bmatrix} 0.008 & 0 \\ 0 & 1.5 \end{bmatrix} \quad R = [0.02] \quad P = \begin{bmatrix} 1 & 0 \\ 0 & 1 \end{bmatrix}$$ (37)

6. Simulation Results

The PMSM model is constructed to verify the speed control and load disturbance rejection using the conventional observer combined with EKF. The simulation is implemented using MAT Lab/Simulink. The parameter of the motor model is given in **Table 1**. Based on optimal control theory, the desired control gain K1 and K2 and optimal observer gain (Jo) are determined and the filter gain is obtained using EKF algorithm. The output drive current and speed are estimated through the observer theory and EKF algorithm is implemented using S-Function block. The input to the S-Function block is taken directly from the machine terminals. The noise-free, accurately estimated output current is fed to the observer as input while the estimated speed is compared with reference speed. At the output, the motor response is checked and the disturbance rejection is observed. The block diagram used in the simulation is as shown in the below **Figure 4** and the simulation results are shown in **Figures 5-10**.

With the reference speed of 200 rad/s, the simulation

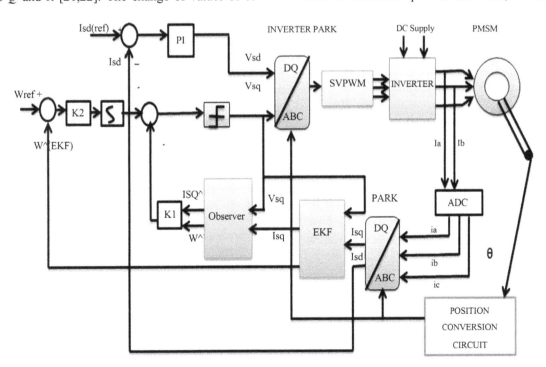

Figure 4. Block diagram of PMSM drive with observer combined with EKF.

Table 1. PMSM parameter.

Variable	Physical Meaning	Value	Unit
R_s	Armature Resistance	0.1127	Ω
L_s	Armature Inductance	3.63e$-$4	H
J	Moment of Inertia	1.2677e$-$4	Kg$\cdot$m^2
B	Damping Coefficient	2.4857e$-$4	N$\cdot$m/rad/s
λ_{fd}	Stator Flux Linkage	0.0131	V/rad/s
p	Poles number	10	
T_{L0}	Static Friction	0.0237	N$\cdot$m

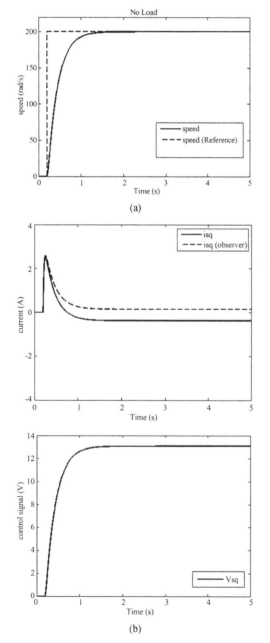

(a)

(b)

Figure 5. (a) Speed response; (b) control signal response for observer acting alone (no load).

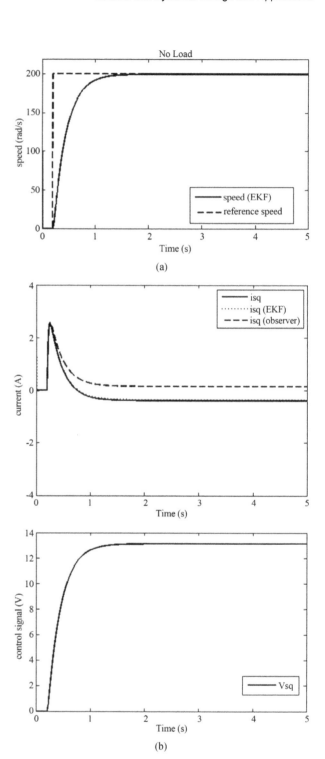

(a)

(b)

Figure 6. (a) Speed response; (b) control signal response for observer combined with EKF (no load).

results with observer acting alone and observer combined with EKF are shown in **Figures 5** and **6**, under no load condition. It is observed that the motor speed tracks the reference speed quickly and smoothly.

To account for the speed estimation performance of the observer acting alone and observer combined with EKF for a step change in steady state operation of PMSM,

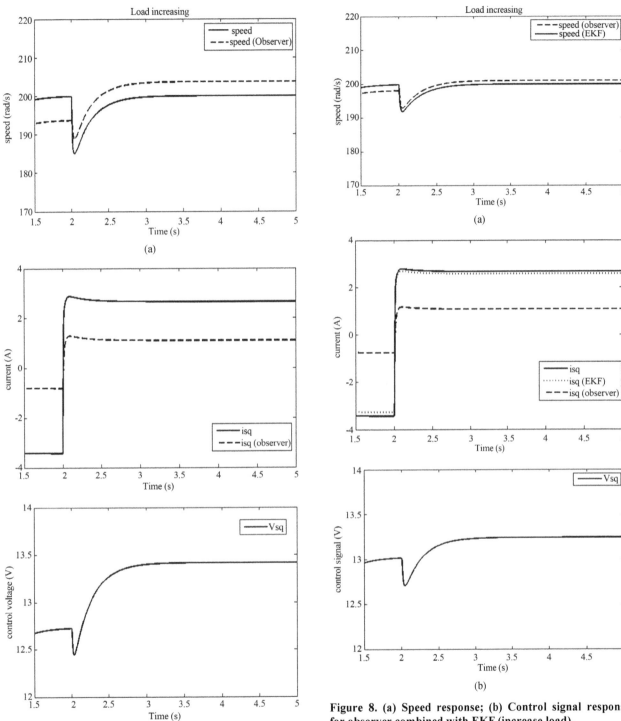

Figure 7. (a) Speed response; (b) Control signal response for observer acting alone (increase load).

the load disturbance is applied at t = 2 s. The simulation results are shown in **Figures 7** and **8** for the increasing load. **Figures 9** and **10** shows the situation for the decreasing load.

From the obtained result, it is evident that the speed

Figure 8. (a) Speed response; (b) Control signal response for observer combined with EKF (increase load).

variation caused by the load disturbance is significantly reduced in the case where the observer is combined with the EKF as compared with the case where the observer is acting alone. Also, as the simulations show, the input signal variation is reduced. The proposed approach mitigates speed deviation caused by the load disturbance variations. Reduction in the transient input signal variation, reduces the risk of potential input signal saturation,

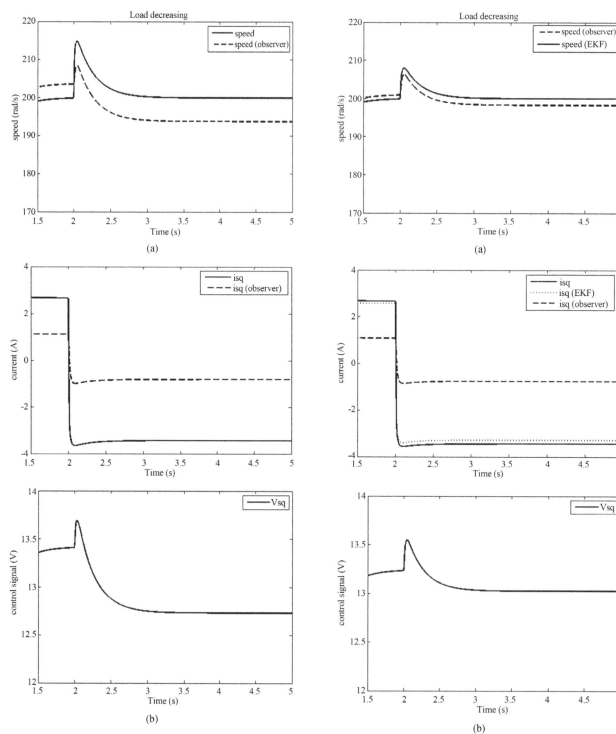

Figure 9. (a) Speed response; (b) Control signal response for observer acting alone (decrease load).

and prevents the deterioration of the system performance. The simulation results are confirms the effectiveness of the proposed method.

7. Conclusion

A novel digital implementation of speed controller for a

Figure 10. (a) Speed response; (b) Control signal response for observer combined with EKF(decrease load).

Permanent Magnet Synchronous Motor (PMSM) with disturbance rejection using conventional observer combined with Extended Kalman Filter (EKF) is proposed. The observer combined with EKF algorithm method attenuates the speed deviation caused by the load disturbance. In addition, the magnitude of the variation in the control signal is much less compared to the situation with an observer alone. The saturation of input and state is reduced effectively and the system performance is enhanced significantly.

REFERENCES

[1] S. Srikanth, B. Ranganaik and M. Srinivas Rao, "Space-vector PWM Techniques and High Temperature Super Conducting PMSM Machines with Multilevel Inverter," *Proceedings of IEEE-International Conference on Advances in Engineering, Science and Management* (*ICAESM*), Nagapattinam, 30-31 March 2012, pp. 522-527.

[2] Y. Luo, Y. Q. Chen, H.-S. Ahn and Y. Pi, "Dynamic High Order Periodic Adaptive Learning Compensator for Cogging Effect in Permanent Magnet Synchronous Motor Servo System," *IET Control Theory & Applications*, Vol. 5, No. 5, 2011, pp. 669-0680.

[3] Y. A.-R. I. Mohamed, "Design and Implementation of a Robust Current-Control Scheme for a PMSM Vector Drive with a Simple Adaptive Disturbance Observer," *IEEE Transactions on Industrial Electronics*, Vol. 54, No. 4, 2007, pp. 1981-1988.

[4] N. Mohan and Electric Drives, "An Integrative Approach," MNPERE, Minneapolis, 2000.

[5] P. Pillay and R. Krishnan, "Application Characteristics of Permanent Magnet Synchronous and Brushless DC Motors for Servo Drives," *IEEE Transactions on Industry Applications*, Vol. 27, No.5, 1991, pp. 986-996.

[6] N. Mohan, "Advanced Electric Drives, Analysis, Control and Modeling Using Simulink," MNPERE, Minneapolis, 2001.

[7] L. S. Shieh, H. M. Dib and S. Ganesan, "Linear Quadratic Regulators with Eigenvalue Placement in a Specified Region," *Automatica*, Vol. 24, No. 6, 1988, pp. 819-823.

[8] Y. P. Zhang, C. M. Akujuobi, W. H. Ali, C. L. Tolliver and S. Leang-san, "Load Disturbance Resistance Speed Controller Design for PMSM," *IEEE Transaction on Industrial Electronics*, Vol. 53, No. 4, 2006, pp. 1198-1208.

[9] F. Benchabane, A. Titaouine, O. Bennis, K. Yahia and D. Taibi, "Systematic Fuzzy Sliding Mode Approach with Extended Kalman Filter for Permanent-Magnet Synchronous Motor," *Proceedings of the IEEE international conference on Systems Man and Cybernetics* (*SMC*), 2010, pp. 2169-2174.

[10] S. Bolognani, S. Calligaro and R. Petrella, "Sensorless Control of IPM Motors in the Low-Speed Range and at Standstill by HF Injection and DFT Processing," *IEEE Transactions on Industry Applications*, Vol. 47, 2011, pp. 96-104.

[11] J. lee, J. Hon and K. Nam, "Sensorless Control of Surface-Mount Permanent-Magnet Synchronous Motors Based on a Nonlinear Observer," *IEEE Transactions on Power Electronics*, Vol. 25, No. 2, 2010, pp. 290-297.

[12] Z. D. Zheng, Y. D. Li, M. Fadel and X. Xiao, "A Rotor Speed and Load Torque Observer for PMSM Based on Extended Kalman Filter," *Proceedings of the IEEE international conference on Industrial Technology*, Mumbai, 15-17 December 2006, pp. 233-238.

[13] Q. T. An, L. Sun and B. Li, "Variable Parameters EKF for Speed Estimation of PMSM," *Electric Machines and Control*, Vol. 11, No. 6, 2007, pp. 559-563.

[14] G. C. Zhu, L.-A. Dessaint, O. Akhrif and A. Kaddouri, "Speed Tracking Control of a Permanent-magnet Synchronous Motor with State and Load Torque Observer," *IEEE Transaction on Industry Electronics*, Vol. 47, No. 2, 2000, pp. 346-355.

[15] T.-J. Kweon and D.-S. Hyun, "High-Performance Speed Control of Electric Machine Using Low-Precision Shaft Encoder," *IEEE Transactions on Power Electronics*, Vol. 14, No. 5, 1999, pp. 838-849.

[16] A. Bado and S. Bolognani, "Effective Estimation of Speed and Rotor Position of a PM Synchronous Motor Drive by a Kalman Filtering Technique," *23rd Annual IEEE Power Electronics Specialists Conference*, Toledo, 29 June-3 July 1992, pp. 951-957.

[17] K. Shedbalkar, A. P. Dhamangaonkar and A. B. Patil, "Speed Estimation Using Extended Kalman Filter for PMSM," *Proceedings of International Conference on Emerging Trends in Electrical Engineering and Energy Management* (*ICETEEEM*), Chennai, 13-15 December 2012, pp. 433-435.

[18] D. Janiszewski, "Extended Kalman Filter Based Speed Sensorless PMSM Control With Load Reconstruction," *Procedings of 32nd IEEE Annual Conference on Industrial Electronic*, *IECON*, 6-10 November 2006, pp. 1465-1468.

[19] E. R. Kalman, "A New Approach to Linear Filtering and Prediction Problems," *Transactions of the ASME–Journal of Basic Engineering*, Vol. 82, No. Series D, 1960, pp. 35-45.

[20] G. Welch and G. Bishop, "An Introduction to the Kalman Filter, Technical Report 95-041," Department of Computer Science, University of North Carolina at Chapel Hill, Chapel Hill, 1995.

[21] R. Dhaouadi, N. Mohan and L. Norum, "Design and Implementation of an Extended Kalman Filter for the State Estimation of a Permanent Magnet Synchronous Motor," *IEEE Transactions on Power Electronics*, Vol. 6, 1991, pp. 491-49.

[22] S. Bolognani, L. Tubiana and M. Zigliotto, "Extended Kalman Filter Tuning in Sensorless PMSM Drives," *IEEE Transactions on Industry Applications*, Vol. 39, No. 6, 2003, pp. 276-281.

28

A Quadrature Oscillator Based on a New "Optimized DDCC" All-Pass Filter

Achwek Ben Saied[1,2], Samir Ben Salem[2,3], Dorra Sellami Masmoudi[1,2]
[1]Computor Imaging and Electronic Systems Group (CIEL), Research Unit (ICOS), Sfax, Tunisia
[2]University of Sfax, National Engineering School of Sfax (ENIS), Sfax, Tunisia
[3]Development Group in Electronics and Communications (EleCom) Laboratory (LETI), Sfax, Tunisia

ABSTRACT

In this paper, a new voltage-mode (VM), all-pass filter utilizing two second-generation current conveyors and tow differential difference current conveyors (DDCCs) is proposed. This filter uses a number of passive elements grounded capacitor. This structure of filter is used to realize a quadrature oscillator. The proposed circuits employ tow optimized differential difference translinear second generation current conveyors (DDCCII). These structures are simulated using the spice simulation in the ADS software and CMOS 0.18 μm process of TSMC technology to confirm the theory. The pole frequency can be tuned in the range of [11.6 - 39.6 MHz] by a simple variation of a DC current.

Keywords: Proposed Current Controlled Oscillators; CMOS 0.18 μm Process of TSMC; Current Conveyor; Differential Difference Current Conveyors

1. Introduction

Differential difference current conveyors (DDCCs) are useful current-mode building blocks and many authors have demonstrated their versatility in CMOS analog circuit esign [1]. Generalized impedance converter, filter, oscillator, quadrature oscillator, floating or grounding resistor and inductance simulation are an important domain of application of DDCCs [2-4]. Indeed, the realization of voltage-mode (VM) first-order all-pass filters is quite recent [5]. These structures present some advantages, such as the possibility to control the frequency or the gain after integration [6-8]. DDCC-based filter or quadrature oscillator presents a good solution to avoid limitations of Surface Acoustic Wave, such as problems of integration, impedance matching, tuning, linearity, etc [3,6].

In order to get tuning parameters for the proposed structure, translinear differential difference second generation current controlled conveyor based structure seems to be the most attractive [9-11]. This DDCC gives a possibility to control the functions [5-8] characteristics by parasitic resistor at port X by means of a current source [12-14]. These DDCCs are extended in CMOS technology to realize a high frequency application such as filters, oscillators, quadrature oscillator and buffer [10,15,16]. To minimize the problem given by the passive element, floating and grounding resistor or floating and grounding capacitor or floating and grounding inductor, DDCC seems to be the most attractive [3,4,14].

This paper is organized as follows: In Section II, we present the proposed all-pass filter which uses two second generation current conveyor and two optimized differential difference current conveyors (DDCCs) and one grounded capacitor. This structure is ameliorated by replacing the grounding capacitor by CMOS Varactors. In Section III, we give the optimized DDCC implementation CMOS 0.18 μm process of TSMC technology. After this, we illustrate the simulation results of the optimized differential difference translinear second generation current conveyors (DDCCs) implemented in 0.18 μm CMOS technology. In Section IV, we illustrate the simulation results of the proposed DDCC all pass filter. In Section V, we present the CCII-based Quadrature oscillator architecture. This application using the proposed filter connected to an integrator in a closed loop. Finally, to validate theoretical analysis, the different circuits are designed and simulated using spice simulation in the ADS software.

2. The Proposed All-Pass Filter

A number of current and voltage mode all-pass filters employing the DDCC have been suggested [17]. However most of these realizations employ floating capacitors and resistors which require a large area to be implemented by MOS transistors. The proposed structure use two DDCC, two CCII and only grounded capacitor. The input of the voltage-mode (VM) all-pass filter is connected to the Y terminal (high input impedance) and its output is connected to the X terminal (low output impedance). For this reason the proposed structure doesn't necessitate a buffer cascade with another bloc. The architecture of the filter is given in **Figure 1**.

The transfer function and the phase of this filter can be expressed by:

$$\frac{V_{out}}{V_{in}} = \frac{1 - jCR_{eq}w}{1 + jCR_{eq}w} \tag{1}$$

$$\theta(w) = -2\,\text{arctg}\left(R_{eq}Cw\right) \tag{2}$$

The pole frequency of the filter is calculated as:

$$f_o = \frac{1}{2\pi CR_{eq}} \tag{3}$$

The type of the filter gives a good solution to realize a controlled Quadrature oscillator [17]. The oscillator frequency can be adjusted by means of the value of the capacitor or the bias current of CCII$_{2,3}$ (the value of R_{eq}). However the capacitor values are not variable after integration, for this reason we present an ameliorate structure for the filter when we replaced the grounding capacitor by CMOS Varactors or by a multiplier capacitor [18]. **Figure 2** displays the architecture of the ameliorated filter.

3. The Optimized Differential Difference Translinear Current Conveyor

The DDCC is a four terminal active block. The symbol and the equivalent circuit of the the DDCC are illustrated in **Figure 3**.

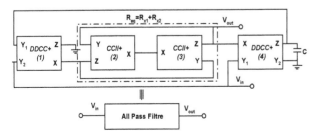

Figure 1. The proposed all-pass filter.

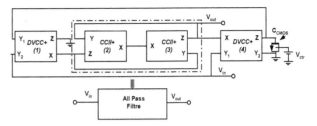

Figure 2. The ameliorated all-pass filter.

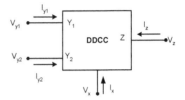

Figure 3. General representation of DDCC.

The DDCC ensures two functionalities between its terminals:

- A Current follower between terminals X and Z.
- A Voltage follower between terminals X and (Y_1 - Y_2).

In order to get ideal transfers, a DDCC should be characterized by low impedance on terminal X and high impedance on terminals Y_1, Y_2 and Z. In this configuration, the relation between terminal voltages and currents can be given by the following matrix:

$$\begin{pmatrix} V_x \\ I_{Y1} \\ I_{Y2} \\ I_z \end{pmatrix} = \begin{pmatrix} 0 & 1 & -1 & 0 \\ 0 & 0 & 0 & 0 \\ 0 & 0 & 0 & 0 \\ \pm 1 & 0 & 0 & 0 \end{pmatrix} \begin{pmatrix} I_X \\ V_{Y1} \\ V_{Y2} \\ V_Z \end{pmatrix} \tag{4}$$

To realize this structure it's necessary to cascade CMOS differential voltage buffer (DVB) with a CCII. An implementation of the CMOS differential voltage buffer (DVB) and the CCII are respectively shown in **Figures 4** and **5** [2-4].

A. CMOS Differential Voltage Buffer

The (DVB) is shown in **Figure 4** [3,4]. The input transconductance elements are realized with two differential stages (M1 and M2, M3 and M4). The high gain stage is composed of a current mirror (M5 and M6). It converts the differential current to a single-ended output current (M7). The output voltage of this amplifier can be expressed as:

$$V'_x = \beta_{y1}V_{y1} - \beta_{y2}V_{y2} \tag{5}$$

where

$$\beta_{Y1} \approx \frac{g_{m7}g_{m1}\left(g_{m6} + g_{d2} + g_{d4} + g_{d6}\right)}{g_{m4}g_{m5}g_{m7} + g_{m6}g_{d7}\left(g_{d1} + g_{d3} + g_{d5}\right)} \tag{6}$$

$$\beta_{Y2} \approx \frac{-g_{m6}g_{m5}g_{m7}}{g_{m4}g_{m5}g_{m7} + g_{m6}g_{d7}\left(g_{d1} + g_{d3} + g_{d5}\right)} \tag{7}$$

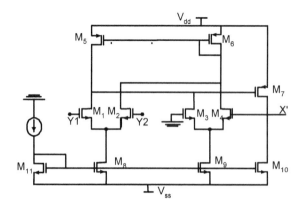

Figure 4. CMOS differential voltage buffer.

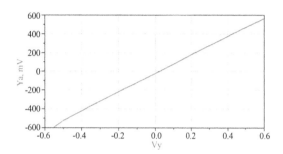

Figure 5. Voltage DC transfer characteristic of the DVB (where $Ya = Vx'$ and $Vy = Vy_1 - Vy_2$).

To determinate the optimal transistor sizes (W and L) for this structure we will use the heuristic methodology [6,7]. This strategy consists on minimizing the impedance output value, assuming that the current mirror has unity gain and closer β_{y1} and β_{y2} to the unity. The output resistor is calculated as:

$$Z_{x'} \approx \frac{g_{m6}\left(g_{d1} + g_{d3} + g_{d5}\right)}{g_{m4}g_{m5}g_{m7} + g_{m6}g_{d7}\left(g_{d1} + g_{d3} + g_{d5}\right)} \quad (8)$$

Simulation conditions are summarized in **Table 1** and the resultant optimal transistor sizes (W and L) are presented in **Table 2**.

The optimized CMOS differential voltage buffer was simulated with Spice simulation in the ADS software. Main obtained results are represented in **Figures 5** and **6**. **Figure 5** displays the DC transfer characteristics of the DVB. The voltage transfer can be linear between −0.6 V and 0.6 V. Moreover, the bandwidths of output terminals are shown in **Figure 6**. The −3dB bandwidths of $V_x' / \left(V_{y1} - V_{y2}\right)$ are located at 3.75 GHz.

The time-domain response of the optimized DVB is shown in **Figure 7**. A sine wave of 100 mV and −100 mV amplitude and 200 MHz is respectively applied as the input Y_1 and Y_2 to the filter. We notice that the output Waveforms are confused with the differential input Waveforms $V_{y1}(t) - V_{y2}(t)$. This result confirms the good functionality of this structure.

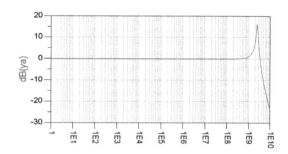

Figure 6. Frequency response of the voltage follower Vx'/ $(Vy_1 - Vy_2)$.

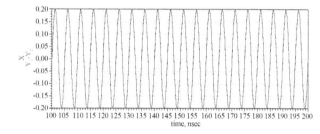

Figure 7. The simulation result of voltage waveforms of Vx' and $(Vy_1 - Vy_2)$.

Table 1. Simulation conditions.

Technology	0.18 μm CMOS
Supply voltage	1.5 V
Bias current	100 μA

Table 2. Optimal device sizing.

Device Name	Aspect ratio W/L (μm)
M5-6	13.725/0.18
M1-4	0.25/0.18
M7	7/0.18
M8-11 (current mirrors)	3.05/0.18

B. Transinear Loop Based CCII Configurations

An implementation of the second-generation translinear loop based current conveyor with a positive current transfer from X to Z (CCII+) is shown in **Figure 8** [7]. In **Table 3** we give the different transistor size.

Table 3 shows the optimal device scaling that we get after applying the optimization approach.

The static and dynamic characteristics of the translinear configuration are summarized at **Table 4**.

4. Simulation Results of the Proposed All-Pass Filter

The VM all-pass filter (**Figure 1**) is simulated with the SPICE program using 0.18 μm TSMC CMOS technol-

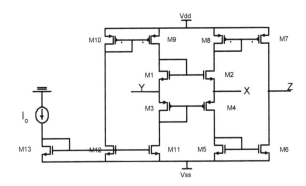

Figure 8. Translinear loop MOS based implementation of CCII.

Table 3. Optimal device sizing.

Device Name	Aspect ratio W/L (μm)
M1, M2	6.1/0.18
M3, M4	27.45/0.18
Mxx (in PMOS current mirrors)	13.725/0.18
Mxx (in NMOS current mirrors)	3.05/0.18

Table 4. Performance characteristics of the optimized CCII with Io = 100 μA and 1.5 supply voltage.

Voltage gain β	0.943
Current gain α	1.1
Fci	2.7 GHz
Fcv	4.33 GHz
Relative current Error	0.15%
Relative Voltage Error	0.093%
Input Impedance (RY//CY)	18 KΩ//87 fF
Input Impedance (Rz//Cz)	24 KΩ//25 fF
Input Resistance Rx	380 Ω
The offset current	−2.2 μA
The offset voltage	13 mV

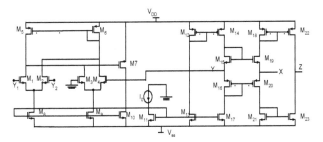

Figure 9. CMOS realization of the DDCC.

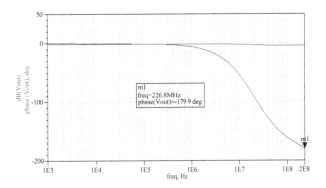

Figure 10. Gain and phase responses of proposed all-pass section.

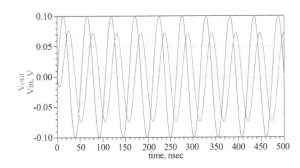

Figure 11. Input and output waveforms for the circuit at 19 MHz.

ogy. The CMOS implementation of the DDCC+ is shown in **Figure 9**. The transistor aspect ratios of MOS transistor were chosen as in **Tables 2** and **3** and the supply voltage was ±1.5 V. The biasing current was taken respectively as 100 μA for the DDCC and 30 μA for the CCII ($R_{eq} = R_{X2} + R_{X3} = 1.5$ KΩ). The simulation results for the magnitude and phase responses of Vout are shown in **Figure 10** where we take $C = 6$ pF. In this figure, the pole frequency of 19MHz is obtained. The pole frequency is 19 MHz instead of 17.7 MHz owing to the effect of the parasitic impedances of the DDCC. The relative error between theoretical and simulation value is equal to 7%.

To confirm this result, the circuit is inputted with a sinusoidal signal of 19 MHz. The input and +90° phase shifted output (V_{out}) are shown in **Figure 11**. **Figure 12**

shows the variability of the pole frequency of **Figure 1** with the bias current $I_{o2,3}$. The pole frequency can be controlled in the range [11.6 MHz, 36.6 MHz] by varying $I_{o2,3}$ in the range [10 μA, 200 μA].

5. Quadrature Oscillator Based on the Proposed All-Pass Filter

To illustrate the utility of the proposed first-order all-pass filter (high input and low output impedances), no buffer is required to connect it to the integrator circuit $\left(V_{out} = -2/(sRC\omega)\right)$ [18]), it is connected in cascade to an integrator in a closed loop [17] to construct a quadrature oscillator, as shown in **Figure 13**. It is seen that the proposed architecture uses three optimized CMOS DCCIIs, tow CCII's, one floating resistor and tow grounded capacitors. The corresponding characteristic

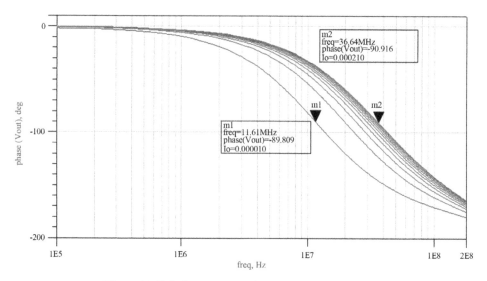

Figure 12. Pole-frequency tuning with bias current $I_{o2,3}$.

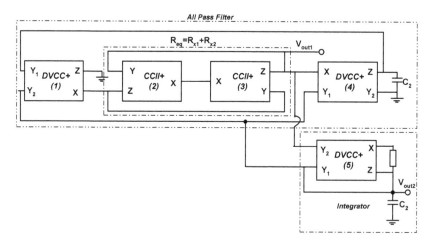

Figure 13. The proposed quadrature oscillator implementation.

equation is given by:

$$s^2 + s\left(\frac{1}{C_1 R_{eq}} - \frac{1}{RC_2}\right) + \frac{2}{C_1 R_{eq} C_2 R} = 0 \qquad (9)$$

This leads to the following oscillation condition and oscillation frequency respectively:

$$f_o = \frac{1}{2\pi}\sqrt{\frac{2}{C_1 R_{eq} C_2 R}} \qquad (10)$$

$$CO : C_1 R_{eq} \geq C_2 R \qquad (11)$$

The confirmed performance of the quadrature oscillator can be seen in **Figure 14**, showing the responses of the oscillator where $C_1 = 6$ pF, $C_2 = 10$ pF, $R = 600$ Ω, and $I_{o2,3} = 30$ μA ($R_{eq} = R_{X2} + R_{X3} = 1.5$ KΩ). The phase difference between two out puts V_{out1} and V_{out2} is 90° and the oscillation frequency is equal to 26 MHz (the theoretical value of the oscillation frequency is 30.5 MHz).

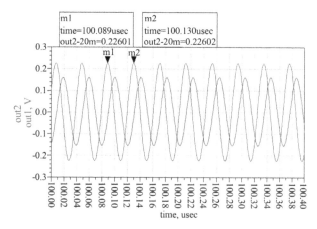

Figure 14. The simulated quadrature output waveforms of V_{out1} and V_{out2}.

The quadrature relationships between the generated waveforms have been verified using Lissagous figure and shown in **Figure 15**.

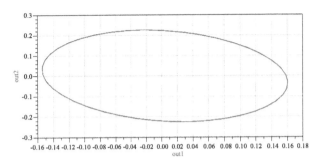

Figure 15. Lissagous figure.

6. Conclusion

In this paper, we have proposed a new design of VM first-order all-pass filter. In order to get high performances of the filter, a translinear DCCII and CCII structures are optimized in 0.18 μm CMOS process of TSMC. The theoretical analysis is verified with the SPICE simulation program. The application example as the quadrature oscillator is included. It shows good usability of the proposed all-pass filter.

REFERENCES

[1] H. Elwan and A. Soliman, "A Novel CMOS Current Conveyor Realization with an Electronically Tunable Current-Mode Filter Suitable for VLSI," *IEEE Transactions on Circuits and Systems* II: *Analog and Digital Signal Processing*, Vol. 43, No. 9, 1996, pp. 663-670.

[2] U. Torteanchai and M. Kumngern, "Current-Tunable Current-Mode All-Pass Section Using DDCC," *International Conference on Electronic Devices, Systems and Applications* (*ICEDSA*), Kuala Lumpur, 25-27 April 2011, pp. 217-220.

[3] S. Wang and H. Chen, "Tunable Voltage-Mode Multifunction Biqaudratic Filter with Grounded Capacitors and Resistors Using Two DDCCs," 3*rd International Conference on Communication Software and Networks* (*ICCSN*), 2011.

[4] M. Somdunyakanok, K. Angkeaw and P. Prommee, "Floating-Capacitance Multiplier based on CCDDCCs and Its Application," *TENCON* 2011-2011 *IEEE Region 10 Conference*, pp. 1367-1370.

[5] H. P. Chen and K. H. Wu, "Grounded-Capacitor First-Order Filter Using Minimum Components," *IEICE Transactions on Fundamentals of Electronics, Communications and Computer Sciences*, Vol. E89-A, No. 12, 2006, pp. 3730-3731.

[6] S. B. Salem, M. Fakhfakh, D. S. Masmoudi, M. Loulou, P. Loumeau and N. Masmoudi, "A High Performances CMOS CCII and High Frequency Applications," *Journal of Analog Integrated Circuits and Signal Processing*, Vol. 49, No.1, 2006, pp. 71-78.

[7] S. B. Salem, D. S. Masmoudi and M. Loulou, "A Novel CCII-Based Tunable Inductance and High Frequency Current Mode Band Pass Filter Application," *Journal of Circuits, Systems, and Computers* (*JCSC*), Vol. 15, No. 6, 2006, pp. 849-860.

[8] A. Bensaied, S. B. Salem and D. S. Masmoudi, "A new CMOS Current Controlled Quadrature Oscillator Based on a MCCII," *Circuits and Systems*, Vol. 2, No. 4, 2011.

[9] A. Khan and A. M. T. Ahmed, "Realization of Tunable Floating Resistors," *Electronics Letters*, Vol. 22, 1986, pp. 799-800.

[10] P. Saaid and A. Fabre, "Class AB Current-Controlled Resistor for High Performance Current-Mode Applications," *Electronics Letters*, Vol. 32, 1996, pp. 4-5.

[11] R. Senani, A. K. Singh and V. K. Singh, "A New floating Current-Controlled Positive Resistance Using Mixed Translinear Cells," *IEEE Transactions on Circuits and Systems-II*, Vol. 51, 2004, pp. 374-377.

[12] G. Wilson and P. Chan, "Floating CMOS Resistor," *Electronics Letters*, Vol. 28, 1993, pp. 306-307.

[13] V. Riewruja and W. Petchmaneelumka, "Floating Currentcontrolled Resistance Converters Using OTAs," *International Journal of Electronics and Communications*, Vol. 62, 2008, pp. 725-731.

[14] M. Kumngern, U. Torteanchai and K. Dejhan, "Voltage-Controlled Floating Resistor Using DDCC," *Radioengineering*, Vol. 20, No. 1, 2011.

[15] P. Beg, I. A. Khan and M. T. Ahmed, "Tunable Four Phase Voltage Mode Quadrature Oscillator Using Two CMOS MOCCIIs," *Multimedia, Signal Processing and Communication Technologies*, Aligarh, 14-16 March 2009, pp. 155-157.

[16] H. O. Elwan and A. M. Soliman, "Low-Voltage Low-Power CMOS Current Conveyors," *IEEE Transaction on Circuits and Systems*: *Fundamental Theory and Applications*, Vol. 44, No. 9, 1997.

[17] S. Minaei and E. Yuce, "Novel Voltage-Mode All-Pass Filter Based on Using DVCCs," *Circuits, Systems and Signal Processing*, Vol. 29, No. 3, 2010, pp. 391-402.

[18] S. Maheshwari, "Analogue Signal Processing Applications Using a New Circuit Topology," *IET Circuits, Devices & Systems*, Vol. 3, No. 3, 2009, pp. 106-115.

29

A 1.8 GHz Power Amplifier Class-E with Good Average Power Added Efficiency

Mousa Yousefi[*], Ziaadin Daie Koozehkanani, Jafar Sobhi, Hamid Jangi
Faculty of Electrical and Computer Engineering, University of Tabriz, Tabriz, Iran

ABSTRACT

This paper presents a 1.8 GHz class-E controlled power amplifier (PA). The proposed power amplifier is designed with two-stage architecture. The main advantage of the proposed technique for output control power is a high 37 dB output power dynamic range with good average power adding efficiency. The measurement results show that the PA achieves a high power gain of 23 dBm and power added efficiency (PAE) by 38%. The circuit was post layout simulated in a standard 0.18 μm CMOS technology.

Keywords: Power Added Efficiency; Power Amplifier; Class-E; Dynamic Range; Polar Modulation; Output Power

1. Introduction

Wireless communication standards are employing power control techniques to reduce interference in the network and saving energy, and power consumption of the mobile device. For design constant envelope modulation schemes such as Gaussian minimum-shift keying or Gaussian frequency-shift keying, switch mode power amplifiers are well suitable. The GSM900 standard for a mobile station specified by European Telecommunications Standards Institute requires the power control range from 24 dB to 34 dB. In the DCS1800 and PCS1900 frequency bands, the standard requires 24 to 36 dB power control range [1]. Power Amplifiers that operate as switches, such as class D and E amplifiers, have the potential for high efficiency [2,3]. However, because the PAs are driven as switches, they have usually been limited to transmit constant envelope signals. Therefore, the vast majority of PAs in modern wireless communication are class AB amplifiers with lower efficiency [4].

There have been several fully integrated implementations of class-E PAs in CMOS reported—see e.g., [5-9]. More recent communications systems are all using both amplitude and phase modulation to increase the data rate and spectral efficiency. The polar transmitter topology allows combining both high efficiency and linearity as-

---
[*]Corresponding author.

suming a highly efficient PA and amplitude modulator is used. The class-E PA is well suited for the polar transmitter, where the input of the PA contains only the phase modulated RF signal [10].

Switch-mode power amplifiers are becoming more and more popular in modern RF transmitter design, especially due to their high efficiency. They are well suited for constant envelope modulation systems such as GSM and Bluetooth. These systems are employing power control techniques to maximize the spectral usage and to reduce the power consumption of the mobile device.

Many power control techniques [4-9] have been carried out before. For example, the conventional power control of a switch-mode PA is implemented by adjusting the supply voltage [11]. **Figure 1(a)** Power control techniques for a constant envelope modulation schemes can be used to improve the efficiency of the PA. For a switch mode PA, the input power is expected to be constant, and therefore a supply voltage power control technique is traditionally employed. High sensitivity to load variations and limited output power control range are main drawbacks of supply voltage power control technique. And also the switch mode power controller is placed in the high power path [6]. Cascode Power Control Technique is another power control technique that is shown in **Figure 1(b)**. The power control signal is applied to the gate of the cascode transistor.

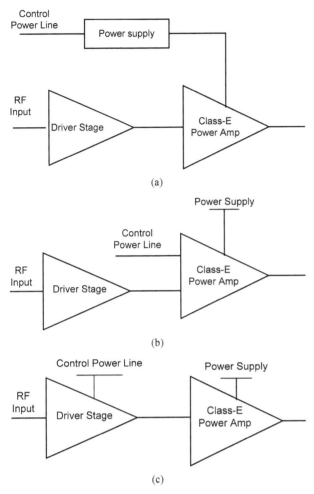

Figure 1. (a) The conventional power control of a switch-mode PA is implemented by adjusting the supply voltage; (b) Cascode Power Control Technique; (c) Block diagram proposed power control technique for class E power amplifier

In [12] a two point modulation technique is proposed. The amplitude modulation is implemented by controlling the current of the PA and simultaneously the supply voltage is adjusted in order to improve the efficiency of PA. Low pass delta sigma modulator with a phase modulated clock is used to modulate the envelope which is another approach [12]. Turing on and off an array of cells according to a digital amplitude control signal, is a digital method for amplitude modulation.

The block diagram proposed technique is shown in **Figure 1(c)**. With this proposed technique, we received the better PAE characteristic. In this structure, output power controlling is accommodated by driver stage. In Section 2 the technique is described.

This paper is organized as follows. Section 2 describes the basic operation and design implementation of used architecture. Simulation results and analysis are presented in Section 3. Finally, the conclusions are presented in Section 4.

2. Proposed Circuit

2.1. Base Structure

Figure 1(c) shows the schematic diagram of the designed two stage fully-integrated PA. It is a two stage class-E power amplifier. The circuit consists of two stages, a class-E output stage and a driver stage. **Figure 2** shows the proposed class-E output stage. Ideally, M1 and M3 act as switch; one-transistor switches on and the other off alternatively in every cycle. The conditions of operation in class-E (hard switching operation and zero-voltage switching condition [8]) allow for a great reduction in power losses, and the tuning of harmonic load impedances is far less sophisticated than in classes relying on tuning of harmonic impedances. The Common Gate transistor is biased so as to be always ON. That keeps the values of on-resistance low, thus limiting the losses and improving efficiency. Traditionally, the self-biased cascode configuration [6] was introduced to optimally divide the voltage swing across the Common Source and Common Gate transistors for higher output power and efficiency within the breakdown limits of the device. The common-source (CS) transistor M1 is designed to operate as a switch that operates in both, saturation and triode region.

The required output power level and the breakdown voltage of the NMOS device set the maximum load impedance RL. The power amplifier is designed to deliver output power for output stage. However, to achieve the desired performance, the output stage requires a high peak voltage. Thus a high gain preamplifier must be designed to deliver the necessary driver level. The large size output stage transistor implies the need for the preceding stage to drive a huge capacitor. Therefore the first stage of the preamplifier needs to be small to minimize the capacitor seen by the mixer and the final stage of the preamplifier must be large to drive the large capacitor presented by the output stage transistors. In addition, to minimize the capacitive loading an inductor can be used at the gate of the large transistors to resonate its capacitor. An inductor with moderate value has reasonable impedance at RF frequency. To maintain the overall efficiency

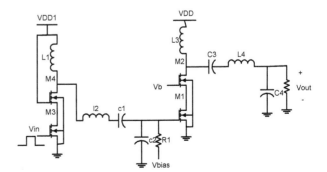

Figure 2. Class-E power amplifier schematic.

close to that of the output stage, the preamplifier DC current need to be small. For controlling output power, in this work power control line is applied to the gate of the M1 transistor common source stage.

2.2. Relations and Equations

Consider Power amplifier shown in **Figure 2**. The input voltage (V_g) is sufficiently low (typically not much greater than the threshold voltage of M1 Transistor), so that M1 is OFF. As V_g is increased, M1 Transistor is ON. Voltage gate of M1 transistor is composed of DC and ac components. DC component is determined by V_{bias} and amplitude of ac component is determined by preamplifier stage.

$$V_g\left(t_1\right) = V_{bias} + V_1 \sin\left(\omega t_1\right) = V_{TH} \tag{1}$$

V_{TH} is threshold voltage of transistor, ω oscillation frequency and V_{bias} is bias voltage of Transistor M1. The transistor M1 is off after t2. Also, duty cycle is

$$D = t_2 - t_1 = \frac{2}{\omega_{in}} \sin^{-1}\left(\frac{V_{TH} - V_{bias}}{V_1}\right) \tag{2}$$

During the time interval D, transistor is ON. The Equation (2) shows that duty cycle (when the transistor is ON) is changed by the voltage bias. **Figure 3** shows duty cycle versus V_{bias}. And also, linear dependence of on duty cycle the bias voltage indicating that duty cycle can be achieved by linearly the bias voltage.

As reported in [14], the Equation (3) states output power change with D.

$$P_{out} = \frac{\beta^2}{2\alpha^2} \frac{V_{DD}^2}{R} \tag{3}$$

In this equation, V_{DD} is power supply and R is load

branch network and α and β is expressed by (4) and (5)

$$\alpha = -\theta_F \theta_c \sin\theta_X + 2\theta_c \sin\frac{\theta_D}{2}\theta_c$$
$$+ \left(\theta_F \cos\frac{\theta_D}{\theta} + 2\sin\frac{\theta_D}{\theta}\right)\cos\theta_c \tag{4}$$

$$\beta = \left[\sin\theta_x + \sin\left(\theta_D - \theta_x\right)\right]^2 \tag{5}$$

The θ_D is the phase duration of the switch on

$$\theta_D = 2\pi D \tag{6}$$

And the phase duration of switch–off is

$$\theta_F = 2\pi\left(1 - D\right) \tag{7}$$

The difference the angle phase θ_X is expressed by

$$\theta_X = \tan\frac{1 - \cos\theta_D}{2\pi - \theta_D + \sin\theta_D} \tag{8}$$

The θ_C can be expressed by Equation (9) as a function of the phase of switch on θ_D.

$$\theta_c = \theta_D/2 - \theta_X \tag{9}$$

Figure 4 shows output power with respect to duty cycle (D). Output power increases as D. We can conclude that power should be changed with change by V_{bias}.

3. Post Layout Simulation Result

The power amplifier complete circuit consists of the output stage and the preamplifier shown in **Figure 2**. Output stage drive is driven by a class E driver stage. In the proposed design, the finite RF choke technique was used and the maximum drain peak is reduced 2.5 V_{DD} [7]. The width and length of transistor M1 is 4600 and 180 μm and also the width and length of transistor M2 is 8200 and 350 μm, respectively. The spiral on chip L2 (2.6 nH) and C1 (6 pF) and C2 (8 pF) are the interstage matching network. The L1, L3 (5 nH) and L4 (5 nH) are

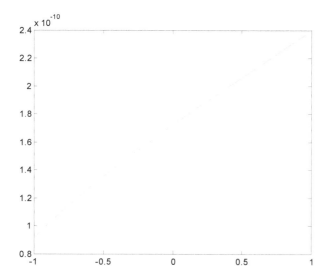

Figure 3. Duty cycle versus Vbais (V1 = 2, f_{in} = 2.4 GHz, V_{th} = 0.55, V_{bias} = −1 to 1).

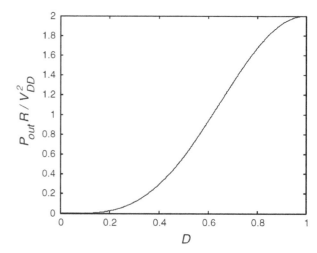

Figure 4. P_{out}R/V_{DD2} with respect to duty ratio D.

realized via bond wire inductor. The proposed power amplifier with output power levels in the range of −14 dBm to 23 dBm and with efficiencies ranging from 0% - 38% has been presented. **Figure 5** shows transient response of voltage gate node transistor M1 versus V_{bias}. DC voltage of gate M1 transistor increases with increasing V_{bias}. **Figure 6** depicts the output power and efficiency versus the variation of the supply voltage VDD. By changing the gate voltage of M1 transistor, to the output stage as shown in **Figure 2**, output power is controllable. **Figure 7** shows that proposed technique provides output power from −14 to 23 dBm whereas; V_{bias} changes from 0 to 900 mv. As a result, Pout dynamic range is 37 dB. In the V_{bias} 700 mv, the maximum PAE power amplifier is 38%. **Figure 8** shows PAE proposed power amplifier versus V_{bias}. The proposed power ampli-

fier has good average power added efficiency with changing V_{bias} from 0 to 900 mv, PAE changing from 0 to 38% and average, PAE is 27% for all of range control voltage (V_{bias}). The results in **Figure 9** show that the proposed modulated PA is more power efficient than the power supply modulated PA and cascode modulated PA. The proposed PA has good average PAE than other techniques. **Figure 10** shows the pout versus normalized control voltage, for changing power supply voltage, voltage gate M2 transistor (cascade transistor) and voltage gate of M1 transistor. PAE and Pout versus frequency for different V_{bias} is plotted in **Figures 11** and **12** respectively. The proposed Power amplifier has 1.2 × 0.6 mm area without pads and bond wire inductors. **Figure 13** shows Layout photo of the proposed power amplifier. **Table 1** shows the comparison parameters of the pro-

Table 1. Comparison Table of power amplifiers

Reference	Frequency (GHz)	Technology (micrometer)	output power(dBm)	Power supply(volt)	Peak PAE (%)	Dynamic range (dB)
[6]	1.9	0.18	32	3.3	40	20
[13]	1.7	0.25	25	1.5	49	17
[9]	2.2	0.18	18	1.6	35	35
This work	1.8	0.18	23	1.8	38	37

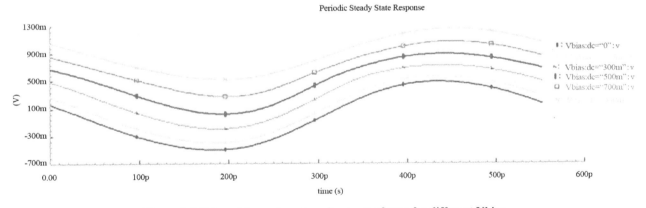

Figure 5. M1 transistor gate node voltage waveforms for different Vbias

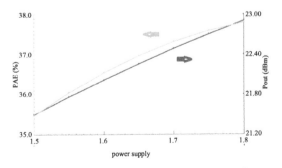

Figure 6. PAE and Pout versus power supply.

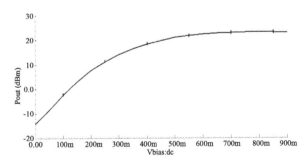

Figure 7. Output power PA across 50 ohm (dBm) versus V_{bias}.

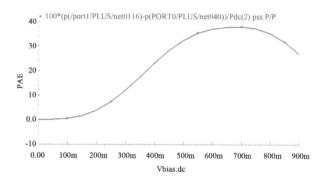

Figure 8. Power added efficiency of proposed power amplifier versus V_{bias}.

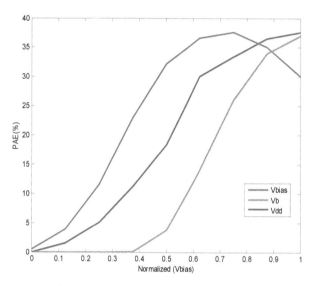

Figure 9. Power Added Efficiency power amplifier versus V_{bias} (0 to 1 v) and voltage gate of M2 transistor (0 to 1.8 v) and power supply (0 to 1.8 v) are normalized.

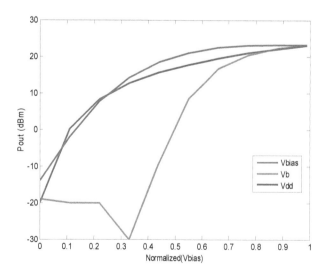

Figure 10. Output power of PA versus V_{bias} (0 to 1 v) and voltage gate of M2 transistor (0 to 1.8 v) and power supply (0 to 1.8 v) are normalized.

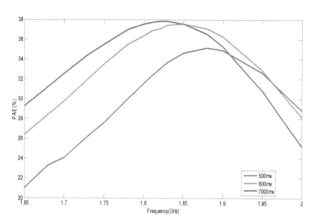

Figure 11. Power Added Efficiency power amplifier versus Frequency.

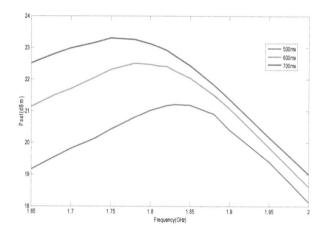

Figure 12. Output power versus frequency.

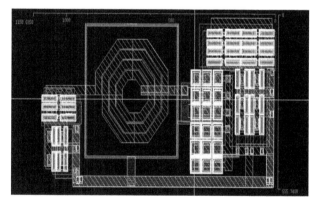

Figure 13. Layout photo of the class-E PA.

posed PA with the published CMOS PAs.

4. Conclusion

This paper presents that the Class-E is suitable for polar transmitter topology. The proposed power control technique is attractive because of the increased average PAE and the switch mode power switch. The post layout simulation has been performed on a 0.18 μm RFCMOS.

This power amplifier is capable of delivering 24 dBm output power to a 50 Ω load at 1.8 GHz.

REFERENCES

[1] C. D. Presti, F. Carrara, A. Scuderi, P. M. Asbeck and G. Palmisano, "A 25 dBm Digitally Modulated CMOS Power Amplifier for WCDMA/EDGE/OFDM With Adaptive Digital Predistortion and Efficient Power Control," *IEEE Journal of Solid-State Circuits*, Vol. 44, No. 7, 2009, pp. 1883-1896.

[2] N. O. Sokal, "Class-E RF Power Amplifiers," *QEX*, No. 204, 2001, pp. 9-20.

[3] F. H. Raab, P. Asbeck, S. Cripps, P. B. Kenington, Z. B. Popovich, N. Pethecary, J. F. Sevic and N. O. Sokal, "RF and Microwave Power Amplifier and Transmitter Technologies—Part 2," *High Frequency Electronics*, 2003, pp. 39-48.

[4] P. Wagh and P. Midya, "High-Efficiency Switched-Mode RF Power Amplifier," *Proceedings of Midwest Symposium on Circuits and Systems*, Vol. 2, 1999, pp. 1044-1047.

[5] P. Reynaert and M. Steyaert, "A 1.75-GHz Polar Modulated CMOS RF Power Amplifier for GSM-EDGE," *IEEE Journal of Solid-State Circuits*, Vol. 40, No. 12, 2005, pp. 2598-2608.

[6] Ch. Park, Y. Kim, H. Kim and S. Hong, "A 1.9-GHz CMOS Power Amplifier Using Three-Port Asymmetric Transmission Line Transformer for a Polar Transmitter," *IEEE Transactions on Microwave Theory and Techniques*, Vol. 55, No. 2, 2007, pp. 230-238.

[7] C. Yoo and Q. Huang, "A Common-Gate Switched 0.9-W Class-E Power Amplifier with 41% PAE in 0.25-_m CMOS," *IEEE Journal of Solid-State Circuits*, Vol. 36, No. 5, 2001, pp. 823-830.

[8] T. Sowlati and D. M. W. Leenaerts, "A 2.4 GHz 0.18-_m CMOS Selfbiased Cascode Power Amplifier," *IEEE Journal of Solid-State Circuits*, Vol. 38, No. 8, 2003, pp. 1318-1324.

[9] D. Sira, P. Thomsen and T. Larsen, "Output Power Control in Class-E Power Amplifiers," *IEEE Microwave and Wireless Components Letters*, Vol. 20, No. 4, 2010.

[10] T. W. Kwak, M. C. Lee and G. H. Cho, "A 2 W CMOS Hybrid Switching Amplitude Modulator for EDGE Polar Transmitters," *IEEE International Solid-State Circuits Conference*, San Francisco, 11-15 February 2007, pp 518-619.

[11] J. N. Kitchen, I. Deligoz, S. Kiaei and B. Bakkaloglu, "Polar SiGe Class E and F Amplifiers Using Switch-Mode Supply Modulation," *IEEE Transactions on Microwave Theory and Techniques*, Vol. 55, No. 5, 2007, pp. 845-856.

[12] A. Shameli, A. Safarian, A. Rofougaran, M. Rofougaran and F. De Flaviis, "A Two-Point Modulation Technique for CMOS Power Amplifier in Polar Transmitter Architecture," *IEEE Transactions on Microwave Theory and Techniques*, Vol. 56, No. 1, 2008, pp. 31-38.

[13] A. Shirvani, D. Su and B. Wooley, "A CMOS RF Power Amplifier with Parallel Amplification for Efficient Power Control," *IEEE Journal of Solid-State Circuits*, Vol. 37, No. 6, 2002, pp. 684-693.

[14] T. L. Yang, J. R. Liang, C. Zhao and D. Y. Chen, "Analysis and Design of Class-E Power Amplifiers at Any Duty Ratio in Frequency Domain", *Analog Integrated Circuits and Signal Processing*, Vol. 67, No. 2, 2011, pp. 149-156.

Permissions

The contributors of this book come from diverse backgrounds, making this book a truly international effort. This book will bring forth new frontiers with its revolutionizing research information and detailed analysis of the nascent developments around the world.

We would like to thank all the contributing authors for lending their expertise to make the book truly unique. They have played a crucial role in the development of this book. Without their invaluable contributions this book wouldn't have been possible. They have made vital efforts to compile up to date information on the varied aspects of this subject to make this book a valuable addition to the collection of many professionals and students.

This book was conceptualized with the vision of imparting up-to-date information and advanced data in this field. To ensure the same, a matchless editorial board was set up. Every individual on the board went through rigorous rounds of assessment to prove their worth. After which they invested a large part of their time researching and compiling the most relevant data for our readers. Conferences and sessions were held from time to time between the editorial board and the contributing authors to present the data in the most comprehensible form. The editorial team has worked tirelessly to provide valuable and valid information to help people across the globe.

Every chapter published in this book has been scrutinized by our experts. Their significance has been extensively debated. The topics covered herein carry significant findings which will fuel the growth of the discipline. They may even be implemented as practical applications or may be referred to as a beginning point for another development. Chapters in this book were first published by Scientific Research Publishing Inc.; hereby published with permission under the Creative Commons Attribution License or equivalent.

The editorial board has been involved in producing this book since its inception. They have spent rigorous hours researching and exploring the diverse topics which have resulted in the successful publishing of this book. They have passed on their knowledge of decades through this book. To expedite this challenging task, the publisher supported the team at every step. A small team of assistant editors was also appointed to further simplify the editing procedure and attain best results for the readers.

Our editorial team has been hand-picked from every corner of the world. Their multi-ethnicity adds dynamic inputs to the discussions which result in innovative outcomes. These outcomes are then further discussed with the researchers and contributors who give their valuable feedback and opinion regarding the same. The feedback is then collaborated with the researches and they are edited in a comprehensive manner to aid the understanding of the subject.

Apart from the editorial board, the designing team has also invested a significant amount of their time in understanding the subject and creating the most relevant covers. They scrutinized every image to scout for the most suitable representation of the subject and create an appropriate cover for the book.

The publishing team has been involved in this book since its early stages. They were actively engaged in every process, be it collecting the data, connecting with the contributors or procuring relevant information. The team has been an ardent support to the editorial, designing and production team. Their endless efforts to recruit the best for this project, has resulted in the accomplishment of this book. They are a veteran in the field of academics and their pool of knowledge is as vast as their experience in printing. Their expertise and guidance has proved useful at every step. Their uncompromising quality standards have made this book an exceptional effort. Their encouragement from time to time has been an inspiration for everyone.

The publisher and the editorial board hope that this book will prove to be a valuable piece of knowledge for researchers, students, practitioners and scholars across the globe.

List of Contributors

Parag K. Lala
Department of Electrical Engineering, Texas A&M University, Texarkana, USA

Assim A. Sagahyroon and Jamal A. Abdalla
American University of Sharjah, Sharjah, UAE

Sheikh Ajaz Bashir and Nisar Ahmed Shah
Department of Electronics & Instrumentation Technology, University of Kashmir, Srinagar, India

Yousif Al Mashhadany, Semeh Jassam, Amead Sami and Hebaa Nassar
Electrical Engineering Department, Engineering College, University of Anbar, Al-Anbar, Iraq

Wagah F. Mohammed, Omar Daoud and Munther Al-Tikriti
Communications and Electronics Department, Faculty of Engineering, Philadelphia University, Amman, Jordan

Aazar Saadaat Kashi, Mahmoud Kamarei and Mohsen Javadi
Department of Electrical and Computer Engineering, University of Tehran, Tehran, Iran

Kavuri Kasi Annapurna Devi
Department of Electrical and Electronic Engineering, INTI International University, Nilai, Malaysia

Norashidah Md. Din and Chandan Kumar Chakrabarty
Department of Electronics and Communication Engineering, Universiti Tenega Nasional, Kajang, Malaysia

Heresh Seyedi and Barzan Tabei
Faculty of Electrical and Computer Engineering, University of Tabriz, Tabriz, Iran

Alireza Ghorbani and Ahmad Ghanaatian
Electronics Department, Iran University of Science and Technology, Tehran, Iran

Maciej Siwczyński and Marcin Jaraczewski
Electrical and Computer Engineering, Cracow University of Technology, Kraków, Poland

Palaniandavar Venkateswaran and Rabindranath Nandi
Department of Electronics & Telecommunication Engineering, Jadavpur University, Kolkata, India

Sagarika Das
B. P. Poddar Institute of Management & Technology, Kolkata, India

Nizar Zrigui and Lahbib Zenkouar
Laboratory of Electronics and Communication (LEC), Ecole Mohammadia d'Ingénieurs (EMI), Mohammed V University — Agdal, Rabat, Morocco

Seddik Bri
Department of Electrical Engineering, Graduate School of Technology, Moulay Ismail University, Meknes, Morocco

Winnie P. Mathews
School of Electrical, Computer and Energy Engineering, Arizona State University, Tempe, USA

Rajitha N. P. Vemuri
School for Engineering of Matter, Transport and Energy, Arizona State University, Tempe, USA

Terry L. Alford
School of Electrical, Computer and Energy Engineering, Arizona State University, Tempe, USA
School for Engineering of Matter, Transport and Energy, Arizona State University, Tempe, USA

Oleg Semenov, Dmitry Vasiounin and Victor Spitsyn
Freescale Semiconductor, Moscow, Russia

El-Sayed A. M. Hasaneen and Nagwa Okely
Electrical Engineering Department, El-Minia University, El-Minia, Egypt

Radwene Laajimi and Mohamed Masmoudi
Department of Electrical Engineering Electronics, Micro-Technology and Communication (EMC) Research Group
Sfax (ENIS), University of Sfax, Sfax, Tunisia

Jin Young Choi
Electronic & Electrical Engineering Department, Hongik University, Jochiwon, South Korea

Takayuki Hayashi and Yoshiyuki Kawakami
Graduate School of Science and Engineering, Ritsumeikan University, Kusatsu, Japan

Masahiro Fukui
Department of VLSI System Design, Ritsumeikan University, Kusatsu, Japan

Dinesh Prasad and D. R. Bhaskar
Department of Electronics and Communication Engineering, Faculty of Engineering and Technology, Jamia Millia
Islamia, New Delhi, India

Yongjia Zhao, Xiaoya Zhou and Xiangliang Jin
Faculty of Materials, Optoelectronics and Physics, Xiangtan University, Xiangtan, China

Kehan Zhu
Electrical and Computer Engineering Department, Boise State University, Boise, USA

Cher-Shiung Tsai and Ming-Shin Lin
Department of Electronic Engineering, Kun Shan University, Yongkang, Chinese Taipei

Kwang-Jow Gan
Department of Electrical Engineering, National Chiayi University, Chiayi, Chinese Taipei

Pedro Bertemes-Filho, Alexandre Felipe and Volney C. Vincence
Department of Electrical Engineering, State University of Santa Catarina (UDESC), Joinville, Brazil

Raghavendra Sharma and Vuppuluri Prem Pyara
Department of Electrical Engineering, Dayalbagh Educational Institute, Agra, India

Mihai Grigore Timis, Alexandru Valachi, Alexandru Barleanu and Andrei Stan
Automatic Control and Computer Engineering Faculty, Technical University Gh.Asachi, Iasi, Romania

Jongdae Kim, Sungchul Lee and Hyunchul Shin
Electrical and Computer Engineering, Hanyang University, Ansan Kyeonggi-do, South Korea

Mamatha Gowda, Warsame H. Ali, Penrose Cofie and John Fuller
Department of Electrical and Computer Engineering, Prairie View A&M University, Prairie View, USA

Achwek Ben Saied and Dorra Sellami Masmoudi
Computor Imaging and Electronic Systems Group (CIEL), Research Unit (ICOS), Sfax, Tunisia
University of Sfax, National Engineering School of Sfax (ENIS), Sfax, Tunisia

Samir Ben Salem
University of Sfax, National Engineering School of Sfax (ENIS), Sfax, Tunisia
Development Group in Electronics and Communications (EleCom) Laboratory (LETI), Sfax, Tunisia

Mousa Yousefi, Ziaadin Daie Koozehkanani, Jafar Sobhi and Hamid Jangi
Faculty of Electrical and Computer Engineering, University of Tabriz, Tabriz, Iran

Printed in the USA
CPSIA information can be obtained
at www.ICGtesting.com
JSHW051439221024
72173JS00006B/1518

9 781632 401007